The Moral Skeptic

Studies in Feminist Philosophy is designed to showcase cutting-edge monographs and collections that display the full range of feminist approaches to philosophy, that push feminist thought in important new directions, and that display the outstanding quality of feminist philosophical thought.

STUDIES IN FEMINIST PHILOSOPHY
Cheshire Calhoun, *Series Editor*

Published in the series:
Abortion and Social Responsibility: Depolarizing the Debate
Laurie Shrage

Gender in the Mirror: Confounding Imagery
Diana Tietjens Meyers

Autonomy, Gender, Politics
Marilyn Friedman

Setting the Moral Compass: Essays by Women Philosophers
Edited by Cheshire Calhoun

Burdened Virtues: Virtue Ethics for Liberatory Struggles
Lisa Tessman

On Female Body Experience: "Throwing Like a Girl" and Other Essays
Iris Marion Young

Visible Identities: Race, Gender and the Self
Linda Martín Alcoff

Women and Citizenship
Edited by Marilyn Friedman

Women's Liberation and the Sublime: Feminism, Postmodernism, Environment
Bonnie Mann

Analyzing Oppression
Ann E. Cudd

Self Transformations: Foucault, Ethics, and Normalized Bodies
Cressida J. Heyes

Family Bonds: Genealogies of Race and Gender
Ellen K. Feder

Moral Understandings: A Feminist Study in Ethics, Second Edition
Margaret Urban Walker

The Moral Skeptic
Anita M. Superson

The Moral Skeptic

Anita M. Superson

OXFORD
UNIVERSITY PRESS

2009

OXFORD
UNIVERSITY PRESS

Oxford University Press, Inc., publishes works that further
Oxford University's objective of excellence
in research, scholarship, and education.

Oxford   New York
Auckland   Cape Town   Dar es Salaam   Hong Kong   Karachi
Kuala Lumpur   Madrid   Melbourne   Mexico City   Nairobi
New Delhi   Shanghai   Taipei   Toronto

With offices in
Argentina   Austria   Brazil   Chile   Czech Republic   France   Greece
Guatemala   Hungary   Italy   Japan   Poland   Portugal   Singapore
South Korea   Switzerland   Thailand   Turkey   Ukraine   Vietnam

Published by Oxford University Press, Inc.
198 Madison Avenue, New York, New York 10016

www.oup.com

Oxford is a registered trademark of Oxford University Press.

Library of Congress Cataloging-in-Publication Data
Superson, Anita M.
The moral skeptic / Anita M. Superson.
    p. cm. — (Studies in feminist philosophy)
ISBN 978-0-19-537662-3; 978-0-19-537661-6 (pbk.)
1. Ethics.   2. Skepticism.   I. Title.
BJ1031.S87 2009
170'.42—dc22   2008022620

9 8 7 6 5 4 3 2 1
Printed in the United States of America
on acid-free paper

In loving memory of my brother,
Thomas Scott Superson
(1963–1996)
who was with me every step of the way.

And to my parents,
Irene and Thaddeus,
who taught me
to know right from wrong,
to stand up for what is right,
and to fight against what is wrong.

Preface

From time to time, everyone wants to know why she or he should be moral. If I need top grades to get into medical school, should I compare answers on my physics exam? As a medical ethics student, should I straighten out a resident who makes crass comments about his female patients? Should I favor my own graduate students when handing out teaching assignments? These are just a few cases that made the question arise for me. For philosophers, of course, this is an age-old topic. Their attempts to answer the question are impressive, to say the least. Yet at the same time I have found them wanting. How could so many serious attempts to defeat the skeptic about acting morally be problematic? Is this kind of skeptic one that philosophers cannot in the end defeat? Most of us, myself included, will not settle for this answer: we want this philosophical skeptic in particular, more than any other, to be defeated. Ethics, after all, is a discipline with significant practical import. Perhaps the failure of the previous attempts to defeat this skeptic lies with what philosophers have taken to be a definitive answer to him, or, better, with what we have taken to be his demands. We need to be on firm footing in attempting to defeat this or any skeptic. For this, we need to know exactly what the skeptic's position is, and hence, exactly what it would take successfully to defeat the skeptic. Defining the position of the skeptic about acting morally is the aim of this book.

My project is in two ways unique. I know of no philosopher who has approached the issue of moral skepticism in the way I do here. Most who write on this topic first defend a moral theory, taking this to be their main goal, and then aim to defeat skepticism within the context of it. Most have not had much to say about how best to construe the skeptic's demands. There is some writing on this, but it is incomplete in ways I argue here. By defining the demands the skeptic can legitimately make on moral philosophers, I hope to aid all philosophers interested in the question of why we should be moral. If my view is correct, we have a complete picture of the skeptic that tells us exactly what it would take for a successful defeat of skepticism. We can then in confidence go on to the project of actually defeating the skeptic.

Notably, there is little if any literature on this issue that is informed by feminism. This is odd, because feminists have a particular stake in defeating skepticism, since women have been, and still are, oppressed, and suffer the harms subsequent to their oppression, including those resulting from sexual harassment and discrimination, rape, and everyday simple assaults to their dignity, such as being cut off when speaking, not being taken seriously by men, being served after men in restaurants and stores, or just being assumed to be stupid. I write this book as a woman, and as a feminist, who has experienced some of these harms. Indeed, it was through my study of feminism and my own experiences of sexism that feminism helped me to see them as such, that the issue of why be moral became most real for me. Feminism gave real meaning to abstract, Hobbesian Foole-type examples that I was not likely to experience myself. Feminism presented examples of real people, being harmed in real ways by those who do not care about acting morally, or who even deliberately want not to act morally. Worse, some could even get away with acting in sexist ways, and even be encouraged under patriarchy to act this way. Why should they be moral? Those of us who find ourselves in the underdog position find this skeptical challenge all the more pressing.

So why haven't feminists taken up this issue? One reason is the "division of labor" common in ethics, but not, say, in epistemology or philosophy of science, where feminism seems to have been incorporated to a much greater degree. Philosophers writing on moral skepticism do not typically work in feminism, and feminist philosophers, though they have said a great deal about normative and applied ethics, have not worked much in this topic, or in metaethics generally. Consequently, the work in either area is insufficiently informed by the work in the other. My project straddles metaethics and feminism. It addresses feminist concerns that have previously gone unacknowledged by metaethicists, including the role of deformed desires in theories of rationality and morality, and whether privilege is a better dichotomy than self-interest against morality. This more inclusive approach to moral skepticism serves to ground a complete defeat of skepticism, according to which no immoral acts—including sexist ones—turn out to be rationally permissible. Further, my hope is that an inclusive setup of the skeptic's position will shape the moral theory we ultimately defend in a way that shows explicitly that acts contributing to women's oppression are wrong.

By importing feminist concerns, I hope to give an age-old topic a new spin. Secondarily, but perhaps as important, my hope is to bring together two groups of philosophers who have for the most part worked independently of each other. We have much to learn from each other. We, after all, share a common goal of pursuing and obtaining truth. I have to think that when we work together, we have a much better chance of reaching this goal. If this book does nothing else but initiate this dialogue, I will consider it to have been a success.

Acknowledgments

Some of the material in this book has appeared in one form or another in various journal articles; thanks to the publishers of *Dialogue: Canadian Philosophical Review*, *Hypatia: A Journal of Feminist Philosophy*, *Journal of Social Philosophy*, and the *Southern Journal of Philosophy* for permission to reprint this material. Specifically, parts of chapter 2 appeared in "The Self-Interest Based Contractarian Response to the Why-Be-Moral Skeptic," *Southern Journal of Philosophy* 28 (3) (Fall 1990): 427–47. Parts of chapter 3 appeared in "Feminist Ethics: Defeating the Why-Be-Moral Skeptic," *Journal of Social Philosophy* 29 (2) (Fall 1998): 59–86, and parts of chapter 5 appeared in "Privilege, Immorality, and Responsibility for Attending to the 'Facts about Humanity'," *Journal of Social Philosophy* 35 (1) (Spring 2004): 34–55. Parts of chapter 4 appeared in "Deformed Desires and Informed Desire Tests," in special issue on Analytical Feminism, *Hypatia: A Journal of Feminist Philosophy* 20 (4) (Fall 2005): 109–26, published by Indiana University Press. Parts of chapter 7 appeared in "Scepticism about Moral Motives," *Dialogue: Canadian Philosophical Review* 35 (1) (Winter 1996): 15–34. Parts of chapter 8 appeared in "The Rationality of Dispositions and the Rationality of Actions: The Interdependency Thesis," *Dialogue: Canadian Philosophical Review* 44 (2005): 439–68.

My professional debts are many. First, I thank the philosophy editor at Oxford University Press, Peter Ohlin, for approaching me at an APA convention about my work, for his patience and very useful suggestions throughout this project, and for his genuine support of feminist philosophical work. I am grateful to have been provided the perfect forum to bring together metaethicists and feminist philosophers to work on one of the most intractable issues in moral philosophy. I thank the series editor, Cheshire Calhoun, for her unflagging enthusiasm about my project from the start, and for her many words of encouragement and good advice along the way. We share a vision about the scope of feminism that promises to close the gap between feminist and "mainstream" philosophers. I also thank my referees, whose extremely useful and detailed suggestions made for a much improved manuscript. Jim Sterba offered comments that time and again struck right at the heart of the issue at hand. I am grateful for his detailed and pressing exchanges on many issues in this book that made me clarify and solidify the entire project. Walter Sinnott-Armstrong generously offered time from his own demanding editing and research duties to give meticulous care and attention to my project. I appreciate his hard work and devotion to the profession in helping me, a complete stranger, make this book the best it could be. David Copp was not only a referee, but my dissertation advisor at the University of Illinois in Chicago. He was, in short, the best advisor one could have. His patience with my very early writing, and the countless excellent comments he has given me over the years on almost all of my written work, all of which I have taken to heart, largely made me into the philosopher I am today. His comments on this work in particular, ones that he describes as "explanatory," turned out in many cases to be anything but, forcing me to rethink a particular issue for at least several days.

Thanks go as well to some of my other mentors and friends. Sandy Bartky's patience with me over my initial skepticism about feminism cannot be repaid. Her comment to me that "feminists were on my side" initially made me open my mind to feminism more than any feminist work I read, and later resulted in much of my work being informed by feminist insights, and being much the richer for it. Liz Anderson has generously offered time to read my work and write letters of recommendation for me over the years. I thank her for being so supportive and contributing to my successes, and for being a model feminist philosopher for the rest of us. I am glad to have had her as a colleague for the one semester I visited at the University of Michigan. Ann Cudd has been my genuine philosophical friend since we first met in Kansas almost two decades ago. Not only has she has helped me think about many of the issues in this book, but she has helped my career in significant ways, and has served as my feminist philosophical compass on countless issues. Many others have either given me comments on some aspect of this book or have been supportive of the project in some other way. These include Louise Antony, Marcia Baron, Anna Bosch, Samantha Brennan, Valerie Brown, Sarah Buss, Joan Callahan, Charles Chastain, Brad Cokelet, Ed Curley, Steve Darwall, Deb DeBruin, Robin Dillon, John Exdell, Jenny Faust, Allan Gibbard, Sandy Goldberg, Sally Haslanger, Carol Hay, David Henderson, Dien Ho, Bob Holland, Lori Holland, Tracy Isaacs, Charlotte Jackson, Diane Jeske, Eileen John, Shelly Kagan, Richard Kraut, Keli Lawson, Oliver Leaman, Jenn Lewin, Hilde Lindemann, Louis Loeb, Duncan MacIntosh, Patricia Marino, Charles Mills, Brad Monton, Amy Mullin, Jan Narveson, Marina Oshana, David Owen, Lois Pineau, Peter Railton, Gina Rose, Russ Shafer-Landau, Pat Smith, Robin Smith, Mariam Thalos, Laurence Thomas, Jennifer Uleman, Helga Varden.

I would also like to thank the audiences at various departments and conferences where I presented versions of some of the material in this book, including the American Philosophical Association, the Society for Analytical Feminism, the Central States Philosophical Association, the Canadian Philosophical Association, the University of Kansas Hall Center for Humanities Gender Seminar, the Society for Women in Philosophy, and the Chicago Chapter of the American Association of University Women, and the philosophy departments at the following universities: Simon Fraser, the University of Illinois at Chicago, the University of Colorado at Boulder, Kansas State University, the University of Kentucky, the University of Cincinnati, the University of Kansas, the University of Louisville, the University of Western Ontario, University of Waterloo, and Lake Forest College. Thanks also to many of my students over the years whose questions sent my research in directions that informed some of the issues discussed in this book.

I owe deep gratitude especially to the American Association of University Women, which awarded me a Postdoctoral Fellowship for the years 2006–7, during which time I wrote significant portions of this book, and to Evelyn Fox Keller, who sponsored my project. The generous support this long-standing organization has offered to women in the academy benefits all women. I thank the University of Kentucky for granting me time away on the Fellowship.

My personal debts are also many. I thank my aunt, Stella, for giving me a clean, quiet place to live in my home town of Chicago. Most of my work on this book, and most of my best philosophical ideas, were nurtured there in a very comfortable place that I will always call home. I thank my parents, Ted and Irene, who taught me the value of hard work, and my brother, Michael, and sisters Luann and Kristin, both for giving me things to think about other than work and for inspiring my work in ways unknown to them. Tom, our brother, fought a valiant fight against cancer that taught us that in any endeavor in life, you should give it your all. We miss him dearly. I thank my cousins, Rita and Judy, and my aunt, Mona, for always asking how my book was coming along, and for giving me welcome breaks from work to go to lunch or strawberry picking. All of my relatives, living or deceased, in some way played a role in shaping me as the philosopher and person I am, and for this I thank them.

Finally, I thank Bob Horsch for allowing me to use his great photo that appears on the cover of this book, one that captures some of my favorite things: Chicago, lighthouses, and the sea. I have often thought that the "life" of a lighthouse is a lot like the enterprise of philosophy. A lighthouse is a lone structure at sea; doing philosophy, for most of us in the profession, is an individual, often isolating, enterprise. A lighthouse faces strong storms and repeated pounding waves; a philosopher's argument is subjected to scrutiny and repeated objections. But a good lighthouse withstands the storms that come its way, boldly shining forth as if strengthened by them, a fortress ready to take the next hit; and a good argument is strengthened by objections, boldly shining forth in the face of further objections, a fortress ready to be made even stronger.

Contents

The Moral Skeptic

1

Introduction

THE ISSUE

I have been thinking about moral skepticism for a long time. I have often been asked whether I am a moral skeptic. I do not know the answer to this question. Happily, for purposes of this book, I do not need to know. While I believe—indeed, there is widespread agreement—that the many cogent attempts that philosophers have made over the centuries at tackling this trenchant issue have failed, I think this does not commit us to skepticism. For it could very well be that the problem lies with how philosophers have been defining the skeptic, what we have taken his demands to be. Philosophers have identified two kinds of moral skeptics: one skeptic doubts whether there is one true moral code, or whether there are true moral statements or moral facts,[1] the other doubts whether we should follow morality, whatever its content—that is, he doubts the existence of moral reasons. Many moral philosophers have been concerned with the former skeptic about theoretical reason. My concern in this book is with the latter kind of moral skeptic about practical reason. More specifically, I want to examine how the traditional picture of the "practical" skeptic (hereafter "the skeptic") has limited the kind of response that philosophers can offer by way of defeating the skeptic. I argue that the traditional view of the skeptic is in some ways too broad yet in other ways too narrow. Each chapter defends a modification of the traditional view. My ultimate goal is to define the skeptic in such a way that a defeat of skepticism would leave remaining no further skeptical challenge about following the dictates of morality.

Why is defeating the moral skeptic so important? The reasons are twofold: theoretical and practical. Demonstrating the rationality of acting morally would strengthen morality by backing it with reason. Here, ethics bears similarity to all other areas of philosophy in which a skeptical challenge is posed to our widely held beliefs and attitudes. A significant part of the entire enterprise of philosophy is justification: if we give up the project of justification, we give up doing philosophy, or the heart of it, anyway. Thus jettisoning the project of defeating the moral skeptic, perhaps because it is too difficult to do so or even because we do not care about the challenge the skeptic poses, would not be a satisfactory response.

3

In addition, demonstrating the rationality of acting morally promises to make headway in achieving the desired effect of people's acting morally. Here, ethics is different from other areas of philosophy. For we do not worry that skeptics about the external world will walk off cliffs or really confuse themselves with brains in vats. We might worry, though, that skeptics about the existence of God will act badly, but then again, many students of philosophy have become such skeptics and have not changed their behavior. But we do worry that skeptics about acting morally will treat others badly, for if moral reasons do not override other reasons for action, then rational persons will do well not to act on them. Indeed, moral philosophers link the theoretical and practical goals: we want people to be moved by the arguments we offer for acting morally, and to act accordingly. It would be no more philosophically satisfying if people acted morally not for the reasons we offer, but out of fear of political sanction, punishment from God, or even just on a fluke, than if people came to hold their beliefs about the existence of the external world or other minds for these reasons and not for sound, philosophical justifications. My claim is not that the reasons for acting morally must necessarily motivate persons, but simply that we want them to do so. I have claimed that the skeptic, as traditionally conceived, has not yet been defeated. Thus these goals have not yet been achieved.

Recently, many philosophers have addressed the issue of the "normativity" of morality, and they divide into roughly two camps. We can characterize the view of those in the first camp to be, roughly speaking, that if there are any moral requirements, they are requirements of rationality. Those in the second camp take it that it is one thing to establish that there are moral requirements, and another thing to establish that moral requirements are normative, or, that the requirements of morality are rational requirements. I am in the second camp. If those in the former group are correct, the "Why be moral?" issue is not intelligible. But if rationality cannot be construed the way these philosophers suggest, then there might not be any moral requirements. So their project is in large part to defend a certain conception of rationality such that morality fits into it. So, for example, David Gauthier aims to develop a theory of morals as part of a theory of rational choice, and boldly asserts: "Indeed, if our defence [of compliance with agreements based on the principle of minimax relative concession] fails, then we must conclude that a rational morality is a chimera, so that there is no rational and impartial constraint on the pursuit of individual utility."[2] Gauthier works within a widely accepted self-interest-based notion of rationality, and he claims that "if we should find that reason is no more than the handmaiden of interest, so that in overriding advantage a moral appeal must also contradict reason . . . then we should conclude that the moral enterprise, as traditionally conceived, is impossible."[3] I agree and disagree with Gauthier here. I am going to take the traditional view of the skeptic as my starting point, and assume that there are conflict cases in which the requirements of morality and the requirements of rationality point in different directions. I will try to stick as much as I can with the traditional picture of the skeptic, and modify it along the way to meet certain concerns related to our effecting a complete defeat of skepticism. But I am not suggesting that if we do not succeed in justifying moral requirements within the context of a certain view of rationality, then there are no moral requirements. Rather, we will need to work harder to develop a moral theory that does provide a complete defeat of skepticism. This is not my project here, nor is my project to defeat skepticism, but to show what it would take for a successful defeat.

Other philosophers have taken a different approach from Gauthier's, but they still fall into the camp of those who believe that if there are any moral requirements, they are requirements of rationality. Michael Smith recently defends the view that a person who asks the question "Why be moral?" does not understand what moral requirements consist in, just as a person who is blind from birth but uses color terms reliably does not understand the concept of "red."[4] At best, she uses the term "red" or "moral reason" in an "inverted commas" sense, figuring out how to apply the term as others do but not genuinely mastering the concept. Smith is trying to establish his view that motivation is built into a moral reason, and I will examine his argument in more detail later on, but I do not want to start my quest by assuming that reason has motivation built into it.

Nor do I want to provide an elaborate account, one set in the context of moral theory, of what it is to give someone a reason to act morally, as do Christine Korsgaard and Stephen Darwall, both of whom work within a Kantian framework. This is another way to approach the skeptical challenge. Korsgaard argues that egoism is a myth because it denies that reasons can be shared. She believes that it is the very nature of reasons that they can be shared.[5] If I ask you to consider how you would like it if someone acted a certain way toward you, Korsgaard says, I am forcing you to acknowledge the value of my own humanity, and impose on you an obligation to respect it. There turns out to be no gap between your reasons and my reasons, as the egoist or skeptic supposes, since if you listen to the argument at all, you have already admitted that each of us is someone, that is, someone who is deserving of a certain kind of treatment. The skeptic, in other words, must not understand what it is to have a reason. Darwall picks up on Korsgaard's point, and claims that when you attempt to give another a second-personal reason, you presuppose that another has second-personal authority, competence, and responsibility as a free and rational agent.[6] A second-personal reason is a reason we give from a second-person standpoint, or "the perspective you and I take up when we make and acknowledge claims on one another's conduct and will."[7] Indeed, according to Darwall, the very validity of a second-personal reason depends on the possibility of the reason's being addressed person-to-person. Moral requirements, then, are connected *conceptually* to an authority to demand compliance.[8] Moral reasons need no independent defense, as they are part of the "circle of irreducibility" of second-personal concepts, which also includes the concepts of responsibility, accountability, second-personal authority, and valid claim or demand. In other words, the skeptic who asks why he should be moral already presupposes that others and himself are engaged in such a way that we see that we have mutual reasons for acting toward each other in ways respectful of our dignity.[9] The skeptic is already "in the game" if he understands what a second-personal reason is. Both Korsgaard's and Darwall's account of the skeptical challenge might turn out to be the best ones we can offer, but, again, I want to stick as much as possible to the traditional view of the skeptic and modify it in light of a complete defeat of skepticism. Further, I do not want to assume up front that moral requirements just *are* rational requirements. If we believe that it is possible that they are not, and that this is just as tenable a position as that they are, then we have to take the position of the skeptic seriously, and not beg the question against him by assuming that moral requirements are rational requirements.[10]

In the other camp are philosophers who separate establishing the existence of moral requirements from establishing the rational requiredness of moral requirements. David Copp, for instance, takes on the challenge of the skeptic who believes in conflict cases where the requirements of morality and rationality part company, that is, where there is a normative conflict between the verdicts of the standpoint of self-interest and the standpoint of morality.[11] Copp argues that neither standpoint overrides the other, and that there is never an overall verdict about which action is required from a standpoint of "Reason" in cases where moral reasons and self-interested reasons conflict. He does not believe that this discredits morality, since self-interest also fails to override morality. David Brink also believes that morality and self-interest part company, and thus that the skeptic's challenge is a real one.[12] He sees "an apparent conflict between living well and living right or morally," and examines some egoist attempts to justify acting morally. He rejects a subjective response, that conceives of the agent's good independently of the good of others, on the grounds that this is not likely to defeat the skeptic. He favors a neo-Aristotelian response that tries to justify the other-regarding aspect of morality in terms of psychological continuity, since this poses the most obvious problem for an egoist justification of morality. Whether Copp's or Brink's accounts are successful or satisfactory for the project of defeating skepticism, I share with each the goal that the skeptic's challenge is a real one for those of us working within the framework of the traditional view of the skeptic who believes that there are conflicts between the requirements of morality and of self-interest, rather than that moral requirements are essentially rational requirements due to the nature of rationality.

So what is the traditional picture of the skeptic? The skeptic adopts the widely accepted theory of practical reason according to which rationality dictates that the agent act in ways that maximize her expected utility, commonly identified with promoting one's own interest, or, satisfying one's desires or preferences. This theory, the expected utility theory of rational choice and action, or, EU, for short, is the received view of rational action. The skeptic challenges the moral philosopher to show that rationality dictates that persons act morally, even when doing so conflicts with their self-interest. That is, the skeptic demands that it be shown that acting in morally required ways, not self-interestedly, is rationally required. If this challenge goes unmet, the skeptic remains undefeated, meaning that rationality requires self-interested action. Yet the fact that the skeptic endorses EU does not mean that he is wedded to it: he will accept a better theory of practical reason, one that includes moral reasons, if one can be defended. This is the task facing the moral philosopher.

Further, on the traditional view, the skeptic believes that it is not rational to have moral desires: a rational person can have any desires but moral ones. Expected utility theory does not rationally assess desires themselves, so that whatever desires a person happens to have, she should maximize their satisfaction. Some philosophers have imposed constraints having to do with coherence, consistency, and transitivity, but otherwise any desires or preferences count. But for purposes of defeating skepticism, philosophers must assume that persons lack moral desires, ones that involve taking an intrinsic interest in the interests of others.

In addition, the skeptic demands a *justifying* reason, not merely a *motivating*, or explanatory, reason for acting morally. A justifying reason justifies the action typically on the grounds that it at least tends to bring about a good state of affairs, while a motivating reason explains why the agent acts the way she does. A justifying reason can motivate, but it need not. And a motivating reason may not be a justifying one, as in the case of the person who acts morally because she wants to look good in front of others, or who has overwhelming feelings of guilt about not acting morally that cause her to act morally. The skeptic seeks a justifying reason, whether or not it is a motivating reason as well.

Finally, the traditional skeptic requires that we show that every morally required action is rationally required, not just that being morally disposed is rationally required. The *action skeptic*, who represents the traditional skeptic, is a skeptic about whether every morally required act is rationally required; the *disposition skeptic* is a skeptic about the rational requiredness of adopting a moral disposition. Both Plato and David Gauthier shift their attempt to defeat skepticism on grounds of self-interest to the level of dispositions, but Gauthier tries to defeat action skepticism, as well, as I will show. On the traditional model, defeating action skepticism alone is sufficient for defeating skepticism fully, since, philosophers believe, no further skeptical challenge would remain once the action skeptic is defeated. As a point of clarification, the action skeptic need not take a stand on the rationality of acts that are merely morally permissible, that is, neither obligatory nor wrong, such as the act of helping someone pick up papers she has dropped. For acts that are morally permissible, rationality might be indifferent between morality and self-interest, which would not threaten the action skeptic's view about rationally required action. The action skeptic is concerned that we demonstrate that when morality requires acting a certain way, rationality follows suit, backing it up with a requirement of rationality. Moreover, the action skeptic is concerned with whether the requirements of morality are rational *requirements*, rather than merely rationally permissible. He wants it to be shown that whenever a morally required act conflicts with a self-interested act, the latter of which he deems to be required by rationality, rationality requires that he perform the morally required act. I will speak at times of "what we have reason to do" or of "what it is rational to do," and here I mean what *Rationality* dictates. But when there is a need to disambiguate, I will clearly say "what rationality requires," or say that "it is rationally required to act in morally required ways."

The skeptic is defined this way for strategic reasons. If the argument against skepticism succeeds, it is supposed to succeed for anyone, regardless of her desires, character, beliefs about moral reasons, and so on. Thus it would not rest on any special contingencies such that it would reach only those in special circumstances. It would not beg the question in favor of morality by assuming that anyone had moral desires on any occasion. And it is supposed to leave open no further skeptical challenge. Finally, it is supposed to defeat the worst-case scenario in opposition to morally required action, which is taken to be self-interested action.

Moreover, we need not worry about extending the justification for acting morally to persons who are in special circumstances, such as when they have no interests at all, or have otherwise perverted interests, such as an interest in not satisfying any of their other interests, or lack sufficient time to dispose themselves to being moral so as to reap any of the benefits from being morally disposed. These cases pose a challenge to morality, but our main concern is to defeat skepticism for ordinary people in normal circumstances. Importantly, these circumstances include ones in which it is possible that morality demands great sacrifices relating to the pursuit of one's own interest.

Having to defeat action skepticism with these restrictions on the skeptic's position of course poses a huge challenge to moral philosophers. Since the skeptic accepts only self-interested reasons, we have to justify acting morally or, at least, being morally disposed, on self-interested grounds. Only self-interested reasons would reach such a skeptic. Indeed, whichever way we set up the skeptic, the setup constrains the kind of answer we can give, determining the range of acceptable answers to the skeptic. Since self-interest and morality are supposed to be paradigmatic opposites, maybe we have set up too big a challenge for ourselves.

Philosophers have made exactly this charge about Descartes's attempt to defeat the epistemological skeptic. Descartes famously digs himself into a very deep skeptical hole, subjecting to doubt everything he has learned from his senses, from his awake state, and even from his own thoughts, since his senses might deceive him, since he cannot tell for certain whether he is awake or dreaming his whole life, and since an evil genius might be deceiving him even about mathematical truths. There is much debate about whether philosophers can and have gotten us out of this skeptical abyss. Of course Descartes himself thought he could, by working out from the existence of his own mind to God's existence to the existence of the external world. But even his argument about the existence of his own mind is flawed, leaving many of us to believe that he dug too deep a skeptical hole. Descartes cast the net too wide by doubting everything. Thus, many philosophers believe that by setting up the skeptic in such a demanding way, the likelihood of success in defeating him is slim to none. A skeptic who doubts everything leaves us with no way to reach him, with nothing to build on.

We might think this is the case in ethics, too: the traditional picture of the skeptic requires too much in demanding that we reach the action skeptic with self-interested reasons. One response is to give up on the project of defeating skepticism. But this is unacceptable if we want to achieve the theoretical and practical goals cited earlier. Making a move parallel to Berkeley's in epistemology by showing that there is nothing to be skeptical about, because the physical world can be reduced to our or God's perceptions, would also not be satisfactory. This merely dodges defeating skepticism, since it does not address what we really want to know, namely, that the external world as we think it is does in fact exist. We want a response to any skeptic that addresses head on what we really want to know is justified. In order to have a complete and successful defeat of skepticism, the trick is then to determine what it is we really want to know.

Unlike those philosophers who believe that Descartes cast the net too wide in epistemology, I believe that philosophers have not cast the net wide enough in ethics. Traditionally, a defeat of action skepticism would be sufficient for a complete defeat of skepticism. Hobbes tried to defeat action skepticism by appealing to reasons of self-interest for each and every action. Gauthier reminds us that this would show too much, since it would make moral reasons otiose. What we really want, Gauthier ultimately argues, is for the skeptic to accept moral reasons on their own, even when they cannot be replaced by self-interested reasons. In response to Hobbes, Gauthier makes a dispositional move, aiming to show that adopting a moral disposition is rational in a self-interested sense. But then he needs to show how the rationality of the moral disposition carries over to the actions expressing it, and in what sense it does. That is, he needs to defeat both the disposition skeptic, who doubts the existence of reasons for being morally disposed, and the action skeptic, who doubts the

existence of reasons for acting morally. So Gauthier does not give up the
project of defeating action skepticism, but needs a way of connecting the
rationality of dispositions and actions. I propose a view according to
which the rationality of dispositions is assessed interdependently of the
rationality of actions. On this view, dispositions and actions are seen as
two sides of a coin, rationally related through the same reasoning on the
part of the agent.

Even if we do defeat action skepticism, and in a way better than
Hobbes's, we will not have shown enough for a successful and complete
defeat of skepticism. In addition, we need to speak to motives, and
demonstrate that rationality requires that we have and act from certain
motives deemed ideal by whatever moral theory we defend, rather than
merely going through the motions. The *motive skeptic* endorses the view
that going through the motions in acting in morally required ways is
rationally permissible. It is important to show that it is rational to *be*
moral, which amounts to being a person who both acts morally and acts
from a certain motive that the moral theory at issue deems ideal.

There is an even deeper skeptical challenge raised about motives. The
amoralist is not moved by moral reasons even though he recognizes their
existence. That is, he sees that there are moral reasons, yet he does not see
their force. Internalists about reasons and motives believe they can indirectly defeat the amoralist by showing that he is either inconceivable or
irrational. I argue against some internalist arguments, and conclude that
we should, indeed, address the amoralist and expand the skeptic's position to include a claim about the rationality of amoralism. Still, if the
amoralist is not moved by moral reasons, I argue that this does not
threaten a successful defeat of skepticism, because whether one is motivated by the reasons one has is a psychological, not a philosophical, issue.
But we should still address the amoralist, in addition to the action skeptic,
the disposition skeptic, and the motive skeptic.

It is not problematic that I reconstrue the skeptic's position in the way
I do. It would be, if my aim were to define the skeptic in a way that would
make it easy for me or anyone to easily refute. But my aim is to define the
skeptic so as to anticipate further skeptical challenges. My strategy is similar
to that of Descartes, who anticipates further skeptical challenges and defines
the epistemological skeptic accordingly. I am introducing deeper kinds of
skepticism, and corresponding ways of referring to The Skeptic (e.g., the
action skeptic, disposition skeptic, and motive skeptic). This is so that were
we to defeat skepticism, we would defeat it completely.

For the same reason, I believe that our setup of the skeptic's position
needs to be more politically sensitive than the traditional one. Just as
some disenfranchised social groups charge that so-called mainstream
moral theories do not explicitly exclude as morally unjustified certain
behavior directed against members of these groups, or worse, even permit
such behaviors, these same groups might charge that a defeat of the
traditional skeptic does not explicitly exclude the same behaviors as

rationally unjustified. The issue is more pressing than ever for women and minorities who in both blatant and subtle ways have had their status as full and equal persons discounted, ignored, or even set back. A complete defeat of skepticism needs to show that behavior that does this is irrational. Part of my project in this book is to address this concern in order to effect a more inclusive defeat of skepticism. I speak mostly in terms of women and feminist concerns since it is this perspective from which I write, but my arguments apply equally to other oppressed groups.

One way that feminists and others might respond to the project of skepticism is to challenge the view that self-interested action provides the biggest challenge to morality for the reason that it is most in opposition to moral action. There are immoral actions other than self-interested ones that, for all we have shown with a defeat of the traditional skeptic, we may be rationally required to perform. Some of these acts take sexist forms. They include doing evil for its own sake, moral indifference, moral negligence, conscientious wickedness, and weakness of will, as well as acts that are performed as part of harmful social practices that may not directly be in the agent's self-interest, but may instead only indirectly benefit the group of which he is a member. The latter include acts that sustain and perpetuate women's oppression, including a man's benefiting from the existence of rape and sexual harassment in virtue of being a member of the group men, even though he himself never rapes or harasses. Any of these immoral acts may be at least as much in opposition to morality as self-interested acts. Since they are not best characterized as self-interested, dichotomizing self-interest and morality runs the risk that they will be left out of the skeptic's challenge, and will leave open whether they are rationally required to perform. But we need to show, for a complete defeat of skepticism, that *no* immoral act has the backing of reason. To meet this charge, then, I argue that we should reconstrue the skeptic's position as one of *privilege* rather than self-interest; privilege includes self-interest, yet goes beyond it. That is, we should take the skeptic to adopt the view that reason requires acting in ways that privilege oneself. This more politically comprehensive picture of the skeptic reflects immoral acts directed against members of oppressed groups that heretofore have been ignored, and also gives us reason to jettison EU.

A related problem is that since EU does not scrutinize desires, it allows for deformed desires, that is, ones deformed by patriarchy. If we justify acting morally in the way contractarians like Gauthier does, by appealing to EU, and if EU allows for deformed desires, we risk recapitulating women's oppression in the resultant moral code. For it might turn out to be rationally and morally required to act in ways satisfying deformed desires. The problem affects any moral theory that aims to defeat skepticism by in some way invoking EU. At the very least, then, we should modify EU to exclude as rational acting on deformed desires. Many philosophers have proposed versions of informed desire tests to eliminate desires based on ignorance of facts, false beliefs, psychological aberrations, and the like, but none of these address deformed desires. I propose a way of doing this, so at the least we should modify EU.

Deformed desires also plague the care ethicists' response to the skeptic. Some feminists endorse the ethic of care as an alternative to self-interest based contractarianism, or, for short, SIB contractarianism, which endorses an individualistic picture of the bargainers to the hypothetical contract from which the dictates of morality emerge. This contractarian model is similar to the traditional view of the skeptic. The ethic of care sees persons as embedded in particular social contexts and as having needs and particular identities. Care ethicists such as Nel Noddings offer an internalist reason for acting morally, whereby the reason is necessarily related to motives the agent has, including deformed desires. Women who come to develop deformed desires from patriarchal socialization and related to the kinds of caring they are expected to do will have reasons for acting on them, and women who lack desires that when satisfied contribute to freeing them from oppression will not have reason to act in these ways. But neither a feminist ethic nor a successful response to the skeptic should allow or perpetuate women's oppression. So this way of responding to the skeptic is problematic.

Suppose we jettison EU. The skeptic's position must be grounded in rationality, since otherwise the skeptical project does not get off the ground. A skeptic whose views are not grounded in a theory of rationality or something like it poses no threat to morality. In line with my view that we reconstrue the skeptic's position along the lines of privilege instead of self-interest, which calls for recognizing everyone's worth as a person, I rely on consistency as a measure of rationality. Specifically, there must be consistency between a person's disposition, actions, desires, maxims, and reasons for disposing herself to morality, as well as in the main tenets of the moral theory to which she subscribes, in that it must account for the intrinsic value of each person. The sense of consistency that I invoke is not that of logical consistency, but what we might call "practical consistency" or coherence. I develop the Interdependency Thesis, which assesses the rationality of moral dispositions and actions interdependently. This thesis allows us to fine-tune the demands of the action skeptic by not focusing just on acts and dispositions in themselves, but on their interconnection. Specifically, our moral assessments should reflect an agent's integrity, which is not just a matter of acting morally and being morally disposed, but of her resolve, her being open to revision, and the like. What is morally required is that an agent act in ways that foster integrity. Our rational assessments should assess the more complex connection between the agent's reasons for adopting a moral disposition, and for having and acting from it, and whether these cohere with her reasons for acting and for wanting to be a morally good person, and the justification for the moral theory or principles she endorses. The measure of rationality should be consistency between these features that reflect moral integrity.

Acts will come in degrees of rationality, as measured by how they contribute to the agent's consistent life plan. This account unites dispositions and actions in a way that provides a fuller, richer assessment of persons and their actions than do other accounts that take EU as a starting point.

In sum, my attack on the traditional picture of the skeptic is threefold. First, the traditional picture is misdirected since it is not sufficiently sensitive to the complexities of morality as just stated. It takes as its target the acts that the moral theory at issue deems to be required. Typically these are defined just in terms of the acts themselves, and whether they meet an independent standard (e.g., maximization of utility). But it needs to include acts that the agent performs yet that make her reflect on her character and firm up her resolve, as well as exclude acts that have no such effect or that are performed by an agent who does not exhibit moral reasoning of the right kind. The traditional picture of the skeptic is too weak because we need to defeat motive skepticism and address the amoralist, in addition to defeating disposition and action skepticism. Thus we need both to clarify and broaden the traditional skeptic's position accordingly. Second, the traditional view invokes EU, which is problematic for the project of defeating skepticism. On EU and the traditional view of the skeptic, for any desire the agent has but moral ones, acting on it is rational. But EU wedges us into a certain answer, forcing us to go the route Hobbes and Gauthier have taken. It does not exclude deformed desires, but takes their satisfaction to be rationally required. And it leaves out too many actions, ones not best characterized as self-interested, that fit better under the umbrella of privilege. Third, the traditional picture of the skeptic is not sufficiently sensitive to issues of gender and the like. Excluding deformed desires as irrational and starting from the position of privilege rather than self-interest will take us a long way toward remedying this. Also, the Interdependency Thesis's judgments are in line with a rich theory of morality and active moral agency, and it is more nuanced to context than the alternatives, all of which are feminist concerns. And the addition of motive skepticism aims to present a better picture of moral agency than one divorced from motives, since it links action and motivation, and assesses the rationality of both. This coherent picture of agency is important for feminism, for example, since if a person acts morally, this still leaves open the possibility of his going through the motions in doing so, and not really respecting the rational agency or humanity of women. Ideally, feminists want both that agents act in nonsexist ways, and that their motives display the same genuine respect for women as for all others.

CHAPTER SUMMARY

The best place to start in tackling the problem of skepticism about moral action is, I believe, with the response to the skeptic offered by SIB contractarians, since their description of the hypothetical bargainers to the contract from which morality is supposed to emerge resembles that of the traditional skeptic, and if their response works, it will have defeated a quite demanding action skeptic who wants it to be shown that every morally required act is rationally required. Gauthier rightly rejects Hobbes's attempt to show that every morally required act is rationally required because it is in the agent's self-interest to perform it. But since Gauthier must reach a skeptic who endorses EU and initially accepts only self-interested reasons for action, he must make the dispositional move, and show that it is rationally required because self-interested to adopt a moral disposition. In addition, if he is to defeat action skepticism, he must show that the rationality of the moral disposition carries over to the actions expressing it. But to do so, he must defend a controversial view— the Dependency Thesis—of the connection between the rationality of dispositions and actions. I take up this topic in chapter 2, where I challenge the skeptic's endorsement of EU on the grounds that it constrains in a problematic way the kind of answer we can give to the skeptic. Chapter 2 also raises the issue of whether we must defeat action skepticism for a successful defeat of skepticism, or whether it would be sufficient to defeat disposition skepticism. In addition, chapter 2 raises problems about moral integrity, specifically that agents are not linked to their reasons in the right way on the Dependency Thesis.

Some feminists have rejected traditional moral theories, in particular SIB contractarianism, in part because of its abstract individualism. According to SIB contractarianism, the true moral code emerges from a hypothetical agreement among self-interested persons who come to the bargain from their current social, economic, and political positions, and who put forward claims to each other and make concessions on the basis of whether doing so best satisfies their desires or preferences. The feminist objection to this view of the bargainers, which is similar to the traditional view of the skeptic, is that (1) it may not be neutral and, if it is not sufficiently reflective of gender, may recapitulate women's oppression; (2) it captures only typically male-male interactions between strangers in a paid workforce situation; and (3) it yields a moral code that is likely to be minimalist in nature. To avoid these and other problems with traditional moral theories, some feminists have proposed and are developing the ethic of care. In chapter 3, I examine the kind of responses to the skeptic that the ethic of care might offer. The most promising one invokes a Humean internalist reason for acting morally that necessarily connects a reason for acting in a caring way with acting from the motive of care. But this motive cashes out in the context of a patriarchal society in ways that recapitulate women's oppression, since the desires associated with women's caring are often deformed by patriarchy. It turns out that the ethic of care is no better off in its aim to defeat skepticism than is SIB contractarianism. If I am right that the ethic of care commits us to internalism in a way that invokes deformed desires and recapitulates women's oppression, it does not meet the aim of feminists and will not successfully defeat skepticism. Chapter 3 raises additional questions about the traditional skeptic, namely, whether we need to defeat motive skepticism in addition to action skepticism because of concerns about motives brought to the fore by care ethicists, and whether we need a fuller account of justification than EU allows that squares with a richer account of morality than SIB contractarianism, one more in line with the ethic of care. In the end, we are left with the traditional picture of the skeptic who endorses EU. In the next couple of chapters, I proceed to chip away at the plausibility of EU.

The topic of chapter 4 is deformed desires and the role they should play in rational and moral theories. Chapter 8 shows that these desires are problematic for successfully defeating skepticism, so we should want to exclude them from a rational choice theory that grounds the skeptic's position. Thus we need to modify the desires we take the skeptic to believe it is rational to have. The traditional picture excludes only moral desires so as not to beg the question in favor of morality. Chapter 4 examines standard informed desire tests that hold promise of showing that deformed desires are irrational. I argue that as they are traditionally construed, they unfortunately fail to do so. I propose an additional condition of rationality according to which the agent recognizes herself as having worth in a Kantian sense. This condition will exclude deformed desires from the skeptic's position, whichever theory of rational choice we take the skeptic to adopt. The fact that EU does not exclude these desires, though, is another factor that counts against it. At the least, then, we should modify EU accordingly, and consequently, the skeptic's position. The upshot for feminism is that since deformed desires will be excluded from the outset as ones it is rational to have and act on, any moral theory that is derived from the theory of rational action with which we begin is one that will not require or deem as morally permissible action that satisfies deformed desires. Neither the moral theory grounded in such a theory of practical reason, nor the theory of practical reason itself, will perpetuate women's oppression for reasons related to women's having deformed desires.

Chapter 5 argues for a further reason to jettison EU, namely, that it is not sufficiently inclusive, particularly when it comes to feminist concerns. It would follow from a successful defeat of skepticism, according to which rationality requires acting in morally required ways, that all immoral acts are irrational. To satisfy feminist concerns about the skeptical project, a defeat of skepticism must show that it is not rational to act in ways covering all sexist behavior, not just sexist behavior grounded in self-interest. The traditional picture of the skeptic, which covers just self-interest, is too narrow in this regard. I argue that all forms of immorality have in common that the agent fails to respect the equal humanity of another person. Privilege covers all these acts, including self-interest. Thus we should expand the skeptic's position to be that rationality requires that one privilege oneself. To defeat the skeptic on this alternative model to EU, we need to show that rationality requires, on grounds of consistency, that we respect the humanity of others: it is inconsistent or contradictory to favor one's own humanity over others' humanity. We can appeal to reasons of consistency rather than self-interested reasons in aiming to defeat skepticism. I develop the consistency model of rational choice and action in chapter 8, though, again, my aim is not actually to defeat skepticism.

Chapter 6 raises a further question about motivation, and develops the objections raised against internalism in chapter 3. Chapter 6 presents the challenge of the amoralist who sees that there are moral reasons, yet denies their force. Internalists of different kinds argue that such a skeptic is either inconceivable or irrational, or just lacks a reason to act morally. I examine and reject several internalist arguments in favor of weak externalism, the view that a reason to act morally may, but need not necessarily, motivate the agent to act. The failure of internalist arguments leaves open the possibility of a rational amoralist. And if a rational amoralist is possible, we must defeat him in order to defeat skepticism fully. This means that we need to broaden the skeptic's position accordingly. I argue that although we need to do so, our failure to defeat the skeptic who believes that amoralism is a tenable position would not count against a successful defeat of skepticism, since being motivated by the reasons one has is a psychological, but not a philosophical, issue.

Still, motives are important to the project of skepticism because most of us believe that the ideal moral person is not one who merely acts morally but one who does so from the right motives. Feminists, for instance, want it to be the case that a person acts morally and does not go through the motions in doing so, but really respects women. The motive skeptic believes that it is rationally permissible for a person to act morally but merely go through the motions in doing so, without acting from the motive the moral theory in question deems ideal. Chapter 7 aims to show that such an agent has reasons and motives that are not in harmony, which is a mark of irrationality. This serves as an indirect defeat of the motive skeptic.

Chapter 8 returns to the theme of chapter 2, the relation between the rationality of a moral disposition and the rationality of actions expressing it. I argue for the Interdependency Thesis, according to which we need to assess the rationality of an agent's actions as ones performed by a certain kind of agent. Here I mean that we should assess the rationality of actions not independently of the agent who performs them, nor should we assess the rationality of actions as ones caused by the agent's having a moral disposition. I defend an alternative model of rationality that invokes various levels of practical consistency, or coherence, existing between an agent's reasons for adopting a moral disposition, the argument for the moral theory or set of principles that the agent adopts that should not be contradictory about the equal worth of persons, and the agent's desires, disposition, and choice to be a moral person as reflected in the maxim the agent adopts. Having a moral disposition entails at least having a commitment to act in ways the moral theory at issue requires, which is to endorse reasons to act in these ways, and to use these reasons in deliberation about acting morally. We are not simply random actors: we act from characters and for reasons. The commitment to morality, then, provides the link between dispositions and actions. I argue that consistency in the sense of coherence in one's disposition and actions partly defines moral integrity. Moral integrity presupposes personal integrity, defined partly by consistency in one's desires to be a certain kind of person, and the disposition one forms and acts from. Moral evaluations of persons and their actions will be a measure of integrity: what is morally required is not just acting in order to meet some standard, but fostering integrity. Interdependent moral evaluations of acts and dispositions measure this best. Rational evaluations of dispositions and acts, too, should be interdependent, and will reflect whether the agent's reasoning is consistently applied. Significantly, the arguments of chapter 8 show that when we defeat action skepticism, we at once defeat disposition skepticism. We should fine-tune the requirements of morality, and thus what needs to be shown to be rationally required, as well as invoke the practical consistency model of rationality, for a complete defeat of skepticism. Doing so holds more promise of defeating action skepticism, and defeating it in a way that speaks to the moral complexity of persons.

To summarize, we need to *broaden* the traditional picture of the skeptic to include motive skepticism and amoralism, and to take privilege rather than self-interest to define the opposition to morality. We need to *narrow* the traditional picture of the skeptic to exclude deformed desires as irrational. And we need to fine-tune the requirements of morality, and consequently, the requirements of rationality, to reflect the complex interplay between dispositions, desires, reasons, and actions. In modifying the traditional picture of the skeptic, the hope is to position ourselves best to defeat fully the skeptic in a way that leaves no further skeptical challenge remaining. Only if we have this revised picture before us will we be confidently poised to put forward a moral theory that has as one of its aims defeating such a skeptic, and only then will each one of us know in the end whether she or he is a moral skeptic.

2

The Self-Interest-Based Contractarian Response to the Skeptic

This chapter examines the self-interest-based contractarian response to the skeptic who is defined in the traditional way as endorsing the expected utility theory of rational choice and action, which identifies rational action with self-interested action, or, the satisfaction of the agent's desires or preferences, and as endorsing the rationality of any but moral desires. Self-interest-based contractarians who reject the Hobbesian strategy of demonstrating that every morally required action is rationally required because it is in the agent's self-interest aim to defeat the skeptic by showing that it is rationally required because in the agent's self-interest to adopt a moral disposition. But then they must demonstrate the rationality of morally required actions that express the disposition. They might defend the Dependency Thesis, according to which the rationality of morally required acts depends on the rationality of the disposition they express. Alternatively, they might defend the Independency Thesis, according to which the rationality of morally required acts is independent of the disposition they express. This chapter argues that neither view offers a successful defeat of action skepticism. It raises at least two questions regarding the traditional skeptic, namely, whether defeating action skepticism is necessary for a successful defeat of skepticism, and whether we should assume that the skeptic endorses EU.

1 INTRODUCTION

The traditional challenge the skeptic presents is for philosophers to demonstrate that every morally required action is rationally required. Rational action is identified with self-interested action, and this is identified with promoting the satisfaction of any of one's desires or preferences but moral ones, or, with maximizing one's expected utility. On the traditional view of the skeptic, then, we must defeat action skepticism by appealing to reasons of self-interest, since these are the only reasons the skeptic will accept until we demonstrate that there are moral reasons and that they override self-interested reasons in cases of conflict.

This chapter examines the SIB contractarian attempt to defeat action skepticism. An SIB contractarian theory is one that has the following three features: it assumes that persons are mutually disinterested;[1] it takes morality to be a set of rules for behavior which would emerge from an agreement among rational and informed persons; and it assumes that to act rationally is to act in one's self-interest, and is concerned to show that at some level morality can be justified on grounds of self-interest. Philosophers who have held this view include Thomas Hobbes, Kurt Baier, Geoffrey Grice, and, most recently, David Gauthier.[2]

One reason to focus on SIB contractarianism is that the first and third features line up precisely with the traditional view of the skeptic. Regarding the first feature, Hobbes, for instance, believes that whatever desires a person has in the State of Nature, he has a right to satisfy them: the desires and passions that persons have, and the actions stemming from them, are in themselves no sin until there is a contract in place constraining their pursuit.[3] Hobbes invokes a subjective and relative notion of the good: "But whatsoever is the object of any man's appetite or desire, that is it which he for his part calleth *good*. . . . For these words of good . . . are ever used with relation to the person that useth them."[4] In the State of Nature, persons act in ways that will promote their own good, that is, in mutually disinterested ways, inevitably leading to an all-out war. Gauthier agrees with Hobbes that in a perfectly competitive market situation, which is a morally free zone, persons exhibit mutual unconcern, and that this should be the starting point for generating a moral theory, since, Gauthier believes, "moral constraints must apply in the absence of other-directed interests."[5] Morality, for SIB contractarians, must be generated from an agreement among mutually disinterested persons.

Regarding the third feature, Hobbes believes that in the State of Nature, everyone is "governed by his own reason" in pursuing the satisfaction of his desires.[6] Gauthier invokes EU because it is a long-standing and well-defended theory of rational action.[7] Both philosophers aim to justify acting morally on grounds of self-interest. Hobbes argues that it is rational for each person to give up his right to satisfy his own desires when others do so as well, since in doing so each person expects to benefit in ways he otherwise could not. Gauthier agrees that "Morality, as a system of rationally required constraints, is possible if the constraints are generated simply by the understanding that they make possible the more effective realization of one's interests, the greater fulfilment of one's preferences, *whatever one's interests or preferences may be*,"[8] but he fine-tunes which interests and preferences persons can enter into the bargain from which the moral contract will be determined. He introduces the assumption of nontuism, the view that the bargainers do not take an intrinsic interest in the interests of those with whom they interact, though they may take an instrumental interest in others' interests.[9] Expected utility theory, together with the assumption of nontuism, gives the SIB contractarian a neutral starting point from which to derive morality that does not beg the question in favor of morality.

A second reason to focus on SIB contractarianism is that it is to date the best-defended attempt to defeat action skepticism that starts with the traditional setup of the skeptic. If successful, it will show that for anyone, even if she lacks moral desires, acting morally is rationally required. Were we successfully to demonstrate that even persons who are considered to be, on the traditional model, as far removed from morality as possible are nonetheless rationally required to act in morally required ways, we will have shown something remarkable indeed, even if other skeptical challenges about motivation and the like can be raised. This chapter concerns mostly Gauthier's theory, since it is the most developed of its kind, and thus provides greatest promise of success in defeating action skepticism.

Indeed, I argue that the SIB contractarian is committed to making what I will call the dispositional move that Gauthier ingeniously makes in response to Hobbes. That is, SIB contractarianism is committed to showing that it is in one's own interest to dispose oneself to being a moral person. If it succeeds in showing this, it will have defeated disposition skepticism, the denial that having a moral disposition is rationally required. But if the theory is successfully to defeat the skeptic, it must also defeat action skepticism. In doing so, it must explain the connection between the rationality of the moral disposition and the rationality of the particular actions expressing this disposition.[10] I argue that Gauthier, or any other SIB contractarian who makes the dispositional move, is committed to the *Dependency Thesis*, according to which the rationality of particular actions depends on the rationality of the disposition they express. More specifically, if adopting a disposition is rationally required, then all the acts expressing the disposition are also rationally required. Unfortunately, the Dependency Thesis is subject to counterexamples, which I discuss in section 3. In section 4, I examine and reject some of Gauthier's arguments for the Dependency Thesis. I argue also that the alternative view, the *Independency Thesis*, which I attribute to Derek Parfit, and according to which the rationality of actions is independent of the rationality of the disposition they express, fares better than the Dependency Thesis. But not until chapter 8 will I defend a third alternative, the *Interdependency Thesis*, according to which the rationality of dispositions and of actions are determined interdependently. This thesis fares better than Gauthier's and Parfit's, for reasons having to do with moral agency, the success of EU as a model of rational action, and the issue of what would constitute a successful defeat of action skepticism.

2 THE SIB CONTRACTARIAN DILEMMA

One clear strength of SIB contractarianism is that it attempts to meet on his own terms the skeptic who believes that the only reasons there are reasons of self-interest. It does so by justifying acting morally, or at least being morally disposed, on self-interested grounds. Unfortunately, though, this strategy ultimately becomes its own downfall, because it limits the response the theory can give to the skeptic. One criticism, then, of setting up the skeptic initially to endorse EU is that doing so risks our defeat of action skepticism.

Self-interest-based (SIB) contractarians can go either of two ways. First, they can focus on the rationality of every particular morally required action rather than on the disposition to be moral. This amounts to showing that on every occasion in which a person acts in a morally required way, she acts in her own interest. But this route seems doomed to failure. It is very unlikely that SIB contractarians will be able to show that for *every* (ordinary) person, acting morally will *always* be in that person's self-interest. For suppose that you could take home some office supplies without getting caught. Or suppose you could jeopardize a colleague's success because you did not like her political views. To show that acting morally is in the interest of even these agents, SIB contractarians undoubtedly will have to buttress their argument in some implausible or otherwise problematic way. They might, for example, build in psychological assumptions such as the assumption that guilt feelings will be so intense that they would deter anyone, even the extreme immoralist, from acting immorally. Alternatively, they might advance a questionable metaphysical view about the nature of a person, such as that offered by Plato, who argues that being moral is in a person's self-interest because only if she acts morally on every occasion will the three parts of her soul be in harmony. A third option is for the SIB contractarian to invoke a Hobbesian Sovereign, or a kind of "moral police force." The moral police force would, of course, have to be extremely clever and powerful in order for it to be against anyone's interest to act immorally on any occasion. It seems likely that any solution SIB contractarians offer will involve obviously false or otherwise problematic assumptions. The point is an empirical one: Sidgwick has it right when he argues that there are two disparate systems of practical reason, namely, morality and self-interest, the complete and universal coincidence of which is improbable.[11] It may of course be logically possible that acting morally always turns out to be in one's own interest.

But even if we could establish the empirical claim that acting morally on every occasion is in one's self-interest, Gauthier rightly claims that the SIB contractarian should not try to show this. Gauthier agrees with Sidgwick that the demands of morality sometimes conflict with reasons of self-interest. Thus, Gauthier writes: "it is only as we believe that some appeals do, alas, override interest or advantage that morality becomes our concern."[12] If we could show that the dictates of morality in fact coincide completely with self-interest, Gauthier's objection would be that there is then no point in developing a morality, for it could be eliminated in favor of a system of prudence: morals would be too useful, or, superfluous.[13]

If we believe that there is a point to morality, we should not aim or expect to show that moral reasons completely coincide with prudential reasons. Recall Hobbes's answer to the Foole that the reneger either will not be allowed into moral interactions with compliant contractors, or will be cast out of society and be back in the State of Nature when his disposition is detected—he cannot expect not to get caught. Gauthier's objection is that the Hobbesian approach is a nonstarter.

Thus SIB contractarians are committed to answering the skeptic some other way while still grounding morality in self-interest. They might attempt to link morality and self-interest by showing that it is in one's interest to adopt a disposition to be moral, that is, to defeat disposition skepticism on grounds of self-interest. This is Gauthier's approach in *Morals by Agreement*. Shifting from action skepticism to disposition skepticism is a promising approach because it avoids the problems involved in showing that every instance of acting in morally required ways is rationally required because in one's interest. Indeed, the dispositional move is the only available option to SIB contractarian theorists, if they are to avoid the problems with the act-by-act approach.

But the dispositional move requires a solution to two problems. First, of course, SIB contractarians must show that becoming morally disposed is rationally required because in one's interest. Second, they must still defeat action skepticism, despite the shift to defeating disposition skepticism on self-interested grounds. In attempting to defeat action skepticism, they must show that every instance of acting in morally required ways is rationally required, *even if not in one's own interest*. Since Gauthier abandons the Hobbesian strategy of demonstrating the rationality of morally required acts on self-interested grounds, he must now show how the rationality of the disposition it is in one's self-interest to adopt carries over to particular moral actions expressing the disposition, making them rational but not because they promote the agent's self-interest.

This is significant for two reasons. First is that Gauthier needs to show in what sense other than self-interest will morally required acts be rationally required. It cannot be in a self-interested sense because he has rejected this in abandoning the Hobbesian strategy for defeating action skepticism. Second, since he rejects the Hobbesian strategy, it is no longer open to him to say that the morally required acts that are in the agent's self-interest are rationally required for this reason. Making the dispositional move precludes this possibility because on it, the rationality of acts will come from the rationality of the disposition they express.

Gauthier argues first that it is in one's self-interest to adopt a putative moral disposition he calls *constrained maximization*. He casts the argument as a choice between this disposition and that of straightforward maximization. A *straightforward* maximizer is one who chooses to act on every occasion in ways that maximize her utility, or, promote her own interest. A *constrained* maximizer is one who compares the benefit of cooperating with what she expects to gain from universal noncooperation, and cooperates if the former provides her a greater expected utility than the latter.[14] Gauthier's argument for the rationality of constrained maximization depends on there being enough others in the population similarly disposed, on people being sufficiently "translucent" so that their dispositions can be fairly easily detected by others, and on the claim that constrained maximizers have a better chance of benefiting than straightforward maximizers by being included in future beneficial interactions. I will pass over this argument, and concentrate in this chapter on the more pressing issue of Gauthier's defense of his claim that the rationality of the disposition of constrained maximization carries over to the particular actions expressing it, or, put differently, that the rationality of morally required actions is dependent on the rationality of the disposition they express.[15] The rational justification of constrained maximization would become significant especially were we unable to defeat action skepticism, and thus forced to settle for defeating disposition skepticism. In chapter 8, I will suggest a way to defeat both simultaneously. The important thing to notice for now is that the rationality of the disposition of constrained maximization is to be determined independently of the rationality of particular moral actions, and on self-interested grounds.

The argument Gauthier offers in *Morals by Agreement* for the connection between the rationality of the moral disposition and of morally required actions consists in attempting to explain away an objector's examples of actions that seem to be irrational even though they are expressions of a disposition it is rational to adopt.[16] One is the case of satisficing, that is, of setting a threshold level of fulfilment and choosing the first course of action that meets the threshold—it may be rational to satisfice rather than maximize. A second concerns wishful thinking—it may be better for us, since we often confuse true expectations with hopes, to choose on the basis of fixed principles rather than to maximize. Gauthier rejects these cases on the grounds that the actor is not perfect: a perfect actor would be a maximizer. A third case concerns threat behavior: the objector believes that if it is rational to dispose oneself to carry out a threat, it is rational to carry out the threat if the time comes. Gauthier rejects this objection on the grounds that threat behavior is irrational and immoral. But Gauthier's dismissing these cases falls short of giving a positive argument for his claim that "If [the constrained maximizer's] dispositions to choose are rational, then surely her choices are also rational."[17] In the next section, I will explore some more convincing counterexamples to Gauthier's view that call for further defense of this claim. I will also examine some arguments that Gauthier offers elsewhere in the context of nuclear deterrence that apply to his views on morality and strengthen his case.

3 THE DEPENDENCY THESIS

We need to get clear on exactly what Gauthier's view is. He offers the following thesis:

> If it is rational for me to adopt an intention to do x in circumstances c, and if c comes about, and if nothing relevant to the adoption of the intention is changed save what must be changed with the coming about of c (such as my hope of avoiding c), then it is rational for me to carry out x.[18]

For our purposes, let us assume that an intention is the same as a disposition—what is relevant is that they are psychological states a person can make herself come to have.[19]

Gauthier's view, at least initially, seems intuitively plausible. Underlying it is a principle most of us accept as true, roughly, "Whenever you act from a disposition it is rational for you to have, you act rationally." This principle is intuitively plausible because it expresses a connection between the disposition a rational person has and the particular actions she performs. We would find it odd indeed if there were *no* connection between the rationality of the disposition and the actions it expresses. And it seems plausible not only for there to be *some* connection, but for there to be this *strong* connection, as the following examples demonstrate. Suppose we could show that it is rational for a person to dispose herself to caring about her parents. Then it seems that every instance of acting in a caring way toward her parents is rational as well. Suppose that caring about truth is rational because truth is good in itself. Then it seems that a person has reason to care about truth on every occasion. Or, suppose the devil exists and is as evil as legend has taken him to be. Suppose there is a pill that you must take every day that will drive away the devil. It seems to be rational for you to dispose yourself to taking the pill every day, and it seems that every instance of taking the pill is a rational action. Likewise, it seems that every instance of driving safely is rational when it is rational to dispose yourself to being a safe driver.

Not only is Gauthier's view intuitively plausible, it is one that we should hope can be defended. For if he can successfully show that the rationality of the disposition to be moral carries over to particular moral actions, he will have defeated action skepticism. Of course, he will have to establish that it *is* rational to adopt a moral disposition—that is, he will have to defeat disposition skepticism. This point aside, his view is better than the alternative view that we are now considering, which in this context—where the rationality of an action is decided independently of the rationality of the disposition it expresses, and the Hobbesian strategy of justifying morally required actions on self-interested grounds is rejected—would have the consequence that action skepticism could never be defeated.

We can take Parfit's discussion in *Reasons and Persons* to represent the alternative view about dispositions and actions.[20] Parfit presents the familiar case of Kate, which is intended to show that even though it may be rational for a person to adopt a certain disposition, not every instance of acting from that disposition is rational. Parfit calls these cases of Rational Irrationality. His discussion centers around a theory of rationality called the *Self-Interest Theory*, or, S. According to Parfit, "S gives to each person this aim: the outcomes that would be best for himself, and that would make his life go, for him, as well as possible."[21] The Self-Interest Theory is similar to EU, which identifies rational choice and action with the maximization of one's expected utility. The person who adopts S as the best theory of rationality might find it rational to dispose herself to act in ways that will make her life go as well as possible. But having this disposition sometimes causes the person to act in ways that do not make her life go as well as possible.

Parfit's example is of Kate, a writer whose strongest desire is to make her books as good as possible. If this desire were not her strongest one, Kate would find her work boring. It is better for her if this is her strongest desire, and if she disposes herself to work hard so that her books will be as good as possible, because only then can she expect her life to go as well as possible. But this disposition sometimes causes her to work so hard that she is exhausted and depressed. Were she to weaken her desire and her disposition so that she works less, she would find her work boring. So she keeps the disposition that is rational for her to have given her strongest desire, even though it sometimes causes her to act irrationally.

To make this a clear counterexample to Gauthier's view, we can expand on the case in the following way.[22] Kate's strongest desire is that her books be good. Given that it is rational for her to have this desire, it is rational for Kate to dispose herself to working hard every weekday. Gauthier's thesis entails that on every weekday when Kate works on her books it is rational for her to do so. Parfit's objection is that, on occasion, say, on Friday of a certain week, Kate will find herself exhausted and depressed from working so hard earlier in the week that working on Friday is irrational because it will not contribute to making her life as good as possible. Kate would be better off taking a break.

Gauthier holds what has been called the Dependency Thesis: the rationality of a particular choice depends on the rationality of the disposition to choose that the particular choice expresses:[23] If a disposition is rational, then every action that expresses it is rational as well. Parfit, in contrast, holds what I will call the Independency Thesis: the rationality of a particular action can be assessed independently of the rationality of the disposition that the particular action expresses.[24]

Gauthier, I believe, is committed to the Dependency Thesis or something like it. Again, he cannot say that particular morally required actions are rationally required because they are utility maximizing, or, interest satisfying, since he denies that we can and should show that. So he and other SIB contractarians must make the dispositional move, grounding the rationality of a moral disposition in self-interest. But then they must explain how the rationality of the disposition carries over to the particular actions expressing that disposition, and the Dependency Thesis seems to be their best option. It certainly seems more plausible from Gauthier's perspective than the Independency Thesis, which would assess the rationality of morally required acts on grounds of self-interest, a move that Gauthier rejects. But in the face of Parfit's counterexample, the Dependency Thesis needs defense. This kind of counterexample needs to be explained away. Let us turn now to Gauthier's arguments.

4 GAUTHIER'S DEFENSE OF THE DEPENDENCY THESIS

4.1 The Inconsistency Argument

One argument Gauthier offers for the Dependency Thesis is that if a person accepts a certain disposition as being rational, rejecting the actions it requires would be inconsistent, and thus we cannot claim that such actions should not be performed.[25] There are two questions: where exactly does the inconsistency lie, since Gauthier himself does not say, and why is it a problem?

David Lewis responds correctly to two interpretations of Gauthier's charge of inconsistency.[26] First, if the argument is that a theory cannot consistently judge the *act* of disposing oneself as rational, while at the same time judge *acting* on the disposition as irrational,[27] it is mistaken, because there is no inconsistency involved in these judgments. They are judgments of two different actions, the act of forming a disposition, and actually acting on it, and so they are consistent. Second, the argument might be that a theory cannot consistently judge *a person* who acts to be rational and irrational. Lewis rejects this view also. The correct judgment we need to make, according to Lewis, is to say that the person is rational in adopting the disposition, but is irrational sometimes in acting on it. A person is a mixture of rationality and irrationality.[28] Since a person has many rational aspects, we can make opposing judgments about her because they are made about different things.[29] Lewis would favor the Independency Thesis.

Lewis's objection raises the issue of the nature of dispositions. The psychology of dispositions might explain the paradoxical nature of the judgment of a person as a mixture of rationality and irrationality. It seems to be the case that many dispositions to act will cause those who act on them to act in ways contrary to the very purpose of adopting the disposition in the first place. It happens in both the case of Kate and in the moral case. Gauthier's constrained maximizer disposes herself to act morally because having and acting on that disposition can be expected to be more self-beneficial than having and acting on the disposition of straightforward maximization. But given that she is disposed to acting morally, she will on occasion act irrationally because she will act contrary to the goal she wants to achieve by disposing herself that way in the first place. This happens on the SIB contractarian schema when she can benefit greatly by acting immorally without risking losing the benefit of being included in further interactions in which others treat her in the ways required by morality.

Other dispositions yield the same result. Consider the person who has a stressful life and who tries to become a calmer person, so she takes relaxing vacations, practices yoga and meditation, and takes up the hobby of reupholstering antique furniture. Despite her efforts, however, she cannot make herself calmer, and, in fact, ends up making herself more anxious because she keeps worrying about the things she ought to be doing that stress her out. The person disposes herself to making herself relaxed, but her disposition causes her to act in ways that frustrate her goal. Or consider the person who disposes himself to be a winner at racquetball. He focuses so hard on trying to win that he loses sight of what he needs to do to win, namely, to perfect his racquetball skills. His disposition, too, causes him to act in ways that frustrate his goal. The same holds in the case of the parent who loves his children a great deal and wants to do what is best for them, so he disposes himself to prevent any harm from befalling his children. But on occasion, such as when his child is trapped in a burning house, the parent risks losing his own life to save her instead of waiting a very short time for firefighters to arrive. Even if he is fully aware of the risk to his own life, and fully expects the firefighters to rescue his child, his disposition causes him to try to save his child. On the worst scenario, he will die, leaving his children fatherless, which is worse for them.

Many dispositions are like this: it is rational to adopt them to achieve a certain goal, yet acting on them does not always help in achieving that goal, or sometimes actually frustrates it. If this is just a fact about dispositions, then it seems wrong to disparage a theory because it can make seemingly inconsistent judgments about a person. If there is an inconsistency in the judgments that a person is rational in one respect, but not in another, it is not a problem. The Interdependency Thesis faces additional problems that I will discuss in chapter 8, but here the point is simply that the inconsistent judgments that it yields merely reflect a fact about the nature of dispositions.

Perhaps Gauthier's point about inconsistency is just that if a person is disposed a certain way, and cannot help but act from that disposition, we would make inconsistent judgments were we to judge him to be rational in adopting the disposition, but irrational in acting on it, given that the action is caused by the disposition. The claim is similar to the statement "Ought implies can": it makes no more sense to say that one is irrational in doing x if one cannot help but do x than it does to say that one ought to do x if one cannot. This is the "mechanism interpretation" of constrained maximization, which takes the disposition to be psychologically compulsive.[30] I will have more to say about this also in chapter 8, specifically about whether this reading of constrained maximization is one we think is a genuine moral disposition. My response to this claim by Gauthier, were he to make it, is that it is at best *wrong* to say that a person ought to do x if he cannot, or that he is irrational to do x if he cannot help but do x. But this does not establish that these judgments are *inconsistent*, which is what Gauthier needs to establish in order to establish the Dependency Thesis.

An objector might claim that because the agent cannot act otherwise, we must judge her to be rational when she acts on her disposition. In Kate's case, we must say that Kate is rational to work on Friday, given that she cannot act otherwise. But, in response, I think that at best we can say that Kate *is caused* by her disposition to work hard on Friday. Yet she is *not justified* in doing so because her working hard on Friday does not lead to a good state of affairs for anyone, especially Kate herself, since she becomes exhausted and depressed. This kind of answer would not satisfy the skeptic in the moral case who demands a justifying reason, not merely a motivating reason, or, psychological explanation for why a person acts as she does.

Although these attempts to dispel Gauthier's inconsistency charge are well taken, there still does seem to be a kind of inconsistency involved in saying that it is rational to be disposed to do x in c, yet when c occurs, doing x is irrational. Consider this case. Suppose you want to be wise in your later years, and have good reason to believe that you will not change. Wisdom will help you know right from wrong, see the things you can and cannot change and help you to know the difference, among other things. Suppose there is a smart pill such that if you take it each year on your birthday, you will be guaranteed wisdom in your later years. Suppose, then, that your disposing yourself now to take the smart pill each year is rational. When your birthday arrives, assuming that you still want wisdom, it would be inconsistent for you to judge that it is irrational to take the smart pill.

Yet consider a case raised by Gregory Kavka.[31] Suppose someone offers to pay you $1 million tomorrow if at midnight tonight you have the readily detectable intention to drink a vial of toxin that will make you very sick for a day. You affirm that you have a reason to form the intention to drink the toxin the next day. You get the money at midnight. The claim is that you would make inconsistent statements if, on the next day, you do not affirm that it is rational for you to drink the toxin. The question, first, is why the inconsistency charge seems to hold in the smart pill case, but not in the toxin case, and second, which case is morality most like?

The inconsistency charge seems to hold in the smart pill case, but not in the toxin case, because the rationality of the disposition seems to carry over to the particular action in the former case, but not in the latter. In the smart pill case, the reason to adopt the disposition is that you want to achieve the goal of having wisdom in your later years, together with the fact that it is *necessary* for you to take the smart pill each year in order to achieve your goal. And the reason to take the smart pill on your birthday is that it is *necessary* for you to do so on this and other occasions in order to achieve the goal of having wisdom. Since your reason for adopting the disposition *includes* the fact that you must act on the disposition, the rationality of the disposition carries over to the particular action expressing it. To be clear, if we asked, "Why adopt the disposition?" the reason is that you want wisdom, together with the fact that it is necessary for you to take the smart pill every year to get wisdom. If we asked, "Why take the smart pill today?" the reason is that you want wisdom, and taking the smart pill on this one occasion, together with the fact that you are disposed to take a smart pill on all your birthdays, will bring you wisdom. The point is that the act gets its rationality from the rationality of the disposition. Your reason to take the smart pill in order to get wisdom is not your reason unless you have the disposition to get wisdom. You might take the smart pill for a different reason, such as that it tastes good. But if your reason for taking the smart pill is that you want wisdom, this reason *comes from* the disposition. So the Dependency Thesis holds in such a case: it is rational for you to dispose yourself to do x in c, and when c occurs, it is rational for you to do x. It would be inconsistent to judge otherwise, assuming, of course, your goals do not change.

The toxin case is different. You form the intention to drink the toxin because you want to achieve the goal of getting $1 million. But if acting on the intention is not necessary to achieving that goal, either because you have already achieved the goal, or because you can achieve it without your acting on the intention on this particular occasion, then it seems that you *can* consistently affirm the rationality of the intention to do x in c, yet when c occurs, judge doing x to be irrational. This is obvious in the toxin case: you have already achieved the goal of having the intention when c occurs. So there is no reason to drink the toxin. You would not make inconsistent judgments were you to affirm the rationality of adopting the intention to drink the toxin at time t1, and at time t2, deny the rationality of acting on the intention.

The toxin case and others like it threaten Gauthier's view. To save it, he or any Dependency theorist needs to establish the inconsistency charge, and, thus, the Dependency Thesis, either by explaining away these cases or by showing that morality is more like the smart pill case than the toxin-type cases. I now want to disarm both disjuncts.

First, the Dependency theorist might explain away the toxin and similar cases by saying that since time passes and circumstances change, it would not be rational to drink the toxin because the *intention* to drink the toxin at time t2 is no longer rational.[32] This move would reduce the threat the toxin case poses to the Dependency Thesis simply by denying that it is a case in which the disposition is rational, and the actions expressing it irrational. Instead, both the disposition and the actions are irrational. More generally, the move amounts to saying that whenever we come across an action that is irrational, we judge that it would be irrational to affirm the disposition it expresses at the time of acting. This preserves the Dependency Thesis.

But this move fails. Granted, it is true that when it comes time to drink the toxin, intending to drink it is no longer rational because you have already achieved the goal of forming the intention. But when you actually do form the intention, it is rational for you to do so because doing so is the only way to get the $1 million. Forming the intention is rational even if you know full well at this time that having the intention will cause you to drink the toxin after you get the money. It is irrelevant that when the time comes to drink the toxin and you are wealthy, the intention to drink the toxin is irrational. What is relevant is that drinking the toxin at time t2 is irrational, but you are caused to drink it by the disposition it is rational for you to adopt at t1. The Dependency theorist cannot explain away the toxin case this way: it is rational to form the intention at t1, yet irrational to act on it at t2.

Moreover, there are cases in which it is rational for you to adopt a disposition at time t1, and in which it is still rational to affirm that disposition at time t2, even though acting on it at t2 is irrational. Consider a modified version of the smart pill case. Suppose you need to take a smart pill only nine out of every ten birthdays in order to gain wisdom. If you have taken a smart pill on your past eight birthdays, and fully expect to on your tenth birthday, it is not obviously rationally required for you to do so on this, your ninth, birthday. This is so because you can achieve the goal of having wisdom without taking a smart pill on this one occasion. Yet your disposition at this time is still rationally justified. Cases like this deny the attempt to save the argument at issue, that if it is irrational to act on a disposition at time t2, it must be irrational to affirm the disposition at that time. This move fails to explain away the toxin and other similar cases.

So let us turn to the second way the Dependency theorist might establish the inconsistency charge, which is to show that morality is more like the original smart pill case than the toxin case. This would amount to showing that there is some goal that ensures the rationality of adopting a disposition to be moral, and whose achievement is accomplished only by acting on the disposition in every relevant instance. Morality would then be like the original smart pill case, in that it would be inconsistent to judge the moral disposition to be rational, and the actions expressing it irrational.

Two things need not concern us in comparing morality to the toxin case: that a moral disposition is different from the intention to drink the toxin because the latter is a one-shot deal, and the former a lifetime or near lifetime commitment, and that having the intention to drink the toxin will cause one clearly to act against one's interest. The former is irrelevant to the issue, and the latter is met by the fact that a moral disposition will sometimes cause one to make sacrifices on a par with, or even greater than, being very sick for a day.[33] Our concern is whether the rationality of the moral disposition carries over to the actions as neatly as it seems to in the original smart pill case, or whether it does not, as in the toxin case.

We might think it does. For on many occasions, a constrained maximizer must act on her disposition in order to achieve the goal of being included in future beneficial interactions. Merely having the disposition is insufficient for achieving this goal: translucency and observing behavior will let the rest of us be fairly certain whether she has it and acts on it. We might want to say, then, that if one affirms it to be rational to adopt constrained maximization, judging acting on it to be irrational would be inconsistent.

However, it is possible to achieve the goal of having the disposition of constrained maximization even without acting morally on a particular occasion. In such a case, the agent can expect to be included in future beneficial interactions despite acting immorally on this occasion. Only if Gauthier were to make the stronger assumption of *transparency*, which he denies, but which would make a person's deceiving us about her disposition impossible, rather than translucency, which he affirms, but which makes us only fairly certain about another's disposition, would this kind of case be extremely unlikely. It would then be consistent for one to affirm at t1 that it is rational to adopt constrained maximization, but at t2, not affirm the rationality of acting on that disposition. This is because the purpose of adopting the disposition could be achieved even without acting on it this time. Thus, morality is more like the modified smart pill case than the toxin case, in that you need to act morally on a number of occasions in order to achieve the goal of being included in future beneficial interactions. And in both cases you would affirm the rationality of the disposition at the time when acting on it is irrational. But morality is *not* like the original smart pill case because in neither case does the rationality of the disposition carry over to *all* the actions expressing it.

As long as there are occasions on which you can act immorally yet still expect others to act morally to you in the future, Gauthier's charge of inconsistency will not hold for *all* instances of acting morally. In these cases, judging it to be rational to adopt a moral disposition at t1, but irrational to act on it at t2, is consistent. But in order to establish the Dependency Thesis, the Dependency theorist must show that the inconsistency charge holds for all instances of acting morally, on the grounds that the rationality of the disposition carries over to the action in every instance. Since the inconsistency charge does not hold for all instances of acting morally, it does not establish the Dependency Thesis. We need a better argument than the Inconsistency Argument to defend the Dependency Thesis, and thus to aid in the SIB contractarian's quest to defeat action skepticism.

4.2 The Impossibility Argument

Gauthier gives a second argument to establish the Dependency Thesis that takes the form of an objection to the kind of view Parfit holds. Gauthier grants for the sake of argument that your forming a disposition that may cause you to act irrationally on occasion is rational. He then claims that if you are rational and know that it would be irrational for you to do x in c, then it would be *impossible* for you to dispose yourself to doing x in c.[34] His point is a conceptual one.

But this argument also fails, for two reasons. First, contra Gauthier and other Dependency theorists, it *is* possible for a person to dispose herself to act a certain way in a certain situation even though she knows it would be irrational for her to act that way when the time comes. People do this all the time. For example, many people are huge sports fans. They really like to watch football, baseball, and basketball, and they believe that being a true fan means watching all the games their favorite team plays. *Since* they have a strong desire to watch sports, it is rational for them to dispose themselves to being true fans. Even so, they know full well that being so disposed will lead them, on occasion, to act in ways that make them less happy. For instance, they may also want to be involved in a relationship with an intimate or friends who may not share their interest in sports. Being a true fan will require giving up these things at least in part, given the likelihood of finding others with a similar commitment to fanhood. But the true fan knows she will be happier if she makes room for these relationships and the commitments they involve. Although she knows that watching all the sports games she is interested in is irrational because it will make her less happy than if she had these relationships and gave up some of the games, and she knows full well that these relationships will conflict with the demands of being a true fan, she finds it possible to dispose herself to being a true fan.

Consider another example. Some people find it rational to dispose themselves to being patriotic because it gives them a tie to their country, a common cause with their fellow citizens, or a sense of belonging. And they dispose themselves this way in the full knowledge that on occasion, a true patriot may be called on to sacrifice her life, say, by enlisting in the armed services during wartime. Gauthier's point might be more persuasive, though, when we consider the case of nuclear deterrence. It might be rational for a country to form the intention to retaliate when its enemy makes the first strike. But if it really thought about the effects of retaliation, it might not be able to form the intention to retaliate. Still, we cannot generalize the point to hold for all cases, as the sports fan and patriot cases show.

A second objection to this argument is that if it were not possible for a person to dispose herself in the relevant way, then it is *never* possible for her to form *any* disposition. Consider again the case of Kate. If Kate forms the disposition it is rational for her to form, given her desire to make her life go as well as possible, she will sometimes act irrationally. The only way for it to be true that Kate will never work to the point of exhaustion is for her to have a much weaker desire that her books be good, and, so, a much weaker disposition to work. But having this disposition will be worse for her, since her books will not be that good, and her life will not go as well as possible. She needs to have the stronger disposition in order to expect to obtain the goals she wants: interesting work, good books, and a good life. And if she forms the *opposite* disposition, clearly she will act in ways that are irrational. Any disposition weaker than the strongest one, but stronger than the one that leads her to avoid working to exhaustion, will lead her to the same problems as the strongest one. Any disposition weaker than the one that leads her to avoid working to exhaustion will be worse for her because it will cause her not to make her books as good as she can. On all the options, she will end up acting in irrational ways. If this is true, and if Gauthier is correct to say that it is not possible to dispose oneself to act in ways one knows are irrational, then one will not be able to form *any* disposition. But this is certainly false, since we all form dispositions of all kinds. Thus we should give up Gauthier's point that disposing oneself to perform an action that one knows it is irrational to perform is impossible.

Gauthier can modify his argument to concede that if one believes it to be irrational sometimes to do x in c, one *can* form the disposition to act that way, but only if one changes one's beliefs about what it is rational to do. One way to do this is for a person to change her desires. In the nuclear deterrence case, for example, a person might come to desire retaliation; in the toxin case, to desire drinking the toxin; in the moral case, to desire acting morally for its own sake. But then Gauthier would have to show that *everyone* forms a desire to be moral, since only those people who actually have the relevant desire would believe that rationality dictates acting in the way the disposition prescribes. But for the person who has not changed his desires, acting morally as the disposition dictates is rationally required. We cannot defeat skepticism by giving a reason to act morally that holds only for people who are already morally disposed because they have moral desires and beliefs, since this would beg the question against the skeptic who claims that not everyone has moral desires and beliefs. Further, such a move relies on a desire-satisfaction theory of rationality for individual moral actions, an account that Gauthier clearly rejects.

Gregory Kavka suggests a different response in support of Gauthier's argument.[35] According to Kavka, an objector might claim that if we admit that some of the actions done in accord with a disposition are themselves irrational, that is reason for doubting the rationality of the *disposition*.[36] This is a reason to prefer the Dependency Thesis to the Independency Thesis, since at least on the Dependency Thesis we might be able to defeat disposition skepticism.

But this attempt to reject the Independency Thesis in favor of the Dependency Thesis also fails. This is because a disposition may still be rational to adopt, even if having it leads a person on occasion to act irrationally, as the modified smart pill case shows. The possibility of Parfit-like cases would not destroy the rationality of the disposition of constrained maximization. Here, too, as in the Kate case, we can rule out all the alternative dispositions as ones it is not rational to adopt. Straightforward maximization is irrational because if one adopts it, one cannot expect to benefit in ways that one can if one is a constrained maximizer. And a weaker disposition to act morally unless one thinks that one can benefit greatly by acting immorally this time is irrational because one cannot expect to receive the benefits a constrained maximizer can expect to gain, since the weaker disposition inevitably will lead one to run the risk of being excluded from future beneficial interactions. The strong version of constrained maximization as Gauthier conceives it still seems to be the disposition it is rational to adopt. Cases of Rational Irrationality, were Gauthier to admit them, should not lead us to reject this disposition as irrational.

Thus the Impossibility Argument fails to defend the Dependency Thesis.[37]

5 SOME FURTHER ARGUMENTS AGAINST THE DEPENDENCY THESIS

Another problem with the Dependency Thesis is that anyone who holds it cannot establish the rationality of the particular choices *independently* of the rationality of the disposition. But this leads to a bizarre result. If someone were to act in a way that, say, a constrained maximizer acts, but *from* an irrational disposition, a Dependency theorist would have to judge this action to be irrational. Suppose a straightforward and a constrained maximizer both perform the same morally required action: keeping his promise to help you put in a floor in your house. The straightforward maximizer keeps his promise because you will help him paint his study—he expects to benefit on this occasion; the constrained maximizer keeps his promise because he expects to benefit from the practice of promise-keeping, even if it means that he might not benefit on this particular occasion, that is, even if you do not return the favor when it comes to his house projects. The point is that the Dependency theorist would have to judge the same acts of promise-keeping differently. Many of us would find it understandable to judge them to be different, morally speaking. But the Dependency theorist's view is that they are different, rationally speaking: only the action caused by the disposition of constrained maximization is a rational action. This is counterintuitive.

The alternative view that I have been attributing to Parfit does not fall prey to this objection because, on it, the rationality of the particular choices can be assessed independently of the rationality of the disposition. And a good thing about this view is that it allows some connection between the rationality of the disposition and the choices expressing it, albeit not the tight one that Gauthier's view has. Consider the disposition that rationality requires one to adopt if one believes in S: one should, rationally speaking, dispose oneself in the way that makes one's life go as well as possible. Certain actions are rationally required on S because they, if performed, contribute to one's life going as well as possible. For example, Kate's staying home tonight to work on her books is rationally required because acting that way contributes to her life going as well as possible. It is because a person wants to act in ways that maximize his utility, or contribute to his life going as well as possible, that rationality requires him to dispose himself in a way that causes him to perform these very actions, even if he knows that having that disposition will cause him, on occasion, to act irrationally. The disposition he adopts is the best available option. And if he has that disposition, he often acts in ways that are rationally required on S, that is, that contribute to his life going as well as possible. The rationality of the disposition and of the particular choices, though the latter can be established independently of the former, go hand in hand. And the actions a person performs caused by the disposition could be judged as being rationally required even if the person does not perform them as a result of having the disposition that rationality requires he adopt. This is more plausible than Gauthier's view. But, as I will argue in chapter 8, even this view faces other problems that are sufficient for rejecting it in favor of the Interdependency Thesis, which favors a stronger, and more plausible, connection between a disposition and the acts expressing it.

Moreover, if Dependency theorists established their thesis, it would mean that the rationality of the disposition carries over to the particular choices in the toxin case, the nuclear deterrence case, and other similar cases, making it rational to drink the toxin that makes you very sick for a day, and for a country to retaliate against another by using nuclear weapons. This is an unpalatable result, which gives us another reason to reject the Dependency Thesis.

We should have expected the arguments in support of the Dependency Thesis to fail. Dependency theorists are faced with the task of showing that morally required acts are rationally required, but not because they are in the agent's self-interest. Their view is that the rationality of an act depends on the rationality of the disposition it expresses, but in some sense other than a self-interested one. Thus they have to explain how it is that a disposition such as constrained maximization is rationally required to adopt because it promotes the agent's self-interest, expresses acts that are rationally required in a non-self-interested sense. This is a formidable task, indeed.

6 CONCLUSION

When all is said and done, SIB contractarians who make the dispositional move are faced with serious problems. The Dependency Thesis must be defended in the face of such counterexamples as the Kate case. But if SIB contractarians cannot establish either the rational requiredness of the disposition to be moral or the Dependency Thesis, they leave themselves open to the charge that it is possible that *no* morally required acts are rationally required. If they cannot show that the disposition is rationally required, then it follows from the Dependency Thesis that they cannot show that all the actions based on that disposition are rational, either. If they can show that the disposition is rationally required, but cannot show why the rationality carries over to the particular choices, they are left in the same position. So they are forced to conclude either that it is possible that no morally required acts are rationally required because acts get their rationality only from the disposition they express, or they have to resort to the Independency Thesis, which allows them to judge morally required acts to be rationally required when they are in the agent's self-interest. The first option is devastating for defeating skepticism. The second, though it would mean that morally required acts in one's self-interest are rationally required, leaves them no better off than they began, for the skeptic wants it to be shown that when morality and self-interest part company, as they often do, rationality dictates acting in morally required ways. And the Independency Thesis leaves the action skeptic undefeated. Indeed, as long as it remains logically possible that there be cases of Rational Irrationality, the action skeptic cannot be answered. But the action skeptic demands that we show that *all* morally required actions are rationally required. The Dependency Thesis held promise because if it were defended, and if we could defeat disposition skepticism, we would defeat this demanding skeptic. But the failure of the Dependency Thesis means that not a single morally required action will be rationally required, since such actions get their rationality from the disposition they express. Thus, on either Parfit's view or on Gauthier's view, action skepticism remains undefeated. One conclusion to draw from this discussion is that if we are to defeat action skepticism, we will need a better theory than either the Dependency Thesis or the Independency Thesis.

Self-interest-based contractarianism's failure to defeat skepticism is particularly disturbing. For one of the main advantages of this theory is that it starts with the assumption that persons do not have any moral motives, and hopes to show that even so, acting in morally required ways is rationally required. The theory thus does not beg the question in favor of morality. Perhaps, though, taking such a strong skeptical starting point, as Descartes does in aiming to defeat skepticism about the external world, at least partly contributes to SIB contractarianism's failure to defeat skepticism. A second conclusion to draw is that this failure calls into question whether we should take the skeptic to adopt the view that rational action is self-interested action. Perhaps the starting point of EU dooms us to failure in defeating action skepticism, unless there is an alternative to Hobbes's and Gauthier's strategies. That is, since the skeptic accepts only self-interested reasons until we demonstrate a better theory of practical reason that includes moral reasons, we are forced to justify morally required actions either directly on self-interested grounds, as in Hobbes's strategy, or indirectly, as emanating from a disposition that itself is in our self-interest to adopt, as in Gauthier's strategy. We might be tempted to conclude that defeating just disposition skepticism is sufficient for fully defeating skepticism, given SIB contractarianism's failure to defeat action skepticism. But I think there is another alternative. The Interdependency Thesis that I will defend invokes a different model of rational action that relies not on self-interest, but on practical consistency or coherence in an agent's dispositions, actions, desires, and justification for the moral theory the agent endorses. This model, I believe, fares better than EU because it does not doom at the start the attempt to defeat action skepticism. Further, it allows us to fine-tune what morality requires in the way of action and make the skeptic's demand responsive to this. The skeptic will still demand that we demonstrate the rationality of every morally required act, yet what is morally required will be assessed in light of the agent's disposition, desires, willingness to correct for mistakes, and so on. The Interdependency Thesis allows the rationality of acts to come in degrees, as measured by the action's contribution to a person's consistent life plan—how she wants to live her life, the kind of person she wants to be, the maxim she chooses to follow, and the like. This will mean that we rationally assess an act in light of the agent's reasoning, the effects it has on the agent's deliberations, and the nature of the act. Thus a person who realizes the error of his ways and tries to correct them acts consistently with his moral disposition, and his acts should be rationally assessed accordingly.

The Interdependency Thesis also gets rid of cases like Kate's, since it judges the rationality of dispositions and of acts interdependently rather than separately. Importantly, together with the practical consistency model of rationality, it links the agent's disposition and actions through her *reasons*. Independent judgments of dispositions and actions are empty in the sense that they tell us only whether an agent or act meets a certain standard, such as whether one's life goes as well as possible, but they do not say anything about our reasons for acting, whether they are linked to moral principles guiding our lives, how they relate to how we want to live, our deliberations about our dispositions, and whether we can change our dispositions. They are, in short, problematic for moral integrity. Dependent judgments are also problematic because it is not clear that they capture the right psychological connection between having a disposition and acting on it: is it mere causation or some strong tendency or what? I will explore these issues in chapter 8 in the context of developing a fuller account of a moral disposition than I discuss here. But in the next chapter, I turn to a feminist critique of contractarianism, and examine whether an alternative theory, the ethic of care, advanced by some feminists offers a better attempt to defeat action skepticism than SIB contractarianism.

3

A Feminist Ethics Response to the Skeptic

This chapter examines three responses to the action skeptic offered by feminists, particularly care ethicists, who reject SIB contractarianism for reasons relating to its assumption of abstract individualism. The most promising response is one that retains the traditional picture of the skeptic, but offers an internalist reason for acting morally, one that necessarily connects a reason for acting in a caring way with acting from the motive of care. But this motive cashes out under patriarchy in ways that recapitulate women's oppression. Thus, we should reject this attempt to defeat the action skeptic. The ethic of care fares no better than SIB contractarianism in defeating action skepticism. This chapter's discussion of the ethic of care raises three questions about the traditional skeptic: first, whether to exclude from EU, the theory of practical reason endorsed by the skeptic, desires deformed by patriarchy whose satisfaction risks recapitulating women's oppression, second, whether we need to defeat motive skepticism in addition to action skepticism for a complete defeat of skepticism, and third, whether we need a fuller account of justification than EU allows, one that squares with a richer account of morality than SIB contractarianism.

1 INTRODUCTION

In the previous chapter, I showed that SIB contractarianism does not defeat action skepticism. One reason, perhaps, is the strong skeptical starting point governing contractarian moral theory, that of mutually disinterested persons who are rational to act in ways satisfying their desires, whatever these may be, excepting moral ones. So perhaps if we start with a different moral theory that does not invoke this starting point, we will have a better chance of defeating skepticism. Some feminists have critiqued SIB contractarianism precisely for reasons relating to its starting point, so the theory they propose in light of these objections seems to be a natural place to start. Indeed, even if SIB contractarianism succeeded in defeating action skepticism, it would be subject to certain feminist objections that render both it and consequently its attempt to defeat skepticism problematic. The theory that feminists have proposed in part to address some of these objections is the ethic of care. Not much has been said, though, either about what a feminist justification for acting morally might look like, or about how the ethic of care itself might respond to the action skeptic. It is important, though, for feminists that we defeat action skepticism, whether or not in the context of the ethic of care, since doing so will back up the charge that an act is sexist with the charge that it is irrational as well, and will take us a long way toward ending women's oppression if people follow the dictates of rationality. Finally, since we want an inclusive defeat of skepticism that covers even sexist acts, it is important to examine whatever feminists have to say about the skeptical project. Feminists claim that such an inclusive defeat of skepticism has not been accomplished by traditional moral theories.

This chapter examines some possible answers that a care ethicist might offer to the action skeptic. After exploring some feminist objections to contractarianism in section 2, and summarizing some of the main features of the ethic of care in section 3, I turn in section 4 to some options that care ethicists in particular might take regarding defeating the action skeptic. One is that we ought to abandon the project of justification for reasons having to do with the rejection of reason due to its being a male-biased concept. Another is that we ought to reject EU, or at least modify it. A third, the most viable for care ethicists, I argue, turns on the care ethicists' insistence that acting from the motive of care is essential to acting morally, a point that separates the ethic of care from traditional rule-oriented moral theories. Care ethicists need to show, in order to defeat skepticism, that rationality requires being the kind of person the theory holds to be ideal: one who acts in a caring way and from the motive of care. One way for care ethicists to show this is for them to be intern-alists about reasons and motives. Very generally, internalism is the thesis that reasons and motives are necessarily connected. I argue that care ethicists ought not to offer an internalist reason for defeating skepticism in the context of patriarchy because this would mean that they link necessarily reasons with motives associated with "women's caring." The danger of having rationality endorse women's caring is that acting ratio-nally would contribute to women's oppression.

2 FEMINIST OBJECTIONS TO CONTRACTARIANISM

In the past couple of decades, feminists have posed many challenges to traditional moral theories, including that they are too focused on the universality of moral rules when they ought to focus on particular moral situations that cannot be codified, that they dictate impartiality when partiality, particularly concerning our treatment of family and friends, is called for, and that they focus on reason to the exclusion of emotion.[1] Perhaps the most telling objection against contractarianism in particular is that traditional moral theory focuses on abstract individuals who are devoid of relations and a social context, instead of on concrete individuals who are socially contextualized and about whom facts are known and matter to our moral obligations. Self-interest-based contractarianism takes as its starting point an abstract individualistic picture of the bargainers to the hypothetical contract that defines the true moral code. As I have shown, the bargainers are in a position similar to that of the traditional skeptic in that they are equally rational in wanting to pursue their own interest as defined by the satisfaction of their desires. These desires, for Hobbes, can have any content, but for Gauthier, are any but moral desires. For contractarians such as John Rawls, who famously invokes the veil of ignorance, the bargainers are explicitly abstracted from their particularities so that we do not know what their particular desires are, the relationships they stand in, and certain features of themselves, including their race and gender, social or class status, intelligence and strength, and the like.[2] For Hobbes and Gauthier, who portray the bargainers as knowing at least their own desires, if not these other features about themselves, the objection is that the bargainers are still abstracted from their real situations in that they are merely hypothetical figures rather than real persons with real particularities that influence their choices in the bargain.

Feminists have identified at least three problems emerging from the objection about abstract individualism. First, the bargaining position is not in fact neutral, despite its being portrayed as such. Its purported neutrality for Hobbes and Gauthier lies with its being designed to show that no matter what a person's (nonmoral) desires, action skepticism can be defeated. Its purported neutrality for Rawls lies with its being designed to show that when no one knows her or his own desires and other self-identifying features about herself or himself, we can reach agreement about our duties, and even defeat action skepticism. The feminist complaint is that features like gender do, indeed, shape the emergent moral code. In a world of unequal power, the Hobbesian contract will never get off the ground, or if it does, it will reflect and recapitulate existing social inequalities.[3] A Rawlsian contract might get off the ground, but it will not be appropriately reflective of gender and other features that matter for our moral obligations. The feminist complaint, then, is that we need to take into account gender in determining our moral obligations. Taking this a step further, if our moral code is not sufficiently reflective of gender, or even recapitulates women's oppression because it leaves gender out, we can expect that any defeat of action skepticism will fall short in this regard—it will not show that all immoral actions are irrational.

A second problem is that abstract individualism is designed to capture typically male-male interactions between strangers in the paid workforce, but not interactions between intimates, which women but not men have historically been associated with, including nurturing children and cultivating social relations.[4] Thus the emergent moral code governs only interactions in the "public sphere" but not those in the "private sphere" of the home. Feminists worry about the implications this has for the moral status of, for instance, child abuse, woman-battering, and rape of female partners.[5] A related point is that the bargainers are assumed to be fully formed adult individuals who are completely independent of each other, with no attention paid to the fact that women bore and nurtured them. The objection, in general, is that contractarianism ignores women's experiences as had under patriarchy, both in the bargainers' status and in the emergent moral code. Again, we can expect that if the moral code is not sufficiently inclusive about the kinds of actions it needs to cover, then the defeat of action skepticism will also not be sufficiently inclusive.

A third problem is that the emergent moral code, particularly for Hobbes, is bound to be minimalist in nature, requiring mainly or only negative duties but not positive duties of helping those in need due to patriarchal, racist, and classist social conditions or just plain biology. This problem is largely the result of everyone's mutual pursuit of his or her own interest and unwillingness to concede any more than is necessary to achieve agreement with the other bargainers. But abstract individualism contributes to there being a minimalist moral code because it means that the bargainers can function as if they have no personal relations, which might make them less receptive to generating positive duties from agreement. But eradicating oppression requires positive duties—for one thing, we need to redress inequalities, and this cannot be achieved simply by duties of noninterference. And demonstrating that rationality demands that we follow the requirements of a minimalist moral code leaves open the rational status of acting in more morally demanding ways, including ways that are essential to eradicating women's oppression.

One way that we can respond to these feminist worries is to reconstrue the skeptic's position from that of self-interest to that of privilege: specifically, we can take the skeptic to hold the view that rational action is action that privileges oneself vis-à-vis morality. I believe that this move will take us a long way toward a successful defeat of skepticism because a defeat of this position will show that many more actions other than self-interested ones contributing to women's oppression are irrational. I will explore this idea in chapter 5. Another response is for feminists to offer an alternative theory to SIB contractarianism that addresses some of these concerns. Feminists have proposed the ethic of care, to which I now turn.

3 THE ETHIC OF CARE

For purposes of this discussion, we need to bear in mind the difference between a *feminist* moral theory that has as one of its aims ending women's oppression, and a *feminine* ethic that gives weight to the experiences and intuitions of women but need not aim at ending women's oppression.[6] Traditional moral theorists might be able to modify their theories to accommodate at least some of the aforementioned feminist concerns, but I will not explore this possibility. Instead, I will focus on the ethic of care because it has been put forward explicitly as a feminist theory. I aim to show that the kind of answer care ethicists might give to the skeptic, however, casts doubt on the theory's being a feminist theory. Much of what I have to say about justification and the ethic of care is speculative, since the theory is still, in the grand scheme of things, in the early stages of development.

By now it is familiar that the ethic of care has roots in Carol Gilligan's psychological studies on how males and females reason about moral conflicts.[7] Gilligan ran the studies in response to Lawrence Kohlberg, who used only male subjects but drew conclusions about the moral reasoning of all people. Gilligan noticed that when she included female subjects, one-third of them reasoned, or "focused," from a certain perspective that she called the "care perspective," as opposed to the "justice perspective" used by all but one of the male subjects in her studies.[8] The justice perspective, which is the perspective of many traditional moral theories, is characterized by a focus on equality, equal respect, autonomy, individualism, individual rights, and the Golden Rule. In contrast, the care perspective is characterized by a focus on sensitivity to the needs of others, responsibility for taking care of others, concern with relationships, attachment to others, and not hurting others. In the justice perspective, rules are taken to be primary; in the care perspective, the rules are secondary and can be changed in order to preserve relationships.

Gilligan analogizes the justice and care perspectives to the duck/rabbit picture familiar from the Rorschach test used to study personality. That is, a person sees moral conflicts in one way or the other, either as an issue of equal respect, or as an issue of attachment. Indeed, Gilligan believes that a shift in perspective denotes a change in the meaning of moral terms—perhaps even the term "justification"—and in the definition of moral conflict and moral action.[9] On her view, then, the justice and care perspectives cannot be unified.

Central to the ethic of care, and, I want to show, crucial to the issue of justification, is the *motive* of care. Indeed, some feminists claim that in order for a moral theory to be a feminist theory it *must* incorporate the motive of care. They charge that traditional moral theories that are based on reason alone and that ignore emotions such as care are sexist when set in the context of a patriarchal society that associates men with reason, and women with emotion. They are sexist because even though under patriarchy women are taught and expected to be caring and nurturing but not primarily rational, moral theories fail to incorporate the traits and concerns associated with care that some women come to have, while revering reason and associating it with men. Virginia Held believes that the history of philosophy reveals a split between reason, which has been associated with men, and emotion, where reason's role is to conquer "female" emotion.[10] In contrasting an ethic based on reason with one based on emotion, Held charges that traditional moral theories such as Kantianism and utilitarianism let reason instead of emotion be the guide for action. But Held agrees with Gilligan that women often pay attention to feelings of empathy and care and let these function as their guides in moral dilemmas. Gilligan's complaint against Kohlberg is that he ranked at the highest stage of moral development attention to rational (male) concepts such as rights, justice, and the like, instead of emotive (female) concepts. Since females' alleged focus on care is ranked at a lower stage of moral development, emotion, and therefore women, get denigrated on Kohlberg's theory.[11]

One feminist response to this data is to give emotion a more prominent role in moral theory than it has been given to date. The ethic of care has been proposed at least partly for the reason that it takes into account and values the care that women are expected to do under patriarchy. An ethic of care that either emphasizes care in favor of justice or aims to unite justice and care in some way[12] might be seen as a feminist ethic because it gives women's concerns due recognition, and values those concerns in virtue of their inclusion in moral theory. In doing so, it aims to end women's oppression.

Held believes that feminists who want to give equal status to women's way of responding to moral dilemmas should stress the development of moral emotions and "embrace emotion as providing at least a partial basis for morality itself, and for moral understanding."[13] Similarly, Seyla Benhabib contrasts justice, by which Hobbes and Locke meant that we ought to do what we rationally agree to do, with the "household of the emotions," which involves nurturing, reproduction, love, and care, and argues that the latter is missing from traditional moral theory and needs to be incorporated.[14] Cheshire Calhoun reads Gilligan's study to be about the difference between women's motive of care and men's Kantian motive to do duty for its own sake, urging the incorporation of women's motives into moral theory.[15] Indeed, many feminists suggest that the best way to interpret Gilligan's results is simply as evidence of yet another area in which women's concerns have been ignored or devalued. Gilligan herself might be making just this point. Annette Baier and Marilyn Friedman also favor incorporating care into justice theories, but Gilligan, Nel Noddings, and Sara Ruddick suggest that we replace justice theories with care.[16]

Care ethicists believe that the best state of affairs, morally speaking, either goes farther than, or is completely different from, overcoming self-interest and respecting rights: it involves caring for others.[17] This could mean a number of different things, among them acting in a caring way, and acting from the emotion of care.[18] Many care ethicists suggest both, and at least one has denied the latter.[19] Others suggest acting out of the emotion of care, but in accord with the dictates of justice at least to some extent, since justice and care are needed to temper each other and since neither justice nor care alone covers all moral situations. Almost all believe that acting from the motive of care is required in order to achieve the best state of affairs, at least partly because they believe that the motive of care is inseparable from, and is supposed to issue in, moral action. Gilligan, for example, takes morality necessarily to involve a mixture of emotion and cognition that are not easily separable: "caring action expresses emotion and understanding."[20] On her view, acting both in accord with care and from the motive of care are essential to acting morally appropriately.[21] The motive of care aids in prompting moral action, and is the difference between merely acting morally and being a moral person in the full sense. Hereafter, I will understand the care ethic's notion of acting in morally appropriate ways to include the motivational component of acting in a caring way.

Care ethicists have additional reasons for making the motive of care central to their theory. Merely acting in caring ways can be construed in terms of rules, but since care ethicists reject rule-oriented theories in favor of a theory that demands that people act in ways that are richer or fuller than merely overcoming self-interest or respecting rights, there must be something distinguishing the ethic of care from rule-oriented theories that cannot be captured neatly in a rule. This is the motive of care. Without it, people could simply go through the motions in acting morally, that is, merely do the right thing by following a rule. Baier nicely summarizes this sentiment by claiming that the human heart is needed for the understanding of morality, and its responses are to particular persons, not to principles of abstract justice.[22] In chapter 7, I will argue that merely going through the motions in acting in morally required ways is irrational, and that a more thorough defeat of skepticism includes defeating the motive skeptic who believes that going through the motions in acting in morally required ways is itself rationally permissible. The ethic of care is thus a step up on other moral theories that may not address motive skepticism, giving us an additional reason to examine its attempt to defeat action skepticism.

Another reason that motives are central to the ethic of care is related to the fact that most care ethicists endorse partialism, the thesis that we ought to give special weight to the desires, needs, and interests of our selves or our social group, including our friends, relatives, and all those in our "inner sphere." Calhoun, for instance, suggests that the motive of care generates special obligations to family and friends that are more likely to figure centrally in women's moral thinking than in men's, probably because women are expected to uphold caretaking roles for family and friends.[23] Noddings, more strongly, claims that even though the feeling of care ought to prompt us to act in caring ways toward strangers, we have no obligation to act in a caring way toward those who are not related to us: "I [an American] am not obliged to care for starving children in Africa, because there is no way for this caring to be completed in the other unless I abandon the caring to which I am obligated."[24]

A view that goes hand in hand with partialism is care ethicists' belief that we need to know people in the "thick sense," to be informed about their particular desires, interests, and needs, in order to know how we ought to respond to them.[25] Benhabib expresses this as a requirement to take the standpoint of the "particular other" in deciding how we ought to act toward this other.[26]

These two points—that care ethicists are partialists and that they require knowledge of people in the thick sense—give us another reason to believe that motives are essential to the ethic of care. People generally care about and know in the thick sense their intimates, and are moved to act in ways favoring them. Lawrence Blum believes that caring is prior to knowing what our moral response to another must be. He reads Gilligan to be saying that "understanding the needs, interests, and welfare of another requires a stance toward that person that is informed by care, love, empathy, compassion, and emotional sensitivity."[27] He suggests that for care ethicists, rules such as "Protect your children from harm" do not go far enough in telling us how we ought to act because they do not say what harm is for a particular child in a particular situation.[28] Caring about the child and knowing her particularities are required for an appropriate moral response; indeed, these are likely to stir up moral emotions that generate moral action.

For at least these reasons, the motive of care plays an essential role in the ethic of care. We need now to examine the response that care ethicists might give to the action skeptic. I will discuss three possible responses, though, again, the literature on the issue of justification in the care ethic is rather speculative.

4 FEMINIST JUSTIFICATION

4.1 Jettisoning the Project of Justification

Undoubtedly the most radical position on justification that care ethicists might take is to reject justification altogether.[29] Perhaps Gilligan would favor this view: a perspective shift might radically change the meaning of terms such as "justification" to mean something completely different from "rational defense." Several arguments can be found in the literature to support the radical position. One is that reason is a male-biased concept being differentiated from, and seen as controlling, unruly "female" emotion, and, as such, it should hold no place in a feminist moral theory.[30] In *The Man of Reason*, Genevieve Lloyd traces the historical conception of reason in philosophy, including ethics.[31] According to Lloyd, reason figures in the notion of important concepts such as that of a good person or even a person itself. Even though reason has been taken "to express the real nature of the mind, in which, as Augustine put it, there is no sex," and that the idea that minds are fundamentally gender neutral underlies many of our moral ideals, the idea of a universal mind, or universal reason, is bogus, according to Lloyd, since historically the feminine has been excluded from this notion, and "femininity itself has been partly constituted through such processes of exclusion." Lloyd cites Kant as a representative dichotomizer who believes that moral acts are those consistent with rational, universalizable principles, and binding regardless of a person's motives, thereby creating a dichotomy between (universal) reason and (particular) emotions. If men are assumed to be rational, and women emotional, then on Kant's theory, what is male must overcome and control what is female. Yet Kant often writes under the guise of the universality of reason.

Lloyd and others[32] have exposed numerous passages from the history of philosophy showing that many philosophers have undoubtedly excluded women from full rational agency, and hence, tragically, from fulfilling the requirements of these philosophers' theories. The historical association of men with reason and women with emotions cannot be denied.[33] And given the wide acceptance of the sexist assumption that men are more rational than women who are primarily emotional beings, we should expect this view to be reflected without challenge in the history of philosophy. Yet because such gender associations have been made does not mean that we should jettison reason, and hence, justification. The main problem, I believe, lies not with something inherent in reason itself, but with the association of men with reason and women with emotion, which is false and sexist.

Still, some feminists suggest that the notion of reason could *never* be neutral, given its firmly entrenched historical associations.[34] Held remarks that "gender has been built into the [concept of reason] in such a way that without it, [it] will have to be [a] different [concept]."[35] This is much like the feminist objection that the courts' use of the notion of a "reasonable person" in the context of sexual harassment and rape cases really amounts to "reasonable man," thereby sanctioning behavior that a reasonable woman would find objectionable, which is unfair and sexist.[36] This point is well taken, but instead of abandoning the concept of reasonable person, we might redefine it so that it is in line with the standards of a reasonable woman. Doing so has the advantage of retaining a concept that can be useful in many contexts.[37] Similarly, feminists might redefine what counts as rational so that the concept of reason reflects the experiences of many women. I will have more to say about this, but for now my point is that Held's objection needs to speak to why the standard conception of reason *in itself* is a bad one that ought to be rejected, since its usefulness may well override its historical association with maleness.

Another argument for rejecting reason, and hence, justification, is that since women under patriarchy are likely to spend their time doing things other than pursuing reason, they are not concerned with it, and so it should not be paramount in a moral theory. Nancy Tuana remarks that "the arduous training and dedication of Descartes' rational man will be obstructed by the daily chores and responsibilities of nurturing children and running a household. The leisure necessary for the pursuit of reason is not available to a wife and mother."[38] Impoverished women will simply find it impossible to pursue Cartesian reason. As it turns out, then, Descartes's rational man is male, European, and upper class.[39] We might conclude, though Tuana does not, that if women do not have the opportunity to pursue Cartesian reason, this way of thinking should not be central in a moral theory.

There is much to be said about this argument. For instance, what is meant by the pursuit of reason? Is it doing professional philosophy? Thinking philosophically about everyday issues? Relying on the laws of logic in everyday life? It certainly is false that women do not use reason in these senses, even if they have been denied the opportunity to pursue Cartesian reason in the paid workplace. A second response to this argument is that if we understand reason in the strong, "Cartesian" sense, very few people, women or men, come to be professional philosophers who employ this kind of reason. Of course, there are even fewer women than men who are professional philosophers,[40] but this seems partly to be a matter of women's not being afforded the same opportunities and encouragement as men to pursue and be retained and promoted in careers like philosophy. There is nothing about women's gender *per se* that prevents them from pursuing Cartesian reason. The solution is to give women the same opportunities and encouragement that we give to men, but not to jettison reason on the grounds that women are not concerned with it, or to decentralize the role of reason in moral theory. Mothers surely play a significant role in the development of their children's rational capacities. Many female office workers use their rational skills to keep male-headed businesses running smoothly. Women in disenfranchised groups such as the indigent and racial minorities have always worked in the paid workforce and used the rational skills this requires.[41] Even "Donna Reed types" have been very politically active and influential about morally charged issues of the day.[42]

Perhaps the real complaint is that women will fall short of rational ideals as defined by different theories because the kind and degree of rationality women have is (allegedly) different from that men have.[43] Since women's concern with sympathy, compassion, and emotional responsiveness is not given a central role in traditional rationalist moral theory, it turns out that according to the standards of traditional morality, women are incapable of leading moral and rational lives.[44]

Feminists have at least two options. They can either (1) keep reason and perhaps change what we take to be rational in light of the experiences of women, or (2) jettison reason on the grounds that women are likely to fall short of its standards as typically construed. I will consider the first option in the next section. The second does not seem to be a plausible way to go because it endorses precisely the assumption that feminists are trying to debunk, namely, that women *are* more emotional than rational and than men. That women are less rational than men is alleged to be due either to their nature or to socialization, either of which is false and problematic. Granted, judging women according to standards of reason they are not encouraged to live up to is unfair. But again, the problem lies with the socialization of women or false assumptions about women's "nature," but not with the standard of reason itself. If we get rid of gendered socialization, and change our beliefs about people's "nature," retaining reason will not be problematic. To give up reason on the other hand is to accept as right the patriarchal patterns of socialization, if not the view that women are not in fact as rational as men.

Tuana takes this last objection to reason one step further. She urges that women, even if they could, *should* not try to live up to the standards of reason because then they "would have to deny all that is seen as female—attachment to individuals, private interests, maternal feelings. . . . [They] must become male."[45] I agree with Tuana that a moral theory's requiring people to deny their individuality under some conditions just to meet its standards is unfair. But not always: the fact that most moral theories require murderers to deny their individuality is unproblematic. But more to the point, Tuana is assuming that women have these and not "male" interests, an assumption that, again, is disputable. Her claim, however, might be that no matter who has such interests, a theory that pegs them as female and for this reason fails to incorporate them into its standards is sexist. This is right. But men who have these interests would not meet the standards, and women who do not have them might, so the theory would not exclude all and only women. It would be sexist, though, in assuming that such interests were female. But then this assumption, and not the standard of reason, should be jettisoned.

Let us consider one last reason feminists might reject reason, and so, justification, namely, that it would be out of place in an ethic of care. Although Nodding's argument is a bit vague, and her final position on this issue is unclear—as I discuss in the next section, she might be endorsing a Humean justification grounded in motivation—she is perhaps the best spokesperson for this view since she is the one care ethicist who addresses the issue of justification head on.[46] Noddings puts forward a moral theory based on care in which we are obligated to maintain and enhance caring relationships between the "one-caring" and the "one-cared-for." She rather quickly dismisses disposition skepticism, arguing as follows. Since moral statements are not truths, they cannot be justified in the way facts are. So, there is no justification for taking the moral point of view.[47] But her argument might be confusing epistemic with practical justification: skeptics about absolute truth in morality, such as relativists and subjectivists, admit that there are moral truths, but believe they are relative to the society or determined by the individual. They can legitimately seek a justification for being a moral person. So for them, skepticism about truth in morality does not entail skepticism about being morally disposed. So perhaps Noddings is a moral nihilist who denies that there are moral facts. Still, practical skepticism does not follow. We might, for example, deny that there are any facts about the rules of etiquette, yet still seek a justification for following them.

On the issue of defeating action skepticism, Noddings believes that traditional approaches are mistaken because they aim at justification rather than motivation.[48] In response to the question "Why should I be committed to not causing pain?" Noddings says that the one-caring receives the one-cared-for and acts in her behalf as she would for herself with similar "motive energy."[49] Caring for another is universally accessible[50] and is a natural feeling[51] when the recipient is a close relative. But Noddings rejects a universal feeling of care because, she believes, it is impossible to actualize and could not be genuine.[52] Whether or not the recipient is a close relative, ethical caring is dependent on an "ideal self," which is developed in light of a person's remembrance both of being cared-for as a child and of caring. Thus the theory is rooted in the ideal caring parent-child relationship. For Noddings, our memories of being cared-for and of caring, and of tenderness, "lead us to a vision of what is good."[53] This vision yields our obligations: a commitment to sustain and enhance this good. Our ideal self, then, is one that sustains and enhances caring. The ethical ideal guides us in our moral decisions and conduct.[54]

So why act morally? Noddings's reply is that situations of caring involving our intimates are natural, or innate, not "moral": we care for them because we love them.[55] In these cases, a person's interest in and caring for her ethical self induces the "I must."[56] First she feels "I must," and then she feels a second sentiment, the genuine moral sentiment that Noddings calls the "I ought," which is that sensibility to which I have committed myself.[57] But with those whom we know less, "we are guided by how we feel, what the other expects of us, and what the relationship requires of us."[58] In such situations involving nonintimates in which the "I must" does not arise, the second moral sentiment, the "I ought," arises "when I realize that the caring relation is superior to other forms of relatedness. I recognize that my response will enhance my ethical ideal."[59] The ethical ideal, then, shapes our moral response to others. Noddings's answer to the question "Why be moral?" is "Because I am or want to be a moral person."[60] Noddings's view is similar to Hume's response to the sensible knave about acting morally. Hume believes that most of us hate treachery and roguery so much that we avoid it for peace of mind and having a good reputation.[61] Hume also believes, as I will discuss more fully in chapter 6, that there are two motives that can issue in moral action: sympathy and a sense of duty. For those persons who are not moved by sympathy on a particular occasion, a sense of duty kicks in and makes them act morally. However, in contrast to Noddings, Hume believes that there is a universal sentiment of sympathy or benevolence. Both ground morality in feelings. I will return to a discussion of Hume, the ethic of care, and internalism later in this section.

Noddings calls her view on justification an alternative to standard views, one that begins not with moral reasoning but with a longing for goodness.[62] At least in these passages, she does not offer a justification, but at best an explanation, for acting morally. The focus shifts from reasons for acting morally to moral sentiments regarding whether one is fulfilled in one's life and in the lives of those to whom one relates.[63]

Noddings's view forces us to remember the importance of justification. Her focus on motivation rather than justification will not rest easy with moral theorists, traditional or not, who believe that we need rationally to justify acting morally. Noddings's account tells us merely how she believes people are prompted to act, and is modeled on an ideal caring relationship between parent and child. Although I believe that her account can be useful in developing a moral theory, that is, in determining our obligations, it falls short of what we demand in the way of justifying abiding by these obligations. Some immediate worries come to mind. One is that many people have not had the ideal caring relationship with a parent or other that for Noddings undergirds our obligations and provides the right sentiments for acting in caring ways. Even those who have had such a caring relationship might not consider it the best one; instead, they might believe that pursuing their own self-interest is best, and consequently use this as a model for goodness that they seek. Or we might have a longing for goodness that amounts to being cared for by others, but never ourselves reciprocate this care. Even persons who consider the ideal caring relationship to be better than others, and long for goodness that amounts to being cared for by others, might never reciprocate this care.

Noddings admits that the tendency to treat each other well is very fragile, making us strive to care.[64] She admits that the natural feeling of care, and the longing to maintain and promote the care we received in infancy, are sentiments a person may lack.[65] Other feminists who endorse some version of the ethic of care recognize many relationships where people lack care, including those in which there is a potential for violence and harm for which most people have the capacity and many have the inclination,[66] those that may not be good, healthy, or worthy of preservation (e.g., abusive relationships and marriages in which one partner lacks respect for the other), and those that are oppressive.[67] Traditionalists who successfully justify acting in morally required ways can judge such conduct to be immoral *and* irrational. By rejecting justification in favor of motivation, Noddings surrenders the right to make these rational judgments. She gives up on trying to defeat the action skeptic, who does not believe that rationality requires that an agent have the moral sentiments of care that she describes. Her theory thus loses the backing of rationality, and thus, of judging immoral conduct to be irrational as well. Noddings's rejection of justification also threatens achievement of the practical goal of people's acting morally, since whether people will act in caring ways is a function of whether they have the relevant sentiment, but not whether they are moved by reasons. Oddly enough, at least in one passage Noddings seems to agree that we need justification: "We should, ideally, be able to present reasons for our action/inaction which would persuade a reasonable, disinterested observer that we have acted in behalf of the cared-for."[68] Since feminists have a lot at stake, theoretically and practically speaking, in defeating skepticism, I believe they should not abandon the project of justification.

4.2 Feminist Models of Practical Reason

Traditionally, the skeptic is taken to endorse EU, and the motive of self-interest that is in accord with EU is taken to be the motive that is most in opposition to morality. Because of the incorporation of care into their moral theory, some feminists might be arguing for a change in this model. In chapter 5, I will take up the issue of the skeptic's endorsement of EU and the motive of self-interest, but here my focus will be on care ethicists' possible rejection of the standard model.

One move that some care ethicists make in responding to the skeptic is to deny that the conflict between self-interest and morality is the paradigm on which to focus in defeating skepticism. They believe that this conflict appropriately captures relationships typical in the public sphere, which is the traditionally male work world, but not in the private sphere associated with women. In the private sphere, where women's relationships center primarily around meeting the needs of those in their care, women's *caring too much* is the proper counterpart to acting morally, as in the case of the overly devoted mother who forgoes the pursuit of her own interest and welfare for the sake of that of her children.[69] Caring too much is one element of women's oppression; thus it should not turn out to be morally or rationally justified. On this model, the skeptic would believe that caring too much, rather than acting self-interestedly, is rationally required. To defeat action skepticism, the care ethicist would need to show that caring to the appropriate extent and in the right way is rationally required.

Yet other models might capture different behavior dichotomized with caring. Perhaps not caring, or disinterestedness, is an even better counterpart, as in the case of the negligent mother who leaves her children home alone in order to go out with friends. Or maybe evil behavior is a better counterpart, as in the case of the mother who deliberately thwarts the interests of her children by physically or emotionally abusing them. The care ethicist would then have to show that overcoming such behavior is rationally required. I examine some of these other kinds of immoral behavior in chapter 5, where I argue that we should broaden the skeptic's position to include them, independent of whether we should endorse the ethic of care as the correct moral theory.

Care ethicists might take another tack, and reject EU on the grounds that its wide acceptance in various disciplines is not a sufficient reason to endorse it for the reason that these disciplines historically have been dominated by men whose interactions that are subject to moral scrutiny are ones taking place in the public sphere. Expected utility theory is more likely to be fairly well worked out than other theories of practical reason that may better describe and apply to interactions in the private sphere that women have traditionally been associated with. Some feminists might explain away EU's intuitive plausibility when it comes to simple cases such as its being rational to go to a football game rather than a soccer game, on the grounds that our intuitions have been shaped by patriarchy. These feminists would favor an alternative model of practical reason that will govern their response to the skeptic.

Jean Hampton provides a nice interpretation of how Ruddick's analysis of mothering might be viewed as such an alternative.[70] According to Ruddick, mothers have to reason in order to decide how best to raise their children. This "maternal thinking" involves a unity of reflection, judgment, and emotion.[71] Unlike EU reasoning, maternal reasoning neither is responsive to preferences or interests nor requires the maximization of their satisfaction, but is instead responsive to demands the mother tries to satisfy for preservation, growth, and shaping of a child who is acceptable to society. Hampton describes reason for Ruddick as being in service to the demands or standards of child-rearing that the mother aims to achieve: it determines the extent to which a given action realizes the standards.[72]

Hampton's interpretation of Ruddick's analysis of mothering is a promising alternative model of practical reasoning. But much more would have to be said to develop fully this account, including whether it is supposed to supplant or merely supplement the traditional model of instrumental reason. Hampton herself believes that Ruddick's view of rational action is *consistent with* EU. Hampton wonders whether we can understand the "demands" to which a mother responds as other-regarding preferences she has, whose mutual satisfaction may not be possible very often.[73] For instance, a mother's choosing between breast-feeding and bottle-feeding her baby often turns on the sacrifices the mother will have to make if she opts for the former, which is a denial of the satisfaction of her preferences. A mother's getting up in the middle of the night to answer her baby's cries instead of enjoying a peaceful sleep is an issue of weighing preferences. Even choosing parenthood with the knowledge that it will demand financial sacrifices for the sake of a child seems best construed on the preference model. Expected utility theory is also useful in that it can show that certain antifeminist behavior is not rational. For instance, the mother who cares too much to the extent of losing her self and her own identity can be shown to be irrational on EU on the grounds that she fails to satisfy her own interests, or even fails to develop preferences that are intrinsically her own. And some instances of people's acting in sexist ways fit nicely under the umbrella of EU in that they are ways of benefiting by satisfying preferences at the expense of women's interests. Still, there are many other, non-self-interested ways of acting, including sexist ones that are not best captured by EU, some for the reason that they are not instances of preference-satisfaction, as, for instance, when men benefit economically and socially from the gender wage gap. Such benefits are the result of systematic forces rather than individual preference-satisfaction. So whether feminists should endorse EU as is or in revised form is not clear. And surely the motive of caring too much, which the ethic of care in particular dichotomizes with morality, does not capture all the sexist versions of immorality needed for a complete defeat of action skepticism.

Duncan MacIntosh suggests a way of retaining EU and defending the reduction of morality to rationality on it, while making it consistent with feminist aims.[74] MacIntosh argues that there are rational constraints on the content and origin of our values such that it turns out, on a Kantian account of rationality involving contradictions in willing and imagining, to be irrational to have malevolent, slavish, bullying, and stingy preferences. Sexist preferences fit into some of these categories. Malevolent values are defined as ones aiming at the nonsatisfaction of the values of others, such as a worker's sexually harassing a coworker to ensure that she does not make it to the top. Slavish values are ones aiming only at satisfying the values of others, such as when a woman devotes herself entirely to the man in her life. I will refer to slavish values as "deformed desires," and I discuss their role in EU in chapter 4, where I offer an addendum to traditional informed desire tests, inspired by MacIntosh's argument, that excludes them as irrational. Bullying values are ones inclining a person to profit at the expense of others, such as men's wanting to keep women in the home serving men's needs while men gain economic power in the workplace. Stingy values are ones inclining a person to withhold aid to another even when it would involve little cost to herself, such as when someone pretends not to notice a woman being beaten by her partner. MacIntosh's proposal is to rule out such preferences as irrational, and then show that given remaining preferences, on the model of EU, acting morally is rationally required. The ideally rational and moral person would be one who aims to satisfy her or his preferences, excepting the foregoing ones.

While some feminists might accept one of these modifications of EU and retain it as the model rational choice to use in defeating skepticism, care ethicists are likely to resist them in favor of an even richer account of rational behavior that goes hand in hand with a richer account of morally required action. One of the main insights of the ethic of care is that the ideal life consists in more than the kind of life each of us would have if we all merely followed the "rules of justice" by respecting rights, satisfying preferences, and so on—that is, the kind of life that we could expect from everyone's conforming to the duties of noninterference designated by a contractarian moral code. The ideal life, for care ethicists, involves (at least) people's acting in a caring way and from the motive of care. Care ethicists want to capture the idea that each of us wants to be cared for and cared about in addition to having our rights respected. Unlike traditional theorists who shy away from this view of morality on the grounds that it is too demanding, care ethicists insist that we can require others to care for and about us.

The skeptical challenge facing care ethicists, then, is to show that we can *rationally* require that people care about us, that is, have a motive of care or some derivative motive and act from it. They believe, as I have shown, that what makes an act morally good or virtuous in the full sense is that it is done in accord with care *and* from the motive of care. Since acting in a caring way must be prompted by the motive of care, to demonstrate the rationality of being a moral person might be to demonstrate simultaneously the rationality of acting in morally required ways—caring *for* people—and the rationality of having and being prompted by the motive of care or some derivative motive—caring *about* people. Indeed, if care ethicists fail to show the latter, they will not have shown that it is rational to be their moral ideal. To defeat skepticism fully, we must not leave any skeptical problem unsolved: not defeating skepticism about acting from the right motive—motive skepticism—is for this theory in particular to do just that (although I think that for any moral theory, we must defeat motive skepticism).

One way that care ethicists might demonstrate the rationality of acting from the motive of care is to defeat action and motive skepticism in one fell swoop. Care ethicists can do this if they are internalists who believe that reasons and motives are necessarily connected. If care ethicists are internalists, and can show either that rationality dictates acting in a caring way or that rationality dictates having and acting from caring motives, they might simultaneously defeat both action and motive skepticism. They might even be able to endorse EU, if they can show that people have *preferences* to act in caring ways, and then demonstrate in addition the rationality of acting from the motive of care, although I doubt that they would make this move, for the reasons cited earlier. In section 4.3, I will discuss the sense in which care ethicists are internalists. I will argue in section 4.4 that, unfortunately, this is a position that they ought not to take within the context of patriarchy. At other points in the book, I will argue that EU needs to be modified, if not jettisoned, and sometimes for feminist reasons.

4.3 An Internalist Answer to the Skeptic

In general, internalism is the view that certain concepts, typically reasons, obligations, and/or motivations, are logically connected. For my purposes here, I will gloss over many of the distinctions I will make in chapter 6 about various versions of internalism and their bearing on defeating skepticism. The kind of internalism that I am interested in here is that which refers to there being a necessary connection between reasons and motivations, specifically, some variation of the following thesis: In order for it to be true that an agent, A, has a reason to do some action, x, A must have a relevant motive, m, either to do x or for some y such that doing x brings about y. For some internalists, this thesis is a biconditional: A has a reason to do x only if A has a relevant motive, and if A has a relevant motive then A has a reason to do x. In his well-known article "Internal and External Reasons," Bernard Williams understands internalists to include both the necessity and sufficiency claim: "A has a reason to ϕ iff A has some desire the satisfaction of which will be served by his ϕ-ing,"[75] though Williams's own version of internalism is much more nuanced than this.[76] In a later article, he explains that he meant only to endorse the necessity claim, though he also believes that having a motive to ϕ is sufficient for having a reason to ϕ.[77] Some internalists take there to be a necessary connection between reasons and motives such that if one lacks the relevant motive, m, one does not have a reason to do x.[78] In contrast, externalists deny that reasons and motives are necessarily connected: on their view, A's having a reason to do x can be independent of A's having the relevant motive. For the externalist, not all motives give rise to reasons, and for any reason, there need be no connection to the agent's desires, though, of course, there may be.

Internalists have modified this thesis to solve several problems, so the best version of the thesis might be a more fine-tuned version of the one just described. For instance, as I will discuss in more detail in chapter 4, Williams offers a version of internalism according to which an agent must go through a process of deliberation in order to ensure that her desires are not based on false beliefs, or to show that she really does have some desire to act in the relevant way despite her denying it.[79] Agents have reasons for action that are not necessarily connected to desires they currently have, but only to ones that would survive deliberation. Thus Williams has a deliberative account of internalism such that he requires only a deliberative connection between desires and reasons: an agent has reason to do some action iff the agent's subjective motivational set is such that sound deliberation would lead the agent to do the act in general. Gilbert Harman, too, modifies the version of internalism stated above, as I will discuss further in chapter 7. Harman offers both strong and weak versions of internalism. On the strong version, the agent must have the motive to act in order to have a reason to act.[80] On the weak version, merely having the *capacity* to be motivated to act gives one a reason to act.[81]

The kind of internalism I am focusing on has roots in Hume, who believes that reason by itself is impotent in the sphere of desire, or, that reason itself cannot prompt action but that the presence of some motive is essential. Here I will present only some of the highlights of Hume's view that bear similarity to the ethic of care, since my main concern is whether care ethicists can defeat action skepticism by endorsing internalism. Hume argues that morality must be based on sentiment, not reason.[82] One of his main concerns is persuasion: in order for a reason, including a moral reason, to persuade a person to perform some action—and Hume believes that reasons must persuade—it must appeal to one of the person's motives. Hume is also an internalist about obligations and motivations, since he believes that awareness of an act as right necessarily means the agent has a motive to do it.[83]

I understand Hume's view about how we determine our duties to be as follows. Briefly, Hume believes that we all have at least the "first seeds" of a universal natural sentiment of benevolence or sympathy, or at least the capacity for pleasant and useful feelings, that enables a person to see that a certain kind of act promotes utility either for the agent's self or for the agent's fellows.[84] The person either approves or disapproves of the act on the basis of whether the moral sense—the capacity to approve or disapprove—finds the feelings accompanying his observation of instances of this kind of act to be pleasant and useful.[85] The rightness of an act is a function of the feeling it produces.[86] For example, honesty, fidelity, truth, manners, and politeness[87] are deemed right or virtuous acts because the agent approves of them and the pleasant and useful feelings accompanying them, but vanity is pronounced a vice because the agent disapproves of it. The sentiment of benevolence or sympathy is essential for kicking off the feeling of approval or disapproval in an agent, and it allows her to determine whether the act is a virtue or a vice.

On the traditional reading, Hume is an internalist about obligations, reasons, and motives: an agent has a reason to act virtuously if and only if she has the relevant motive of approval generated by the sentiment of benevolence or sympathy. This is best seen in Hume's answer to the sensible knave, who, like the skeptic, believes it to be rational "to take advantage of the exceptions," that is, to act immorally when doing so is to his benefit. Although Hume cites reasons why the knave should act morally, including that acting morally is often in one's self-interest, promises peace of mind, and does not forfeit one's reputation, he admits that there is nothing further to say to the knave who rejects these reasons: "I must confess, that, if a man think, that this reasoning much requires an answer, it will be a little difficult to find any, which will to him appear satisfactory and convincing."[88] On one reading of this passage, Hume is saying that since reasons must appeal to some motive in order to be convincing, if one lacks the motive (or perhaps merely the capacity to be motivated), then one lacks a reason to act in the relevant way. The knave lacks the motive and hence the reason—and presumably the obligation—to act morally.

We can read into care ethicists' account of morality a version of internalism, though not explicitly stated, that is in places similar to Hume's. A feminist defeat of action skepticism, then, might *retain* most of the traditional view of the skeptic rather than adopt an alternative, but insist that justification take the form of an internalist reason.

Like Hume, care ethicists ultimately want to ground morality in some sentiment, though for them it is the motive of care. The motive of care has been characterized in the following ways: a natural feeling of empathy, care, and compassion;[89] love;[90] sympathy and solidarity;[91] supportiveness, concern for others, an ability to help others grow and develop, concern with human relationships, and nurturance;[92] taking an interest in another person;[93] and caring for a person for that person's sake and not as a means to one's own interests.[94] It is these feelings, rather than some desire or preference, or feeling of approval or disapproval, that care ethicists link with reasons and obligations.

Some care ethicists, such as Rita Manning, seem implicitly to endorse the Humean claim that reason is impotent in the sphere of desire. In response to the question "Why be moral?" or, in this case, "Why act in a caring way?" Manning agrees with Noddings, who says that we naturally care, and adds that if we do not care, then we should simply strive to become more caring persons: no reason can be given.[95] We might read Manning to be saying, with Hume, that if a person does not have the relevant motive—in this case, care or some feeling generated by care—no reason to act morally will persuade her so to act. That is, Manning endorses the internalist view that having a reason necessarily entails having the relevant motive of care. One who lacks the motive of care can only try to become a caring person who has the motive of care and other desires generated by care, because only then can she be persuaded that she has reason to act in a caring way.

Noddings's account of how obligations arise is similar in some ways to Hume's. According to Noddings, our natural impulse to care gives rise to an interest in moral behavior.[96] This natural impulse to care is likened by Noddings to the Humean natural sentiment of benevolence, in that it is universally accessible and natural, and it forms the basis of morality.[97] As I have shown, for Noddings, morality requires two feelings: the sentiment of natural sympathy we feel for each other, and our longing to nurture and maintain the caring moments we once experienced in being cared for and in caring for others.[98] Both the natural impulse of caring itself and the ethical ideal that strives to maintain care "guide us in moral decisions and conduct," that is, generate our moral obligations.[99] In Noddings's metaphorical language, the "I must" that arises with either natural caring or the remembrance of being cared for and caring for carries obligation with it.[100] Moral behavior amounts to "meeting the other as one-caring,"[101] which means genuinely responding to the perceived needs, and, I believe she would add, interests and preferences, of the other[102]—whatever it takes to maintain and enhance caring.[103] Thus Noddings, like Hume, believes that our obligations are ultimately generated by some sentiment, though of course Noddings and Hume differ about the process by which we determine our obligations.[104]

For Noddings, reasons and motives are connected in the following way. Contrary to her rejection of reason and justification that I discussed earlier, Noddings elsewhere appeals to reasons. She claims that women give reasons for their caring actions, but the reasons "point to feelings, needs, situational conditions, and their sense of personal ideal rather than universal principles and their application."[105] At another point, she claims that "our reasons for acting have to do with the other's wants and desires and with the objective elements of his problematic situation."[106] Hume grounds reasons in pleasant and useful feelings associated with an agent's approval of an act arising from universal sympathy or benevolence, but Noddings grounds reasons in feelings, desires, wants, and needs—motives, more generally—connected to care. Another person's motives of care supposedly generate reasons for us to respond according to care, though Noddings to my knowledge never defends this claim. But more along the lines of a Humean view, Noddings believes that since we have a duty (and want to) achieve, maintain, and enhance the ethical ideal that consists in maintaining and enhancing the caring relation, that is, the caring moments we experienced when young, we must *ourselves* have desires, preferences, and interests, the satisfaction of which promotes the caring relation. But Noddings believes that we cannot require the initial impulse of care that arises as a feeling, since it is a feeling, and one that arises naturally at that.[107] So reasons for action must not be based directly on it. Instead, the motives that are generated *by* our sentiment of care give us reasons for acting. To clarify, suppose that my obligation "to meet the other as one-caring" amounts to comforting her after her son has died. The natural caring I (ideally) have generates this obligation, as well as a desire for a certain state of affairs, namely, to maintain the caring moments we once experienced, which in this case cashes out as a desire to comfort the mourner. I have a reason to act on *this* desire. If I am reading Noddings correctly, she seems to endorse internalism biconditionally. Like Hume, she believes that a person has a reason to do x only if she has the relevant motive, that is, natural caring. But also, she believes that if a person has the relevant motive, which in this case is the desire to maintain the caring moments we once experienced, then she has a reason to do x. Thus, the care ethicist endorses internalism between motives, reasons, and obligations. The care ethicist's answer to the skeptic would be that acting in morally required ways, or, maintaining and enhancing the relation of care, is rationally required if and only if the agent has a motive of care. Their view, were care ethicists to defend it adequately, has the advantage that it would at once defeat both action skepticism and motive skepticism. That is, it would show that acting in a caring way, and that acting from the motive of care, are each rationally required.

4.4 An Argument against Internalism

But there are problems particular to the ethic of care if it gives this kind of internalist answer to the skeptic. These problems are ones similar to those raised by other feminists who have argued against incorporating care into moral theory on the grounds that in the context of patriarchy, doing so would put expectations on women that, when met, would perpetuate women's oppression. I now want to argue that were care ethicists to make the internalist move about reasons, obligations, and motives that they seem to, they will run into the same problems.

Let us first consider the charge made by some feminists that incorporating care in a moral theory perpetuates rather than ameliorates women's oppression. The source of the problem is the gender-based kinds of caring that are socially expected of women. It is a common feminist complaint that the *kind* of caring women are expected to undertake, which is tainted by patriarchal expectations, and the traits associated with women's caring, are believed to be part of women's essential nature, and thus the associated roles are ones they cannot escape from without censure. Women's caring as reflected in roles such as mother, nurturer, and caretaker is different from and ranked lower than the caring that men are expected to undertake in their more "rigorous" roles associated with the justice theory. For instance, while fathers are expected to show their care for their children by earning a paycheck to provide them with life's essentials, mothers are expected to engage in emotional work, including tending to a child's wounds, meeting others' emotional needs, and even being supportive to a partner in any circumstances. Men's caring has to do with protection and material forms of help, which men control but women believe they need. The care men give to women "manifests, consolidates, and perpetuates male power with respect to women."[108] Men's caring is not believed to be part of their essential nature, allowing them to opt out without penalty. The care women give, in contrast, involves admitting dependency and sharing or losing control.[109] In effect, women's caring contributes to their oppression. It leads to stress, drug abuse, and alcoholism;[110] it reinforces the suppression of self and leads to a denial of one's autonomy and authority and masks the unequal power of a wife and husband;[111] it prevents a woman from seeking the same emotional support she provides for others;[112] it makes a mother judge her success solely in terms of the success of her children, and makes her lose touch with her own needs;[113] it leads women to protect their oppressors and not to resist their own oppression;[114] it makes mothers instill patriarchal values in their children and runs the risk that male children will come to expect caring treatment from all females, thereby subjecting women to exploitation;[115] it defends traditional relationships and puts women into sex roles;[116] and it increases the likelihood that women will adopt patriarchal values and stereotypical traits when they adopt gendered roles.[117]

For at least these reasons, incorporating this kind of care into a moral theory might make the theory feminine, but not feminist, since doing so will only perpetuate but not help eradicate women's oppression. Were the ethic of care to include patriarchal women's caring, the dictates of the ethic of care would have it that women will be morally obligated to engage in the very behaviors that are caused by and contribute to their own oppression.

I have similar worries about care ethicists endorsing the kind of internalism I have described, according to which an agent has a reason if and only if she has the relevant motive. The first problem concerns the necessity claim that the agent has a reason to do x only if she has the motive of natural caring. As I have shown, for Noddings this motive gives rise to our obligations to act in caring ways. But this alleged "natural" caring that Noddings alludes to might very well be gendered. If so, it can lead to gendered obligations grounded in care. For example, women, but not men, might be obligated to act in overly nurturing ways that cause them to lose touch with their own needs. Feminists are right to resist including such obligations in a moral theory, and they should also insist that it is not the case that reason requires acting in these ways.

The second problem concerns the sufficiency claim, that if the agent has a motive to act, she necessarily has a reason to act. Not only are women and men expected to engage in different kinds of caring, but under patriarchy, women are likely to develop desires and preferences that when satisfied support oppressive conditions and practices. These are called "adaptive preferences" or "deformed desires." I will have more to say about such desires and their role in defeating skepticism in the next chapter, but for now, let me give some examples in connection with the ethic of care in particular. Many women want to get married and have children because they believe they will be unfulfilled if they do not, and want to avoid the stigma of being childless or single. Others who believe that a husband or lover will protect them from violence that men on the street pose end up staying with abusive partners because they care about and want to protect them from the authorities. Many women want to be self-sacrificing for men, not only for economic survival but for acceptance. And many become self-sacrificial for their children, too, because they believe that a good mother behaves this way. This is not to say that women do not have *other* desires for their own welfare that inevitably conflict with desires deformed by patriarchy. The point is that it is problematic for care ethicists, for purposes of defeating skepticism, to endorse an internalist view according to which having a motive is sufficient for having a reason, when the motive of care at issue is genderized in this problematic way. Having a reason to satisfy such desires means that rationality endorses "women's caring," which contributes to women's oppression.

On the flip side, under patriarchy women are socialized *not* to have certain motives. For instance, in unreciprocated ego-feeding and wound-tending, women lose their *own* interests. Sandra Bartky describes women as first having to beg for their man's attention, but then merging with the man psychologically so that their interests become one and the same.[118] Also, many women believe that oppression is unchangeable, and come to see feminism as a threat to them and their lifestyle.[119] Or, they do not even recognize their oppression, and see feminism as futile. As a result, they do not develop desires whose satisfaction would contribute to their freedom from oppression. These include desires for economic and emotional independence, for having a career that gives them an identity distinct from their roles as wives and mothers, and even to learn to do house repairs or to drive long distances or go out to dinner alone. But if internalism is true, and motives necessarily yield reasons for action, where the relevant motives are lacking, the agent lacks a reason to act. It will be the case, then, that women who lack desires that when satisfied would contribute to freeing them from oppression will not have reason to act in these ways. If the ethic of care is to be a feminist ethic, it should not, morally and rationally speaking, be one that allows or perpetuates women's oppression. Thus care ethicists have reasons not to endorse the kind of internalism at issue, at least not when the motive of care is understood in genderized ways as it is under patriarchy. Alternatively, they might invoke an informed desire test such that only desires surviving it would be rational, and hence candidates for rational and moral action. For instance, on Williams's version of internalism, patriarchal desires that are based on false beliefs would be subtracted from one's desire set, while other desires associated with nonsexist or feminist states of affairs might be added to the set.

5 CONCLUSION

In chapter 2, I showed that the SIB contractarianism response to the skeptic failed. I turned to the ethic of care in response to feminist concerns about contractarianism regarding both the content of the moral code and the starting point it takes to generate it. The ethic of care holds promise of being a feminist theory having as one of its aims ending women's oppression. I examined a variety of responses to the skeptic that care ethicists might make, the most promising of which is an internalist reason that necessarily links obligations, reasons, and motives. An internalist reason can link acting in a caring way with acting from the motive of care, both of which care ethicists take to be essential to a plausible moral theory. But since women's care under patriarchy is likely to take the form of behavior that sustains rather than contributes to ending women's oppression, care ethicists should not offer the kind of internalist reason that they might to defeat skepticism.

Assuming that care ethicists insist that motives are central to their theory and must play a role in justification, perhaps a better approach is that they require two levels of justification: (1) show that every morally required action is rationally required, and (2) show that having and acting from the motives associated with care but that do *not* perpetuate women's oppression when satisfied is rationally required. Care ethicists can rationally require certain motives if they show both that a person can come to acquire motives she lacks and that lacking certain motives is a mark of irrationality. In chapter 7, I will argue that people can acquire motives they lack, and that we should defeat the motive skeptic in order to defeat skepticism fully. One way to defeat the motive skeptic is to show that there is a disharmony, which is a kind of irrationality, between the agent's motives and reasons in the case of the agent who merely goes through the motions in acting morally but who does not acquire and act from motives the theory in question deems ideal. Care ethicists need not be internalists but can be externalists about reasons and motives, yet demand that people act from motives that are associated with care but that do not, when acted on, perpetuate women's oppression. Alternatively, in light of feminist objections to the ethic of care itself, not just its attempt at justification, feminists might not endorse the ethic of care unless it is clear that the theory can rule out ways of caring that contribute to women's oppression. They might pursue ways of incorporating feminist concerns into other, non-SIB contractarian theories, and invoke strategies of justification that would also satisfy feminist concerns.

In the end, the internalist attempt at justification that care ethicists might favor does not fare much better than SIB contractarianism's attempt to defeat action skepticism. Yet it raises important issues that we need to address, including the problem of deformed desires, and whether we should broaden the skeptic's position beyond EU such that when we defeat skepticism, we defeat it in the context of a richer view of morality than SIB contractarianism allows, given the constraint put on it by the starting point of the preference-satisfaction account of rational action. A richer view of morality would include positive duties, would be sensitive to the people's social position, and would directly address oppression. I offer a fuller account of the justification of moral dispositions and actions in chapter 8 that I believe supports such a view. But first I turn to the issue of the role of deformed desires in a theory of rational choice.

4

Deformed Desires

This chapter argues that since the formal version of EU does not exclude desires deformed by patriarchy as irrational, the traditional picture of the skeptic who adopts EU runs the risk of recapitulating women's oppression in the emergent moral code. Demonstrating that acting in ways that might contribute to oppression is rationally required obviously does not constitute a satisfactory defeat of skepticism. Informed desire tests hold promise of excluding from EU deformed desires as irrational. But, as traditionally construed, they fail to do so. Such tests require the addition of a condition of rationality according to which the agent recognizes herself as having intrinsic worth. Excluding deformed desires from EU or any theory of rational choice we might take the skeptic to adopt takes us some way toward narrowing the skeptic's position in order to effect a satisfactory defeat of action skepticism.

1 INTRODUCTION

I showed in the previous chapter that under patriarchy, women are likely to develop desires that when satisfied support oppressive conditions and practices, and that according to internalism, which care ethicists might adopt, women have reasons for acting on their deformed desires, and lack reasons for acting in ways that contribute to freeing them from oppression when they lack such desires. One way to avoid these problematic links between reasons and desires is for care ethicists to exclude deformed desires as ones that necessarily yield or necessarily reflect reasons for action. Expected utility theory also needs to exclude deformed desires, since otherwise it, too, can be criticized for allowing acting on deformed desires to be rational. Indeed, in its formal version EU does not distinguish desires that are deformed by certain social practices and institutions from ones that are not, but typically requires only that desires be consistent and properly ordered.[1] Yet if we want to use EU as a foundation for constructing a moral theory in the way SIB contractarians do, or even if we want to aim to defeat the skeptic who believes that EU is the best theory of rational action, we should want to exclude deformed desires from EU as irrational. "Informed desire tests" are one way to do so: only those desires surviving any such test are rational, and thus are candidates for rationally and morally required action. This chapter examines whether some of the conditions of rationality invoked by traditional informed desire tests can be used to exclude deformed desires from theories of rationality, and ultimately, theories of morality.

The main concern about deformed desires in this book is their impact on defeating skepticism. Several worries arouse suspicion that an attempt to defeat skepticism without excluding deformed desires would be unsatisfactory. One is the problem, already mentioned, of recapitulating women's oppression. Self-interest-based contractarianism is particularly affected: including as rational deformed desires that contractors may bring to the bargaining table in Gauthier-type schemes presupposes that the powerful will win out. For now, the burden falls on the moral contract that emerges from agreement to exclude the satisfaction of such desires because satisfying them leads to unjust results. We are likely to have our hopes disappointed that SIB contractarianism would generate such an agreement, partly because the privileged often take deformed desires as evidence that women *like* to be in subordinate roles. Their belief is rooted partly in the view that any desires a person has she has autonomously, and that, when satisfied, they will promote what she judges to be best for her. So on an SIB contractarian scheme, if a hypothetical woman bargainer puts forward claims that reflect her deformed desires, these claims will be treated just like any other claims she puts forward in bargaining, and the emergent agreement over everyone's claims will reflect all such desires. Moreover, moral theories other than SIB contractarianism may be affected by deformed desires, since in order successfully to defeat action skepticism, they must answer to a skeptic who endorses EU. Even if these theories are not grounded in EU like SIB contractarianism, EU might constrain their content.

A second problem concerns the neutrality of the skeptic's position. As I have pointed out, philosophers have defined the skeptic's position broadly, allowing it to be rational for a person to have any but moral desires so that a defeat of skepticism will cover all persons in all situations, will not beg the question against those who may not have moral desires on every occasion, and will not rest on any special contingencies such that it would reach only those who have moral desires. This explains the neutrality of the skeptic's position. Yet if deformed desires are not excluded from EU, since their satisfaction advantages some over others, the deck is loaded from the start: the skeptic's position only appears neutral. This is because oppressive states resulting from women's having and satisfying their deformed desires either will emerge from the moral code or at least will not be caught by it. Thus the moral code will not address oppression when it should, or it will recapitulate it.[2] The neutrality objection is specific to Hobbesian contractarian theories where bargainers know their desires— Rawlsian bargainers are behind the veil of ignorance where they lack knowledge of certain features about themselves, including perhaps desires, that are arbitrary, and that may bias their choice of the principles of justice.

Third, willing deformed desires affronts one's rationality. Deformed desires, I shall argue, are both a cause and a result of one's not seeing oneself as having intrinsic worth, as in the case of a woman who believes she needs to be with a man to be fulfilled and so becomes partnered with a man, which in turn makes her not desire independence. In general, social practices and institutions can make a person come to see herself as having inferior status, and the servile preferences she subsequently forms reinforce this view. But having desires that make one see oneself as inferior to others contradicts the intrinsic worth that Kant believes we all have in virtue of our capacity for rationality. Endorsing these desires is not rational; we would choose to have them only when coerced by unjust social conditions. Deformed desires are ones the agent would not otherwise, in the absence of such conditions, choose to have. If deformed desires, like other irrational desires resulting from lack of or false information, nonreflection, or psychological disturbances, are not excluded from a theory of rational choice, a defeat of skepticism that is grounded at least partly in them would be unsuccessful because it would amount to having a situation that it is not rational to act on. A successful defeat of skepticism cannot demonstrate the rational requiredness of acting in ways that contradict rational choice. My focus will be on deformed desires because I am concerned to clarify the skeptic's position in such a way that were we to defeat the skeptic, we would have no further skeptical challenge remaining, and our defeat would be inclusive. In section 4, I propose an addendum to traditional informed desire tests that aims to eliminate deformed desires from the theory of rational choice the skeptic takes to be right. My view, roughly, is that when an agent recognizes herself as having intrinsic worth, consenting to deformed desires would not be rational because they would affront her rationality by being inconsistent with her worth as a person. I now turn to a more detailed analysis of deformed desires.

2 DEFORMED DESIRES

Desires influenced by patriarchy include ones supporting female slavishness, exemplified by characters such as the Deferential Wife, who caters to her husband and family because she believes it is women's proper role;[3] the marianismo woman, who is the submissive and self-denying counterpart to machismo man;[4] and the right-wing woman, who adopts a traditional lifestyle either because of religious, antiabortion views or because she believes that she has few or no economic and social options.[5] These women may be, in the words of Uma Narayan, the "dupes of patriarchy," who buy wholesale into patriarchal values and principles, having desires that are all deformed by patriarchy.[6] Others are mere "bargainers with patriarchy," who are not completely duped by patriarchy but still buy into some of its practices; they have both deformed and nondeformed desires, and recognize external constraints that patriarchy places on them and choose in the face of these constraints. Bargainers with patriarchy include the surrogate mother who wants to be pregnant because she believes that only pregnancy will give her self-worth,[7] but does not like the effects of pregnancy on her body; the woman who plays the "dating game" because she wants to be with a man because she believes that being with a man will bring her security and happiness, but wants also to be independent; and the Pirzada Muslim woman who veils herself for reasons of security, obedience, modesty, and identity, but dislikes veiling because it is uncomfortable and risky to her health.[8]

There is controversy among feminists over whether and to what extent women's desires are deformed. Christina Hoff Sommers, a self-proclaimed feminist, believes that none of women's desires are deformed because women are no longer the victims of undemocratic indoctrination, and that admitting to the existence of deformed desires is illiberal and a threat to democracy.[9] Marilyn Friedman, who believes that women can have autonomy only when they have more than one option and full information, would take many of women's desires under patriarchy to be deformed, since in spite of the advances made by women, coercion, constraint, and undue restriction of options still exist.[10] Martha Nussbaum agrees with Friedman and John Stuart Mill, and believes that women can have deformed desires even in a democracy, due to a legacy of social hierarchy and inequality that has made women adapt their desires to the options, beliefs, and norms they tend to have under patriarchy. Narayan herself believes that women have both deformed and nondeformed desires and choose autonomously even if they choose to act on the former. She believes that most women are bargainers with patriarchy who have deformed desires but that these desires "reflect realistic assessments of options open to them to get the things they currently want out of life."[11]

Surely Sommers's view is far too simplistic, since it fails to recognize that women can still be oppressed even though they have achieved equality in some areas. As Ann Cudd cogently argues, women are still victims of systematic violence and the threat of violence, they are stereotyped, which harms them economically and psychologically, and they are harmed economically through employment discrimination, group-based harassment, opportunity inequality, and oppression by choice.[12] I agree with Narayan's complex picture of reality: many women both want and do not want to participate in patriarchal practices, and when they do, they often do so for complex reasons even while understanding the political significance of their actions. For instance, for many women dressing fashionably presents a dilemma about making oneself an object of sexual attraction and dressing to get ahead or even to fit in. The choice to shave one's legs often comes out of a struggle between a desire to be "feminine" and a desire to resist patriarchal standards of beauty. And the choice not to speak out against job discrimination is often the result of an interplay between a desire to stand up for oneself and get what one rightfully deserves and a desire not to make waves. The picture is complicated by the fact that we cannot read off a person's desires just from her behavior—does the woman who conforms to the dictates of fashion and beauty, but just to get ahead in the business world, have deformed desires? I will outline five features of deformed desires. While I do not deem each to be necessary and/or sufficient for a desire to be deformed, we can be fairly certain that most deformed desires have most of these features. Thus, desires are deformed when they meet at least most of these conditions. That plenty of women have deformed desires is obvious. But while Narayan believes that most women are bargainers with patriarchy, I believe that women fall into all categories. Some exhibit "active agency" in considering whether to participate in patriarchal practices, others who reject wholesale feminist ideology buy into patriarchy because they are duped by it and have no vision of alternatives, and still others fall somewhere in between. The category any woman falls into is determined by the reasons she engages in conformist behavior, the principles she adopts, and the like. We need not settle this empirical issue, but just decide whether *any* deformed desires should be included in a rational or moral theory.

Sandra Bartky offers a rich description of repressive satisfactions, or, deformed desires, as those that

> fasten us to the established order of domination, for the same system which produces false needs also controls the conditions under which such needs can be satisfied. "False needs," it might be ventured, are needs which are produced through indoctrination, psychological manipulation, and the denial of autonomy; they are needs whose possession and satisfaction benefit not the subject who has them but a social order whose interest lies in domination.[13]

I want to identify five features of deformed desires, the first three of which emerge from this passage. The first feature is that the source of deformed desires contributes to their deformation. Arguably all desires are formed in a social context; deformed desires are formed by and in response to *unjust* social conditions, including patriarchal ones where men are deemed superior, women inferior.[14] Jon Elster defines the "sour grapes" phenomenon to explain how women acquire deformed desires by adaptation to their subordinate state.[15] Just as the fox's conviction that the grapes he wants to eat are out of his reach causes him to believe that they are sour and to come to prefer not to eat them, women adapt their preferences to a social position that affords them few options. This is not to say that unjust social conditions *necessarily* issue in deformed desires, since many women resist acquiring them, or if they do acquire them, they rid themselves of them on reflection, reprogramming, or desensitization. Still, social influences are strong, as evidenced by the fact that even some feminists have admitted to having rape fantasies.

Nussbaum elucidates three general factors present in patriarchy that produce deformed desires and that represent ways in which women are indoctrinated, manipulated, and denied autonomy. These are (1) lack of information or false information about fact; (2) lack of reflection or deliberation about norms; and (3) lack of options.[16] Indoctrination occurs when, for example, widely accepted sexual mores and customs, endorsed by the judicial system, instill the myth that women who get raped deserve it because of the clothes they wear, the places they visit, or the times they go out. Deformed desires about rape stem from either lack of reflection on norms governing heterosexual behavior, which allow a great deal of latitude to men but not to women, or false information about "women's nature," including the belief that all women want to have sex even if they resist, or even lack of options, such as when women agree to be made sexual partners in exchange for economic security. Women come to desire restrictive behavior that labels them as "good," and to seek traditional roles of faithful wife and mother. Manipulation occurs when, for instance, the media pressures women to be feminine at the expense of developing their intellectual capacities.[17] Deformed desires about femininity also can stem from lack of information about women's intellectual capacity, or lack of reflection on social norms requiring women but not men to cultivate the "fashion-beauty complex," or women's not having the option to resist cultivating beauty norms for job security or social acceptance. Women come to want to engage in beauty practices because doing so makes them feel good. Finally, denial of autonomy occurs when a person loses her capacity for self-directedness or self-authorship over her life. It also reflects the three factors Nussbaum lists, as in the case of the Deferential Wife, who believes that women's proper role is to serve her family and comes to desire this kind of servility. Note that there need not be an identifiable person or group that intentionally manipulates, distorts facts, or holds back information; these more subtle forms of coercion systematically deform women's desires.

A second feature of deformed desires that we can identify in the passage from Bartky is that they benefit not their bearers, but the privileged and patriarchy itself. There is an oddness to this feature, since typically when a person desires something, she believes that satisfying this desire will benefit her, and it often does. Indeed, the Hobbesian view, prevalent in liberal thought, is that a person's good is defined in terms of her desire-satisfaction. But a person's beliefs about such expected benefits sometimes do not square with the harms that result from satisfying certain desires. For example, slavish values aim only at satisfying the values of others, typically to the disadvantage of the "slaves."[18] Such is the case when women lose themselves in caring for others as I described in the previous chapter—here, others benefit—or when women desire to conform to the fashion-beauty complex that leaves them with an inferiorized image of their bodies, unnecessarily demands their time and money, pits them against other women, and keeps them out of jobs they rightly deserve—here, the system benefits.[19] Obviously, in order to legitimize these claims, we must appeal at some level to an objective notion of the good. I will return to this point in section 3.

We can attribute women's belief that they benefit from the satisfaction of their deformed desires to their being deceived about the benefits that they or women as a group receive from deformed desire-satisfaction. Deception is a third feature of deformed desires. Some women believe that they benefit from subservience to men because men find this attractive. Some women believe that denying abortion rights benefits women as a group by discouraging permissiveness about sex, thereby preventing rape. Deception thus explains the insidiousness of deformed desires, which is that it causes the nonprivileged to contribute to their own maltreatment due to their perception of benefit. Indeed, the nonprivileged must be convinced that their subordination is self-beneficial; otherwise they would aim to rid themselves of deformed desires. Elster remarks that what brings about the subordinates' resignation in the case of sour grapes "is [their belief] that [the satisfaction of desires] is good for the subjects."[20] At the same time, we should admit that women *do* benefit from conformity: many feel good conforming to the fashion-beauty complex, conformists avoid hassle and are more easily promoted than their "rebel" sisters, and those who play out "feminine" roles often "catch" a man. But these benefits are at best short-term and shortsighted: the fashion-conscious woman wastes a lot of time and money and may even damage her health, the conformist usually does not get to the top or does so by leaving intact a sexist system that perpetuates sexist stereotypes that harm all women, and the partnered woman is often expected to conform to autonomy-denying, "feminine" roles, or worse, even suffers abuse. Such "benefits" are false because they are accrued in non-self-respecting ways that are at odds with and outweighed by the decided disadvantages of contributing to women's oppression. Women are deceived, then, about two things: that desire-satisfaction is just about receiving the "false benefits" of conformity, and that deformed desire-satisfaction makes women incur harms of oppression.

A fourth feature of deformed desires, one not mentioned in Bartky's account, is that deformed desires often conflict with their bearer's desire to promote her own welfare. Feminists such as Lois Pineau and Catharine MacKinnon suggest that deep down, despite patriarchy's influence on their desires, women—perhaps excepting the complete dupes of patriarchy—really do want their own welfare. Pineau believes that women know which sexual encounters are enjoyable, and thus consensual;[21] MacKinnon suggests that women who are sexually harassed find it devastating to their self-respect and health, that pornography models operate not from free will but from constraint and inequality, and that rape victims who appear disinterested are not indicating desire but silence.[22] Women with deformed desires may have a confused desire set, one that is not, after all, entirely at odds with their welfare, objectively determined. Preferring at once what is in one's own welfare and "ilfare" is inconsistent, but women's preferences can take more tangential routes either toward or away from their own good. Cudd's useful explanation of the phenomena of conflicting desires is that it is not the case that women come to prefer oppression to justice, and subordination to equality, but that they come to desire the kinds of social roles that lead to their oppression and subordination.[23] The marianismo woman, for instance, need not prefer to be subordinate, but wants to uphold a religious tradit-ion of the veneration of the Virgin Mary that relegates her to such a role. But she may at the same time desire to promote her own welfare, which is determined independently of deformed desires.

A fifth feature of deformed desires is that at base they involve a person's not having the appropriate regard for herself as an intrinsically valuable human being. Here I rely on the Kantian notion that each of us has intrinsic worth, or dignity, just in virtue of having the capacity for rationality. Kant believes that no one can lower or raise the intrinsic value of another or of himself or herself.[24] But while many men under patriar-chy believe themselves to be superior in value, many women, being at least partly duped by patriarchy's messages of inferiority directed at them, believe themselves to be inferior. Recognizing one's value, however, is necessary for one's believing oneself worthy of self-directedness and for having full agency. Deformed desires jeopardize autonomy and thus full agency because their satisfaction aims to lower their bearer's value. Sexist social practices and institutions cause women to believe they are inferior, and the servile preferences they consequently form reinforce their belief in their inferiority.

We now need to find a way to exclude deformed desires from rational and moral theories. I will next examine some informed desire tests, and argue that they do not successfully eliminate deformed desires as ones it is not rational to have. In the last section, I propose an addendum to the standard tests that relies on the foregoing analysis of deformed desires to deem them irrational.

3 INFORMED DESIRE TESTS

Standard informed desire tests involve a process of deliberation under which an ideal observer would reject certain desires as irrational. A quick survey will show some conditions of rationality that philosophers have imposed on desires. Bernard Williams invokes deliberation to exclude as irrational both desires that are grounded in false beliefs, such as a desire to drink from a glass you believe contains gin when it contains petrol, and desires that have their source in either ignorance of facts, such as a desire to stay in a building that is about to be bombed, or ignorance about one's desires, such as a desire to lie low when you do not realize that you like to be in the limelight.[25] Michael Smith expands on Williams's list by excluding desires that are "wholly and solely the product of psychological compulsions, physical addictions, emotional disturbances ... depression, spiritual tiredness, accidie, illness, and the like."[26] Richard Brandt deems a desire irrational if "the person would not continue to have the desire if he got before his mind vividly [i.e., focused his attention with maximal vividness and detail with no doubt about the truth of the information],[27] with firm belief, not necessarily just once but on a number of occasions, all the *relevant* propositions the truth of which can be known to him, at the very same time at which he was *reflecting on the object in a desiring way.*"[28] Brandt invokes "the canons of inductive or deductive logic," and facts or "publicly available evidence which could now be obtained by procedures known to science."[29] Peter Railton also offers a full information account, defining what he calls "objectified subjective interest" as what a person would want when he had "unqualified cognitive and *imaginative* powers, full factual and nomological information about his physical and psychological constitution, capacities, circumstances, and history, and about his environment, and whose instrumental rationality was in no way defective."[30] James Griffin and Elizabeth Anderson offer more inclusive accounts that assess a person's entire life rather than what is rational to do in a particular situation.[31] According to Griffin, the informed desire account must reflect what he calls "the structure of desire." This is a desire to live a certain life that is valuable to the person who lives it as measured in terms of her well-being. It includes higher order desires (e.g., desires about desires) and global desires about life itself, as well as ordinary local desires, including, for my purposes, deformed desires. Griffin's test has both subjective and objective elements; it includes desires a person has and ones she should have because an objective observer who has experienced a different life judges that they will make her life better. On Anderson's account, we judge desires according to a social norm or standard that tells us whether they adequately express people's drives for certain states of affairs. The standard varies with our purposes: different standards allow us to judge whether a person is a good philosopher, a good mother, or even has a good life. We determine the standard by a hypothetical procedure in which we offer reasons to each other for why we value what we do. We can check others involved in the procedure as to whether their values involve inconsistency, ignorance, partiality, confusion, double standards, insensitivity, or self-defeat.

Despite the differences in these informed desire accounts, they have in common two goals: (1) promoting the agent's good, defined either subjectively and relatively, or objectively, and (2) protecting the agent's autonomy. Consider some ways in which an agent's desires stand in the way of her welfare and self-determination. She can have desires grounded in false beliefs, such as when she wants not to brush her teeth because she falsely believes that not brushing her teeth will preserve them. She can have desires grounded in psychoses, such as when her depression keeps her from wanting to pursue the ambitious career she studied hard for in favor of a menial job that does not boost her self-esteem and end her depression. And she can have desires grounded in logical error, such as when she is obese and wants to keep overeating because she makes an exception for herself to the rule that overeating causes obesity. Philosophers, particularly those working in the liberal tradition, assume that the agent's acting on whatever desires she has that survive deliberation is rational because acting this way promotes her own good. Yet, I shall argue, traditional informed desire tests do not exclude deformed desires from the desire-based theory of rational choice. And these desires also stand in the way of the agent's welfare and self-direction by being a cause and a result of her not seeing herself as having worth. The reasons they do not exclude deformed desires are threefold: (1) the nature of deformed desires, (2) the nature of deliberation, and (3) problems with both relative and objective notions of the good. I will discuss each in turn.

3.1 The Nature of Deformed Desires

For several reasons, it seems doubtful that at least Williams, Brandt, and Railton intend their deliberative tests to extend to deformed desires. None explicitly mentions deformed desires. The examples they offer, such as Williams's case of the person who mistakes petrol for gin and desires to drink the former, and Railton's case of Sheila, a journalist in the Northwest who is offered a job in the East from a great metropolitan newspaper but has a strong desire to stay at her current job, are not ones involving a person's failure to recognize her own worth.[32] In addition, what I will call the Kantian "facts about humanity," or, the worth that all persons have in virtue of their capacity for rationality, are not scientifically provable facts, so Brandt's test would not exclude desires that do not recognize them. Railton's requirement that a person have full information about his capacities does not clearly extend to the Kantian assumption of persons' intrinsic worth, which is grounded in the capacity for rationality. Rather, as I understand it, it is meant to exclude desires based on misinformation about a person's talents and abilities, and only insofar as these affect her choices but not because they ground her status as a moral entity. Finally, traditional theorists give no indication that their informed desire tests are intended to exclude desires based on the logical error of inconsistency involved in seeing men, but not women, as deserving of respect, instead of logical errors about more factual matters.

Nor do I think we can extend the conditions of rationality invoked by traditional informed desire tests to cover deformed desires, for the reason that these desires are significantly different from other irrational desires. While deformed desires may involve logical error or false beliefs or mistaken facts at some level, the confusion really concerns the integral nature of persons, or, the bearer's own value as a person, which are deep Kantian facts that are more fundamental than the value a person may have in virtue of either her personal attributes such as activities and career (e.g., upholsterer, professor) or her group membership (e.g., gender, race). Getting straight about one's value as a person is hardly the same as getting straight about whether the glass contains petrol or gin. The fact that traditional informed desire tests focus on a person's choice about how best to act only on particular occasions is further evidence that they are not designed to extend to deformed desires. Griffin's and Anderson's broader tests come closer to excluding deformed desires by extending to a person's choice about how best to lead her life, but I believe that neither gets at the underlying nature of deformed desires, namely, their connection to the agent's worth.

This feature of deformed desires distinguishes them on two counts: (1) their effect on the agent's self-directedness, including her having individual interests and making them her own, and her being self-directing about her agency, and (2) their effect on the agent's other desires and life as a whole. I will examine these features of deformed desires in this subsection.

Since deformed desires involve the agent's lacking the appropriate regard for her worth, we need to give an analysis of what it is to have worth. I endorse a Kantian analysis that I will elaborate on in chapter 5 in connection with my account of privilege. Kant believes that each person has intrinsic value, or dignity, which is grounded in her capacity for rationality, which in turn is marked by her having desires, interests, goals, and plans.[33] This explains the commonality of rationality. But rationality also distinguishes each person from all others, for it is from one's rationality that one's individuality stems, as evidenced by the unique set of desires, interests, goals, and plans that each person has that mark her rationality.[34] Certainly Kant must have meant to emphasize that a person's desires, interests, and such be *individual* in nature—that is, be the person's *own*—for otherwise we would be following heteronomous law in satisfying ones that really belong to others. Kant must have meant to exclude deformed desires as markers of a person's rationality, since deformed desires, when satisfied, benefit those in the dominant group at the expense of the nonprivileged.

Individual interests are central not only to rationality but also to understanding morality, as Judith Thomson argues.[35] Thomson grounds the right against bodily intrusion, one of our most fundamental rights, in two related features of persons, namely, that we have what she calls "inherently individual interests," and that we are subject to the moral law. Thomson rejects the Hobbesian state of nature in which there are no moral or political laws, on the Kantian grounds that "the capacity to conform your conduct to the moral law is a necessary and sufficient condition for the moral law to apply to you."[36] But in order to have the capacity to conform her conduct to the moral law, that is, to understand morality and to follow it, a person needs to have inherently individual interests. For Thomson, morality ought to allow us to cherish our inherently individual interests, such as bodily integrity and life. If a person lacks such interests, Thomson questions whether she even understands morality. Thomson's point, I believe, is that morality is often opposed to self-interest, and only if a person understands that she ought to perform some action when performing it is not necessarily in her interest can she understand what it is to make a moral sacrifice. In short, a person's individual interests are ones that matter to her in such a way that not satisfying them as morality requires is sacrificial. Thus Thomson rejects ethical egoism on the grounds that it requires only that we act in ways that best promote our own interest but not that we respect others' rights. And she rejects act utilitarianism on the grounds that it requires an agent to sacrifice her rights even to her own bodily integrity for the sake of the good of the majority. Thomson, I believe, would agree with Kant that a person's having interests is essential for his or her being in the "moral game." I would add to Thomson's list of rejected theories any moral theory that requires the satisfaction of deformed desires that benefit the dominant group, since these desires are heteronomous but not inherently individual interests that would put their bearer in the "moral game" of having legitimate rights and obligations.

Having inherently individual interests is essential to one's autonomy. Being a fully autonomous agent requires not just having desires, plans, and such, "attached," as it were, to a person, but their bearer's making these things her own. Indeed, this is what *makes* them inherently individual interests. Now, prima facie, deformed desires seem to be the very antithesis of inherently individual interests, since they seem to belong more to "the established order of domination" than to the individual. The problem is that sometimes their bearer believes they *are* her own: the prostitute insists that she really wants to sell her sexual services, and the homemaker with few options insists that she would rather devote all her time to raising a family than pursuing a career. So we need a way to decide when a person's desires truly become her own.

Harry Frankfurt offers one. Frankfurt famously argues that what makes an entity a person is the ability to form second-order desires and second-order volitions, which involve the capacity for reflective self-evaluation about one's first-order desires. A first-order desire is simply a desire to do or not to do one thing or another.[37] A second-order desire is wanting to have or not to have a certain first-order desire. To have a will, or, a second-order volition that is essential to being a person, is to want one of one's first-order desires to be effective, that is, to motivate or prompt one's action. Wantons, in contrast to persons, lack second-order volitions. They are unconcerned with the desirability of their desires themselves, and pursue whatever course of action they are most strongly inclined to pursue. Thus the unwilling drug addict who is a person has conflicting first-order desires to take the drug and not to take the drug, and is not neutral with regard to them: he wants the latter desire to be his will, to be his effective desire. Both desires are his own, but, according to Frankfurt, he *makes one of them more truly his own,* and in doing so withdraws himself from the other. That is, he *identifies* himself, through the formation of a second-order volition, with one rather than the other desire. In contrast, the addict who is a wanton is unconcerned about which desire moves him to act, though he, too, may experience a conflict in his first-order desires. What distinguishes him from the person is that he does not care that one of his first-order desires rather than the other should be his will. Crucially, he has *no identity* apart from his first-order desires. He cannot and does not care which of his first-order desires wins out, because either he lacks the capacity for reflection, or he is indifferent to evaluating his own desires. He is moved simply by the strength of one of his first-order desires.

Frankfurt's analysis of what it takes for one to make one's desires one's own, unfortunately, leaves wide open the content of these desires and second-order volitions. On his account, it is possible for a woman who is a person in Frankfurt's sense to want to make her deformed desires more truly her own than other desires she may have, and so to identify herself with her deformed desires. Unlike the wanton, she might care which of her desires wins out when there is a conflict, or which ones she identifies herself with even in the absence of any conflict. But I question whether she really can make her deformed desires her own and will them to be effective. My initial thought is that the prostitute, no matter what she says, does not really want to sell her sexual services, but has to deceive herself that this is really what she wants.[38] She does not autonomously choose to make her deformed desires more truly her own than desires she may have for her welfare. And if she does not have these desires, we should question what makes her not desire her welfare, and whether these factors interfere with her autonomy. I will flesh this out in the context of Narayan's account, which, unlike Frankfurt's, specifically addresses deformed desires.

Narayan believes that women *can* make deformed desires truly their own by "bargaining" with patriarchy. She understands, for instance, Muslim women's choice to veil as a "'bundle of elements,' some of which they want [e.g., ones reflecting their commitments to various aspects of their own religious, social, and communal identities] and some of which they do not want [e.g., one's reflecting restrictions placed upon them by patriarchy], and where they lack the power to 'undo the bundle' so as to choose only those elements they want."[39] Narayan portrays deformed desires to be the result of a struggle between desires in full knowledge that some are caused by patriarchy, thereby indicating women's active agency. She denounces feminists such as Catharine MacKinnon and Andrea Dworkin for representing women as capable only of "zombielike acquiescence to patriarchal norms," and their agency as being "completely pulverized" by patriarchy.[40] Narayan's view, in short, is that since women's deformed desires reflect realistic assessments of the options available to them to get what they want out of life, they are their own desires.

I agree with Narayan that women make choices even within the constraints of patriarchy, and I believe that all but the complete dupes of patriarchy exhibit agency. The Deferential Wife, I believe, is influenced, but not determined, by her social circumstances, which can confuse her about her worth. I believe further that she is not responsible for her servility, not because of her socialization, but because there is reason for her to do what she believes morality requires her to do, which is to be servile. Freeing her from responsibility on these grounds preserves her agency.[41] But I remain skeptical that any deformed desires are truly their bearer's own just because the agent can bargain about them and they in the end reflect realistic assessments of their options. I should think that the veiling woman who realizes that her options are limited under patriarchy would yet not want to have desires deformed by patriarchy. I want to suggest that the person who retains deformed desires even after "bargaining" with patriarchy doubts her self-worth, and that such desires cannot truly be her own.

According to Narayan, women's wearing the burqa outside the home signifies womanly modesty and propriety.[42] The woman who chooses veiling after bargaining over her conflicting desires partly because she believes that she needs to send a message to men about her sexuality lacks sufficient belief in her self-worth to insist that men be the ones to change their attitudes toward women who do not veil, rather than women concede by donning restrictive, uncomfortable, and dangerous veils. In this respect, she is not much different from the Deferential Wife, who believes that women should serve their families, in that her *principles*, not just her desires, are wrong. The veiling woman who struggles with patriarchy, and yet concedes partly for patriarchal reasons, shows that she is still under its grip. On Frankfurt's account, the veiling woman turns out to be a person, not a wanton, because she cares which of her first-order desires wins out. On Narayan's account, the veiling woman is a person whose identity lies with her deformed desires. Narayan notes that the values, attitudes, and choices that are impoverished by patriarchy "are in fact the values, attitudes, and choices that define for these women the lives they currently have and value, and the selves they currently are and in many ways want to remain."[43] My complaint is that on both Frankfurt's and Narayan's accounts, the veiling woman's will, or second-order volition, that makes her deformed desires more of her own than her other desires, and so ultimately identifies her, is *itself* deformed by patriarchy. This sheds doubt on whether her choice to be governed by her deformed desires is autonomous, and whether her deformed desires really are her own. So we need a better account of what it is to make a desire one's own, since having one's own desires is essential for having autonomy.

I propose the following constraint on willing: in order for a person's desires to be her own, they must meet the condition that they be in keeping with her intrinsic worth as a person in the Kantian sense. It is this feature that makes a person, but not a wanton, care which of her first-order desires wins out. The person who truly exhibits full agency does not sacrifice herself, but *maintains* a sense of self *through* her inherently individual interests. Although Thomson does not speak much about the content of such interests, her rejection of act utilitarianism on the grounds that it does not respect these interests but instead requires a person to sacrifice herself for the good of the majority, is telling. Again, Thomson seems to be agreeing with Kant that a person's interests must not belong to others, since we would be following heteronomous morality in satisfying them. An act utilitarianism requires a person to act on an interest in maximizing pleasure for the majority even at the expense of her own pleasure. This interest cannot be a person's own because it is too self-sacrificial. Self-sacrifice and self-worth are related, as Robin Dillon explains. Following Kant, Dillon remarks that "self-abnegation is incompatible with self-respect insofar as it involves not paying attention to oneself in the first place, insofar as one never attends to one's intrinsic worth as a person nor to one's own needs, desires, projects, and so on."[44] In order for interests to be one's own, then, I suggest that they must be ones that a person can choose consistent with her own worth as a person. Deformed desires fail in this regard because, when satisfied, they aim to lower one's own value as a person. A person has to value herself appropriately, which involves knowing, acknowledging, and asserting her worth as a person. This means that she must have and assert her inherently individual interests, but not ones that belong to others or to the system of domination.[45] This is exactly what Thomson believes makes a person a member of the moral community. Thus, contra Narayan, the veiling woman does not make deformed desires more truly her own than other desires by bargaining about them. Rather, she needs to *rid* herself of them since they conflict with her self-worth, if she is to assert her individualism and worth as a person, which is necessary for her being a bearer of rights and a member of the moral community.[46]

An additional argument for the view that a person cannot make deformed desires her own is that she cannot freely choose to have desires that are themselves the product of coercion, since this would be like freely consenting to slavery, which Mill was right to think could not be done. Deformed desires are autonomy-restricting; to choose them would be paradoxically to use one's autonomy to give up one's autonomy. Indeed, a second-order volition that selects deformed desires over other desires fails to capture the essence of Frankfurt's view, namely, that having second-order volitions allows a person to have freedom of the will, or, in his words, to be free to want what one wants to want.[47] Thus I believe that Narayan's representation of the bargainers with patriarchy offers a false sense of control or autonomy a person has over her self. A person who exhibits full agency and self-direction cannot choose to have desires that are coercive, ones making her act in ways she otherwise would not. The veiling woman does not freely choose to have a desire to veil and to have it win out over her other desires, even if she recognizes that the former is deformed by patriarchy.[48] She cannot freely make these desires her own, and if she has them, she cannot be fully self-directing.

Whether had by the dupe of, or the bargainer with, patriarchy, deformed desires benefit "the established order of domination," but not their bearers, or benefit their bearers only in ways that are shortsighted and not self-respecting. This also bears on whether deformed desires diminish the agent's self-directedness. The woman who wants to be self-sacrificing because she believes that women have a duty to serve their families has a deformed desire whose satisfaction benefits the system, not herself.[49] A student who wants to have sex with her married professor because she is attracted to his power, even though she knows he will go back to his wife after the fling and, she tells herself, she sincerely does not mind being used, has a deformed desire that when satisfied supports a system that favors women's dependence on men, and conflicts with her intrinsic worth, which requires satisfaction of her sexual needs on terms of equality. In the typical case, the agent who seeks to satisfy her own desires does so in order to benefit in some way, thereby contributing to the agent's self-directedness. But to the degree that an agent has deformed desires, she cannot be self-directing because the true benefits of their satisfaction are "turned over," as it were, to the system or to others.

Deformed desires have a deeper impact than other irrational desires on their bearer's self-directedness about her own agency: they affect the agent's choice to be a moral person, as exhibited in the following features of moral agency. Deformed desires stand in the way of the agent's assessing her actions and disposition, her reasons for adopting a moral disposition, and for having and acting from it. For if the agent lacks a sense of her self-worth, she cannot make good choices about being morally disposed and acting morally. Deformed desires stand in the way of the agent's engaging in reflective deliberation. They affect her moral reasoning, making it unclear whether she has the right reasons for the choices she makes and the actions she performs. Deformed desires stand in the way of her having a second-order desire about being a moral person, and then squaring this with her first-order desires, interests, and beliefs, especially when these conflict with her self-worth. Finally, deformed desires stand in the way of the agent's reflecting on the moral maxim she chooses to guide her life by, and the justification for the moral principles or theory that yields the maxim. All of these choices and facets of deliberation, which I will elaborate on in chapter 8, are essential to being a morally good person, but cannot be undertaken appropriately by a person who does not acknowledge her own intrinsic value. Such a person is likely to endorse a moral theory that does not give appropriate weight to her self and her desires, but requires undue self-sacrifice or deference from her and members of her group, which risks recapitulating women's oppression. Her political and religious values, which together with her moral values form the core of her identity, are likely to go the same way. Deformed desires' impact on the agent's self-directedness is much more far-reaching than that of other irrational desires because they concern her own agency, not just confusion over facts or even choice of career. Deformed desires even shape a person's worldview, which subsequently shapes her other desires and choices, which can further restrict her autonomy.

In conclusion, the nature of deformed desires, particularly their relation to the agent's value as a person, is one reason to doubt that traditional conditions of rationality in standard informed desire tests, such as having full information and not suffering psychoses, could be used to exclude deformed desires as irrational. Perhaps another feature of traditional informed desire tests might protect the agent's worth and so serve to eliminate deformed desires. Rational deliberation is a candidate.

3.2 The Nature of Deliberation

Traditional informed desire tests, such as Brandt's "cognitive psychotherapy," which "relies simply upon reflection on available information, without influence by prestige of someone, use of evaluative language, extrinsic reward or punishment, or use of artificially induced feeling-states like relaxation,"[50] describe a fully rational person reflecting on her desires in a "cool hour," adding and subtracting ones in light of standards of rationality. But is this kind of reflection sufficient for excluding deformed desires as irrational?

Kant presumably would say yes, since he believes that when fully rational, persons *necessarily* respect themselves,[51] which amounts to one's acknowledging one's intrinsic value, and, I believe, acknowledging that one's deformed desires are irrational since they are grounded in a failure to recognize one's worth. One who, on reflection, fails to recognize his or her worth, is, for Kant, irrational. But Kant's view is problematic. For one thing, it is not sensitive to the fact that women under patriarchy are continually sent strong messages of inferiority through behaviors such as rape, woman-battering, and sexual harassment that can easily counteract conflicting messages that one has intrinsic worth as a person.[52] Reflection is unlikely to clear up the resulting confusion about one's worth. Holding the patriarchal woman responsible for her self-conception is unfair, given her social situation. Further, deeming as irrational the abused woman who has a deformed desire to stay with her abuser is insulting since she is hardly ever in a "cool hour" to reflect, and reflection alone is unlikely to overcome the effects of her circumstances to get her to see her worth and her desire as deformed. In addition, contra Kant, her capacity for reflection is not impaired; rather, she gets the facts about her worth wrong, concluding from her experiences that she is inferior to men. She consequently does not realize that her desires are deformed. So Kant is wrong to think that reflection would make any rational person recognize her worth and thus see when her desires are deformed.

When ordinary reflection fails to exclude irrational desires, as may be the case for the patriarchal woman, theorists such as Williams and Railton extend deliberation to include imagination. The idea is that the agent who reflectively deliberates about her desires can rely on imagination in addition to the conditions of rationality to determine whether her desires are ones it is rational for her to have. For Williams, the agent should exercise his imagination sufficiently to see what it would be like were he to satisfy the desire in question, or to see what it would be like to have different desires and satisfy them.[53] For Railton, the agent uses imagination to tell him what he would want his nonidealized self to want were he to find himself in certain circumstances,[54] or, what he would want himself to want or seek if he knew what he were doing.[55] The patriarchal woman would either imagine what it would be like were she to satisfy her deformed desires, or were she to have different desires and satisfy them, or she would imagine whether she would want to satisfy her deformed desires were she now to know what she was doing. Imagination holds promise of getting the patriarchal woman to see that she has intrinsic value, and consequently, that her desires are deformed.

Williams's extending the process of deliberation to include imagination supports his internalism, for if an agent lacks the relevant motivation, we simply extend the process of deliberation to include imagination so that any reasons for action always appeal to some desire in the agent's motivational set. Indeed, internalists *must* resort to something like imagination if they are to have hope of excluding deformed desires as irrational, since on a simple version of internalism, having deformed desires is both a necessary and a sufficient condition of having a reason to act in ways satisfying them. Imagination holds promise of severing the necessary connection between reasons and deformed desires.

But I am skeptical that deliberative imagination will exclude deformed desires for internalists such as Williams. Recall from the previous chapter that Williams believes that an agent, A, has a reason to ϕ if and only if A has a set of motivations, S, such that A could be led to desire to ϕ by sound deliberation from the motivation that she has in her actual motivational set, including the set of her desires, evaluations, attitudes, projects, and so on.[56] Williams's commitment to internalism stems from his belief that only internal reasons can explain action. He gives the example of Owen Wingrave, who has no motivation to join the army and has desires that all point in another direction. When his father tells Wingrave that he has a reason to join the army, he must, says Williams, mean an external reason. If Wingrave does join the army, his action cannot be explained in terms of an internal reason, since he lacks the relevant motive, and since no motivation is generated by his deliberating about joining the army. But Williams dismisses external reason statements as false, incoherent, or something else misleadingly expressed. Reasons for action, for internalists like Williams, must be tied to the agent's motives, and when motivation is lacking, deliberation must bring it about. Note that Williams does not think of S as "statically given," such that my motivation must already be in S and deliberation just brings it out. Rather, deliberation can add new desires as well as subtract ones that the agent thinks she should not have.[57] Still, I take Williams to be saying that any new desires the agent comes to have as a result of imagination must be at least loosely related to S, because otherwise Williams's view is externalist, and because reasons would lose their explanatory power.

The problem is that Williams can extend imagination only in ways still tied to elements of the agent's motivational set, S. Thus, the test is not likely to work for the dupes of patriarchy, who do not recognize their own worth. The elements in S are ones that in people like the dupes of patriarchy will not aid the agent in deliberative imagination to rid herself of deformed desires or to add new nondeformed desires. Her motivational set, S, is itself sufficiently corrupted to limit her imagination. However, imagination has a better chance of working in the bargainer with patriarchy, since the bargainer has a mixed motivational set containing both deformed desires and ones that when satisfied respect women's value.

To put the point another way, one that cuts across the internalism/externalism debate, imaginative deliberation involves a person's being imaginative about her *desires* or something in her motivational set, S. To repeat, for Williams this includes "dispositions of evaluation, patterns of emotional reaction, personal loyalties, and various projects, as they may be abstractly called, embodying commitments of the agent."[58] But the patriarchal woman needs more than imagination to see that her deformed desires are irrational or to add nondeformed desires to her motivational set. She needs to be *visionary*, and not just about her desires, but about her *self*. Being visionary is more extensive in scope and more complex than imagination. The visionary patriarchal woman will see herself as having intrinsic value, and consequently will be reflective from the ground up, much like the Catholic who challenges her beliefs not from the standpoint of her religion but in a radical way that cuts to their very foundation. The visionary person will conceive of herself not only with different desires, but with different *values* and *principles* that both underlie and shape her desires. She will come to believe that she has a right to act on her desires, and not adopt and act on ones that benefit others only. She will question her own ideal of a worthwhile life and the standards by which she judges her life as such. She will see her opportunities and choices in a new light, and will see herself as part of the moral community and as an individual in her own right who is deserving of respect. She will change her worldview, which affects every aspect of her life.

Consider an abused woman who becomes visionary. Williams's and Railton's tests are limited to her imagining that she does not want to stay with her abuser or developing new desires that when satisfied would be at odds with her staying with her abuser. On the visionary model of deliberation, she will envision herself as having intrinsic value, as not being deserving of abuse, as not having principles that endorse women's servility to men, and as asserting her right to act on desires that she has that will promote her own welfare rather than satisfy her abuser's interest in "keeping her in line." An informed desire test has to be more radical in these ways in order for it to exclude in a wholesale way deformed desires as irrational. I propose that we incorporate into traditional informed desire tests the notion of being visionary. The way to do this is to build in as a condition of rationality that the agent acknowledge her intrinsic worth. This condition, then, will stand alongside being fully informed, not suffering psychoses, and so on. Next I will argue that in addition, we need to import objective value into informed desire tests.

3.3 Subjective, Relative Good versus Objective Good

In the spirit of liberalism, which deems persons to be the best judges of their own good, and having the goal of protecting autonomy, many traditional informed desire tests, including those offered by Railton,[59] Brandt,[60] and Williams, as well as the desire-satisfaction theory of rational choice endorsed by the skeptic, identify value with the satisfaction of a person's wants or desires, that is, with a subjective, relative notion of the good. But this account of value seems to stand in the way of excluding deformed desires as irrational. Consider again that for Williams, deliberation holds promise of bringing about a desire that a person may have but does not recognize she has and that gives her a reason to act. But Williams adds the caveat that only when ϕ-ing is *rationally related* to the relevant desire will that desire provide a reason for A to ϕ—desires in the unconscious might not count.[61] That is, deliberation might reveal some rationally related desire that the person had all along, but we cannot go too far from a person's desire set that is "before her mind." Williams's commitment to internalism, according to which reasons must explain action, constrains the desires and so the reasons that deliberation can bring about.

Consider the woman who wants to play the "dating game," and who might have a desire for her welfare that would be revealed in deliberation and yield a reason for action. Suppose we adopt an objective notion of the good, according to which the good is independent of what persons deem to be good but is decided by some objective measure. If the woman in the example is a dupe of patriarchy who does not know deep down what is objectively good for her, then acting on an objective notion of welfare would of course not be rationally related to the desire she is ignorant of. Thus it violates Williams's constraint and cannot be used by Williams to rule out deformed desires as irrational. The woman lacks a desire, and so a reason, to act in ways that promote her objective welfare. Alternatively, on a subjective, relative notion of the good, the woman determines *for herself* whether playing the dating game promotes her welfare. But this leaves it open as to whether deliberation will exclude deformed desires— it will not, in the woman who meets the conditions of rationality but who still believes that conformity to sexist roles promotes her welfare. Also, for Williams, this kind of patriarchal woman has reason to act on her *deformed* desires, since these desires do not conflict with but are in line with her desire for her welfare as defined by her, and so deliberation does not exclude them. For these reasons, relative good does not eliminate deformed desires from theories of rational or moral action.

The alternative, objective notion of the good, then, bears the burden of ruling out deformed desires in informed desire tests invoking it. But like many philosophical concepts, it is notoriously difficult to defend. Both Griffin and Anderson[62] have recently offered rich attempts to do so in the context of their informed desire tests. Griffin invokes objective, "prudential" values such that if one has and acts on them, one's life will be better than it would be in their absence. But he does not say how he derives his list of prudential values, or what makes up each one. And there will be disagreements over some of them, such as autonomy, particularly in connection with whether satisfying deformed desires promotes autonomy.

Anderson defends a plausible "expressive theory" of rational action that accounts for a multitude of ways of valuing persons, animals, inanimate objects, and states of affairs, including honoring, being in awe of, respecting, and liking. Through a hypothetical process, we justify our valuations by offering reasons for them to each other. People's attitudes are rational to the degree that they respond properly to the reasons they give each other for why they value what they do. Anderson sets several constraints on the procedure, such as the requirement that everyone be included, and that each is consistent in his or her reasons and not confused, insensitive, or partialist. She deems it to be objective if it is progressive, that is, when it gets people to have self-understanding about the kind of lives they want to lead and persons they want to become, to become more consistent, and to carry on their commitments more fruitfully than before. Yet it seems that the privileged might be able to escape even these strong constraints, either by not engaging, because they believe they meet Anderson's goals and already live according to an ideal, or because they do not engage with the nonprivileged on genuine terms of equality. So Anderson's test, though it invokes objective value, might not yet exclude deformed desires.

Even feminists, who are most concerned about deformed desires because of the role they may play in the recapitulation of women's oppression, are divided about whether to endorse subjective or objective value. Some feminists worry that importing objective good goes against the grain of liberalism and sanctions the long-standing tradition of the privileged determining what is best for the nonprivileged. Hobbes and Mill attempt to avoid the problem of the powerful determining the interests of the powerless in their liberal theories by invoking subjective value. More radically, and speaking more to feminist concerns, recall that Sommers believes that to criticize women's preferences is patronizing, illiberal, and undemocractic.[63] Less radically, Susan Estrich objects to rape laws in the United States for the reason that they sanction a man's deciding what a woman wants when it comes to sex by turning the issue of *mens rea*, or, the man's prohibited state of mind, into one of whether the woman consented, as measured by whether she showed "reasonable resistance" to the sex, but not by whether she said "no."[64] The feminist fear about the powerful group's imposition of value is grounded in the fact that women historically have been denied their own voice about what they value, having had their own "good" determined for them by men. But there is reason for feminists to be skeptical about subjective value. Recall that the privileged often take deformed desires to be evidence that women like to be in subordinate roles, and the privileged believe that whatever desires women have, they have autonomously, and that when satisfied, their desires will promote what women judge to be best for themselves. Among the feminists who are skeptical about subjective value are Mary Gibson, Jean Hampton, Susan Moller Okin, and Martha Nussbaum, all of whom endorse objective value.[65]

The debate among feminists comes down to the issue of whether women's autonomy is promoted by their having and acting on whatever desires they do. Those of us feminists who endorse objective value deny that it is. I have argued that deformed desires threaten a person's autonomy by constraining her in much the same way that the unjust social conditions causing them do, coercing her to act in ways she otherwise would not. They even *take the place of* unjust social conditions in coercing action. A person must rid herself of deformed desires in order to be self-directing and assert her individualism, which, as I have shown, is the basis of morality. Making women aware of their deformed desires is autonomy-promoting, just as removing coercive external factors is, and *all* feminists urge that we do this. The former is achieved, I believe, only by appeal to objective good, which, when introduced in informed desire tests, can free women by showing them that they are harmed by having deformed desires, despite what they may believe. Feminists should not resist objective value wholesale, since they *must* appeal to objective good in order for claims about women's oppression and the ways they are harmed by it even to have meaning. When women are denied rights to equal pay for equal work and to bodily self-determination, or the opportunity to advance in the workplace because of sexual harassment, or the freedom to walk down the street alone at night or to hike in the woods alone at any time, they are objectively harmed, such harms being facets of their oppression. Having deformed desires is also a facet of women's oppression, and claims about them are meaningful in virtue of their referring to the objective harm they bring to their bearers when satisfied.

Thus, objective good matters to the rationality of desires, so it should be invoked in an informed desire test that aims to exclude deformed desires. The trick is to come up with an account of objective value that avoids the feminist worry about the privileged determining for women what is in their own good, since such a notion of the good runs the risk of contributing to women's oppression as much as some subjective notions. In the next section I propose an addendum to traditional informed desire tests that invokes a weak sense of objective value—one that is not morally loaded—that meets the feminist objection. An informed desire test must rule out desires that are *inconsistent* with ones the agent would have were she visionary and were she to acknowledge her intrinsic worth, since recognizing her worth is necessary for her autonomously deciding what is in her interest. This is a point about *individualism*, that is, about having inherently individual interests that are properly one's own and that make one a player in the moral game, as Thomson and Kant argue. As such, it is a rational, not a moral constraint, so importing it into a theory of rational choice does not beg the question against the skeptic who seeks to demonstrate the rationality of acting in morally required ways from nonmoral grounds. This constraint appeals to objective value in supposing that desires that are inconsistent with ones the agent would have were she visionary and were she to acknowledge her intrinsic worth are ones that, when satisfied, do not promote the agent's welfare. The inconsistency in the agent's desires is what makes deformed desires fail the informed desire test. An informed desire test must rule out non-self-respecting desires as ones the agent would not rationally choose, since having them would be to make herself inferior in worth. For example, a woman's desire to occupy roles in which she is subservient to men is inconsistent with the fact that she has intrinsic value that ought not to be compared to others' value and outweighed by it. The Muslim woman who wants to veil herself out of obedience or to send men a message about her sexuality has desires that conflict with her intrinsic value as a person that flies in the face of servility. Non-self-respecting desires cannot be universally willed because having them affronts the agent's rationality.

4 A PROPOSAL

The very features of deformed desires outlined in section 2 show that these desires are ones that an agent under ideal conditions of rationality would not have. Thus the fully stated addendum to traditional informed desire tests I propose is the following: under ideal conditions where the agent recognizes her intrinsic worth, consenting to desires having the features outlined would not be rational because they would affront the agent's rationality by being inconsistent, when satisfied, with her worth as a person.

Let us examine how the five features of deformed desires show that these desires affront the agent's rationality. First, desires that have their source in denial of autonomy, indoctrination, or manipulation involve surrendering the capacity of deciding for oneself what one chooses to desire, in favor of having one's desires defined by others for oneself. Others' desires are imposed on one. Again, this is what worries some feminists enough to endorse subjective value. But instead of endorsing subjective value, we can show that desires grounded in the agent's belief that she is inferior in worth are inconsistent with desires she would have were she to acknowledge her worth. Women's humanity, like men's, requires that they be able to control their lives in these respects, to be their own persons with inherently individual interests. Allowing oneself to be ruled by others' desires is inconsistent with acknowledging one's own worth.

Second, desires that when satisfied benefit the privileged and the system that maintains inequality but not the nonprivileged or even at their expense, fail to respect the humanity of the nonprivileged by failing to see them as "likes" who are equal beneficiaries of desire-satisfaction. Acquiring such desires would affront women's rationality because it would make their desires servile to men's, and thus treat inconsistently the humanity of self and others.

Third, it would not be rational for women to acquire desires that make them believe falsely that they and/or the group, women, benefit when they are satisfied—this would be to consent to being deceived. In this case, women would let others—namely, the privileged—decide for them whether they benefit from the satisfaction of these desires. They would give up being self-directing about their agency, since they would be treated merely as a means to the ends of the privileged. This would be to treat them as beings who are rationally incapable, and so, as inferior to others, thereby denying their intrinsic worth.

Fourth, deformed desires affront the rationality of women who desire their own welfare, for the reason that they conflict with this desire. Women's acquiring desires that conflict with their desire for their own welfare is not rational because the former deny their intrinsic value while the latter reflect it. For the dupes of patriarchy who lack a desire for their own welfare, consenting to deformed desires is not rational because these desires are the product of deception. They fail for the same reason the third feature fails.

Finally, since deformed desires are both a cause and a result of a person's not seeing herself as having intrinsic value, consenting to them is not rational for anyone who has intrinsic worth. Having deformed desires makes a person wrongly see herself as inferior in value when she is not. Suppose that a woman has a desire to be a stay-at-home mother that is deformed by her belief that women should fulfill their "natural" nurturing role. This desire conflicts with a woman's intrinsic value, which when respected would not relegate her to gender roles. It would instead play out as her having a desire to stay in the paid workforce after having children because she believes that women should have economic independence and a choice about their lifestyles.

5 CONCLUSION

To summarize the argument of this chapter: I began by raising the threat that deformed desires pose to the defeat of skepticism, namely, that not excluding them from EU would mean that a defeat of skepticism grounded in EU would be unsatisfactory because it is likely to recapitulate women's oppression. I turned to traditional informed desire tests as a way to exclude deformed desires as irrational, and so, when satisfied, as ones that do not maximize expected utility. I showed that traditional informed desire tests do not exclude deformed desires, due to the nature of these desires, the nature of deliberation, and problems with subjective and heretofore objective accounts of the good. Deformed desires are integrally related to the agent's worth as a person, which is reflected in the agent's having individual interests that she makes her own, and which bears on her autonomy. Standard conditions of rationality, such as having full information and not being mistaken about facts, are not likely to exclude deformed desires as irrational. Reflective deliberation, even when extended to imagination, is also unlikely to exclude deformed desires because it is not sufficiently strong. A dupe of patriarchy is unlikely to have a motivational set such that imagination will get her to subtract deformed desires or add better ones. This calls for being visionary. Finally, although traditional informed desire tests invoke a subjective, relative notion of the good, they need to invoke objective good in order to exclude deformed desires. I proposed an addendum to traditional accounts: that as a condition of rationality the agent acknowledge her intrinsic worth. Desires that when satisfied are inconsistent with an agent's worth—and this is an objective test—are not rational, and thus should be excluded from EU. Modifying EU in this way removes the risk of recapitulating women's oppression, at least for the reason that the emergent moral code, grounded in EU, will not reflect deformed desires. There might yet be other feminist reasons for jettisoning EU.[66] In the next chapter, I want to justify invoking an alternative to EU that relies on privilege instead of mere desire- or preference-satisfaction. The privilege account includes as rational, in addition to desire-satisfaction, various ways of benefiting that contrast with morality. In doing so, it offers a more promising way to achieve a complete defeat of action skepticism.

5

Self-Interest versus Morality

This chapter argues that privilege provides a better contrast with morality than does self-interest. The traditional model of the skeptic dichotomizes morality with self-interest, both in the theory of practical reason the skeptic is assumed to endorse (EU) and in the motives he believes it rational to have, ones that are most in opposition to morality (selfish, or, nontuistic motives). But there are immoral acts other than self-interested ones that are at least as much in opposition to morality; a successful defeat of skepticism must show that all immoral acts are irrational. Privilege covers all these acts. They all have in common that the agent fails to respect the intrinsic value of another person. This chapter examines the reasons philosophers contrast morality with self-interest, and argues that privilege serves their purposes while at the same time represents in a more inclusive way the skeptic's position. The chapter examines a number of different kinds of immorality, and shows how each is different from nontuism or is not covered by EU. Finally, it addresses the problem that privilege comes apart from EU: the assumption of nontuism serves merely as a constraint on the preferences it is rational to satisfy, but the assumption of privilege aims to capture more cases in opposition to morality than nontuism. An alternative model of the skeptic's position, that acting in ways that privilege oneself vis-à-vis morality is rationally required, fares better than the expected utility model. On it, the skeptic assumes that it is rational to privilege oneself, which amounts to being inconsistent about his own and others' humanity. To defeat skepticism on this broader model, we need to show that it is rationally required, because consistent, to respect the humanity of others. We appeal to reasons of consistency rather than self-interested reasons.

1 INTRODUCTION

Philosophers traditionally have taken acting in one's self-interest to be the paradigm case against morality. This is not of course to deny that philosophers have recognized the coincidence of acting morally and acting self-interestedly: character-oriented theorists such as virtue ethicists, for one, construe self-interest in such a way that acting in morally required ways is in one's self-interest in that it promotes the good life, and even action-oriented theorists believe that the demands of morality and self-interest in a desire-satisfaction sense often coincide. David Copp distinguishes two views of self-interest that surface in the large body of literature on this topic. In general, something is in a person's self-interest just in case it would be good for the person. On a subjectivist view, "a person's life is going well for her to the extent that her desires are being satisfied or her values are being fulfilled," while on an objectivist view, whether a person's life is going well for her is a matter independent of such psychological states, but judged on the basis of a more "objective standard," such as whether the person is developing her talents.[1]

Nor is this to deny that people often favor their families or even country over their own self-interest, as in the case of the Deferential Wife and the patriot. Still, many philosophers take self-interest to pose the biggest threat to morality. But they often conflate two meanings of "self-interest." On the one hand, as I have been saying, self-interest refers to *a theory of practical reason*: historically, many philosophers, including Plato, Hobbes, Bentham, Sidgwick, and Hume, have taken the skeptic to endorse a theory of practical reason that identifies rational action with self-interested action. The moralist must then demonstrate that we are rationally required to act morally, and thus that moral reasons override reasons of self-interest in cases of conflict. Gauthier, as I have shown, formulates this most precisely in the language of EU: the skeptic is assumed to adopt this "weak and widely accepted conception of practical rationality,"[2] according to which a person's expected utility is measured by the satisfaction of his or her desires or preferences. On the other hand, self-interest refers to *motives*: philosophers such as Plato and Hume have taken the skeptic's challenge to be prompted by *selfishness*. In Plato's tale of the ring of Gyges that makes its bearer invisible, Glaucon argues that "no one is just of his own will but only from constraint."[3] Hume contrasts the selfish and social sentiments, and to the sensible knave, who has "lost a considerable motive to virtue," he offers a litany of motives to prompt virtuous action, including peace of mind, antipathy to treachery and roguery, consciousness of integrity, and enjoyment of character.[4] Selfishness is assumed to be the motive that is most in opposition to morality, which requires that persons be other-directed; one is selfish when the ends of one's actions refer only to one's self. Gauthier believes that we need not make an assumption as strong as selfishness to capture motives in opposition to moral ones. He takes the assumption of nontuism to be sufficient for this purpose. Nontuism is the view that persons take no interest in the interests of those with whom they interact, though they "may take an interest in states of affairs that cannot be specified except with reference to others."[5] Nontuism allows persons to take an *instrumental*, but not an *intrinsic*, interest in others' interests. While the selfish person has only interests *in* the self, which take oneself as an object, the nontuist seeks to maximize interests *of* the self, which are held by oneself as a subject but can refer to the interests of others, or even be self-destructive.[6] Still, since for the nontuist the interests of others have only instrumental value, they are not properly other-directed in the way morality requires.

Strictly speaking, nontuism is, for Gauthier, a limitation on the kinds of interests or preferences that the skeptic believes it is rational for a person to have. Gauthier talks in terms of *preferences*, since he believes that preference is "even more clearly subjective and behavioral than interest."[7] Preferences take as their objects alternative possibilities realizable in action. They relate states of affairs, such as preferring the eating of an apple to a pear, which are not direct objects of choice, but rather are possible outcomes of the actions among which one chooses. Although Gauthier speaks loosely in terms of advantage, benefit, or satisfaction, EU defines utility in terms of preference (utility being a measure of preference) and identifies rationality with the maximization of utility. Gauthier notes that preferences do not depend solely on the qualities of experience, such as enjoyment.[8] This seems to be what distinguishes desires and preferences for Gauthier, who does not take preference to be a mental state.[9] Unlike desires, preferences do not refer to feelings, though they, like desires, can serve as motives that bring about action. I will understand the notion of being motivated nontuistically to mean that a person seeks to maximize interests of the self.

These two meanings of "self-interest" are united in the following way. The skeptic—and here our concern is the action skeptic—endorses the best available theory of practical reason, according to which it is rational to satisfy one's desires or preferences. Nontuism serves as a further constraint on what these desires or preferences can be, being imposed so that a defeat of skepticism does not beg the question in favor of morality by importing moral desires at the start. Gauthier is right to want to generate his moral theory without introducing prior moral assumptions.[10] Were we to assume, or even to leave it open, that a person has moral desires, it would of course fall out of EU that it is rational to act in morally required ways because one desires to do so. But there are plenty of situations where persons lack moral desires, and the skeptic's position is designed to cover these. But although Gauthier begins with an "initial presumption against morality,"[11] he later clarifies that "nontuism offers a worst-case scenario,"[12] being most in opposition to moral action. We can understand the skeptic's position, then, to be that rationality requires acting in ways that satisfy one's nontuistic preferences, since these are believed to be the farthest removed from morality.

One upshot of this description of the skeptic's position is that the instrumentalist motive of nontuism is taken to be the worst-case scenario against morality but only *as constrained by, or, within the parameters of,* EU. That is, we assume the skeptic endorses EU, and then set constraints on what ultimately measures rational action, namely, preferences. But this constraint limits our attempt to defeat skepticism. For even if we demonstrate the rationality of acting in morally required ways in cases where morality and self-interest conflict, we will not have fully defeated action skepticism since there are immoral actions other than self-interested ones whose performance, for all we have shown, may be rationally required. These actions will thereby escape the skeptic's challenge and response to it. Such actions express (1) preferences that are consistent with nontuism but that take different forms that nontuism does not adequately capture, such as moral indifference; (2) worse preferences than nontuistic ones, such as having a negative intrinsic interest in others' interests, or, doing evil for its own sake; (3) behaviors that are entirely different from ones motivated nontuistically and that are not best described as preferences, such as succumbing to emotion, as in weakness of will and moral negligence; or (4) behaviors that need not make reference to the agent's desires or preferences that are not directly in the agent's self-interest, but only indirectly benefit the group of which the agent is a member, and that are performed as part of harmful social practices, such as when a white person who does not harbor racist attitudes nonetheless enjoys the privilege of being able to buy "flesh-colored" bandages, or even when men benefit from the practices of rape, and sexual harassment and discrimination, and when whites benefit from the practice of hate speech. The last group of acts challenges the skeptic's endorsement of EU: EU links rational action with desire- or preference-satisfaction, but these are cases where the benefits the privileged person enjoys are indirect, resulting from an unjust system rather than from any immoral motives he has and actions based on them that he performs. Such indirect systematic benefits are not properly covered by EU, which covers only benefiting by desire-satisfaction.

Nontuism does not cover the first three of these cases of immorality, and EU does not cover the last. Were we to dichotomize morality and self-interest, whether we understood self-interest to refer to motivation or to rational action, we would run the risk that the acts not covered would be left out of the skeptic's challenge. This would leave open whether rationality requires performing these acts instead of morally required acts in cases of conflict. If we defeat skepticism on the traditional picture of the skeptic, all we will have shown is that when *self-interest* and morality conflict, acting morally is rationally required; we will not have shown that other immoral acts are overridden by morality on rational grounds. Of course, it would not follow automatically from a defeat of traditional skepticism that these other immoral actions are rationally required; the worry is that since we will not have shown that they are *irrational*, they might turn out to be either rationally required, or at least rationally neutral, when they conflict with moral action. But even the possibility of rational neutrality threatens our defeat of skepticism. To defeat action skepticism fully, we want to show decisively that all immoral acts are also irrational. Of course, this is not the strategy we follow in defeating skepticism; rather, we aim to demonstrate that every morally required act is rationally required, and it follows from this that immoral acts are irrational, since whenever acting morally conflicts with acting in ways opposed to morality (and not just self-interestedly), reason will require acting morally.[13] We want the defeat of skepticism ultimately to be a victory over *all* immoral acts, not just self-interested acts. For only then will we have shown that any immoral act does not have the backing of reason, and once we have shown this, the skeptic cannot claim victory when non-self-interested but otherwise immoral acts are not shown to be irrational.

There is a tension, then, between the requirement that the skeptic's position be grounded in a theory of rational action and the requirement that it capture motives most in opposition to morality. If we enforce only the former requirement, the victory over skepticism will be incomplete because EU can be constrained by nontuism but not other immoral motives, and because EU does not capture cases of benefiting from an unjust system. If we relax the former requirement so that the defeat of skepticism covers all acts in opposition to morality, not just nontuistic preference-satisfying ones, we risk not having the skeptic's position grounded in a theory of practical reason. My aim is to diffuse the tension between these two requirements. In the remainder of this chapter, I will first examine why philosophers have dichotomized self-interest with morality. Next I will examine a taxonomy of cases of immorality and analyze them in Kantian terms, as failing to give the appropriate treatment to another person on the basis of his or her status as a person. I will argue that *privilege* captures the reasons philosophers dichotomize self-interest and morality, and that it provides a better contrast with morality than self-interest since it underlies all the immoralities I will examine. By "privilege" I mean that a person favors his interests and his reasons over others and their interests and reasons by failing to respect their intrinsic worth. The skeptic's position, then, should be broadened along the lines of privilege. Finally, I will discuss a problem that arises if we shift from nontuism to privilege. Nontuism is grounded in EU because it is merely a restriction on the preferences the satisfaction of which, on EU, is rational. Privilege, though, since it is more than, and different from, a restriction on the preferences the skeptic takes to be rational, and covers far more cases removed from morality than does nontuism, comes apart from EU. We could go one of two ways: either revise EU to include as rational acting in ways supporting or sanctioning a position of privilege vis-à-vis morality; or drop the requirement that the skeptic endorse EU or any theory of rationality in favor of a less rigorous requirement of rationality. Later in this chapter, I will explore the view that it is rational to take the humanity of others to give you a reason not to privilege yourself when privilege and morality conflict; it is rational to endorse a moral theory that is itself consistent in its dictates, meaning that it must be impartial in the sense that it acknowledges that all persons are equal in virtue of their intrinsic worth.

The issue of whether self-interest is the paradigm case against morality is significant for any moralists who acknowledge the existence of evils aside from nontuism and who want to defeat skepticism completely. Particularly feminists, race theorists, and others who argue against the oppression of certain groups should be alarmed that many acts contributing to oppression are ones that, even with a successful defeat of the traditional skeptic, would not turn out to be irrational. So in addition to their attack on traditional moral theory for the reason that it does not pay the attention it should to the oppression of women, feminists ought to charge that under the historical conception of self-interest as the paradigm case of immorality, acts of oppression might escape as *rationally* permissible.

Feminists should be suspicious of the self-interest/morality dichotomy for some of the same reasons that have made them reject SIB contractarianism. Were we to show that morally required actions are rationally required because in one's self-interest at the level of dispositions or actions, we would sustain the individualistic, atomistic, androcentric view of people as self-interested that some feminists find objectionable, a critique familiar from chapter 3. Further, the self-interest/morality dichotomy captures mostly interactions among strangers who have no intrinsic interest in each others' interests, but who see others as competitors for the same scarce goods, as in a Hobbesian or paid workforce situation. Relatedly, Elizabeth Anderson argues that this dichotomy views decision-making from a male perspective, ignoring "more feminine" ways of making decisions.[14] Gauthier would defend the self-interest model partly because he believes that we need only to address the defeat of skepticism to interactions between strangers, since, he believes, friends and family members are generally tuistic toward each other. But of course, the reality is that family members are notoriously nontuistic, though the kind of immorality they exhibit need not be self-interest. And covering only stranger-stranger interactions leaves out too many interactions that ought to be covered by morality, even if they are not motivated by self-interest but instead are allegedly naturally tuistic. By reconstruing the paradigm case against morality as privilege instead of self-interest, I hope to meet these charges.[15] A defeat of skepticism that has moral reasons overriding reasons relating to privilege promises to be more thorough than a traditional defeat that has moral reasons overriding reasons of self-interest.

2 THE ASSUMPTION OF SELF-INTEREST

Why have philosophers pitted morality against self-interest? There are at least four reasons, the first three of which are related: (1) self-interest describes the way persons naturally act, (2) it is taken to be the worst-case scenario in opposition to morality, (3) it does not beg the question in favor of morality when used as an assumption in the context of defeating skepticism, and (4) it is part of a long-standing theory of rational action. I will have more to say about EU later, but for now I want to say more about the first three reasons, which refer to motives. I am going to argue that pitting morality against privilege captures the same reasons and offers a more thorough position against morality.

Some philosophers dichotomize morality and self-interest, exemplified in various versions of skeptical positions they describe, because they believe that persons naturally behave self-interestedly in the absence of moral and political constraints, suggesting that our natural self-interest— or, more accurately, selfishness[16]—is in direct opposition to acting morally, and thus presents the worst-case scenario against morality. Philosophers who dichotomize morality and self-interest typically assume a subjectivist view of self-interest, and they believe that the desires one has are nontuistic, if not selfish.[17] They believe we are naturally motivated to act this way. In Plato's tale of the ring of Gyges, Glaucon remarks that "if we grant to both the just and the unjust license and power to do whatever they please . . . we should then catch the just man in the very act of resorting to the same conduct as the unjust man because of the self-advantage which every creature *by its nature* pursues as a good."[18] Hobbes affirms this idea in his description of persons as they would exist without moral constraints. In this hypothetical State of Nature, persons are equal in strength and equally prudent with an equal hope of attaining their own ends. Each has the right to self-preservation, which can never be given up voluntarily, since all voluntary acts aim for one's own good. Competition for scarce goods will, "in the nature of man" and under these conditions of equality in the State of Nature when each pursues his or her own good, result in life for each that is solitary, poor, nasty, brutish, and short.[19] But even though Hobbes often speaks as if persons are naturally self-interested, he says that there has never been a time where men were in a condition of war against one another, suggesting that he postulates a hypothetical State of Nature and the characters in it as a strategic move for purposes of defeating action skepticism.[20] Indeed, Hume denies that persons are naturally self-interested, but believes instead that they are motivated by sympathy rather than self-interest, and generally will act morally.[21] But, like Hobbes, Hume makes a strategic move to present the worst-case scenario in opposition to morality, and describes the sensible knave as one who believes he can benefit by generally following the rule of acting justly, but on occasions when he expects not to be caught, to take advantage of the exceptions to the rule. That is, he wants to act in self-advantageous ways rather than morally.

Whether persons naturally (actually) are self-interested, Hobbes and others assume that we are, at least in certain circumstances, so as to set up the worst-case scenario against morality in order not to presuppose that we have other-directed motives. We need not decide the empirical issue of what persons' actual motives are in order to defeat skepticism. Whether persons are naturally self-interested does not affect the theoretical issue of justifying acting morally: the justification stands no matter what persons' motives are. Even the practical issue is not affected. We might think it is, because we might believe that our defeat of skepticism would have to be grounded in self-interested reasons only, since these are the only reasons that could motivate naturally self-interested persons. But being self-interested by nature does not mean that persons cannot change, and act against what it is natural for them to do. To think otherwise presupposes a static, and false, view of human nature.[22] Even naturally self-interested persons can accept and act on non-self-interested reasons for acting morally.

Self-interest is bad both as a motive, expressed in a bad maxim describing how one is supposed to act, as well as in its effects. When cast as the motive of selfishness, self-interest is in itself, according to many moral philosophers, as far removed from morality as we can get, since selfish persons take only their own ends to be the object of their actions, while morality requires that persons act for the sake of others' ends. Even nontuistic persons take at best an instrumental but not an intrinsic interest in others' interests, which flies in the face of morality. The self-centered person, according to S. I. Benn and Ron Milo, who have independently identified a number of immoralities that I will discuss in the next section, knows what is wrong but out of self-love and a ruthless unconcern for the good of others pursues his own good.[23] He follows a maxim that tells him to act thusly; what makes the maxim bad is his bad preference for his own good to be advanced even at the expense of others' good. The nontuistic person might also dismiss the interests of others in cases where her own interests are not served when satisfying the interests of others.

Self-interest is bad in its effects, too. When Plato's Lydian shepherd in the ring of Gyges tale makes himself invisible, he commits adultery with the king's wife, and with her help kills the king and takes over the rule, making himself "a god among humans."[24] For Hobbes, the bad effects of acting in one's self-interest are displayed at two levels, as the Prisoner's Dilemma shows: when *everyone* acts self-interestedly instead of cooperatively (morally), and when an *individual* free rides in a cooperative state by reneging on the moral contract.[25] Hobbes argues that if all or most people act self-interestedly, we all end up in the state in which life is poor, nasty, brutish, and short. Each person would be worse off than she would have been had everyone cooperated, yielding a state where each would achieve certain benefits that are attainable only through cooperation, including peace, well-being, security, and certain goods and services. Cooperation requires sacrifices to one's interest; specifically, it requires that one "lay down some of one's rights as long as others do so as well," and this means that one is likely to forgo satisfying some of one's desires. Still, mutual cooperation yields a much greater expectation of benefit than does mutual pursuit of self-interest. Further, the Prisoner's Dilemma, when applied to Hobbes's schema, is supposed to show that laying down some rights and cooperating is in each person's interest. But even if most persons cooperate, if one person such as Hobbes's Foole free rides by breaking his contract because he can escape detection, the persons with whom he interacts, if they are unable to detect his disposition, will suffer the effects of his acting self-interestedly by having the satisfaction of their own desires thwarted. In the worst case, if the Foole has a desire to kill others, and he free rides by breaking his contract requiring him not to kill, he will thwart others' desire for self-preservation, which Hobbes believes is our strongest desire.

Some philosophers have criticized philosophers such as Gauthier, who most explicitly says that one of his reasons for dichotomizing morality and self-interest is that "nontuism offers a worst-case scenario." Peter Vallentyne believes that the case where people are highly negatively concerned for others, desiring that they be poorly off, is far worse than that of mutual unconcern.[26] Vallentyne believes, that is, that taking a *negative* intrinsic interest in others' interests is worse than nontuism. Benn calls this "malignant wickedness," or, taking the suffering of others to be an end in itself and a reason for action.[27] Christopher Morris believes that envy, spite, hatred, and intolerance threaten morality more than self-interest does.[28] I will describe other immoral motives, including moral indifference, perverse wickedness, conscientious wickedness, and moral negligence, that are at least as much in opposition to morality, both in themselves and in their consequences, as nontuism.

Gauthier agrees with Morris that in a world where people have envy, spite, hatred, and intolerance of or for their fellows there would be no morality since persons would prefer conflict with each other to mutual constraint. But Gauthier believes that humans could not live very long in this world. Thus he prefers the assumption of nontuism because it represents a more realistic world in which "some persons much of the time, and almost all persons some of the time, are moved by negative, other-directed interests."[29] In addition, he believes that the evil persons Morris describes "should be treated as enemies, lacking any moral standing, because their interests render them unfit to be participants in 'a cooperative venture for mutual advantage.'"[30]

But first, I believe there is no reason to think humans could live very long in a world of *nontuists* either, since having no intrinsic interest in the interests of others can lead to the same bad consequences as other immoral motives. People who enslave others out of self-interest, for example, can cause just as much harm as people who are indifferent to others' enslavement; drivers who never service their cars out of self-interest, or who cause accidents to collect insurance money, can cause just as much harm as drivers who never service their cars out of negligence. Second, it seems to me that a realistic world is one in which some people at least some of the time, and some people a lot of the time, engage also in non-self-interested, but otherwise immoral behavior, including negligence, indifference, and malignant wickedness: such characters are precisely the ones we have to worry about. People's general complicity in racist and sexist systems of oppression, which often stems from these other immoral motives, is evidence that we in fact inhabit such a world right now. If we want to set up the skeptic to represent realistic cases of immorality, then we need to cover these cases, too.

To be sure, Gauthier might have the following worry. In setting up the skeptic, we start with someone who on a particular occasion asks why he should act morally rather than self-interestedly. To cover every such case, we assume that persons are nontuistic in their *character*, and not just on a particular occasion, for then the argument reaches anyone who on any occasion may have only nontuistic motives. Gauthier's concern might be that the same strategic move, when applied to immoral motives other than nontuism, will portray a caricature *too* far removed from morality, and hence, unrealistic, for it would have us assume that persons are always indifferent, or always malignantly wicked, and so on. But to assume this seems to be no more problematic than it is to assume that persons are nontuistic in their characters, not just on the occasion. The bolder assumption is also purely a strategic move; we need not believe that real persons have such immoral characters. Gauthier himself admits that although he makes use of the notion of "economic man," that is, one who is nontuistic in character and actions, this notion is merely a caricature that has "useful explanatory and normative purposes." Real persons, he admits, are constrained by tuistic interests in the pursuit of their asocial concerns, but they share some of the characteristics of economic man.[31] Moreover, I am going to propose a way of setting up the skeptic that *unites* all the immoralities by what they have in common, which is that they disrespect the humanity of others. The aim of my proposal is to avoid Gauthier's worry and at the same time meet the strategic goal.

Gauthier's more serious objection to Morris is that immoral but non-self-interested persons cannot be participants in morals by agreement. In other words, Gauthier's contractarian framework constrains his view of the skeptic; the goal of cooperation rules out other immoralities. Gauthier is not clear about why this is so, but my speculation is that if the skeptic is characterized as believing that nontuism is rational, moral philosophers can aim to defeat skepticism by appealing to reasons of self-interest, since the nontuist adopts EU. If we defeat skepticism, and if persons act on this self-interested justification, then the benefits of cooperation will be secured—cooperation can be achieved only by reaching immoralists who see that cooperation is in their self-interest on a subjective view of self-interest that Gauthier accepts. Of course, we would have to show that cooperation is in their interest, no matter what their desires. But other immoralists need not accept self-interested reasons for acting morally—unlike nontuism, other immoralities are not best described as constraints on desires set in the context of EU. Indeed, it is not clear that non-self-interested immoralists endorse any particular theory of practical reason. So there is no set of reasons to appeal to, to offer a skeptic who endorses the rationality of actions that are grounded in immoral motives other than nontuism, though we would have to assume that this skeptic's position is backed by reason, since the challenge is to defeat immoral but rational action with rationally justified, morally required action. Since this skeptic does not necessarily accept self-interested reasons, the benefits of cooperation cannot be secured even if he accepts reasons for acting morally. This is my earlier point about EU and nontuism going hand in hand, and that philosophers' traditional defeat of skepticism is constrained by EU. The skeptic is assumed to be rational in that he adopts the best-defended theory of rational action, one that happens to be on its face opposed to morality; it, together with the assumption of nontuism, presents a case in opposition to morality. The problem, then, if we are wedded to the contractarian framework and its expected benefits of cooperation, is that we will not completely defeat action skepticism because there will be cases of immorality that are not necessarily irrational on EU; the skeptic can claim victory. If we want a complete defeat of action skepticism, we will need to drop the requirement that the skeptic adopt EU, and assume something weaker. One alternative measure of rationality might be the requirement that the skeptic merely be able to *understand reasons* for action and the basic rules of logic, which would allow him to accept moral reasons were the justification of morality successful. I will show that all the examples of immoral persons I shall discuss, with the exception of the psychopath, can be reached by rational argument. Either they are able to understand that their actions are wrong, as in the case of the malignantly wicked person who deliberately attempts to set back the interests of others for its own sake, or they suffer only temporary lapses of rationality, as in the case of the weak-willed person who lets emotion overcome reason. Since these immoral persons can understand the justification philosophers offer, philosophers should expand their goal of offering reasons for acting morally that are acceptable to the nontuist, to offering reasons that are also acceptable to other immoralists. I will pursue this topic further in section 4, but turn now to the notion of privilege.

3 IMMORALITY AND PRIVILEGE

3.1 Privilege

Suppose we relax the assumption that the skeptic endorses EU. Since nontuism is a constraint on the desires it is rational, on EU, to satisfy, if we do not take the skeptic to endorse EU, we can open the skeptic's position to include preferences other than nontuistic ones, as well as behaviors that need not be grounded in preferences. This holds promise of a more thorough defeat of skepticism. In this section, I want to show that the assumption of nontuism does not cover other immoralities that we would want to be covered for a complete defeat of skepticism. I also want to show that acts that are part of harmful social practices, while they may be self-beneficial, are not best captured by the desire- or preference-satisfaction view of self-interest. Finally, I want to argue that a better way to capture the skeptic's position, one that goes beyond nontuism to cover all of these cases of immorality including nontuism, involves privilege. Before discussing the cases of immorality and how privilege factors into each one, I need to say what I mean by privilege.

My account of privilege relies on Kant's notion of humanity. So I need first to explain this, and then use this analysis to explain what I mean by privilege. Many moral philosophers take as one mark of a moral theory that it must be consistent in its main tenets, one of which requires that it be impartial in the sense that it acknowledges that all persons are equal in certain respects, and that no special preference be given to one's self or one's family or friends or special group in determining the course of right conduct.[32] John Cottingham named the Impartiality Thesis the view that we ought not to give any special weight to the desires, needs, and interests of our social group, such as friends, relations, and those in our inner group.[33] These are the features that place persons in the "moral game," rendering them both the bearers of obligations and the recipients of moral treatment. Of course, partialists disagree. The ethic of care, a partialist theory, requires care for persons or groups related to us, but not for others, *because* they are related to us. Care ethicists seem to believe that if everyone acts in caring ways toward their relations, everyone will be taken care of. What separates partialists and impartialists, I believe, is that impartialists do not want it to be the case that properties a person comes to have as a result of luck disfavor the person. John Rawls, a paradigmatic impartialist, sets up the "original position" from which persons are to decide the principles of justice, to correct for the arbitrariness of the world.[34] For Rawls, persons should not be disfavored on the basis of their inclinations and aspirations, conception of the good, financial status, or any arbitrary contingency that might allow people "to be guided by their prejudices."[35] Gender would be one such contingency. Settling the debate between partialism and impartialism would take me too far afield.[36] But I want to note that I find it ironic, then, that care ethicists like Noddings are partialists, since gender is a feature that we come to have as a result of luck, and feminists argue that a moral theory ought not to disfavor persons on the basis of gender. The same reasoning should apply, we should think, to the property of being related.

For impartialists, the respect in which persons are equal is of course different for different theories. For instance, for Bentham, each sentient being's ability to experience pleasure and pain is the feature that determines our duties to them. Bentham put forward his version of act utilitarianism in response to the despotic leaders of his time, arguing that morality requires that each person count for one, no more and no less, and that every sentient being's pleasure and pain should be weighed equally in the hedonic calculus.[37] Kant, though, another impartialist, explained best *why* each person counts: each has dignity or intrinsic value in virtue of his or her capacity for rationality, which is marked by having desires, interests, goals, and plans. So each should be treated with the same respect as others. These features I will call "the facts about humanity."[38] Recall that rationality simultaneously marks a feature common to all persons, yet distinguishes each person from all others. As I explained, a person's interests, desires, and the like that mark her rationality must be individual in nature. Moreover, it is not just that we *have* interests and the like, but, as I will explain shortly, it is important for rationality that they be ones that a person *cares* about and is ready to *assert* when necessary. This is the idea that, I believe, Thomson tries to capture in her account of "inherently individual interests," which are essential for a person's understanding and following morality. The idea, again, is that having individual interests allows a person to understand what it is to make a moral sacrifice, which involves doing something that she ought when it is not necessarily in her interest. Recall that Thomson rejects both act utilitarianism and ethical egoism because neither moral theory allows us to cherish appropriately these interests. These theories seem to stand in the way of our having rationality in the fullest sense, since they require that we or others too readily give up satisfying interests we care about and want to protect. Interestingly, contractarianism has been at the center of debate on this issue. On the one hand, it would seem that Hobbesian contractarianism aims to protect inherently individual interests by recognizing that persons have them and care about them, and by allowing persons to assert them in bargaining. But some feminists have leveled yet another objection against contractarianism, that since we all come to the bargaining table with different starting points, the disenfranchised might have to sacrifice interests that are grounded in gender, class, and race, just to get others to enter a bargain and then follow it. The emergent moral code is likely to be sexist, racist, or classist. A feminist attempt to resolve this debate has been proposed by Jean Hampton. It involves modifying Hobbesian contractarianism along Kantian lines so that persons bargain in ways that would maximize the satisfaction of their interests, but with the constraint that each is accorded intrinsic worth in the Kantian sense.[39] Hampton's account is promising because it preserves the idea that we care about and are justified in asserting the interests that mark our rationality, yet we should constrain the pursuit of their satisfaction in ways respectful of everyone's intrinsic worth.

Kant's Principle of Humanity of the Categorical Imperative requires that we respect our own and others' humanity. Stephen Darwall offers a useful way of expanding the notion of the "facts about humanity," arguing that it is not simply this notion that makes us candidates for moral treatment, but the "deep idea" underlying it, what Darwall calls "second-personal authority," or, the fact that we all have *the same standing to make claims and demands of each other and to hold one another accountable*.[40] This, he suggests, is what Kant means when he says that a person's dignity is that by which he "exacts *respect* for himself from all other rational beings in the world."[41] Darwall's insight is reflected in Kant's notion of co-legislation. Kant argues that we must respect each person *as a potential co-legislator* of morality, and engage only in conduct with which we would expect all reasonable people to agree.[42] Potential co-legislators are those of us who are in the moral community in exactly the sense Darwall attributes to Kant.

Darwall's proposal bears similarity to Christine Korsgaard's analysis of Kant's view of humanity, which I will explain shortly.[43] I want to unite Darwall's and Korsgaard's views in the following way. What connects having interests, desires, and the like with authority and accountability is *reasons*. So, to relate Thomson's point to this, it is not just that we have interests and desires, but that we see their connection with autonomous action, that is, that we are prepared to assert to others *reasons* for our ends and actions that are typically motivated by our interests and desires. For Kant, reason-giving is what ultimately gives us authority; what makes us accountable to others is that they are seen as authoritative in this sense.

Let me briefly highlight Korsgaard's analysis. For Kant, the characteristic feature of humanity, or rational nature, is the capacity for setting an end, and doing so out of free choice. As rational agents we will choose good ends, which are ends that can be shared with others. These "objective," morally obligatory ends complete and perfect the capacity for reason; they make the same claim on *all* rational beings, and so are completely justified. That is, all rational beings will agree on the ends as a result of our giving to others practical reasons for them and for our actions related to them, and so they yield a duty to bring them about.[44] The significant passage linking Korsgaard's to Darwall's views is the following:

> If you view yourself as having a value-conferring status in virtue of your power of rational choice, you must view anyone who has the power of rational choice as having, in virtue of that power, a value-conferring status. This will mean that what you make good by means of your rational choice must be harmonious with what another can make good by means of her rational choice—for the good is a consistent, harmonious object shared by all rational beings.... The unconditioned goodness of anything is rational nature, or the power of rational choice. To play this role, however, rational nature must itself be something of unconditional value—an end in itself. This means, however, that you must treat rational nature wherever you find it . . . as an end.[45]

To treat someone as an end in itself is to regard that person as one who confers value on the objects of her choice.[46] This idea is similar, I believe, to Darwall's notion of second-personal authority: being able to confer value on one's end is to be able to put forward reasons for your ends (and actions), which is to be authoritative. Korsgaard concludes that for Kant, the possession of humanity and the capacity for the good will, whether or not it is realized, *is enough to establish a claim on being treated as an unconditional end.*[47] That is, it is just your having the capacity to put forward reasons—and so your capacity to have interests that you care about and are prepared to assert—that are recognizable to other rational persons, whether or not you exercise this capacity, that is sufficient for making you a being we ought to respect. In Darwall's terms, your authority is sufficient for making you a being we ought to respect.

I now need to relate Korsgaard's analysis of Kant's view about humanity to the notion of privilege. When an agent fails to respect others' humanity, he either does not recognize others' humanity when he should or disregards their worth, or acknowledges it and seeks to set it back, or fails to focus on it, or does not care about it. He flouts morality, or takes it to be optional for him. Flouting morality essentially amounts to flouting others' interests. In flouting morality, the agent makes himself an exception to the rules; he violates the Universal Law Formulation of the Categorical Imperative, which requires that one follow only those maxims that one can will—both imagine and want—to be a universal law. He instead follows a maxim that others would consent to only if they were coerced, and in so doing violates the Principle of Autonomy of the Categorical Imperative, which requires that one follow only those maxims that one imposes on one's own will when one is universally legislating, that is, when one is deciding to adopt rules for the guidance of one's and others' conduct. The nontuist, for instance, takes only an instrumental interest in others' interests, and puts his interests ahead of others' unless one of his interests is to promote those of another. The nontuist *privileges* himself by making himself count for more than one, and thereby going against a fundamental tenet of morality. Essentially, the nontuist privileges his *reasons* for action. On EU, one's interests, desires, or preferences give one reasons to act; the nontuist takes his self-interested reasons to count for more than moral reasons, which reflect the intrinsic value of others, which is tied to their interests. The nontuist does not take the worth of others, represented by their interests, to give him a reason not to privilege himself. Now, one can privilege oneself not only by being nontuistic but also by not adequately focusing on the rational agency of another but letting one's passions get the best of one (immorality caused by lack of rational self-control), by not caring about the interests of others (immorality caused by lack of moral concern), or by disregarding others' interests or disrespecting their humanity (immorality stemming from bad preferences or values). These three categories of immorality, which I will discuss more fully in the next section, have in common that the agent privileges himself or his own interests and reasons over others and their reasons by not taking others' worth to give him a reason not to privilege himself by making his interests and reasons count for more than those of others.

It turns out that privileging oneself is exactly what Kant takes to be arrogance, which he considers to be the worst vice and the deepest source of evil in human nature. Here I will follow Robin Dillon's thorough

examination of Kant's account of arrogance to aid my account of privilege. According to Dillon, arrogance in general involves a person viewing
himself as superior in status to others and hence as being entitled to treat
others as his inferiors.[48] Dillon identifies two kinds of arrogance that Kant
describes: interpersonal and primary. Interpersonal arrogance deals with
the attitude a person takes toward others. In particular, the interperson-
ally arrogant person (1) does not regard others as equals; (2) wants to
heighten his own self-esteem; and (3) demands that others value themselves much less than they deserve, as having lower status, and that they
sacrifice their self-respect in order to advance the arrogant person's self-
interest. The first of these features will be clearly evident in all the
immoralities that I will discuss—it is just what I said privilege involves.
The second means that the arrogant person wants to make himself superior in worth to others. Kant, of course, believed that no one could raise or
lower their own or another's intrinsic value or status, but the arrogant
person takes the attitude that he is superior to others, which is exactly
what happens when a person ignores, discounts, does not care about, or
fails to focus on others' humanity—in Darwall's terms, the arrogant
person believes that he does not have to be *accountable* to others. The
arrogant person signals that his worth must be treated with respect, while
the worth of others may be disrespected in one of these ways. A poignant
example comes from Hampton, regarding rape. The rapist expresses the
idea through rape that women are even lower than chattel, being mere
"objects" who are there to be used whenever the male feels the need to do
so. Further, rape is a moral injury to all women because "it is part of a
pattern of response of many men toward many women that aims to
establish their mastery *qua male* over a woman *qua female*."[49] The message it sends is: "As a woman, you are the kind of human being who is
subject to the mastery of people of my kind." The third feature of
interpersonal arrogance might not be obvious: does the immoralist demand that others value themselves less than they deserve? To see that he
does, consider that his maxim is one that others would not consent to
unless they were coerced. Since the immoralist cannot universalize his
maxim, he hopes that others do not regard themselves as having worth
and asserting their interests, for then he can carry out his maxim without
resistance, or even with others' compliance.

Primary arrogance, which underlies interpersonal arrogance, is the view
that the arrogant person's wanting something gives him a right or entitle-
ment to it, and so he shall have it.[50] The arrogant person's badness, for
Kant, lies with his attempting to incorporate what he wants into his
maxim, thereby making his inclinations the condition of compliance
with the moral law, which Kant deeply opposes: he is able to pass off
what he *wants* to do for what he *ought* to do, turning his subjective desires
into objective reasons.[51] This way he can think that he is doing his duty. He
attempts to have power over morality and reason itself in order to boost his
own worth. Note that this view, however, is inconsistent with my earlier

claim that in privileging himself, a person takes morality to be optional. The way to make these views consistent is to recognize that the arrogant person *cannot* actually change the moral law: he can never lower others' moral status, nor can he get them to consent to maxims grounded in his inclinations unless they are coerced, typically by force or deception.[52] So his maxim is not really universalized. But he *tries* to make it become the moral law. The true moral law, consisting of universalizable maxims, he considers to be optional; that is, he can opt out of it unless he can change it to incorporate his inclinations. When a person cares negatively about another's humanity and wants to discount it or render it void, or does not care about another's humanity, or fails to focus on it, he follows a maxim that incorporates his own—but not others'—interests, or incorporates others' interests but in inappropriate ways.

Any agent can take a privileged stance toward morality and others regardless of his social position. However, being in a position of *social* privilege relating to gender, race, class, and the like, allows, if not encourages, the agent to take a privileged stance toward morality and others, and he sometimes does so in ways related to these features. Consider gender. The agent who exhibits a sexist form of immoralism privileges himself and tries to render women inferior in virtue of their gender, or at least does not take their worth to give him reasons not to privilege himself. He fails to treat women as equal in humanity, but instead either degrades them or stereotypes them as being essentially some x, where x is a property that is deemed inferior, such as one associated with the body but not rationality. For example, the man who makes catcalls to women passersby objectifies women in terms of their body parts, and stereotypes them as being solely bodily objects available for his sexual pleasure. To respect women, though, is to respect, not renounce, their individuality, or, their inherently individual interests. The agent who privileges himself in the way I am describing fails to respect women's individuality while seeing members of the privileged group as individuals in their own right. In a patriarchal society, the socially privileged agent's taking this stance of privilege is sanctioned and often rendered invisible because social privilege is systematized and hidden in institutional structures. The upshot is that the socially privileged agent's privileging himself is too often viewed as being morally permissible. Consider again that in rape, U.S. law currently takes the issue of mens rea, or, the mental state of the perpetrator, to turn on the issue of whether the victim consented, and this becomes a matter of whether she engaged in resistance sufficient to make it clear that she was not consenting to the sex. Women's saying "no" to the sex does not normally count in the court's eyes as sufficient resistance. The law requires physical resistance, even when circumstances are such that it would not be wise for the woman to fight off her attacker, or when she cannot do so. Here women are treated as if they do not know their own minds when it comes to sex, and men are deemed to know better than women when women have consented to sex. The stereotype of women as less rational than men gets played out and sanctioned in rape laws.[53]

An agent's taking a privileged stance toward morality and others displays an inconsistent regard for the agent's own worth and that of others, either as individuals or as members of a social group. If we identify the skeptic's standpoint more broadly as privilege rather than more narrowly as nontuism, then in order to defeat skepticism, we need to show that it is rationally required or at least permitted because *consistent* to respect the humanity of others, that is, to have the reasons for their ends and actions count equally to the agent's own. Privilege disallows this. I want next to examine how privilege plays out in various kinds of immorality.

3.2 Immoralities

3.2.1 Immorality Not Captured by Nontuism

I will use the categorizations of immoral behaviors that have been independently identified by Milo and Benn.[54] There are three categories of immorality that are not all captured by nontuism, including immoral acts stemming from (1) bad preferences or values, (2) lack of moral concern, and (3) lack of rational self-control. Arguably, nontuism can take different forms, some of which may play out as many of the kinds of immoralities I will discuss, as when the agent has a desire to satisfy and so acts out of weakness of will or in a morally indifferent way. Expected utility theory invokes a subjective account of the good that allows the satisfaction of any desire to count as promoting one's self-interest. Nevertheless, these other immoralities can stand on their own, as cases that are different from ones of desire-satisfaction. What separates them from nontuism is that in the latter, the agent has a first-order maxim to promote her self-interest, whereas in the former, the agent need not be governed by this maxim. The main issue is that while the consequences of these other immoralities can be just as bad as those from nontuistic acts, the motives, intentions, and maxims of the agents performing them are in some cases arguably worse than those of the nontuist. For each immorality, I will explain the role of privilege, and show how the immorality differs from nontuism. The upshot is that we need to broaden the skeptic's position beyond nontuism to cover these kinds of immorality for a complete defeat of skepticism.

3.2.1.1 Bad Preferences or Values. Included in the first category, acts stemming from bad preferences or values, are self-centered behavior ("preferential wickedness"), malignant wickedness, and perverse wickedness. In each case, the agent focuses on others' humanity, but cares negatively about it in wanting to discount it or render it void. Preferential wickedness is the closest position to nontuism: the self-centered, or preferentially wicked, person knows what is wrong but out of self-love and a ruthless unconcern for the good of others pursues his own good.[55] He has one maxim, always to act in ways promoting his own good. The nontuist seems to be a different kind of character, one who does not take an intrinsic interest in others' interests. Still, the nontuist is ready to drop others' interests if promoting them does not promote her own, suggesting that she, too, lacks compassion. Neither has to, but may, take an instrumental interest in the interests of others. Thus preferential wickedness is synonymous with nontuism. Examples include the person who blasts music in the yard all day without any concern for his neighbors who repeatedly ask for peace and quiet, and the "deadbeat dad" who chooses to spend his money on himself rather than on his children with no concern for the financial sacrifices the family is thereby forced to make. Their bad preference is that they prefer their own good even if satisfying their preference means setting back others' interests. In acting on their bad preference, they privilege themselves by disregarding others' interests, and so discounting their humanity, with full knowledge that others are deserving of respect. They privilege their reasons to promote what is best for them over moral reasons requiring equal consideration for everyone's interests. The preferentially wicked person is indifferent to others' welfare; when his immorality is the product of social privilege, he is complacent about a hierarchical system that allows such indifference, as is the case when white persons are indifferent to the effect of segregation in housing on educational opportunities for minorities.

The malignantly wicked person, whom Milo labels "Satanic,"[56] is motivated by envy or resentfulness, and knowingly does evil for its own sake. The opposite of the Kantian ideal, who does duty for the sake of duty, he does what is morally wrong just because he believes it to be wrong. His bad preference is that he takes the suffering of others to be an end in itself and a reason for action, which is reflected in the maxim according to which he guides his life.[57] Both Benn and Milo portray malignity as the worst kind of immorality; while the nontuist has only an instrumental interest in others' interests, the malignantly wicked person has an intrinsic interest in others' interests, but it takes a *negative* form. Both the self-centered and the malignantly wicked person know that others are deserving of respect equal to that given to those they might favor, but the former chooses to ignore this, while the latter chooses to render it void. In doing so, the latter privileges himself by thinking of himself—his interests and reasons—as superior to those of others: he makes himself an exception to the rules of morality, which require that each count for one. An example of this character who is influenced by social privilege is the misogynist who sees women getting ahead in his workplace and then goes out of his way to set them back. He may at first have only selfish concerns, not wanting women to threaten his position, but later he forgets these because his position is secure. He might seek to destroy the career of one woman whose success makes him intensely envious—perhaps she is junior to him and progressing at a faster pace. But then he extends his maxim to all women, even those from whose failure he has nothing to gain; he is concerned simply with seeing them suffer and takes their suffering to be an end in itself, perhaps because he convinces himself that women are in certain respects fundamentally different from men and thus not deserving of relevantly similar treatment. An even *worse* character, I believe, is the malignantly wicked person who tries to get his victim to be complicit in his own warped beliefs, as is the case with the slaveholder who convinces his slaves to be subservient and even to enjoy their position, and the misogynist who with the help of the system rewards women for their complicity by getting them to believe that they do not need feminism, that their value lies in their being attractive, and so on. This character hopes that others do not regard themselves as having intrinsic worth so that he can universalize his maxim with their consent. The workplace misogynist may spread rumors about the competence of a female colleague, which effectually makes her work suffer and causes her to doubt her merit. He knows well that it is hard to overcome psychological damage but proceeds with an intent to destroy her well-being. By intending to make his victim suffer for the sake of suffering, he clearly devalues women and displays disregard for their equal personhood status—their ability to put forward reasons for wanting to have career success.

The perversely wicked person knows basic moral principles such as "Killing is wrong," but his ignorance that a certain act is an instantiation of a given principle makes him act wrongly.[58] He fails to believe that what he does is wrong, and believes that it is right. He has bad derivative moral principles. He willingly does something wrong because though he is ignorant that his act is wrong, his ignorance is unreasonable. Perverse wickedness is different from nontuism: while the nontuist may set back others' interests when promoting them interferes with promoting his own, the perversely wicked person is unreasonably ignorant that his acts set back others' interests. Consider the socially privileged person who knows the basic moral principle, "Rape is wrong," but, perversely and unreasonably, is ignorant that date rape is an instantiation of it because he subscribes to patriarchal assumptions surrounding heterosexual courtship practices in which the man plays the dominant role. At base is his belief—and bad value—that women are sex objects to be used for men's pleasure, rather than autonomous persons whose sexual preferences and reasons for acting on them ought to be respected. His bad values blind him to the wrongness of his acts and prevent him from taking a positive intrinsic interest in others' interests when it is reasonable to expect persons to do so. On this score he is as bad as the nontuist. But he is worse, in the sense that he can have really bad values that blind him to the wrongness of many of his acts—he might, due to his bad values, always set back others' interests, though he need not do so for its own sake. Like the other immoral characters in this category, the perversely wicked person makes himself an exception to morality. He privileges himself and his reasons because his unreasonable ignorance about the moral status of his acts and his bad values lead him to discount the interests and reasons of others. In the case at issue, society's failure to acknowledge the seriousness or even the existence of date rape through its failure to accord women autonomy in sexual matters allows the perversely wicked person to privilege himself in this way. In order to defeat skepticism fully, we need to broaden the skeptic's position to cover all cases of bad values, not just nontuism.

3.2.1.2 Lack of Moral Concern.   The second category of immorality, that caused by lack of moral concern, occurs when an agent is either unaware of or indifferent to the wrongness of his act, which, for Milo, amounts to a lack of concern for the interests or welfare of others.[59] Moral considerations play no role in his practical deliberations, at least regarding the act in question, and moral beliefs do not motivate him to act. The amoral agent is or can reasonably be expected to be fully aware of the personhood status of others but simply does not care about it. At least three kinds of immorality fall into this class: psychopathy, moral indifference, and conscientious wickedness.

Psychopathy is the most extreme case. Here I will rely heavily on an excellent account of psychopathy defended by Antony Duff, and backed by empirical evidence.[60] According to Duff, the psychopath lacks moral concern because he lacks the concept of moral wrongness, and this is due to his lacking emotions such as love, and values and interests that are critical to moral understanding and being a part of a moral world. Hervey Cleckley, a psychiatrist, cites empirical evidence that psychopaths are affectively impaired.[61] He notes that psychopaths have a pathological egocentricity and incapacity for love made evident in part by an absolute indifference to the hardships they bring to those they claim to love. They display a poverty in major affective reactions, showing only halfhearted emotions. And they exhibit unresponsiveness in interpersonal relations, as when they do not appreciate special consideration or kindness. More recently, Shaun Nichols states that empirical studies have shown that the difference between psychopaths and other groups that fail to distinguish moral from conventional violations is not a difference in rational capacities, but in affective response. The data shows that psychopaths have an abnormally low responsiveness to pictures of faces of people in distress.[62] Nichols believes that psychopaths use moral terms in an "inverted commas" sense, that is, in a way that reveals that they lack true understanding of the meaning of moral terms but use the terms according to convention, offering reasons of convention for all kinds of wrongs (e.g., jaywalking and bank robbery).[63] Duff, though, believes that the psychopath may understand simple moral notions such as that pain is bad both for himself and for others, but that where he goes wrong is in understanding more complex moral issues such as the concept of insulting a loved one, which involves being rude to someone who trusts him to be kind.[64] The psychopath appears, especially to those who do not know him well, to be self-interested. He can deliberate instrumentally, and often acts self-interestedly. But just as often he passes up excellent opportunities to promote his interest.[65] He sometimes acts morally, but it is unpredictable when he will go astray—he acts immorally in both serious and trivial matters.[66] He finds unintelligible any first-order maxims that include others' interests because he is too self-absorbed to appreciate in any deep sense the difference between good and evil. Unlike the nontuist, though, he does not act on a self-centered higher-order maxim, but just does not have non-self-directed, lower-order maxims. Nor does he knowingly act on an evil maxim.[67] He does not see that he is acting immorally when he does, since according to Benn, he is unable to see things from an objective perspective, or, another's point of view, which is consistent with his lack of remorse or shame for moral failure.[68]

Significantly, unlike the selfish person who understands how others' welfare can yield reasons for action but does not act on these reasons, according to Duff the psychopath fails to see how moral or other concerns, values, or interests generate *reasons* for action for others or even for himself. He can see *that* others have certain values, such as caring about their families and friends, but he does not get what it means for them to *have* (deep, complex) values and emotions, and fails to see how these values yield reasons for action for them. This is because he fails to understand the emotional significance that these values have for others. His real problem is that he himself lacks rational values, concerns, and interests, since he is missing the emotional component of what it is to have such things.[69] He has no emotional responses or concerns on any level deeper than that of immediate feeling.[70] At best he can apply moral rules, but he often gets them wrong; he is unable to explain and criticize them, or to apply them to new cases, due to his own lack of values and interests. Duff rightly claims that the psychopath neither acts nor is a person, in the full sense. In short, he lacks moral understanding, which for Duff has an emotional component and requires that one *have* values and interests, though they need not be shared with others.[71]

Unlike the nontuist, the psychopath does not fully appreciate that he privileges his own interests over those of others when he acts self-interestedly, because he fails to understand at a fundamental level what he is doing. He does not understand the Kantian notion of authoritativeness, or reason-giving ability, because he does not see how a person's interests and values yield reasons for action for them, even in his own case. His failure to recognize others' intrinsic worth stems from his failure to recognize his own intrinsic worth. Although he may at times appear to have and act on similar preferences to those of the nontuist, nontuism does not sufficiently capture this kind of immorality.

I have been arguing that we need to broaden the skeptic's position beyond nontuism to include other immoralities. But psychopathy is the one kind of immorality that I believe cannot be covered by the skeptic's position, since, in defeating skepticism, we need to assume that persons are rational at least to the extent that they can see that moral concerns can generate reasons for action. And we need to assume that the skeptic is ready and willing to accept moral reasons, should a good argument be given for acting in morally required ways. But this requires a higher level of rationality than the psychopath can reach. We do not fail to defeat skepticism if our argument for the rationality of acting in morally required ways does not apply to a character who lacks interests in the full sense and cannot ever be part of the moral game because he cannot be responsive to moral reasons.

It is interesting to note that in the course of his discussion on psychopathy, Duff criticizes theories of rationality that identify rational action with maximizing the satisfaction of one's interests but without requiring that the agent have interests in the full sense and see their connection with reasons for action. Such theories, one of which undoubtedly is EU, are consistent with psychopathy: on EU, the interest-satisfying actions of the psychopath are rational. This is yet another strike against the formal version of EU. In addition to its failure to exclude deformed desires as irrational, the formal version of EU does not require that interests be full-fledged, with the result that satisfying even "psychopathic" interests is rational. Duff concludes that we need a more robust theory of rational choice that insists that interests, and, I would add, preferences and desires, be full-fledged ones. This should be the kind of theory that informs the skeptic's position. The theory of rationality I favor as one that holds more promise of defeating skepticism relies on practical consistency as a mark of rationality. My view is that the agent must have interests and values in the full sense in order to engage in the complex reasoning required for making sure that there is consistency or coherence in her dispositions, actions, maxims, moral theory, and so on. I will return to this point in chapter 8.

There are agents other than the psychopath whose immorality is caused by lack of moral concern, but who fully understand the nature of their immoral acts. The morally indifferent person knows what it is for an act to be morally wrong, but fails to have the appropriate "con-attitude," or negative attitude, toward his act because he lacks concern for the interests of others and feels no remorse or guilt about his indifference.[72] He does something that he believes is wrong simply because he is indifferent to, or does not care about, the fact that it is wrong, which for Milo amounts to his not caring about the interests of others. Or, as Milo says, he fails to be motivated by what he judges to be wrong.[73] A white person who prior to the Rosa Parks case routinely sits in the front of the bus while blacks are relegated to the back, and who knows that segregation is wrong, is still indifferent to its wrongness and to the interests of blacks who suffer its harms. In this case, his social position, which favors whites allows him to be indifferent; he does not care about blacks' interests because he does not have to care. His indifference to others' interests is a form of privilege whereby he knowingly disregards their intrinsic worth while allowing his own interests and reasons to count.

The same is true of the morally indifferent woman who sees an elderly person who needs help crossing a busy street, knows she could help, but goes her own way, without remorse or guilt, because she does not care about the needy. She makes herself an exception to the rule that we should care about morality and others, and believes that she is entitled to be indifferent. Indifference is consistent with nontuism in that the indifferent person may end up acting in self-promoting ways. And she may even have a preference not to expend effort and attention in helping needy people, or more generally, caring about the interests of others. In these cases, moral indifference is compatible with nontuism. Yet it can be different from nontuism. The morally indifferent person might act in ways that are indifferent to the interests of others but do not yet promote her own interests. Or she might not have a preference not to care about others' interests, but just not consider their interests. The white bus rider in the example might not be motivated by self-interest, as the nontuist would be, but just be going about his business as usual.

The third kind of lack of moral concern is conscientious wickedness. The conscientiously wicked person, according to Benn, governs his actions by a primary goal or principle that can reasonably be seen as *good*, but does so "at the cost of a callous insensitivity to evil done by the way," which he knows or could reasonably be expected to know yet systematically disregards.[74] An employer who subscribes to the seemingly neutral and fair principle "Justice means giving to each what he deserves" ends up knowingly favoring men in hiring because men, but not women, are encouraged to and often do develop traits and skills needed for traditionally male jobs. He knows or ought to know that he fails to accord women due respect by denying them opportunities readily granted to men. His insensitivity is a form of indifference to the wrongness of his act, though his principle seems innocuous. Like moral indifference, conscientious wickedness is consistent with nontuism because the conscientiously wicked person might end up acting in self-promoting ways. Yet it is different from nontuism, as Benn explains: the conscientiously wicked person does not have a self-centered higher-order maxim, but believes that any considerations that are not directly validated by his primary ideal goal or principle are necessarily outweighed by it when they conflict with it.[75] His ideal might genuinely be good, but he pursues it ruthlessly to the exclusion of other goods that ought to be taken account of. Benn gives the example of believing with the Irish Republican Army that only through indiscriminate violence can a united Ireland arise, *and* that to go through with it one must stifle sensibility to the horrors through one must wade to bring it about.[76] The conscientiously wicked person is not best described as having a preference to ignore other factors that ought to be taken into account, and so as self-interested; rather, Benn attributes his insensitivity to "a sense of mission so great or an arrogance so overwhelming that he can desensitize himself [or] school himself to a callous disregard."[77] The unfair employer who hires only men might benefit because he avoids offering additional training that women might need to do the job, but he acts not out of self-interest but from a single-minded pursuit of his principle and insensitivity to fairness to women. He privileges his own interests over women's by effectually giving them less than they deserve and want when he does or ought to know better but is insensitive. This kind of lack of moral concern should also be captured in our setup of the skeptic.

3.2.1.3 Lack of Self-Control.   The third category of immorality, that caused by lack of self-control, takes the forms of weakness of will and moral negligence, the latter of which includes impulsiveness, carelessness, recklessness, and self-deception. Here the agent is or should be aware of the facts about others' humanity but fails to focus on this, succumbing instead to emotion. Philosophers traditionally have defined the weak-willed person as one who knows what the right thing to do is yet acts contrary to it by succumbing to emotion. But Donald Davidson, in his well-known article on the subject, takes weakness of the will to be a form of irrationality, where the agent joins together all of his reasons into a set of "reasons all things considered," and acts contrary to what he judges to be best on the basis of all available reasons.[78] Although weakness of will, for Davidson, may be the *result* of emotion, he explains it in nonpsychological terms, as the agent's acting against what he judges he has reason to do, all things considered. Weakness of will is possible, then, because the agent has no reason to do what he does when he acts akratically. On either the traditional or Davidson's definition, weakness of will is compatible with nontuism in cases where the agent succumbs to self-interest against her moral principles. Yet weakness of will is different from nontuism: the nontuist follows a higher-order maxim of self-interest, while the weak-willed person has a higher-order moral maxim that he acts against, usually due to emotion, and not always out of self-interest. Put another way, the nontuist does not fail to focus on others' humanity; rather, he focuses on it, but puts his own interests first, taking only an instrumental interest in others' interests. The weak-willed person on occasions of weakness fails to focus on others' humanity when he should, acting contrary to reasons he himself believes he has for respecting others' humanity. He privileges his own interests and reasons on these occasions. The person in a traditional marriage who has an affair out of weakness of will privileges her own interests over those of her spouse by failing to focus on his interest in having a faithful spouse. Sometimes weakness of will is encouraged by social privilege. For instance, attempts to justify rape and woman-battering typically point to ways in which the woman allegedly provoked the wrongful behavior, such as dressing provocatively, inviting the rapist in, or saying the wrong thing, thereby causing the perpetrator's weakness of will—"I couldn't help myself"—about acting contrary to reasons he believes he has to respect the intrinsic worth of his victim. Such justifications are sanctioned by a sexist culture and even the law on rape, which as I have said puts the burden on the victim to show she did not consent to the sex. The perpetrator's social privilege, which all men are granted in a patriarchal society, encourages him to fail to focus on his victim's humanity, when morality requires that he be against her interest in and reasons for not being harmed.

Note that weakness of will has in common with psychopathy the feature of being a lapse in rationality. But since in weakness of will this lapse is only temporary, and the weak-willed person understands the complexities of morality, has the right emotions and has full-fledged values and interests, and sees their connection to reasons, the argument we offer to defeat skepticism can reach such a person. Thus we should broaden the skeptic's position accordingly.

The morally negligent person fails to act in accord with his own moral principles, is ignorant due to his negligence that what he does violates these principles, wants to avoid wrongdoing and prefers its avoidance to what he does, and is inclined to feel remorse on reflection.[79] Milo categorizes three kinds of moral negligence. First is carelessness, which is failing to pay attention to the wrong-making features of an act. A professor who tries to be funny in class without seeing that he insults certain students is careless. Second is recklessness or impulsiveness, which is violating a duty to check to make sure that one's acts do not violate one's moral principles. A person who subscribes to the principle "Do no harm" but who fails to have her brakes checked and, without reasonable deliberation, takes the risk that her car will not hit anyone is reckless. So, too, is the person who harbors sexist or racist attitudes in a sexist and racist climate, because he fails to pay attention to whether his attitude will prompt others to act on their sexist or racist attitudes.[80] The third kind of negligence is self-deception, which is failing to realize when one could and should that one's act is of the sort that one believes is wrong. The mother who verbally cuts off her daughter when the latter tells her that her father raped her deceives herself about her husband's goodness, when the appropriate response is for her to take responsibility and comfort her daughter.[81] In general, the morally negligent person fails to take precautions against her tendency to ignore others' humanity, or even takes a risk with others' humanity. Her ignorance about the wrongness of her act stems from her negligence about the fact that she effectually counts her own worth more than the worth of others. Again, as with many other kinds of immorality, negligence, recklessness, and self-deception might be motivated by self-interest, in which case they are compatible with nontuism. Yet there are instances of each of these immoralities that are not prompted by desire-satisfaction, distinguishing them from nontuism: the careless professor might insult his students in the absence of a desire to be funny or another desire, and the reckless driver might not think about having her brakes checked and whether her failure to do so squares with her moral principle to do no harm. The self-deceived mother might seem to be satisfying a desire to have a good marriage, but she is not doing so; rather, she is merely making herself falsely believe that she has a good marriage. The negligent person follows a different maxim from the straight nontuist: she does not follow a higher-order maxim of self-interest, but has good moral principles, though she violates them for reasons other than self-interested ones. The skeptic's position needs to represent this kind of immorality also.

3.2.2 Immorality Not Captured by EU

There is one other class of actions that escape the traditional picture of the skeptic.[82] These are the ways that various social practices advantage or privilege the members of one social group (typically men, whites, the upper class) while disadvantaging the members of another (typically women, minorities, the working class). In the context of the immoralities I have outlined, I have already discussed various ways in which members of privileged groups might act immorally due to their social privilege, and have shown how each as an individual may benefit from doing so. Now I have in mind those members of privileged social groups who do not themselves engage in immoral actions, do not know and may reasonably not be expected to know of the disadvantages or harms suffered by those in the disadvantaged groups, or at least cannot in any simple way eradicate these harms by their own actions, yet who nonetheless benefit in an undeserved way from the unjust systems (sexism, racism, classism) in virtue of other groups being disadvantaged. The agent who in this way participates in systematic injustice does not aim to satisfy his desires or preferences. Yet he benefits indirectly, in virtue of institutional or system-atic injustice. The benefits the members of advantaged groups reap are shared by all members of their social group; an individual member of the group need not do anything but just be a member of the group to enjoy these benefits. Their *having* privilege, though different from the ways other immoralists *privilege themselves*, shares with them the feature that some persons' intrinsic value is not appropriately acknowledged.

Separating cases of undeserved benefiting from cases of individual malfeasance is often difficult.[83] Some examples will help to illustrate what I have in mind. Consider the practice of rape. Men who never rape women still enjoy the systematic benefits of the existence of the practice of rape, which are directly proportional to the harms that women as a group suffer. Rape harms women as a group in at least the following ways. It stifles women's freedom to do simple things such as go out alone, at night, in strange places, or even to respond to assaults on their dignity that come by way of catcalls. It makes women live in fear of men, since men can use rape as a weapon against women who "get out of line." The practice of rape divides men into good (nonrapists) and bad (rapists), and it does so along racial lines (black men being seen as rapists, white men as nonrapists).[84] It forces women to seek protection from "good" men and increases their dependence on them. Rape makes women suffer degradation by perpetuating sexist stereotypes of women as passive, weak, in need of protection, and as sexually available to all men. Rape costs women money, making them select better neighborhoods to live in, buy cars instead of using public transportation, buy locks for their windows and doors, and take self-defense classes. Men benefit socially and economically from the practice of rape: they enjoy freedom of movement, power over women, independence, the ability to move ahead in the workplace uninhibited by fears and economic burdens that rape imposes on women, a positive image as fully human beings, and peace of mind. Men who do not rape do not strictly speaking do anything wrong by benefiting in these ways, and indeed, most probably never thought about having these benefits. Arguably they reasonably cannot be expected to recognize such systematic benefits because their experience in the world is deemed to be the status quo. Yet women as a group are disadvantaged at the same time men are advantaged, both in virtue of their gender.

The practice of sexual harassment works similarly. Even though a particular man may never sexually harass a woman, he will in virtue of his group membership enjoy the benefits of this practice. Street harassers curtail women's freedom to take direct routes, and degrade women by reducing them to mere sex objects, and men who harass women on the job effectually keep women out of top positions and male-dominated professions. When women are degraded and kept out of jobs, all men benefit by having much greater freedom and increased opportunity to get ahead economically, socially, and politically.

Members of advantaged groups also enjoy "wild card" privileges from systematic racism or sexism rather than particular practices associated with such systems. Peggy McIntosh outlines forty-six privileges that whites enjoy at the expense of blacks and other minorities.[85] They are "wild card" privileges because their recipients can pull them out at any time and use them to bring themselves even further privileges. McIntosh's list includes being able to see wide and positive representation of people of her race in the media, being able to protect her children most of the time from people who might not like them, never being asked to speak for all the people of her race, being reasonably assured that the police or IRS agents she deals with will be people of her race, and being able to buy bandages in "flesh" color that match the color of her skin. Men enjoy similar privileges vis-à-vis women. All such cases exemplify the fact that members of the disadvantaged group are devalued in their humanity.

Surely a white person's buying "flesh-colored" bandages, or a man's being able to stay out late in unfamiliar neighborhoods, are not by themselves instances of immoral actions. Yet an institutional injustice has occurred, and we need to pronounce moral and rational judgments about it. The issue is how this fits into the project of defeating skepticism. EU takes rational action to be that which aims to promote the satisfaction of an agent's desires or preferences. Benefiting from institutional injustice in the ways described is not equated with desire- or preference-satisfaction, so it does not come under EU's umbrella. Expected utility theory does not pronounce the acts associated with institutional injustice to be rational or irrational. Yet all of the "acts"—I put this in scare quotes because the agent typically need not act in order to benefit, but just be a member of a certain social group—that maintain institutional injustice, even if they are not in themselves immoral and are not performed by an identifiable guilty agent(s), are ones we may not want to be rationally neutral because they, along with instances of individual malfeasance, aid in maintaining unjust systems that indirectly harm all members of a social group (e.g., when all women are harmed by the practice of rape), and directly harm individual members of the group (e.g., when a particular woman is raped). This suggests that setting up the skeptic to endorse EU is not the best way to go because EU leaves out ways of benefiting that are not properly actions, and not instances of preference- or desire-satisfaction. Suppose we assume that the skeptic endorses EU, and we defeat skepticism. We can do so either on EU's terms by showing that every morally required act is ratio- nally required because in one's self-interest, or that morally required acts are rationally required in a self-interested sense because they emanate from a rational disposition; or not on EU's terms by showing that acting in morally required ways is rationally required in a non-desire-satisfying sense. The first way is problematic at least for the reason that it makes moral reasons otiose, in the case of Hobbes, and that it cannot explain the connection between the rationality of a moral disposition and the acts expressing it, for Gauthier. But if we take the second route, and defeat skepticism, and so EU, we will not have shown anything about the rational status of benefiting from institutional injustice. Benefiting in this way gets left out of the traditional skeptic's challenge, due not to the narrowness of the assumption of nontuism, but rather to the narrowness of EU, which speaks only to acting in preference-satisfying ways. Such a defeat of skep- ticism would be incomplete because it may not cover all immoralities.

The question is whether cases of benefiting from systematic injustice are immoral, and hence, targets for inclusion in the skeptical project. The issue is complicated. On the one hand, each of the ways that members of dominant groups benefit from systematic injustice functions to sustain our unjust system, and it is a feature of oppression that when one group is advantaged, another group is disadvantaged.[86] It is wrong for some people to be disadvantaged unfairly because of their race, gender, and the like. Certainly moral philosophers interested in social justice want to pro- nounce these systems of oppression morally wrong. They have a stake in showing that all forms of racism and sexism, even those hidden and obscured by various structures, are not backed by reason. The question is whether each and every act or benefit sustaining them is also morally wrong. Some of the factors complicating the issue are the following. One is that, as I have said, it is difficult to separate cases of merely benefiting from systematic injustice from cases of individual malfeasance. The latter cases can be classified as one of the kinds of immoralities I discussed earlier. These acts violate moral requirements, and are ones we should want to show to be irrational. For example, if we can contribute to moral indifference by not doing anything about the fact of a man's being hired instead of a woman who is at least as competent, then this is a case of individual malfeasance. Other cases are more difficult to sort out: does a man who enjoys the freedom of being able to go out late at night act indifferently toward his privilege and toward women's humanity?

Another factor that makes it difficult to determine the moral status of benefiting from social injustice is that one person's actions typically will not have much of an effect on the system. A white person who buys flesh-colored bandages does not do very much to sustain racism. Her act is not as directly related to the harms of racism as, say, Hitler's preaching hatred for the Jews. And the one act by itself does not do much to sustain the system; rather, all the acts, the instances of benefiting, and the ways in which the system becomes institutionalized together function to sustain the system.[87]

I think that deciding this issue turns on what we think is morally required, and this should be decided on a case-by-case basis. Some factors that may play a role are the following: the person's degree of responsibility for maintaining the unjust system; what the person is able to do to counteract the injustice; the strength of the connection between the benefit and the maintenance of the unjust system; and whether the person cannot reasonably be expected to know that he benefits from an unjust system. The last factor is a matter of knowing that others share in the basic facts about humanity, or that they have intrinsic value. I have argued elsewhere that knowing this about others is a very simple thing.[88] So even though we might initially exonerate a white teenager who buys flesh-colored bandages because she cannot reasonably be expected to know that in doing so she benefits from and perpetuates an unjust system, we might think that she should at least acknowledge her privilege, if not even try to change things by writing a letter of protest to the bandage company. Similarly, even if we initially exonerate a man who benefits from the practice of rape, we might think that he reasonably should be aware of his benefiting, and try to make his male friends aware of the disadvantages women incur, or try to convince his employer that women should be paid more than men enough to compensate them for living in safer but more expensive neighborhoods, or at least not to try to prevent the women he interacts with from feeling like fully human beings rather than passive, weak beings in need of protection. A more complex issue than seeing that others have legitimate desires and interests that they do not want thwarted is figuring out how a person's humanity is violated even by mere participation in an unjust system. Once we settle on what is morally required in cases of benefiting from an unjust system, we will know whether a particular case is an instance of immoral behavior that we want to establish in our defeat of skepticism as irrational. Some ways of benefiting will turn out to be morally and rationally permissible, even if they contribute to an unjust system. Others will not. A robust defeat of skepticism would not leave open the rational status of these actions. Thus, philosophers need to expand the skeptic's position not only beyond nontuism but also beyond EU, to include as (initially) rational various ways of benefiting that contrast with morality but that are not instances of desire- or preference-satisfaction. Only then will a defeat of (at least) action skepticism be complete.

4 A NEW MODEL: CONSISTENCY AND PRIVILEGE

I have been arguing for expanding the assumption of nontuism to accommodate non-self-interested versions of immorality. In addition, I have raised the case that is not captured by EU of benefiting that is the result of institutional injustice rather than individual malfeasance. I have shown that the various immoralities that are different from nontuism are best captured by privilege. The advantage of describing the skeptic's position in terms of privilege is that a successful defeat of skepticism would show that acting in any of these immoral ways, not just acting self-interestedly in a nontuistic sense, is irrational. The problem remaining is the tension between the skeptic's endorsing EU and taking privilege rather than nontuism to be the worst-case scenario against morality. Unlike nontuism, privilege does not serve merely as a constraint on EU; it goes beyond EU in this regard since it incorporates behaviors that are best described other than as constraints on preference-satisfaction. The disadvantage of broadening the assumption of nontuism to privilege is that the latter is not backed by EU, or by any other theory of rational choice and action. Thus we are hemmed in: the skeptic's position needs to be at least prima facie a rational one. The skeptic serves as the philosophers' device for testing the rationality of acting morally. The strategy is to have the skeptic already accept the ongoing theory of practical reason, one that does not include moral reasons, with the caveat that he would accept an even better theory of practical reason that includes moral reasons were one to be found. To capture the idea that the skeptic who rejects moral reasons holds a rational position, philosophers couch the skeptic's position in a theory of practical reason, allegedly the best defended one. Skepticism about acting morally is just like skepticism in epistemology on this score: the former is the denial of the existence of moral reasons, and the latter is the denial that there is good reason to believe that the external world exists. The epistemologist must show that our belief in the external world is justified according to some standards of justification that we would accept. The moral philosopher must show that moral reasons are justified because either they fit into the ongoing theory of rational action or they are part of an even better theory of practical reason. The skepticism project does not get off the ground unless the skeptic endorses a plausible theory of practical reason. There is no point defeating a skeptic whose position is not rational, for the reasons that this skeptic provides no challenge to morality, and our defeat of skepticism would not have to be grounded in reason by appealing to reasons the skeptic can accept.

Historically, many philosophers engaged in the project of defeating skepticism have invoked some version of EU, so it may be difficult to give it up. Hobbes asserts that the laws of nature are *precepts of reason* forbidding a person to do that which is destructive of his own life.[89] He believes that all voluntary acts aim at a person's own good, and that persons cannot voluntarily or rationally give up their right to self-defense since doing so would be destructive of one's own life. But persons rationally should give up other rights when others do so as well, in order to have security, peace, and well-being. Hobbes invokes the notion of expected utility in his answer to the Foole in arguing that it is not rational to perform an action that the agent cannot expect will be self-beneficial, even if in fact, through some turn of events, the action turns out to be so.[90] So under threat of punishment from the Sovereign, acting immorally would not be rational even if the agent believes he can escape detection, because doing so does not maximize the agent's expected utility. Hume takes the sensible knave to identify rational action with self-interested action, claiming that a person conducts himself with most wisdom when he takes advantage of the exceptions to the rules about acting virtuously.[91] Sidgwick, too, links self-interest with a rational choice theory: "the calm desire for my 'good on the whole' is *authoritative*; and therefore carries with it implicitly a rational dictate to aim at this end."[92] But Sidgwick ends up endorsing both the "maxim of Prudence" and the "maxim of Rational Benevolence" as ways it is rational to act, since he believes that it is rational for a person to promote the good or satisfy the desires of all, not just of oneself.[93] More recently, Gauthier takes the skeptic to adopt EU because it is a long-standing and well-defended theory of rational action: "the maximizing conception of rationality is almost universally accepted and employed in the social sciences.... It lies at the core of economic theory, and is generalized in decision and game theory. Its lesser prominence in political, sociological, and psychological theory reflects more the lesser concern with rationality among many practitioners of those disciplines, than adherence to an alternative conception."[94]

The deeper question is why rational action is identified with self-interested action, or, desire- or preference-satisfaction. The hope is that acting from privilege is sufficiently similar to count as rational action. Here I will rely on Hampton's thorough investigation of EU. Hampton claims that EU has roots partly in Bentham's idea "that in order to understand value as it originates in the subject, we require the concept of utility, understood as a cardinal (and interpersonal) measure of pleasure or happiness experienced by an agent when his desires are satisfied, and something that ought to be *maximized*."[95] In essence, to experience something as good is to be favorably aroused by it.[96] Bentham directly links value, or the good, with the maximization of the satisfaction of a person's wants or desires. Bentham believes that "a man is said *to have an interest in any subject*, in so far as that *subject* is considered as more or less likely to be to him a source of pleasure or exemption."[97] Our actions, then, are motivated by an interest in producing pleasure or preventing pain. Bentham believes further that self-interest overrides the interests of others, and that it is the only motive that can always be counted on, claiming that the human race would have ended long ago had each person not been primarily interested in his or her own well-being.[98] The Principle of Utility, which counts each person's pleasure and pain equally, would maximize utility in the world when followed by all. Contemporary game theorists tweak Bentham's notion of value, taking utility to be a measure of one's preferences rather than desires. Gauthier's version of EU counts as the basis of rational choice only considered preferences, coherent preferences, preferences that are revealed in action and speech, and preferences that are stable under experience and reflection. For Gauthier, but not for Bentham or Hampton, preferences do not depend solely on the qualities of experience such as happiness or enjoyment.

Aside from its intuitively plausible link with the good for a person, EU is favored by others because they believe both that it best explains and predicts behavior, and that every human reasoner uses it.[99] According to Hampton, the early proponents of EU, von Neumann and Morgenstern, deliberately designed it to be purely *predictive* of how a person with certain preferences would choose under risk. But many of its proponents have taken it to be an accurate description of how humans actually reason, thereby lending it scientific authority because it explains behavior. However, EU has been criticized on this score. Hampton believes that since the numbers in the von Neumann and Morgenstern function represent only utility but not welfare that is supposed to underlie our preferences, EU does not describe behavior. That is, utility simply measures preferences, so EU is purely predictive, not descriptive or normative. Thus for Hampton, EU is *not* a theory of *reason*, but only a way of predicting behavior.[100] Elizabeth Anderson objects to EU on the grounds that people do not always care about their own good, that desiring certain things might not be good for them even if we think it is, and that it is not clear whether it is their own well-being or their self-interest considered selfishly that they care about.[101] Anderson also believes that we cannot read off values from a person's preferences, since, for instance, a person might just happen on a whim to want something, and that our whims, appetites, compulsion, habits, and so on make us seek things that we find bad. Anderson's objection sheds doubt even on EU's *predictability*. Anderson debunks EU also on the grounds that we value things in many more ways than desiring, such as being in awe, loving, liking, appreciating, and admiring.

My aim in this book has not been decidedly to debunk EU, though I have offered some critiques of it in relation to the project of defeating skepticism. These include that it unduly constrains the kind of answer we can give to defeat skepticism by grounding it in self-interest, and making it difficult to explain the connection between having a rational disposition and acting in a rational way from this disposition; that its formal version does not exclude as irrational deformed desires, thereby risking recapitulating women's oppression when attempting to defeat skepticism with EU as a starting point; and that it is consistent with psychopathy because it does not require that the agent have desires and interests in the full sense, seeing their connection to reasons for action.

Even if we could resolve these problems with EU, other problems arise concerning the moral code generated from a defeat of skepticism grounded in EU. Hampton argues that grounding the skeptic's position, and hence morality, in EU will inevitably yield a morality that allows us to treat people as instrumental: "if you ask me why I should treat you morally, and I respond by saying that it is in my interest to do so, I am telling you that my regard for you is something that is merely instrumentally valuable to me; I do not give you that regard because there is something about you that merits it, regardless of the usefulness of that regard to me."[102] Hampton believes that this flies in the face of what morality requires, which is that we owe persons respectful treatment simply in virtue of the fact that they are persons. I have been arguing that we need to define the skeptic's position to represent a myriad of ways, in addition to acting self-interestedly, that agents may fail to treat others with this Kantian view of respect.

An additional and related objection familiar from chapter 2 is that defining the skeptic to adopt EU as in SIB contractarianism, where the bargainers are assumed to be self-interested and will accept a moral code that each of them could rationally accept only because it is in their self-interest, is likely to lead to a minimalist morality such as Hobbes's or Gauthier's. Having mutual cooperation as their goal, each bargainer will find it in his or her interest to make only minimal sacrifices, giving up, for Hobbes, the rights to kill, harm, steal, lie, and so on, resulting in a moral code that includes only duties of noninterference. While these duties are important, they are insufficient for ensuring that we act in ways respecting others as having intrinsic value, which often requires carrying out positive duties such as ones directed at satisfying basic needs. And as I have said, showing that fulfilling only negative duties is rationally required is not sufficient for defeating skepticism. These and other critiques, then, render EU a suspicious starting point for the project of defeating skepticism.

We need an alternative to EU that will get us what we need for a successful defeat of skepticism. The alternative should not beg the question in favor of morality by assuming at the outset that the skeptic endorses moral reasons, but should compete with morality. It should capture Bentham's plausible insight that value has to do with being favorably aroused, and is directly linked with the satisfaction of a person's desires, and that reasons for action ultimately all arrive at pleasure. Privileging oneself is tied to what is good for a person in Bentham's sense. It is similar to self-interest in that it is advantaging oneself, but it is richer in the ways I have described. It encompasses a variety of ways that an immoralist disrespects another's humanity, and it covers benefiting from institutional injustice. I propose that we take the skeptic to endorse the view that rationality requires one to act in ways that privilege oneself vis-à-vis morality. That is, it is rational to privilege oneself in the sense of advantaging oneself, including doing so in ways that disrespect others' humanity.

I do not think that for purposes of defeating skepticism we need to defend a full-fledged theory of practical reason that replaces EU but is grounded in privilege. Rather, we need simply to ground actions that are in opposition to morality in some kind of rational basis that captures the good things about EU and avoids at least some of the problems EU presents for defeating skepticism. An account of rational action grounded in privilege is arguably better than EU at predicting and explaining be-havior, if only because it covers a greater variety of behaviors in which people do in fact engage. The privilege account fares better than EU also because in not dichotomizing morality and self-interest, it allows for the case that sometimes morality should *not* demand that we act against our self-interest, as when women give too much of themselves in caring for others and lose themselves to the interests of others. Dichotomizing morality and privilege allows for morality to require that we act in self-interested ways when doing so is self-respecting: it is rational for others not to privilege themselves by taking advantage of women, and it is rational for women to act in self-respecting ways even if self-interestedly.

If the modified skeptic's position is that it is rational to act in ways that privilege oneself by disrespecting the humanity of others, to defeat the skeptic we now need to show that rationality requires not privileging oneself by disrespecting others' humanity, but instead acting in morally required ways. That is, the moralist has to show that rationality requires taking the worth of others to give one a reason not to privilege oneself. This reason, I am suggesting, is not a self-interested reason. Nor is it the case that to defeat skepticism, we need to ground moral reasons in "reasons of privilege," to parallel grounding moral reasons in self-interested reasons. I have argued that privileging oneself, or in some cases being privileged by the system, displays an inconsistency in treating the humanity of self and others. It involves caring negatively about others' humanity by either rendering it void or discounting it, not caring about others' humanity, not being aware of others' humanity by failing to focus on it and succumbing to emotion instead, or even enjoying undeserved benefits from an unjust system. One promising alternative to the model of EU and self-interest is that of consistency. We might assume that the skeptic's position is backed by reason in the sense that it requires understanding the basic laws of logic, including the principle of consistency. There are *reasons of consistency* to which we can appeal that a person who is rational and in a position of privilege can ultimately accept. Rationality requires not being inconsistent. To defeat skepticism, then, we need to show that rationality requires, on grounds of the principle of consistency, that we not disrespect others' humanity; it is inconsistent in the sense of being contradictory, and so irrational, not to respect others fully, but to respect one's own humanity and to expect that others do so as well.

Promising though it is, a defeat of skepticism grounded on the principle of consistency faces a charge similar to that given by the universal egoist to the individual egoist. Thomas Nagel defines "egoism" as the view that the only *source* of reasons for action lies in the interests of the agent.[103] Individual egoism is the view that "all practical requirements are derived from the overall interests of just one *particular individual*."[104] The problem with individual egoism is that it cannot explain how a characteristic such as the fact of promoting one's self-interest serves as a reason for one person but not for another. That is, individual egoism takes it that one's own desires or good give(s) one reasons, but denies that the desires or good of others give(s) one reasons. There is an inconsistency, or a contradiction, involved here, unless the egoist can explain what is so special about the one person that only her desires give her reasons.

Universal egoism attempts to diffuse this inconsistency. According to universal egoism, *each* person's desires give that person a reason; the principle of egoism should be universalized to everyone. While each person might not *want* others to follow the principle that each ought to do what best promotes her own interest, for the reason that others' following it is likely to result in one's own interests being set back, each can still universalize this maxim. Thus the universal egoist avoids the inconsistency charge facing individual egoism.[105] In universalizing the maxim of egoism, one claims that one's welfare is no more important from the perspective of the universe than anyone else's: each person's good is the source of reasons for herself. So there is no inconsistency.

An objector might claim that my argument about consistency in respecting one's own worth and the worth of others is similar to that given by the individual egoist, and is subject to an objection similar to that given by the universal egoist that diffuses the inconsistency charge. In essence, the skeptic can claim that there is no inconsistency in privileging oneself, so it is not irrational to do so. According to the objector, my argument is that the person who privileges himself takes it that his humanity gives him a reason to respect it, but he denies that the humanity of others gives him a reason to respect it. Only my worth gives me a reason to respect it. This claim is similar to that made by the individual egoist. And it is inconsistent, or contradictory, in the same way: it allows that one person's worth, but not anyone else's, gives that person a reason. To diffuse this inconsistency, the privileged person, or skeptic, can follow the reasoning of the universal egoist and reply that taking oneself to have a reason to privilege oneself means that it is rational for each to privilege himself and that this view gives each person the same status. That is, the person who privileges himself takes it that his worth is the exclusive source of reasons for himself, and universalizes this principle so that every person's worth is the exclusive source of reasons for himself. Thus, the privileged person can escape the inconsistency charge, and thus the charge that privileging oneself is irrational.

The objection to the inconsistency model of rational action takes it that we all have the same worth, but that I favor my reasons having to do with my worth more than the reasons of others having to do with their worth. This is one way of construing the egoist's or privileged person's position. But I have been arguing for another view, according to which the privileged person takes it that he has more worth than others—his worth counts for more—and this is why he can favor his reasons over others'. On my account, privileging involves not regarding others as equal in worth by discounting, ignoring, rendering void, or, in general, not appropriately acknowledging their humanity. It involves privileging one's reasons for action over moral reasons, which reflect the intrinsic value of others.[106]

The question is whether the inconsistency charge still holds on my account of the privileged person, even if it can be diffused on my objector's account. I think it does. The reason is that these accounts trade on two different kinds of consistency. On my account, the privileged person aims to make another inferior in worth by discounting her worth in one of the ways exhibited by the immoralities I discussed. I have said that morality requires that each counts for one, without favoritism of one or a group. When one discounts another's worth, one acts immorally. There is an inconsistency that explains immorality, which is a violation of *impartiality*, which on my analysis requires treating equally everyone's worth and not favoring one's own over another's. Morality requires this kind of consistency.

My objector construes inconsistency not as a violation of impartiality, but as a violation of *universalizability*. Here the inconsistency charge is mounted against favoring one's own reasons, and not taking others' reasons to factor into one's own. The objector is able to diffuse the inconsistency charge by claiming that each person's good gives that person a reason. That is, we can universalize the principle that one's own desires or good give(s) one a reason. But this does not diffuse the violation of impartiality, which requires that we treat everyone's worth equally.

The point I am making is a more general one about morality and rationality. Many of us think of the dictates of morality as impartial, and as universalizable. But many of us think of the dictates of rationality only as universalizable—certainly the egoist or nontuist or skeptic can say they are. We do not think of the dictates of rationality as being impartial; indeed, EU requires favoring the satisfaction of one's own desires over those of another. It would be interesting to explore why we have such different takes on morality and rationality, and I think that an attempt to defeat skepticism that invoked reasons of consistency as I am suggesting should do so. I am not going to conjecture any answers since my goal in this book is not to defeat skepticism but merely to set out the terms under which a complete and satisfactory account should be given. I merely want to suggest that reasons of consistency promise to be better than reasons of self-interest for grounding the rationality of acting in morally required ways.[107]

One further advantage the privilege account of rational action has over EU can be seen in connection with Duff's charge that EU is consistent with psychopathy. Suppose we defeat action skepticism. In order to avoid Duff's charge, we want moral reasons to be ones the agent gets in a strong way such that they are connected to values and interests the agent has in the full sense and cares about asserting appropriately. I have argued in chapter 4 that since deformed desires are heteronomous, ones the agent could not have as her own, they should be excluded from a theory of rational choice that would ground morality. I will argue in chapter 7 that in demonstrating the rationality of acting morally, we also need to show that rationality requires not only acting in morally required ways, but from certain motives—merely going through the motions will not suffice for a successful defeat of skepticism. The person who merely goes through the motions is not a moral agent in the full sense, one who cares about morality and has moral desires that motivate moral action. I will argue in chapter 8 that the moral person assesses her character from time to time in light of her actions, and rejects acts that are out of line with a moral character. She understands morality and has an interest in following it, and adopts a moral disposition for the right reasons. She has to be cognizant of her reasons for acting in order to be able to change or to firm up her resolve. Being a moral person involves reflection on both the maxim one adopts, and on the reasoning or the justification for the moral theory or principles that yield the maxim. Maxims involving privileging oneself over others fail to be consistent in the way I have described. The moral person understands reasons and their connection to values and interests in the strong way that Duff claims EU does not require. I favor the view that rationality is a matter of the agent's being consistent in the sense of having coherent desires, dispositions, and actions, as well as the maxim or moral theory she adopts being consistent in the sense of not being contradictory in the treatment it requires.

Thus a defeat of skepticism on my account will invoke full-fledged, rich reasons for being morally disposed and for acting morally, and these can be had on an account whereby rationality is grounded in the principle of consistency. Agents with deformed desires would fail to be rational, as would agents who merely go through the motions in acting morally. Any defeat of skepticism, such as one grounded in EU, that falls short of the agent's having reasons in the full sense, and seeing their connection to interests and values that he has, would be unsatisfactory. The privilege theory sits better than EU with the agent's being able to understand moral reasons in the right sense. Privileging oneself requires that one *has* full-fledged interests. The agent who privileges himself makes his interests and reasons stemming from them—his worth—count for more than that of others, which means that he *gets* the significance of interests and sees that they are connected to reasons for action. Acting out of privilege means being inconsistent, but (possibly) not at a psychopathic loss about one's humanity and the humanity of others.

5 CONCLUSION

I have argued for broadening the skeptic's position from that of self-interest to that of privilege in order to effect a successful defeat of skepticism that covers all immoral acts. Thus far, we have fine-tuned the action skeptic's position in the following ways. We have questioned whether action skepticism even needs to be defeated, given our doubts about defeating it on grounds of self-interest. We have seen the failure of two theories—SIB contractarianism and the ethic of care—to defeat action skepticism. At the very least, if we are to start with the traditional picture of the skeptic as endorsing EU, we must modify EU or whatever theory of practical reason we endorse, and thus our depiction of the skeptic, in ways that exclude deformed desires. This chapter has argued for the most radical revision of the action skeptic's position from that of its being rational to act in self-interested, preference-satisfying ways to its being rational to act in ways that privilege oneself vis-à-vis morality such that one advantages oneself in ways that disrespect others' humanity. Our task in defeating skepticism is to show that there are reasons of consistency according to which it would be irrational not to respect others' humanity, reasons that a skeptic who endorses the view that it is rational to privilege oneself can rationally accept. Before developing further the ways in which consistency comes into play in a model of rationality, I want to move beyond action skepticism and raise the challenge of the amoralist, who sees that there are moral reasons, but remains unmoved by them.

6

The Amoralist

This chapter examines and rejects several internalist arguments defending the view that we need not address the skeptic who believes that amoralism is a tenable position, for the reason that the amoralist is either inconceivable, irrational, or simply lacks a reason to act morally. The amoralist recognizes that he has a reason to act morally, but denies the force of moral reasons. This chapter defends a weak externalist view, according to which recognizing a reason to act morally may, but does not necessarily, motivate the agent. The failure of internalist arguments leaves open the possibility of a rational amoralist. Thus, we should address the amoralist in attempting to defeat skepticism, and broaden the skeptic's position accordingly. However, even if we do not defeat the amoralist because he remains unmoved by moral reasons, we will not have failed to defeat skepticism wholesale, because whether one is motivated by the reasons one has is a psychological, not a philosophical, issue. Still, philosophers may help in achieving the practical goal of people's acting morally in ways other than justifying acting morally.

1 INTRODUCTION

Although the traditional conception of the why-be-moral skeptic portrays the skeptic as one who denies merely the *existence* of moral reasons, some philosophers have noted the possibility of an even more challenging skeptical position, according to which a person, when he ultimately recognizes the existence of moral considerations, remains unmoved.[1] Call this skeptical position amoralism, and the person who actually fails to be moved by his reasons the amoralist.[2] The question I seek to answer in this chapter is whether, in order to defeat skepticism fully, philosophers must address their argument for the rationality of acting morally to the amoralist, who denies the *force* of moral reasons, or whether they may (or even should) address their argument only to someone who is already somewhat disposed to morality and so likely to be motivated by the argument, or to someone who may lack prior moral motives but who is moved by moral reasons when they are offered. If the former, we will need to broaden the skeptic's position beyond action skepticism and disposition skepticism to include amoralism. I will argue that we should not restrict the skeptic's position by assuming that people are already disposed to morality, and that we should not rule out broadening it to include the assumption of amoralism, at least not for reasons that internalists offer. Up front, I want to distinguish the amoralist from the motive skeptic who believes that it is rationally permissible merely to go through the motions in acting morally. The amoralist denies that reason has motivating force either in the sense that the reason to act morally itself must motivate the agent to act, or in the sense that the agent has a prior moral motive that makes her see the reason to act and prompts moral action.

Defeating the amoralist and the skeptic who endorses amoralism is to defeat an even stronger character than the mere action skeptic, who demands only a reason for acting morally whether or not it be motivating, thereby giving us a more comprehensive defeat of skepticism. Amoralism threatens the defeat of skepticism insofar as it thwarts our success in achieving the practical goal of people's actually acting morally. Philosophers link the theoretical and practical goals: we offer reasons at least partly because we hope to convince people to act on them. For moral philosophers in particular, achieving the practical goal is salient because the stakes are higher when people are not convinced about morality than when they are not convinced to have certain epistemological beliefs. Most of us do not worry that skeptics about the existence of the external world will step out in front of moving trains, but we do worry that skeptics about morality, no matter how philosophically sophisticated, will use, oppress, or otherwise harm others. And if our arguments by themselves convince people to act morally and they actually do so act, we will have turned a purely philosophical project into one with a profound effect on the world. So prima facie, we have reason to address the skeptic who endorses amoralism.

However, prominent philosophers such as Aristotle believe that we should address the argument for the rationality of acting morally only to those who already have their foot in the door of morality, but not to the amoralist, for reasons of persuasion. Myles Burnyeat, for instance, is one commentator who believes that Aristotle is giving a course in practical thinking to enable someone who already *wants* to be virtuous to understand better what he should do and why, and that such understanding, for Aristotle, is more than merely cognitive.[3] In one passage, Aristotle suggests that the student of ethics *must be brought up in good habits*:

> there is a difference between arguments from and those to the first principles.... Presumably, then, *we* must begin with things known to *us*. Hence any one who is to listen intelligently to lectures about what is noble and just and, generally, about the subjects of political science must have been brought up in good habits. For the fact is the starting-point, and if this is sufficiently plain to him, he will not at the start need the reason as well; and the man who has been well brought up has or can easily get starting-points.[4]

The student of ethics must be brought up in good habits because certain premises used in arguments for acting morally, such as those invoking the first principles, will be understood and accepted only by such people. Aristotle would have to throw out too much of the first principles were he not to direct the argument only to persons who are already tending to virtue.[5] Aristotle's worry is that those who do not understand the first principles are unlikely to understand and accept the argument for acting morally because they will be stuck on the premises invoking the first principles. In terms of defeating skepticism, Aristotle is suggesting that we can broaden the range of acceptable answers to the skeptic if we take him to believe that it is rational to be already somewhat disposed to morality, which would increase the likelihood of defeating action skepticism. We would not be limited, for instance, to grounding the rationality of morally required action in self-interest, but could appeal to values that are amenable to morality because we could persuade to act morally those brought up in good habits.

One problem with defining the skeptic as one who believes that it is rational to be already somewhat morally disposed, or to have moral desires, is the obvious one of begging the question in favor of morality: on EU, it is rational to act on any desires, including moral ones, so the rationality of acting morally would be easily demonstrated. Directing the argument only to those who already care about virtue and want to be virtuous might be advantageous for motivational reasons, but risks compromising a successful defeat of action skepticism. What we gain on the persuasion issue, we lose by not addressing a skeptic who accepts only self-interested reasons, or reasons of privilege on my account, and denies the existence of moral reasons. A related problem with this construal of the skeptic is that we will leave out a lot of people who either do not have a foot in the door of morality, or do not have a foot in far enough—we will not give them a reason for acting that may be motivationally effective. The skeptic needs to represent this position, not only because the skeptic should represent the worst-case scenario against morality but also because setting up the skeptic this way, I believe, captures reality. Aristotle himself worries that our arguments "are not able to encourage *the many* to nobility and goodness" because they act morally only out of fear of punishment, suggesting that he believes that many of us, at least on occasion, lack moral motivation.[6] Other philosophers, such as Gregory Kavka, are more optimistic. Kavka insists that the vast majority of humankind fall into two classes of people to whom we should direct our arguments about morality: (1) those already endowed with a conscience and moral motivations, who will get satisfaction from acting morally and suffer guilt when they act wrongly, and (2) those who are capable of developing into moral persons without excessive cost, including immoralists who are not fully committed to an immoral way of life, and children.[7] Kavka excludes only immoralists and hardened cynics from those capable of being persuaded by rational argument. No matter which position turns out to be empirically true, we should set up the skeptic to cover even the possibility that there will be persons who are at least on occasion not morally motivated, so that a defeat of skepticism will be complete.

Note that the amoralist is not pigheaded in the sense of not even being open to persuasion. Again we can draw on Aristotle, who worried about addressing pigheaded people. He says:

> it is enough in some cases that the *fact* be well established, as in the case of the first principles; the fact is the primary thing or first principle. Now of first principles we see some by induction, some by perception, some by a certain habituation, and others too in other ways. But each set of principles we must try to investigate in the natural way, and we must take pains to state them definitely, since they have a great influence on what follows.[8]

Aristotle is suggesting that we should address our arguments about morality to those who understand and accept the first principles. If a person has been brought up in bad habits, he will be pigheaded in arguments because he is not willing to accept the first principles. He will be committed, but just fight the argument.[9] There are two readings of this passage, depending on the meaning of the phrase "to have a great influence on what follows": (1) a person who lacks the first principles will not even *understand* the argument, or (2) he will understand it but not be *motivated* by it because he does not accept the first principles—he fights the argument. Aristotle is right not to address his argument to the pigheaded person since this person will have no chance of being motivated by the argument. But a person need not have the first principles in order to understand or be motivated by the argument for the rationality of acting morally. We have to assume that the skeptic can understand the argument and is not cognitively impaired, and that he is open to accepting moral reasons should they be offered. Similarly, the amoralist need not be psychologically aberrant about motivation—he just denies the force of moral reasons, but is open to persuasion by them. The skeptic believes that it is rational to be moved by other reasons, particularly ones that might issue in immoral behavior, such as self-interested reasons or reasons about one's alleged superiority in worth. So let us take the skeptic to endorse amoralism. In order to defeat the skeptic fully, we have to defeat the amoralist who denies the force of moral reasons.

Internalists about reasons and/or obligations, and motivation, believe they can show that the amoralist is either inconceivable, or lacks a reason to act morally, or does not understand that he has a reason, or is irrational. Any of these internalist responses would serve indirectly as a defeat of the amoralist. For if the amoralist is inconceivable, then it makes no sense to set up the skeptic to endorse amoralism; if he does not understand that he has a reason, then we need not address our defeat of skepticism to him; if he lacks a reason to act morally, then we need not worry about defeating him because he remains an action skeptic; and if the amoralist is irrational, then we will have defeated the skeptic who endorses amoralism. This chapter focuses largely on the internalism/externalism debate since it lies at the heart of the issue of whether philosophers need to defeat the amoralist in order fully to defeat skepticism. I believe that the internalism/ externalism debate is one of the most intractable in moral philosophy, due partly to the intuitive force of either side of the debate. It is certainly one of the most confusing, due partly to the myriad of nuanced ways these terms are used in the literature, which I will try to sort out. The main kind of internalism at issue here links reasons and motivation *necessarily* (though internalism about obligations and motivation plays a role in a response Hume might give to the amoralist), while externalism denies the necessary connection. Various versions of "reasons" internalism provide different accounts of the ways in which the amoralist's position is problematic, and they divide up in two main ways. *Humean internalism* is the view that if a person is motivated by a reason, it must be because she has some prior motivation. This thesis is described in a variety of ways in the literature. Recall Williams's description of Humean internalism as the view that A has a reason to ϕ iff A has some desire the satisfaction of which will be served by his ϕ-ing. Charlotte Brown, following Nagel, defines internalism that has been associated with Hume as the view that "if an agent perceives that a certain course of action is the right one, this necessarily means having some motive to do it."[10] Christine Korsgaard says that "Hume seems to say simply that all reasoning that has a motivational influence must start from a passion."[11] And Stephen Darwall defines Humean internalism as being "that a condition of a consideration's actually being a reason is its capacity to motivate."[12] There are subtle differences between these ways of putting the thesis, but the main feature I want to highlight now is that having a reason entails having some preexisting motive, since, as Hume believes, reason by itself cannot motivate, being only the slave of the passions.[13] The presence of a motive is essential for a reason to prompt action or to persuade. Hume's belief that reason is impotent in the sphere of desire is what drives his internalism about reasons and motives. Reasons for acting morally must be tied to some feeling the agent has: the reason persuades only those who have the relevant feeling, and the motive explains why the person acts morally. But since Hume believes that actions cannot properly be assessed as rational or not since they are prompted by motivation, not reason, this view is more properly termed *neo-Humean (reasons) internalism*. This kind of internalism has its roots in Humean moral sentimentalism, the view that an agent is motivated to do the right thing because her moral sentiments provide her with an awareness of her duty (or moral concepts or moral knowledge) and her motive for acting in light of her duty.[14] I want to contrast neo-Humean reasons internalism with another kind of internalism that has its roots in rationalism.

Rationalism is the view that the agent is motivated to do the right thing because of a rational awareness that it is the right thing to do.[15] A *rationalist internalist*, then, believes that reasons necessarily motivate the person who has a rational awareness that an act is the right thing to do. A version of this is *Kantian internalism*, according to which a reason necessarily motivates the agent to act—but provided that the agent is rational.[16] Were the agent rational, she would be motivated by pure practical reason. Kantian internalists believe, that is, that one need not have a prior motive to be motivated by the reason for acting morally, but insist, against externalists, who deny the necessary connection between reasons and motivation, that the reason *itself* necessarily motivates a rational agent. If Kantian internalism is true, then the amoralist's reason to act morally should also serve as his motive: if he has and/or recognizes the reason,[17] he will necessarily be motivated to act on it.

In this chapter, I will examine several internalist responses to the amoralist and reject them in favor of a weak externalist response. Weak externalists hold the view that recognizing that one has a reason to act morally may, but does not necessarily, motivate the agent. If internalist responses to the amoralist fail, this means that philosophers still need to address the amoralist in defeating skepticism.

Internalism, at first glance, provides a neat way of possibly uniting the theoretical and practical goals of defeating skepticism—and of achieving the practical goal by indirectly defeating, or, discounting, the amoralist—by necessarily linking having a reason and having a motive to act. I say "possibly" because being motivated need not issue in action, though not being motivated probably means not acting in the relevant way. Yet I find problematic the arguments that internalists offer in connection with amoralism, and my challenges to these arguments leave open the possibility of a rational amoralist. As I have said, I will endorse, though not fully defend, weak externalism about reasons and/or obligations, and motivation. My view is that if we broaden the skeptic's position to amoralism, or at least not rule out the amoralist for internalist reasons, even if the reason to act morally does not motivate a person to act morally, we are not left in a problematic position regarding skepticism because this psychological issue is, as Korsgaard puts it, "beyond the purview of philosophy."[18] The possibility of a rational amoralist, though it leaves open a skeptical challenge, does not after all threaten a successful defeat of skepticism; the skeptical challenge it leaves open is merely a psychological issue. Thus we should address our argument about the rationality of acting morally to a skeptic that we assume is cognitively rational in the sense that he understands the argument, but who believes that it is rationally permissible not already to be morally motivated. We can assume, in other words, that the skeptic endorses amoralism.

Before examining the arguments offered by some internalists, I need to say more about internalism and externalism, since these terms are used in a variety of ways in the literature, some of which overlap, and my critiques of internalism will turn on the nuances of the varieties of internalism I will distinguish.

2 INTERNALISM AND EXTERNALISM

I have described internalism in chapter 3 as the view, in general, that there is a logical or necessary connection between two concepts, typically reasons, motives, and obligations; externalism is a denial of this logical connection. We can be internalists about reasons and obligations, or reasons and motivation, or obligations and motivation, and externalists about any of these pairs, or we can hold a two-step internalism necessarily linking all three concepts. William Frankena defines externalism as the view that obligation (or reason) represents a fact or requirement that is external to the agent in the sense of being independent of his desires or needs, whereas internalism regards motivation as internal to obligation (or reason).[19]

Significantly, internalism is a logical thesis: motivation is logically internal to moral considerations such as reasons.[20] Internalists put this point in various ways: motivation is built into moral thought or perception;[21] knowing what is the right thing to do or recognizing a reason to do the right thing entails, or just means, having a motive (actual or potential) to do it;[22] the reason that an act is right is both the reason and the motive for doing it—it is a practical reason.[23] Leaving aside other ways that internalism is nuanced (e.g., Williams's version, according to which one has a reason only if one has a motive that one could reach by sound deliberation, and Kantian internalism, according to which one is necessarily motivated by a reason), the general point is that internalism is a claim about the very *concept* of morality, that it is in virtue of the concept of morality that moral considerations necessarily motivate.[24] Since internalism is a conceptual issue, the motivational power of morality is a priori, and does not depend on things like facts about agents.[25]

We can differentiate versions of internalism and externalism not only according to where motivation comes in but also along the lines of strength of the motivation. In general, externalists about reasons and motivation believe that (moral) knowledge is one thing, motivation another.[26] Against internalists, externalists deny that moral knowledge or a reason necessarily motivates a person. A *strong externalist* about moral reasons believes that moral reasons never motivate since they are desire-independent; motivation must come from some source external to the agent. A *weak externalist* about moral reasons believes that moral reasons can motivate—and perhaps this is the usual case—but denies that they necessarily do so; motivation may sometimes come from the agent. Some philosophers use the terms "internalism" and "externalism" more broadly, to apply to reasons in general rather than just to moral reasons.[27] So strong externalism about reasons *simpliciter* is the view that *all* reasons are desire-independent. Weak externalism about reasons *simpliciter* is the view that *some* reasons are desire-independent, while others depend on desires. A weak externalist can believe that, for instance, prudential reasons are desire-dependent and moral reasons desire-independent, or even that some prudential reasons are desire-dependent, but others desire-independent, and so on. Except when noted, I will be talking about strong and weak externalism about moral reasons and motives. I will defend weak externalism in the context of critiquing internalism.

A weak version of internalism holds that having a reason to act morally implies having a motive that need not be overriding. A strong version holds that having a reason to act morally implies the existence of an overriding motive. A strong internalist must demonstrate either that the moral motive is stronger than any other motive the agent might have or that there is something about a moral reason that it implies having this strong motive. A further assumption of strong internalism is that the overriding motive actually issues in action when there are no other factors interfering. Only a successful defense of strong internalism would achieve the practical goal of people's acting morally.

Internalism can be differentiated along another dimension, namely, that of the agent's awareness of the reason or obligation. David Brink identifies three kinds of internalism along these lines. *Agent internalism* is the view that in virtue of the concept of morality, moral obligations motivate (or provide reason for) the agent to act morally. Although Brink links obligations and reasons, we can use a two-step internalism to link obligations and reasons, and reasons and motivation, to apply Brink's definition to the issue I am concerned with, whether moral reasons motivate. Agent internalism would then be the view that in virtue of the concept of morality (or a moral reason), moral reasons motivate the agent to act morally. The significant point here is that agent internalism is objective: it ties motivation to a moral consideration independent of anyone's recognition of her obligation or reason. What we mean by having an obligation or moral reason is just that it motivates.[28] *Appraiser internalism* is the view that it is in virtue of the concept of morality that moral belief or moral judgment provides the appraiser with a motive (or reason, on two-step internalism) for action. Appraiser internalism conceptually links moral belief or moral judgment with being motivated to act; it is subjective in the sense that it links the appraiser's motives to her beliefs or judgments about moral considerations independent of whether the beliefs or judgments are correct or justifiable.[29] Thus merely believing that one has a reason or obligation to act entails having a motive to act. Finally, *hybrid internalism* is the view that it is a conceptual truth about morality that the agent's recognition of a moral obligation motivates (or provides a reason for) the agent who recognizes the relevant moral consideration to act. On a two-step hybrid internalism, the agent's recognition of a moral reason motivates the agent to act. Brink believes that hybrid internalism is both objective and subjective—objective presumably because the moral obligation (or reason) is correct or justifiable, and subjective because the agent has to recognize the obligation (or reason) in order for her to have the relevant motive.

Another source of ambiguity in internalism has to do with the precise connection between reason and motivation. Internalism is ambiguous between two views: that a reason just *is* a motive, and that the agent is necessarily *moved by* a reason. Neo-Humean internalism is generated by the view that since reason itself cannot motivate, the agent needs to have a prior motive that both makes her see that she has a reason to act and itself prompts action. Kantian internalists believe that reason itself can motivate action—indeed, it necessarily does in the rational agent. When seen as a response to neo-Humean internalism,[30] Kantian internalism is the view that the agent who has a reason necessarily is motivated *by* the reason—that is, that reason itself can motivate. Internalists often speak this way. Rachel Cohon describes internalism as saying "If S has the desire that gives rise to his reason to A, knows the facts of his situation, and deliberates rationally in the light of these, he can and probably will be moved *by* his reason to do A, because desires are inherently motivating states of mind."[31] Korsgaard calls "the internalism requirement" the view that "practical-reason claims, if they are really to present us with reasons for action, must be capable of motivating rational persons," and defines true irrationality as "a failure to respond appropriately to an available reason," suggesting that rational agents are moved *by* their reasons.[32] But saying that one is necessarily motivated *by* the reason one has is different from saying that a reason for action just *is* a motive. The former suggests that the agent recognizes the reason and then is moved by it— two different steps—while the latter suggests that the reason and the motive are one and the same thing.

Both views are problematic. The former view seems in the end to be a kind of externalism, a point that can be brought out by a distinction between neo-Humean internalism and what Brown calls "the trigger view."[33] Neo-Humean internalism is the view that having a reason entails having a prior motivation, while the trigger view is an externalist position according to which the agent's being aware that she has a duty or reason will move her to act by *triggering an antecedently given desire* to do what is right.[34] The suggestion is that the trigger view, though it closely resembles neo-Humean internalism, is an externalist position because the agent is moved to act by a prior desire to do what is right that gets *triggered by* her recognition of a reason or duty, making the reason or duty one thing, and the motive to act on it another, and thereby making it possible to have a reason or duty and not be moved by it. On neo-Humean internalism, the agent's reason for acting just *is* her motive. If Kantian internalism means that the agent is motivated *by* the reason (the agent's cognitive awareness that something is her duty or reason), it seems to be a kind of trigger view because it leaves open the possibility that the agent can recognize a reason and lack the motivation. But this is not acceptable to internalists, who link necessarily reasons and motives. Alternatively, if Kantian internalism is the conceptual view that having a reason just is having a motive in rational persons, or, that what we mean by having a reason is that it necessarily motivates rational persons, it avoids the possibility of a split between one's having a reason and not being moved, but it no longer serves as a response to neo-Humean internalism about whether reasons can motivate, which is the claim that the agent is motivated *by* the reason rather than needing to have a prior motive. Kantian internalists might try to collapse these views in the following way: a rational agent is motivated by the reason just in virtue of the reason's being a motive—the reason functions like a desire in that it motivates. But I think this is double talk, for the reason that we can separate the notion of being motivated by a reason from the notion of a reason's being a motive. My point is that internalists should sort out and clarify along the dimensions discussed the sense in which they necessarily link reasons and motives.

I now want to examine the ways in which some representative internalists might respond to the amoralist.

3 NEO-HUMEAN INTERNALISM

3.1 Hume's Response to the Amoralist

There are two answers Hume might give to the amoralist, and each depends on a different version of internalism from the one Hume is standardly taken to hold. The first response, which I do not take to be the received view since it does not address head on the amoralist who denies being motivated in the presence of reasons, stems from Hume's moral sentimentalism. It is in this context, specifically in his view of how rightness gets determined, that Hume displays his internalism about obligations and motivation.

The details of Hume's moral sentimentalism are complex. Reason, for Hume, is concerned with abstract relations of ideas or objects, such as with logic or mathematics, but it neither yields conclusions about actions nor gives us our ends, nor rationally assesses these ends—preferring the destruction of the world is on a par with preferring to scratch one's finger.[35] Hume believes that since morality is necessarily practical, and that it would be in vain to inculcate it if it had no influence on the passions and actions, it must not be derived from reason.[36] Morality excites passions, and produces or prevents actions, and since reason by itself cannot do these things, the rules of morality are not conclusions of reasons. By this Hume means that morality must be based on sentiment, and further, that we come to know our duties not through reason alone, but from having some motive.[37]

The universal sentiment of benevolence or sympathy that Hume believes we all have at least the "first seeds" of enables the agent to see that a certain kind of act promotes utility, either for the agent's self or for the agent's fellows.[38] In order to avoid bias that may arise in a situation in which the agent is directly involved, the agent is supposed to take the position of an impartial observer and observe a number of instances of a particular act present in situations in which the agent is not involved. The agent either approves or disapproves of an act or character on the basis of whether the capacity to approve or disapprove finds the accompanying feelings of benevolence or sympathy to be pleasant and useful.[39] For instance, the agent approves of taking care of one's children and of the feeling of sympathy or benevolence accompanying this act, since approval generates pleasant and useful feelings in the agent. After approving of a number of instances of this kind of act, the agent then pronounces the act to be virtuous. Having a duty to take care of one's children implies having a motive of approval of the act and of the accompanying feeling. In contrast, observing a number of instances of acts of disutility, such as one person's inflicting pain on another, generates disapproval and allows the agent to pronounce the act a vice. This process is not merely a description of the feelings we have when we observe acts and character traits, but is normative in that it determines our duties. The rightness of an act is a function of the feeling it produces: only right acts are produced by useful and pleasant feelings. For Hume, we do not first see that some act is right, and then become motivated by this fact;[40] rather, our motives determine our duties. We act from a nonmoral feeling of approval of an act. Since we all have at least the "first seeds" of the universal sentiment of benevolence, we should all have, or at least have the capacity to have, pleasant and useful feelings generated by acts of which we all approve, and thus arrive at the same duties.

Hume's internalism about obligations and motivation seems not to be agent internalism, since this view is objective in the sense that it ties motivation to a moral consideration independent of anyone's recognition of it. Hume's view that having the feeling of approval determines one's duties suggests that the agent must *recognize* her duty—approving of an act as right entails recognizing it to be a duty. This subjective element suggests that Hume holds either appraiser or hybrid internalism about obligations and motivation. Hume's introduction of utility as a measure of the rightness of a kind of act provides an objective element that makes the obligation correct or justifiable; that is, we can justify the rightness of a kind of act in virtue of the utility it produces, and this can be "measured" objectively. This suggests that Hume is a hybrid internalist. We can express his internalism about obligations and motivation as follows: recognizing a duty of virtue implies having the relevant motive, which is the complex connection between approval, benevolence, and feelings of usefulness.

Hume's sentimentalism and internalism about obligations and motives might prompt him to claim that the amoralist is inconceivable: since the amoralist lacks the moral sentiments that motivate him to act morally, he cannot believe that he has moral duties, and so obviously does not recognize having a reason to act on these duties. Anyone who recognizes that he has a duty and a subsequent reason to act virtuously would be motivated to act morally, and everyone in fact does recognize a duty and subsequent reason, in virtue of having the nonmoral sentiment of approval. The alleged amoralist who acknowledges his duties and subsequent reasons does so because he shares with the rest of us the sentiment, or "first seeds" of the sentiment, of sympathy or benevolence that accompany feelings of approval of both virtuous acts and these sentiments. Hume's assumption that the sentiment of sympathy or benevolence is universal precludes the possibility of the amoralist: if a person recognizes his duty, then he must have had the relevant feeling generated by the universal sentiment of sympathy or benevolence.

Were Hume able to dismiss the amoralist in this way, then the amoralist would pose no threat to our attempt to defeat skepticism, and we would not need to address him. But Hume's response is unsatisfactory. His argument turns on the dubitable premise that everyone has at least the first seeds of sympathy. Empirical assumptions about people's psychology are difficult to establish and subject to refutation by competing theories. If Hume cannot establish the empirical premise about universal sympathy or benevolence, then the amoralist can deny that he has it, but still insist that he recognizes his obligations and reasons to act morally without being motivated to act this way. Of course, the amoralist would have to recognize his obligations and reasons for them in some other way than Hume describes, such as through reason rather than motivation. Hume denies that this could be done, since he believes that only motivation can give us our duties and knowledge of them. This point aside, one way Hume argues for the universality of sympathy or benevolence is to ask whether we would consider the interests of a person who has gouty toes when we decide whether to walk over them. Hume says that if you have nothing to gain by stepping on them, then you will consider the pain he would have if you stepped on them and be moved by it. Hume concludes that in *all* cases, the interests of others will have authority over your sentiments.[41] But of course Hume's conclusion does not follow: a better test case would be one of a genuine conflict of interest, where a person has something to gain by setting back another's interests. Clearly, the number of these cases where persons pursue their own interests in such cases of conflict casts doubt on any empirical evidence for universal sympathy. So the amoralist can insist that he lacks the relevant motive because he lacks the alleged universal sentiment of sympathy or benevolence, even though he recognizes his obligation and reason to act virtuously. The upshot is that the amoralist is not inconceivable, and Hume is wrong to dismiss such a character by invoking claims about universal sentiments.

Moreover, it would be odd for Hume to dismiss the amoralist as inconceivable, because Hume himself acknowledges cases in which a person is not motivated to act morally. Such cases cast doubt on the existence of the universal sentiment of sympathy or benevolence. It turns out that the complex way in which we determine our duties is Hume's description of what happens only in a naturally morally sound person, one who has the natural feelings of sympathy and benevolence. The unsound person, however, lacks these feelings. But since, for Hume, obligations (and reasons) must be tied to motives, in the unsound person some other motive must kick in. In cases where the unsound person acts morally, Hume believes that the sense of duty motivates.[42] I want to focus on a case that is closer to that of the amoralist, who, since he lacks a motive to act morally, is not likely to act morally. This is Hume's case of the sensible knave, who lacks the natural feelings of sympathy and benevolence, and has "lost a considerable motive to virtue," and acts immorally when doing so promotes his self-interest.[43] The case of the sensible knave threatens both Hume's internalism about obligations and motives and neo-Humean internalism about reasons and motives, because the knave recognizes his obligation and reason, but lacks the motive to act morally. How can Hume explain this case and maintain his internalism about the necessary connection between recognizing obligations and motivation?

One possible response is Hume's claim that the sensible knave approves of a kind of act as a general rule, for example, that honesty is the best policy, but like the skeptic, believes it to be rational and wants "to take advantage of the exceptions" and act immorally when it is to his benefit. Thus the sensible knave recognizes his obligations insofar as they are general rules that when generally followed promote utility. What he approves of, then, must be the rule. He is appropriately motivated when it comes to the rule, but lacks the motive to follow the practice on occasions in which following it is not in his interest to do so. On hybrid internalism, which I have said that Hume holds when it comes to obligations and motivation, if one lacks the relevant motive, one must not recognize the obligation. We might think that Hume's response to the sensible knave who lacks the motive to be honest on the particular occasion on which he stands to benefit from acting dishonestly, and presumably his response to the amoralist, is that they must not recognize their obligation on this occasion. But Hume does not say this; instead, he offers a better reason that the sensible knave *would* recognize and be persuaded by because it appeals to some motive he has. In doing so, Hume shifts his answer from one embedded in internalism about obligations and motivation to one that relies on neo-Humean internalism about *reasons* and motives. Hume offers to the knave self-interested reasons for acting virtuously: acting virtuously provides peace of mind, consciousness of integrity, and a satisfactory review of one's own conduct, and does not risk forfeiting one's reputation.[44] Self-interested reasons persuade the knave because they appeal to his desire for the promotion of his own interest or happiness.

But a passage I cited in chapter 3 is crucial both to the response Hume might give to the amoralist and to his view of internalism. In it, Hume admits that there is nothing further to say to the knave: "I must confess, that, if a man think, that this reasoning much requires an answer, it will be a little difficult to find any, which will to him appear satisfactory and convincing."[45] This passage is ambiguous. On one reading, Hume is saying that the sensible knave does not recognize that he has a reason to act morally even if such a reason is grounded in self-interest. The knave goes wrong in his failure to recognize a reason, and there is nothing more we can say to him. We do not need to address such a person in our attempt to defeat skepticism, because he fails to recognize reasons for acting morally. Since the sensible knave lacks the motivation, he must not recognize his duty, and so of course he does not recognize a reason for doing his duty. But this does not serve as a response to the amoralist, since the amoralist, by hypothesis, does recognize that he has a reason to act morally but is not so moved—he will insist that this is possible, himself being a case in point.

On a second interpretation of this passage, Hume is saying that we cannot offer the sensible knave a reason for acting morally that will persuade him or anyone else like the amoralist, who is also unmoved by moral reasons. But since all reasons must persuade—that is their point— this means that the sensible knave or anyone who is unmotivated simply does not *have* a reason for acting morally. But reading Hume in this way in this passage supports Hume's being an *agent* internalist who believes that having a reason implies having a motive independent of whether the agent recognizes it. That is, the agent—to wit, the sensible knave and the amoralist—who is not persuaded by the reason for acting morally lacks the reason for acting morally because he lacks the motive. Hume's response to the amoralist, then, may be that he does not have a reason for acting morally.

Brink raises a problem in connection with a charge that internalists level against externalism. The charge is that externalism threatens morality on the grounds that it makes motivation separate from moral considerations and dependent on external facts, and thereby makes us lose assurance that moral considerations will motivate. But Brink responds that, ironically, agent internalism threatens morality. For if agent internalism is true, and if some people lack the motive to act morally, "then agent internalism forces us to revise our [belief about their moral obligations.]"[46] The objection is that this version of internalism—and here Brink is referring to agent internalism about obligations and motivation—leaves off the moral hook anyone who on any occasion lacks a motive to act morally. For Brink, the problem is that agent internalism makes us compromise the moral demands themselves. I would add that agent internalism compromises our defeat of *action* skepticism. Agent internalism frees the amoralist not only from his obligations but also from his rational requirements when it connects necessarily reasons and motives. Either it is the case that the agent such as the amoralist who lacks the motive to act morally lacks the reason to do so; or the agent who lacks the motive to act morally lacks an obligation, and then there is no need rationally to justify acting on the obligation in his case. But responding to the amoralist in the way suggested by agent internalism—by freeing him from his obligations and rational requirements—is merely to dismiss action skepticism, not to defeat it, much as Berkeley dismisses skepticism about the external world by simply reducing the physical world to perceptions. Neither view is a satisfactory defeat of skepticism, which would meet the skeptical challenge head on.

In sum, Hume's attempt to defeat the amoralist by showing either that the amoralist is inconceivable or that he lacks a reason to act morally, is unsuccessful.

3.2 Smith's Response to the Amoralist

Brink believes that the way out of the threat agent internalism about obligations and motives poses to morality is for the internalist to invoke appraiser or hybrid internalism, according to which recognizing that one has an obligation entails having a motive to act on it. On these versions of internalism, as I have shown, if the agent lacks the motive to act morally, she lacks merely the *recognition* that she has the obligation or reason. This removes the threat to morality that plagues agent internalism: were the agent to recognize her obligation, she would be motivated. Likewise, we might think that the way out of the threat that agent internalism about reasons and motives poses to the defeat of skepticism is to invoke appraiser or hybrid internalism, according to which recognizing a reason to act morally entails having a motive. Were the agent—the amoralist, in particular—to recognize a reason for acting morally, he would be motivated.

However, the amoralist is someone who by definition recognizes a reason to act morally yet remains unmoved. Thus, hybrid or appraiser internalists must be challenging the possibility of the amoralist by attacking the notion that someone could genuinely recognize her reason for doing her duty and still remain unmoved. The problem with the amoralist is that despite what he says, he fails to recognize that he has a reason to act morally. Michael Smith, who defends a more sophisticated nonagent version of neo-Humean internalism than Hume's own, and offers much richer arguments than Hume's, describes the amoralist in exactly this way: "the *very best* we can say about amoralists is that they try to make moral judgements but fail."[47] Smith believes that the amoralist fails to make moral judgments because he does not understand them, and I would add, his failure to understand them impedes his recognition of them. For Smith, the amoralist does not understand moral judgments because he lacks the appropriate motivation. Consistent with his view is Smith's internalism (which he calls "the practicality requirement"), which says that "it is a platitude that an agent has a reason to act in a certain way just in case she would be motivated to act in that way if she were rational" and that it follows from this that the agent who lacks the motivation is practically irrational, that is, suffering from weakness of will or some other irrationality.[48] Thus, although Smith does not explicitly say, his argument must be addressing an amoralist who does not suffer from weakness of will or "other similar forms of practical unreason on his motivations."[49] He is concerned to show what goes wrong in this kind of amoralist.[50] If Smith is right, then we do not need to address the amoralist in attempting to defeat skepticism—there is no need to address someone who does not (and cannot) understand his reasons.

Smith defends his view in response to Brink, who acknowledges the possibility of the amoralist who understands moral considerations yet remains unmoved. Brink charges that internalists cannot make sense of a genuine amoralist; rather, they can admit that the amoralist is possible only in the sense that the amoralist understands the moral sense of terms in an "inverted commas" sense.[51] That is, for the internalist, the amoralist remains unmoved by moral considerations only because he regards them in a conventional sense, taking them to be only what others, but not himself, regard as moral considerations. Brink believes that this is wrong, since he acknowledges the possibility of a genuine amoralist who understands and accepts moral considerations yet remains unmoved.

Smith argues against Brink by invoking an analogy comparing the amor- alist to a person who is blind from birth who uses color terms reliably.[52] Suppose that the blind person uses a sophisticated machine that allows her to feel "color" through her skin. When she says "Fire engines are red," according to Smith she must be using the term "red" in an inverted commas sense, namely, that "Fire engines are 'red.'" She does not possess the concept of red, and so does not master the term, even though she uses it reliably when she makes color judgments. In order to possess the concept of red, she needs to be in the relevant psychological state to make color judgments, and this entails having the appropriate visual experience. Reliable use of color terms does not indicate full mastery of these terms. Similarly, for Smith, the amoralist does not make genuine moral judgments, though he might use the right terms. Making genuine moral judgments involves being in the appro- priate psychological state of being motivated. Smith accuses Brink of begging the question against the internalist by assuming that the amoralist has mastered moral terms since he uses them reliably. But as in the color case, one needs to have the relevant motivation in order to master fully moral terms. Lacking the motivation, the amoralist does not understand what it is to have a reason to act morally, though on Smith's view, and in contrast to agent internalism, he still has a reason. Smith is able to say this because he separates motivating reasons and normative reasons, a point to which I will return.

But I believe that Smith himself begs the question against the extern- alist by assuming that a person needs to have the relevant motivation just to master moral terms like "reason." While it is clear in the color case that one needs to have the experience of seeing red to use the term "red" in a knowledgeable way, it is not clear in the moral judgment case that one needs to be appropriately motivated in order to use moral terms in the right way. What is it about making a genuine moral judgment that necessarily entails being motivated? The burden is on the internalist to explain this assumption, which seems mysterious to the externalist. To assume that mastering moral terms entails having the appropriate motivation is to assume the truth of internalism, which is just the issue. An externalist like Brink would reject this analogy, and require the internalist to offer an independent argument for what counts as mastery of a moral term rather than merely assume that motivation does. Smith, I believe, anticipates this objection and offers such an argument, but first let me raise an additional objection to Smith's analogy, since the debate does not get moved along any farther when each side begs the question against the other.

Smith compares the amoralist who is never motivated by his moral judgments to the person who has never directly experienced color. But I think that the comparison is not the right one. The amoralist can be motivated by other *non*moral judgments—he denies only the force of moral reasons. The amoralist who initially is also skeptical about the rationality of acting in morally required ways will, as traditionally depicted, be motivated by self-interested reasons. So it is false that the amoralist can ever use the term "reason" in the right (internalist) way. Only a strong externalist denies that moral reasons or judgments can be motivational. A weak externalist believes that we *can* be motivated by moral judgments, but just denies that such judgments or reasons and motivations are necessarily connected. Smith's analogy must be comparing a person blind from birth who never has a direct experience of color to a person who is *never* moved by *any* reasons, that is, a strong externalist about reasons *simpliciter*. But the amoralist can be both a strong externalist about moral reasons, and a weak externalist about reasons in general, in virtue of his being moved by reasons other than moral ones. Smith's argument does not address about reasons *simpliciter* the weak externalist, who by Smith's lights can use the term "reason" in the right way when it comes to nonmoral reasons. Smith makes the amoralist a stronger character than he needs to be.

This point aside, to avoid begging the question against the externalist, Smith offers another instructive argument intended to establish that mastery of moral terms involves having the appropriate motivation.[53] Smith claims that when a person changes her moral judgment about a matter, she reliably changes her motivation. He asks us to suppose that a person judges that he should vote for the libertarians and is motivated to do so. But the person becomes convinced by another that he should vote for the social democrats, and forms the relevant judgment that he do so. If he is good and strong-willed (i.e., does not suffer from weakness of will or some other such malady), he will subsequently have a change in motivation. There are two ways to explain the reliability of the connection between judgments and motivations: internally, according to which the motivation follows directly from the content of the moral judgment itself, and externally, according to which the connection follows from the content of the motivational dispositions had by the good and strong-willed person. On the former, internalist reading, the agent acquires a *nonderivative* concern for social democratic values: the judgment either causes or just is the expression of a nonderivative desire—that is, a desire that is not derived from some more fundamental judgment about what it is right to do in certain circumstances. On the latter, strong externalist reading, since there is no necessary connection between a judgment and a motive (these are separate), the agent's having a new judgment does not give him reason to change his motive, and he might still be motivated to vote for the libertarians. The only way an externalist can explain a change in motivation when there is one, according to Smith, is that a good person has a derived motivation "to do the right thing." Smith finds this externalist explanation problematic because it suffers from, in the words of Williams, "one thought too many." In Williams's well-known case, a man saves his wife from drowning "because she is his wife," a motive that lacks the feelings of direct love and concern for his wife. Being a good person, for Smith, means that you have direct concern for what you think is right, and not that you follow an abstract, or as Smith says, de dicto rule that you do the right thing. Since externalism commits us to the latter view, it ought to be rejected in favor of internalism.

But again, Smith's objection stands against only strong externalism. A weak externalist can admit that the motive often does come from the judgment, but simply deny that it necessarily does. Also, for an externalist, even a good and strong-willed person might remain unmoved when her judgment changes, as in the case of the meat-eater who forms the new judgment that she should become a vegetarian, yet still eats meat. If she eats meat often enough, we are right to question whether she has the relevant motive. Granted, a strong externalist has to explain why it is that a person's motivation changes when it does. Smith explains it in terms of a derivative motive to do the right thing, but I think he is wrong to reject this motive as being problematic because it suffers from "one thought too many." For suppose that a married person considers having an affair, but does not have one because she has a commitment to be committed. This abstract (de dicto) rule can motivate when direct concern for one's partner does not, and having it shows that the agent has reflected in a meaningful, morally praiseworthy way on her character. A derivative motive need not be a bad thing, morally speaking.

Moreover, Smith's own view is problematic in the way he thinks externalism is, namely, in the way that it disconnects reasons and motives. To see this, let us examine the Humean Theory of Motivation, which Smith endorses and formulates as follows:

P1: R at t constitutes a motivating reason of agent A to ϕ iff there is some ψ such that R at t consists of a desire of A to ψ and a belief that were he to ϕ he would ψ.[54]

P1 is the Humean claim that motivation has its source in the presence of a relevant desire and means-end belief. P1 insists, that is, that reason by itself cannot motivate, but needs a desire and a belief to do so.

P1 is a thesis merely about *motivating* reasons, and is *silent* about the conditions under which the agent has a *normative* reason. To say that one has a normative reason to f is to say that there is some normative requirement that one f, and so to justify one's acting thusly from the perspective of the normative system generating the requirement.[55] Normative reasons hold independent of one's desires. Importantly, Smith believes that motivating and justifying reasons may come apart:

> [the agent] may well be motivated to do what he is required to do (that is, he may have a motivating reason to do what he has a normative reason to do), he may be motivated to do something that there is no normative requirement for him to do (that is, he may have a motivating reason to do what he has no normative reason to do), and there may be a normative requirement that he do what he has no motivation to do (that is, he may have a normative reason to do what he has no motivating reason to do).[56]

Smith suggests that normative and motivating reasons are two different things, and that the agent is not motivated *by* a normative reason, though he may have a motive to do what his normative reason dictates. The agent is motivated instead by a prior motivation. And Smith's definition of a normative reason makes no reference to desire. Smith's point is really much stronger than he says: it is not that motivating and justifying reasons *may* come apart, but that a normative reason (by itself) *cannot be* a motivating reason. Smith means to separate them by definition. The Humean internalism instantiated in P1 is merely about motivating reasons; it says of the reasons that motivate that they must have a desire and a belief present.

Separating reasons in this way provides Smith with yet another way to avoid the objection raised against agent internalism that if one lacks the motive to act morally, one lacks the duty and the reason. Smith is able to say that those persons lacking the motivation, including the amoralist, still have a normative reason to act morally. But splitting reasons in the way Smith does separates the theoretical and practical goals in defeating skepticism. On Smith's internalism, and on neo-Humean internalism in general, agents cannot be motivated *by* the normative reason, but their motivation must come from some prior desire they have. At best, the motive will get the agent to see that there is a reason to act morally, but the motive itself is what actually prompts action. But we want agents to be motivated *by* the reason for acting morally, since otherwise there are better ways of achieving the practical goal than by a defeat of action skepticism, including moral education or even brainwashing—whatever it takes to instill motives to act morally. Importantly, and ironically, neo-Humean internalism is subject to the problem raised against strong externalism, that we lose our assurance that moral considerations will motivate. For the neo-Humean internalist, the prior motivation, but not the moral consideration itself, motivates. Moreover, if a nonmoral motive—either the complex connection between the feeling of approval, benevolence, and usefulness, for Hume, or a desire to ψ, together with a belief that were the agent to do what he has reason to do, he would ψ, for Smith—motivates an agent to act, then the agent's act does not have moral worth, which involves having an awareness that this is what morally ought to be done.[57] But then we lose too much of a connection between what motivates us and the requirements of morality. Smith's separating motivating and normative reasons is at least as problematic as strong externalism's disconnecting reasons and motives.

Thus I find Smith's rejection of the amoralist problematic. In sum, Smith believes that the amoralist does not understand that he has a reason to act morally because he lacks the appropriate motivation. If the amoralist does not understand that he has a reason to act morally, then there is no need to address him in attempting to defeat skepticism. If he insists that he understands, and is still unmoved, Smith believes that it is only because the amoralist understands terms like "reason" in an inverted commas sense, just as the person blind from birth understands the term "red" without ever having experienced the color. Smith is suggesting that it is impossible for there to be a rational amoralist who understands that he has a reason to act morally and remains unmoved.[58] Merely acknowledging the impossibility of the amoralist is sufficient as a defeat of amoralism—no further defeat of the amoralist is necessary to defeat skepticism fully. But I have argued that Smith's argument fails. Thus, the amoralist who understands that he has a reason to act morally and remains unmoved is possible, and we need to address him in aiming to defeat skepticism, unless there is a better argument against doing so.

4 KANTIAN INTERNALISM

4.1 Korsgaard's Response to the Amoralist

Brink believes that if the amoralist is possible, then internalists have to give up the necessary link between a moral consideration and actual motivation. Korsgaard, in agreement with Smith's "practicality requirement," offers another option: build in a condition of rationality such that *only for rational agents*, recognizing a moral consideration entails having a motive to act on it. That is, having a reason to act morally entails having a motive *in a rational agent*. Korsgaard offers the "internalism requirement" for practical reason, which says that "practical-reason claims, if they really are to present us with reasons for action, must be capable of motivating *rational* persons."[59] Thus she defines a practical reason in terms of whether it is a deliberation that is capable of motivating a rational person.[60] On Korsgaard's view, if an agent is not motivated to act morally, it follows not that he lacks a reason to act morally, or that he does not recognize such a reason, or does not understand it as Smith argues, but that he is not rational. The amoralist, then, is irrational, but conceivable.[61] His irrationality does not falsify internalism.

Korsgaard rejects both neo-Humean internalism and Hume's view that reason by itself cannot prompt action, in favor of Kantian internalism, the view that having a reason to act morally is itself capable of motivating every rational person who recognizes it.[62] Against Smith, who separates normative and motivating reasons, against Williams, who believes that external reasons (those not necessarily related to motives) are false or incoherent, and against Hume, who on an agent internalist reading believes that one's lacking a motivation means that one lacks the relevant reason, Korsgaard argues that skepticism about practical reason (whether reason motivates) need not entail skepticism about pure practical reason (whether there is a reason to act morally). Just as a person's lacking a motivation to do what is in her greater good throws no doubt on the argument that preferring one's greater good is rational, it is also the case that a person's not being motivated to act morally throws no doubt on the argument for doing so. Korsgaard's general point about reasons is that the extent to which people are actually moved by rational considerations "is beyond the purview of philosophy," which can at most tell us what it would be like to be rational. If we were rational, we would be so moved, but if we are not moved, then we are not rational.[63]

Although I endorse Korsgaard's conclusion that motivation is beyond the purview of philosophy, I want to raise some objections to her arguments. The central argument is her powerful analogy comparing practical and theoretical reason that is intended to show that a person who recognizes a reason to act and remains unmoved is irrational. According to Korsgaard, being *motivated* by a reason (practical reason) is just like being *convinced* by an argument (theoretical reason): "For me to be a theoretically rational person is not merely for me to be capable of performing logical and inductive operations, but for me to be appropriately *convinced* by them: my conviction in the premises must carry through, so to speak, to a conviction in the conclusion."[64] Korsgaard cites Aristotle's example of the novice in scientific studies who can repeat the argument but lacks the right conviction until he really understands it. Many things—passions, distractions, illnesses—might cause a person not to be motivated by a reason or convinced by a good argument. But a good argument is just that, and an agent's failure to be convinced by it is indicative of her irrationality, according to the internalism requirement for theoretical reason. Similarly, according to the internalism requirement for practical reason, an agent's failure to be motivated by a reason is indicative of her irrationality. The necessity or compellingness of both a good argument and of a moral consideration lies in the consideration or argument, but not in the agent.

Before addressing the analogy itself, let me speak first to theoretical rationality, and clarify what I take to be Korsgaard's point. Consider the following pairs of questions. Does theoretical rationality require merely that *if* you believed the premises of an argument, you would believe the conclusion? Or does it require that when you actually *do* believe the premises, you should, on pain of being irrational, believe the conclusion? Put another way, does theoretical rationality say that if you were convinced *that* the premises of an argument were true, you would be convinced *that* the conclusion were true? Or does it say that if you were convinced *by* the premises, you would be convinced *by* the conclusion? The first question in each set does not require that the agent have any belief about, or commitment to, the premises; it refers only to a hypothetical belief that the agent may have. The second question in each set requires that the agent have a further psychological, dispositional component; it poses a stronger requirement about the agent's being engaged in a certain way, psychologically, with the argument. On the strong requirement, the agent actually acquires the belief (she has a disposition to believe x, or in the case of practical reason, to do x). The strong requirement seems to be the sense in which Korsgaard understands theoretical reason: there is a psychological, dispositional component to theoretical rationality, such that actual, but not mere hypothetical, belief carries through from the premises to the conclusion in a rational agent. The point is not about the argument—how the premises are linked to the conclusion—but about the agent, his psychological relation to the premises and the conclusion. The strong requirement is more resistant to counterexamples, so it better supports Kantian internalism, but it exposes a weakness in the analogy, as I will try to show.

To illustrate further the difference between the strong and weak versions of the theoretical requirement and the weakness in the analogy, consider the familiar argument demonstrating the problem of evil: (a Judeo-Christian) God is all-powerful, all-knowing, and all-good; but evil exists; therefore, (a Judeo-Christian) God does not exist. The weak requirement of theoretical rationality affords the person who hears this argument the opportunity to be more objective about it because he understands it hypothetically, as an "observer" who lacks the relevant psychological commitment. Were the argument to commit him to something he did not want to believe, he would find it easier to resist than he would on the strong requirement, say, by denying that he believes all the premises, denying that he believes them as stated, and so on. The strong reading requires the person who actually believes the premises to believe the conclusion: the belief carries through from the premises to the conclusion. If the person resists the conclusion, but remains convinced by the premises, we, along with Korsgaard, charge him with being irrational. What lies behind the charge of irrationality is that the resistant person has inconsistent beliefs, since in a valid argument the conclusion is contained in the sum of the premises. The person believes the premises, yet believes the denial of the conclusion: he believes that God exists. Having inconsistent beliefs establishes why it is odd—and irrational—to be psychologically committed to the premises of an argument but not to its conclusion.

Let us now turn to Korsgaard's analogy comparing practical rationality to theoretical rationality. The analogy is designed to show that the agent who is unmoved by a moral consideration is irrational in the same way as the agent who is not convinced by the conclusion of an argument whose premises he believes in. My objection is that in the case of a failure of practical rationality, there does not seem to be an inconsistency of any kind that would explain the agent's supposed irrationality. There is no psychological or dispositional component in just recognizing a practical reason that fails to carry over to the motive to act on it. Now Korsgaard might mean to suggest that there *is* such a psychological component, one that would explain an inconsistency. She defines being practically rational as being appropriately *motivationally responsive* to a reason for action.[65] But being appropriately motivationally responsive is ambiguous. It might mean that the agent is psychologically disposed in such a way that when she recognizes the reason, she will be motivated; the agent who recognizes the reason but lacks the motivation displays a motivational inconsistency. But this builds in motivation in a question-begging way because it implies that recognizing the reason already means having motivational responsiveness. It implies the strong reading of the requirement of practical reason, which is that the agent is engaged with the reason because she is already motivated: recognizing the reason means the agent is motivated to act on it. Further, this view is similar to neo-Humean internalism, a view that Korsgaard rejects, so it is not open to Korsgaard.

Alternatively, being appropriately motivationally responsive to a reason might mean being psychologically disposed to it in such a way that when the agent recognizes the reason, she will be motivated. But this does not establish the internalist's point that the rational agent will *necessarily* be motivated. After all, a weak externalist can define practical rationality as being appropriately motivationally responsive to a reason in the sense that a practical reason can, but need not, motivate the rational agent. Thus despite the initial power of Korsgaard's analogy, it does not demonstrate that the agent who fails the internalism requirement for practical reason is irrational.

Korsgaard supports her view that the agent who fails the internalism requirement for practical reason is irrational with an example that suggests another way to explain an inconsistency underlying a failure of practical reason. She believes that a failure in means/end rationality exemplifies *true irrationality*, which is a failure to respond appropriately to an available reason.[66] If an agent recognizes the reason for having a desired end, and believes that certain means will achieve the end, she should be motivated to take these means. If she is not, she is irrational. There is supposed to be an inconsistency here: the agent is motivated by a certain end, but is not motivated to take the necessary means to achieve the end.

But, in response, not all cases of failures in means/end rationality are obvious cases of irrationality. Suppose that I am in Lexington, Kentucky, and very much want to be in Chicago in a couple of hours. The only way for me to get there in such short time is to fly. But I despise flying: I dislike the treatment I routinely get from airport security personnel, I am afraid of heights, I dislike sitting next to bothersome people, and so on. My fear of heights cannot be dismissed out of hand as irrational: I might know about air safety requirements, how often planes are inspected, and how they are fixed, and be aware that anything mechanical can fail at any time and that planes do on occasion go down, and just not like the sensation of being up in the air. It is not obvious that my recognizing that I have a reason to take a plane to Chicago and wanting to be in Chicago in a short time motivates me to take a plane or means that I want to do so. If I do become motivated and eventually get on the plane, my motivation certainly does not come from the reason, but more likely from my trying to convince myself that my fears and dislikes are exaggerated. Similar things can be said about wanting to be slimmer or to have healthy teeth, but not wanting to take the necessary means to do so: there is nothing irrational about not liking dieting or fearing the pain of a dentist's drill. Even if these cases did show that it is irrational to want the end but not the means, and thus that there is an inconsistency in motivation, this does not establish that recognizing a reason and failing to be motivated is like this, because in the latter case there is no inconsistency in motivation, as I have just argued.

Korsgaard supports her view that reasons necessarily motivate in yet another way that is independent of inconsistency: she discounts as a kind of irrationality any failure to be motivated by a reason that an agent— presumably including the amoralist—has. Some of the things that might interfere with the motivational influence of a given rational consideration include rage, passion, depression, distraction, grief, physical or mental illness, failing to observe rational connections, being "willfully" blind to them, being indifferent to them when they are pointed out, self-deception, rationalization, and weakness of will.[67] Korsgaard admits also that it is unclear when a reason is "available to us," since there are cases in which we do not know about the reason, or we could not possibly know about it, or we deceive ourselves about it, or we have some physical or psychological condition (as those just listed) that makes us fail to respond to it. She admits that as we move down the list, "there is progressive uneasiness about whether the claim is becoming external," but the test for the reason's being internal is that "if a person did know and *if nothing were interfering with her rationality*, she would respond accordingly."[68] Thus an amoralist who claims not to be moved by reasons for acting morally presumably is, for Korsgaard, irrational in one of these ways.

One problem with this defense of internalism is raised by Jean Hampton. Hampton objects that building in so many exceptions concedes too much to the externalist, since (Kantian) internalism then "does not require that a motive *actually* accompany a reason, but only that it ought to do so."[69] Hampton thinks that externalists can accept the claim that motives ought to accompany a reason; they dispute only the claim that motives *must* accompany reasons. Korsgaard and Hampton might end up at loggerheads over this issue, but in order to refute Kantian internalism, we need to show the possibility of a rational person's recognizing a reason without the reason's being motivationally efficacious. If we can show this, then we can admit the possibility of a rational (or at least, not obviously irrational) amoralist. In the next section, I examine a case that I believe is one of a rational person who recognizes a reason but is not motivated.

4.2 The Case of the Deferential Wife

To be clear, such a counterexample to Korsgaard's view does not speak to the conceptual issue of what a reason is, but to the substantive issue of whether there are instances of rational persons who are not in every case motivated by the reasons they have. A Kantian internalist might insist that since internalism is a conceptual issue about the meaning of the term "practical reason," no counterexample succeeds in defeating it. But even conceptual claims can be challenged. For instance, although we define "bachelor" as an unmarried male, the existence of Catholic priests and young boys legally ineligible for marriage challenges the definition because these persons lie outside the institutional norms to which the term traditionally applies. Challenging conceptual points is even more appropriate when there is a serious dispute over the meaning of terms, as there is in the internalism/externalism debate. Moreover, resorting to a conceptual point as a way of dismissing any purported counterexample would be an unsatisfactory defeat of the amoralist. For on it, the amoralist would necessarily be irrational—just look and you will find the way in which he is—and the kind of skeptical challenge he raises would never arise. On these internalist positions, were we to defeat action skepticism, we would automatically, by a definitional move, defeat the amoralist, since the amoralist who remains unmoved when he has reason to act morally is irrational or, on a view like Smith's about a rational amoralist, fails to understand what a reason is. But this is too quick. Certainly a similar kind of move would not be an acceptable defeat of *action* skepticism: attempting to defeat the skeptic who believes that acting rationally is acting self-interestedly merely by defining rational action as (including) moral action is not sufficiently attentive to the details of the debate and calls out for defense.

Thomas Hill's case of the Deferential Wife, which I mentioned in chapter 4, serves, I believe, as a counterexample to the view that all instances of a failure to be motivated by a reason are cases of irrationality.[70] As Hill describes her, the Deferential Wife is servile, or lacks self-respect, because she does not acknowledge her own worth; rather, she is utterly devoted to her husband, tending not to form her own interests, values, and ideals, and when she does, counting them as less important than her husband's—which she dutifully satisfies. Curiously, she believes that women are mentally and physically equal, if not superior, to men, but that their proper role is to serve their families, which she is glad and proud to do. This case displays a symmetry between Korsgaard's view about practical reason and Kant's view that when fully rational, persons necessarily respect themselves.[71] Recall that Kant suggests that a rational agent need only engage in rational reflection to see herself as having intrinsic worth, and would put aside conflicting factors such as social influences that would make her not be self-respecting. Putting this in terms of the internalism debate, presumably Korsgaard and Kant would say that were the Deferential Wife to recognize a reason for being self-respecting, she would, if rational, be appropriately motivated. I will argue that her confusion about her worth is what prevents her from being motivated by the reason to be self-respecting, but that this need not impugn her rationality.

The fact that the Deferential Wife does not acknowledge her own worth makes her prima facie irrational, according to my earlier argument. In chapter 4, I argued that informed desire tests need to add another condition of rationality, that a person acknowledge her intrinsic worth. To be clear, I built this in as a constraint on the desires it is rational for a person to have. But this is an ideal condition, and it is consistent with this that a person not recognize her own worth and yet not be irrational. Such is the case sometimes when circumstances prevent a person from acknowledging her intrinsic worth, as in the case of the Deferential Wife whose confusion about her worth stems from the social circumstances in which she has lived her life.

Here I will elaborate on the case as Hill describes it. Under patriarchy, the Deferential Wife may have been harmed by direct and indirect acts of sexism. Statistically speaking, she may have been a direct victim of rape, sexual harassment, battery, and devaluation by her teachers, which would have threatened her belief in her worth even if she at the time had it.[72] She is indirectly harmed in virtue of being a member of the group, women. The existence of rape and sexual harassment, for example, harms all women by degrading their image and perpetuating stereotypes that women are weak, helpless beings in need of protection. Finally, the Deferential Wife is the victim of institutionalized sexism, which occurs when, for example, employers perceive women as less reliable workers— and so pay them less or do not hire them—because they opt out of the paid labor force to raise children because of the gender wage gap.[73] These and other forms of sexism prevalent in a patriarchal society devalue women by attempting to degrade them and establish men's dominance over them. They often mask their message of inferiority as the right way for people or states of affairs to be, which contributes to the Deferential Wife's confusion about her worth. The Deferential Wife is likely to believe that *morality* requires servility over self-respect: commonsense morality, which reflects the ongoing ideology of her society, gives us the wrong view about what self-respect requires, namely, that women stand by and nurture men while sacrificing their own interests and needs, and even some philosophical moral theories require excessive altruism.[74] The Deferential Wife internalizes the message of degradation, and becomes a "bargainer with patriarchy," who knows patriarchy's influence on her desires and options, has conflicting deformed and autonomous desires, and chooses in ways that best uphold her identity.[75] She ends up being servile because she legitimately doubts her own worth. Kant's view is that were the Deferential Wife rational, she would put aside these strong social influences and overcome her confusion about her worth. The Kantian internalist's view is that were the Deferential Wife rational, she would recognize that she has reason to be self-respecting and be appropriately motivated.

I deny both views. I agree with Cynthia Stark that labeling the Deferential Wife as irrational for not being self-respecting is too harsh, and that setting the bar for rationality this high is to engage in victim-blaming, since judgments of rationality are often used to marginalize groups whose members' identities are constructed by "institutions and ideologies that function systematically to impede the development of a robust sense of worth" in them.[76] That is, instead of blaming the sexist social norms, practices, and institutions, the Kantian judgment that a victim of such circumstances is irrational places the blame for failing to be motivated by a reason squarely on the victim and her rational capacities. It says that there is something wrong with *her*, or more accurately, her reasoning skills or motivational capacities. But this is false: the Deferential Wife reasons correctly, understands what it means to have intrinsic worth, sees that if a person had intrinsic worth she would respect herself, but gets the facts about her worth wrong in her own case due to her experiences. On enough occasions, she is sent the message that women are inferior in worth to men, and this legitimately confuses her about her value and makes her conclude that she is inferior in worth. Thus, I agree with Stark that a person can genuinely and sincerely, but mistakenly, conclude that she has little or no self-worth, and, I would add, doing so does not impugn her rationality. She is like any patriarchal woman who cannot shake her deformed desires using reflection in a "cool hour," as I discussed in chapter 4. Were she to live in a different world, and have different experiences, she *would* acknowledge her own value and not be confused about it. Kant is being idealistic (or unfair) in thinking that anyone, *no matter what her circumstances*, would on reflection acknowledge her worth, or be motivated by a reason she had to be self-respecting. The Deferential Wife's confusion, after all, is about her worth, which is fundamental to her identity and governs her worldview and her choices about career, politics, and even having children—she is confused about *herself*.

This confusion, rather than any of the conditions of irrationality Korsgaard lists, is what prevents her from being motivated by the reason she has for being self-respecting. As Hill describes the case, the Deferential Wife does not have any of the psychological failings of rage, passion, and so on. Clearly she is not indifferent about her moral status or her reason to be self-respecting, because she believes that women are mentally and physically equal, if not superior, to men, and holds the (bad) moral principle that a woman's duty is to serve her family. She really believes she is doing the right thing. Of course, she cannot really believe both that women are equal to men and that they should serve their husbands, so she must be thinking they are unequal in *worth*. This is to be mistaken about Kantian equality, which is confusion, not indifference. Nor is she negligent: we are not assuming that she does not rationally reflect on her moral status or on her reason to be self-respecting when she should. She merely comes up with the wrong answer—getting it right requires being visionary and scrutinizing her principles in addition to her preferences. Nor is she self-deceived, which typically involves a person's lying to himself that he is still a good person in spite of his failure to live up to his moral standards. The Deferential Wife lives up to the servile principle she believes in, and would be able to face her intrinsic worth were she to come to see it fully. She is not self-deceived about having a reason to be self respecting—she just gets confused about her worth, and her confusion gets in the way of her being motivated by her reason to be self-respecting, which is a perfectly rational response to her circumstances. It is much like the case that Susan Wolf describes, of the Victim of a Deprived Childhood, who was given no love and was beaten by his father and neglected by his mother, and later in life embezzles money.[77] Wolf argues that he could not have had reason not to embezzle, even though there were reasons around, because his reasons are determined by his circumstances.[78] As Wolf says, the problem is not with the functioning of his reason, but "that his data were unfortuitously selected." The Deferential Wife is not weak-willed, which requires that she recognize her worth but succumb to emotion and not be self-respecting. When it comes to her "wifely role," she is confused about her worth. And she does not rationalize, which also requires that she recognize her worth but tell herself a story that it is false. She acknowledges that if someone recognizes his worth, then, when rational, he will be motivated by the reason to be self-respecting, but because she herself does not believe that she has intrinsic worth, she fails to be motivated by the reason. My view is that in the Deferential Wife's case, her *circumstances*, not a failure of rationality (i.e., the state of her rational powers), are what legitimately stand in the way of being appropriately motivated when she has a reason to be self-respecting.

The case of the Deferential Wife shows that it would be too quick to impugn a person's rationality if she fails to be motivated by reasons she has. There may be circumstantial or even political or other reasons for not being so motivated. Consider again the problem-of-evil argument concluding that God does not exist. A person who is convinced by the premises but still believes that God exists has inconsistent beliefs, but might nonetheless have good reason to believe in God, such as when a close friend or relative suffers from a serious illness or has just died and believing in God provides comfort to the believer, or when the person is a priest or nun and jettisoning his or her belief in God would eradicate too much of his or her identity. These cases raise the issue of whether there are other factors involved in determining (practical) rationality in addition to the link between having a reason and being motivated. Clearly, we do not want to concede too much here, since one reason to offer arguments is to convince and motivate others, and being convinced or being motivated are indicators of rationality. The weak externalist would agree. My point is merely that we ought to be careful in excluding as irrational anyone who is not motivated by the reasons they have.[79] Moreover, the factors that Korsgaard lists as ones that might interfere with a person's rationality defined in Korsgaard's way as being appropriately motivationally responsive to practical reasons may actually be ones that prompt a response that is rational in some other sense. Consider passion. Consider the case of a woman who has been repeatedly seriously physically abused by her husband, who has no good options available, and kills him in self-defense. Even though she suffers psychologically from the abuse, and kills out of passion, there is nothing irrational or psychologically wayward with responding to a threat to one's life in this way, and with recognizing that one has a reason not to kill and not being motivated. Indeed, passion might be exactly what prompts a rational response.[80]

4.3 Further Thoughts

An advantage that externalists have over Kantian internalists is that they do not impugn people's rationality in every case that they fail to be motivated by the reasons they have. Kantian internalists have two options: either impugn people's rationality when they fail to be motivated by the reasons they have, or deny that people have certain reasons. Kantian internalists might take the second route when, for instance, there are actions that are too demanding to motivate necessarily a rational agent. The worry is that it is open to the internalist to resist reasons, for instance, for avoiding sexist behavior, when persons are not motivated by these reasons and internalists do not want to impugn their rationality. Korsgaard would probably deny this, and insist that if there are reasons, there are reasons, and it is not up to the internalist to resist them. But this is the only option for a Kantian internalist who does not want to impugn people's rationality when they are not appropriately motivated. The list of rational, morally required actions may be restricted to ones that rational agents are capable of acting on in the sense that their not being motivated and not performing these acts will not impugn their rationality.

While the case of the Deferential Wife raises the possibility of a rational person's recognizing a reason and remaining unmoved, an objector might insist that it does not defend the possibility of a rational *amoralist*. To do this, we need to show that *the amoralist* is not irrational despite his not being motivated by moral reasons. One way the internalist might support the charge of irrationality is to show that one of the factors Korsgaard lists interferes with the rationality of the amoralist. But as I have described his position, none of these factors is obviously present—we just know that he is not moved by moral reasons. But if one of these factors is present, it is likely that the amoralist is also an immoralist, and so his *acts* are irrational on the grounds that they are instances of his privileging himself by trying to make himself superior to others, as in weakness of will, indifference, and self-deception. Internalists might support the irrationality charge by claiming that the amoralist is *never* motivated by any reasons. But only a strong externalist about reasons *simpliciter* is never motivated by reasons, and as I have shown, the amoralist is motivated by self-interested reasons. And just like the action skeptic who is open to the rationality of acting morally, the amoralist is open to being motivated by moral reasons were we to demonstrate the rationality of being so motivated. An internalist might find it odd—and irrational—for the amoralist to be selectively motivated, and demand an explanation as to what it is about moral reasons that are not motivating for him. But an internalist would have to explain what it is about only moral reasons in particular that they necessarily motivate.[81] For if all practical reasons necessarily motivate, then internalism has not made any headway in achieving the practical goal: we can be equally motivated by self-interested and moral reasons, and neither is decisive about how we will act. Only strong internalists, who believe that moral reasons yield overriding motives, have a shot at achieving the practical goal, but then they have to explain why moral reasons have overriding force.

The internalist who believes that a rational amoralist is conceptually impossible will want the externalist to explain what a reason is if it is not a motive, to show that reasons and motives can be split in a rational agent, and to show what motivates a rational agent if a reason does not. Interestingly, Hobbes, whom Korsgaard and Nagel take to be a paradigm internalist, has, I believe, an externalist view that can answer these questions. Hobbes describes the rational agent who moves from the State of Nature to the cooperative state with the rules of a contractarian morality in place and generally followed. The case of the rational Hobbesian agent shows additionally that the agent can, and not in an odd way, be moved by a separate motive, "what serves me best." And it shows why we still want people to be moved by their reasons, even if they are not necessarily so moved.

On internalism, the reason that a person does an act and the reason that the act is right are one and the same thing—the reason just is the motive.[82] Korsgaard believes that Hobbes is an internalist because self-interest both motivates and justifies the Hobbesian agent's actions. Korsgaard collapses justifying and motivating reasons in a rational person: a person is *moved by* self-interest (a motivating reason), and self-interest *justifies* the act in question (a justifying reason). An externalist denies this identification: even though both the justification and the motive are self-interest, either they can be split, on weak externalism, or they are split, on strong externalism. Hobbes believes that we are all naturally motivated by self-interest, a desire which we do not lose when we move from a State of Nature to a cooperative state. What does change, however, when we move out of the State of Nature, is the Hobbesian agent's view of what is in his self-interest. That is, the Hobbesian agent in the State of Nature believes that satisfying his desires, no matter what they are, promotes his self-interest. He might desire to lie, cheat, break his promises, even kill, and when he and others with similar desires act on their desires, an all-out war ensues. To get out of the State of Nature, each rational Hobbesian agent lays down rights that all others agree to lay down, and in doing so sacrifices satisfying some of his desires that he once believed, when satisfied, would best promote his own interest. He sees that it is better for himself to strive for the benefits of cooperation if others do so as well, even though cooperating requires him to give up the pursuit of some of his desires. In essence, he goes from having short-sighted self-interest in the State of Nature to having enlightened self-interest in the cooperative state. The content of his justifying reason in the State of Nature thus becomes more sophisticated in the cooperative state. However, nothing changes about his desire or motive: he still wants to do what serves him best.

Since the content of the Hobbesian agent's reason changes, but his motivation does not, this is a case where the agent's reason is not the same as his motive. His motive must be a separate one, such as: "because it is serves me best." This motive, since it is general, does not reflect the content of his reason. We have seen that Smith rejects the agent's having a general motive, "because it is right," on the grounds that it invokes "one thought too many." Korsgaard also rejects the agent's having such a separate motive, but on the grounds that it is as odd in the case of practical reason to require a special psychological mechanism (a desire to do one's duty) that motivates, as it is in the case of theoretical reason to require a belief (that the conclusions of sound arguments are true) that convinces.[83] But since the content of the Hobbesian agent's reason changes, but his motivation does not, there is no oddness in the externalist position that he may be motivated by a separate motive, "because it serves me best." The fact that the Hobbesian agent acts on this motive, and not on his justifying reason, does not obviously impugn his rationality. In addition, the case of the Hobbesian agent shows that the agent is not motivated *by* the reason he has; that is, he is not motivated by the content of the reason, but by the separate motive. Recall the ambiguous way that internalists describe their position, that the reason just is a motive on the one hand and that the agent is motivated by the reason for acting on the other hand. This example shows that either reading of internalism is incorrect.

Admittedly, it would be bad for the project of defeating skepticism were there no connection between reasons and motives. The Hobbesian agent has the motive of self-interest all along, in both the State of Nature and in the cooperative state. It is possible that this motive prompts action independent of the justification. When the agent moves from the State of Nature into the cooperative state, he might recognize the new content of his justifying reason, and think "Great, the justification I have for acting in the cooperative state is still in line with my motives." He treats the justification as an afterthought. I have argued that philosophers want the reasons they offer to motivate. The weak externalist can have this point in a way that is sufficient for uniting and achieving both the theoretical and practical goals. Unlike strong externalists, who hold reasons to be desire-independent, weak externalists merely deny that reasons are desire-dependent. Weak externalists can, with Korsgaard, define a reason as a consideration that motivates a rational agent, but simply deny that it necessarily does. They believe that having a practical reason can be determined by external factors not related to the agent's desires. They admit the possibility that a rational person can sometimes be motivated by things other than reasons, such as passion, a general rule about the rightness of acts, or even the authority of reason,[84] or not even be motivated at all.

5 CONCLUSION

Internalist arguments, were they successful, would show that the amoralist is inconceivable or irrational or just lacks a reason to act morally, and thus that we should not try to defeat the amoralist for a successful defeat of skepticism. I have tried to show that these arguments are not conclusive. This leaves open the possibility of a rational amoralist. Since a rational amoralist is possible, we should broaden the skeptic's position to include amoralism. What implications does this have for a successful defeat of skepticism?

Korsgaard is right that whether people are in fact motivated by their reasons is beyond the purview of philosophy. But she and I differ in the conclusions we reach. Korsgaard's view is that philosophy gives us reasons, and whether they motivate us determines whether we are rational, because we begin with the *conceptual* claim that practical reasons are reasons that necessarily motivate rational persons. My view is that philosophy gives us reasons, and whether we are motivated is strictly a *psychological* issue that is beyond the purview of philosophy. Since I do not endorse the conceptual claim, I do not draw a conclusion about a person's rationality. Regarding the amoralist, then, Korsgaard would write him off as irrational and of no threat to the defeat of skepticism. I have argued that the failure of internalist arguments leaves open the possibility that the amoralist is not irrational. But the possibility of a rational amoralist, though it leaves unmet a skeptical challenge, does not jeopardize a successful defeat of skepticism, because whether reasons motivate is purely a psychological issue. In the end, we should not, for internalist reasons, deny the amoralist's challenge; we can broaden the skeptic's position to amoralism. But we should not deem our defeat of skepticism to be a failure if it does not convince the amoralist.

We might think that philosophers are helpless in achieving the practical goal if we fail to defeat the amoralist because he will remain unmoved by reasons to act in morally required ways. But this is false. The point about motivation being beyond the purview of philosophy is that unless the amoralist is in his position for a reason that philosophers can legitimately address, and not for some psychological reason, such as being indifferent, pigheaded, or resistant, then we do not have to defeat him in order to defeat skepticism fully. It may very well be that the reasons people are not moved by moral reasons are themselves legitimate subjects of philosophical scrutiny. For instance, there may be political and sociological reasons, in addition to reasons concerning psychology and morality, that some people are not moved by reasons for being nonsexist. Philosophers can redirect their arguments to making institutional changes, say, by analyzing the notions of privilege and structural sexism and their role in the lack of motivation. Changing the structure of unjust social institutions is likely to effect changes in people's motivations. So, too, is "world-traveling," which gets others to see things from the perspective of the oppressed.[85] For instance, since men have never had women's experience of being degraded in virtue of their group membership, "world-traveling" might help them to understand the psychic harms involved in this kind of degradation, including loss of self-esteem or feeling inferior or helpless, and to see how these harms can affect job performance, leading to loss of economic equality.[86] Thus there are other ways that philosophers can aid in achieving the practical goal than offering reasons for acting morally.

Finally, in labeling the issue of motivation as a mere psychological one, I do not mean to dismiss the role of motives in defeating skepticism. I believe that rather than aiming to defeat the amoralist for whom moral reasons are not motivating, we should aim to defeat what I will call the motive skeptic. Motive skepticism is concerned with whether in acting morally the agent must act from a certain motive, as dictated by the moral theory, rather than merely going through the motions. I turn to this issue next.

7

The Motive Skeptic

This chapter examines whether we need to defeat motive skepticism in addition to action skepticism for a complete defeat of skepticism. The motive skeptic believes that it is rationally required to act in morally required ways, but believes that there are no rational requirements on the relevant motives, but that it is rationally permissible merely to go through the motions in acting morally, without acting from the motive that the moral theory in question deems ideal. One reason not to extend the project of defeating skepticism to motives is that we cannot acquire motives we do not have. But then we should have the same worry about actions we cannot perform. Some internalists believe that the project of defeating skepticism extends only to those with the relevant motives. But there are problems with this version of internalism. So this reason does not count against our having to defeat the motive skeptic. One possible way indirectly to defeat the motive skeptic is to show that having reasons and motives that are not in harmony is a mark of schizophrenia of the kind that some philosophers believe plagues modern moral theories. This kind of disharmony is a mark of irrationality, which shows that having a rational requirement to act in morally required ways while believing that it is rationally permissible merely to go through the motions is an untenable position.

1 INTRODUCTION

In the previous chapter, I argued that we should aim to defeat the amoralist in our attempt to defeat skepticism, but that if we fail to do so, this is not problematic for our defeat of skepticism, since whether a person is motivated by reasons she has is mainly a psychological issue. Yet whether a person *has* certain motives is not (just) a psychological issue. I distinguish the amoralist from the motive skeptic: the amoralist denies that moral reasons necessarily motivate, while the motive skeptic believes that it is rationally permissible merely to go through the motions when acting in morally required ways. The motive skeptic denies that rationality requires that one have and act from the motives the moral theory at issue deems ideal. I argue in this chapter that going through the motions when acting in morally required ways leaves the agent in a position of irrationality, which serves as a defeat of the motive skeptic.

Although philosophers have had things to say about motives, they have traditionally ignored whether and how motives might fit into the project of defeating skepticism. In chapter 2, I showed that in attempting to defeat skepticism, Gauthier makes the dispositional move, and aims to defeat both disposition and action skepticism. But dispositions are different from motives. I will have more to say about dispositions and their relation to actions in chapter 8, but for now, a disposition is a tendency to act a certain way, while a motive is what actually prompts action. In chapter 3, I showed that care ethicists are concerned with acting in caring ways and from the motive of care, but I had to embellish their view about motives and their connection to reasons in terms of defeating skepticism. Most moral theorists join care ethicists in identifying a motive they take to be ideal, one that makes a person a moral person in the full sense rather than one who just performs right actions. These are the motives at stake in defeating motive skepticism. I will highlight three different motives deemed ideal by the relevant theories and that are at the center of the debate. They represent theories that are Kantian internalist, neo-Humean internalist, and externalist, emphasizing the fact that motive skepticism cuts across the internalism/externalism debate and is an issue for any moral theory that deems a certain motive to be ideal. The internalism/externalism debate, however, will surface once again in section 2, where it is central to the argument that we need to defeat motive skepticism for a full defeat of skepticism. I shall first say a bit about the motives at issue.

First is what Kant calls the moral motive, or acting for the sake of duty. This is the motive of respect for morality itself. The Kantian motive prompts the agent to act, but the agent must first know what her duty is, which is determined by the Categorical Imperative. I have shown that Kantian internalism is the view that reason, or knowing one's duty, necessarily motivates a rational person. The motive the reason generates is the moral motive. To flesh out what the moral motive amounts to, Barbara Herman argues that Kant does not endorse "rule-fetishism," whereby the agent's motive is to act in conformity with duty. Instead, the agent's motive is to do the particular act in question—for example, to keep her promise to her friend to take him to dinner. According to Herman, the agent "is not trying to bring about 'kept promises' or even 'her kept promises.' [The agent is] trying to do what [she] promised, because [she] promised to do it." The duty is: "Keep your promises." The object of the agent's action is to take her friend to dinner. The motive, then, is to fulfill a promise to take her friend to dinner, as this is morally called for.[1] Kant is concerned to defend the moral motive because he believes that other motives, such as caring for others, self-interest, and other inclinations, are likely to lead the agent astray by causing her to do other than what duty requires.[2] Indeed, only the moral motive will not have this effect because it has rational content, meaning that the agent must know her duty in order to act for its sake. Marcia Baron defends the Kantian motive against criticism that it is too cold or abstract on the grounds that being a responsible moral agent requires that one have some conception of why the things one lets be one's guide in deliberations about conduct are good guides; the agent who acts from the motive of care "lacks a higher order aim of 'doing what is right.'"[3]

Care ethicists, though, agree with Michael Stocker, who believes that the motive of care is essential for caring for others noninstrumentally and not treating them as replaceable.[4] They deem the motive of care to be ideal: without this motive the person is morally remiss because she does not feel emotion toward others themselves.[5] Recall Noddings's view that we should act out of care or concern for a particular person rather than compassion in general, emphasizing being related in a certain way to "the other," that is, having and maintaining close personal relations among family and friends.[6] Recall that Noddings suggests that we do not have obligations to care for those with whom we are not in close relationships because there is no way that caring for them can be completed without abandoning the caring in personal relationships that is our obligation.[7] Noddings's aim is to develop a theory that "preserves our deepest and most tender human feelings,"[8] which are present only in close relationships. She claims that the test of one's caring lies partly in how fully one receives the other.[9] We have seen in chapter 3 that care ethicists are neo-Humean internalists who believe that having a reason to act necessarily entails having the motive of care: acting in a caring way must be prompted by the ideal motive of care.

A third representative ideal motive is that offered by John Stuart Mill. Mill believes that people are not motivated by his argument for the principle of utility, but by utilitarian feelings that are acquired from moral education. Mill believes further that cooperating with others gives a person the feeling that the interests of others are her own interests, and that sympathy and the influence of moral education can lay hold of the smallest germs of this feeling. This utilitarian feeling is the ultimate sanction of the greatest happiness morality.[10] Korsgaard characterizes Mill as a strong externalist about reasons and motives, since the reason or argument for the principle of utility does not motivate the agent to act in utilitarian ways, but the agent is motivated by something completely external to this reason.[11]

These and other moral theories morally require that agents have and act from the motives they each deem ideal. Presumably, each would also make this a rational requirement, though as I say, there is not much discussion of the rational requirement in the literature. The motive skeptic denies the rational requirement: he believes that it is not rationally required to have and act from (ideal) motives, neither in their own right nor by the falsity or defeat of action skepticism. Let us assume for the sake of argument that we have defeated action skepticism, and that the agent acts morally. The question is why he acts morally. The motive skeptic's position about motives might be that they do not matter: as long as one acts morally, it does not matter what prompts that action. But given our assumption that we have defeated action skepticism, the agent's motive should be one that is likely to issue in moral action on many occasions. Self-interest will not suffice because of the occasions on which self-interest and morality conflict. Feeling threatened also fails because threats can be removed. Not reflecting but acting morally because one has been raised to do so comes close, but runs the risk that the person will one day reflect and choose to act otherwise. The aim is to describe the motive skeptic as one who believes that it is rational to act morally, but that a person who only acts morally is not a moral person in the full sense.

So instead of thinking of the motive skeptic as believing that it is rational to have one of the motives just described, let us take him to believe that rationality requires that he act morally but that it is rationally permissible for a person to do his duty but only halfheartedly. An SIB contractarian scheme is useful in explaining his position further. The motive skeptic believes that it is rationally permissible for an agent to acquire a moral disposition, and that her disposition prompts moral behavior even when she can expect to get away with acting immorally. What prompts her to become morally disposed is that she thinks morality is necessary to achieving a better world: she sees that we are all better off in general if we act morally than if we do not, and becoming morally disposed is likely to issue in moral action. She not only sees that the world is a better place in a utilitarian sense, but she sees that she herself has a greater probability of benefiting in such a world, as compared to a world in which most people do not follow the dictates of morality. Moreover, she believes that her becoming morally disposed is necessary for making others believe that she is a morally good person. She can then expect to benefit, for only if others take her to be a morally good person will they treat her in morally good ways. Once she has adopted a moral disposition, she acts on it. So because of her disposition, she acts morally even when she can expect to benefit from reneging, unlike the purely self-interested person. But because morality often requires her to make sacrifices, she deems it to be a necessary evil: it is necessary for the world's being good and for her convincing others that she is moral in order to get the benefits of morality, such as similar treatment from others.

At the risk of trivializing the moral case, I compare her to the person who eats vegetables in order to benefit himself yet does not acquire a taste for them. He prefers junk food because he likes the taste of it but disposes himself to eat vegetables because of the benefits he expects to get from eating them. He eats vegetables halfheartedly, unlike the person who actually likes them. He is not a healthy eater in the full sense because he lacks a real commitment and the motives that go along with it. Both the junk food lover and the person who lacks moral motives but acts morally have motives that in some way fall short of the best they could be.

Even though the halfhearted agent is morally disposed, what prompts her to do her duty is none of the motives I have described: neither care for others nor mere recognition of her duty, nor motives generated from moral education. Instead, she views morality as a constraint, and is rational to do so, according to the motive skeptic. If morality would not contribute to the world's being a better place, and if the agent's acting morally would not have any chance of convincing others she is a moral person, she would neither dispose herself to act, nor actually act, morally. Thus, she is unlike all of the following: the Kantian agent who respects morality for its own sake and is motivated to do his duty because it is his duty, the follower of the care ethic who acts from the motive of care for others independent of the consequences, and the utilitarian who Mill describes, who is motivated by his utilitarian upbringing. Like the person who acts out of self-interest or out of habit, or because she feels threatened, the agent merely goes through the motions in acting morally. I describe her this way because she neither cares about others nor respects morality, nor is motivated by a moral conscience acquired from a proper upbringing, but is indifferent to these things. She is unlike Gauthier's "liberal individual," the person on whom morality takes an affective hold, who comes to value morality and other moral persons.[12] She is likely to act morally most of the time, even though she is not a moral person in the full sense. She is prompted to act from her disposition, which she acquires because of the expectation of benefits from the moral world and from convincing others that she is a moral person. But technically, in a way she is motive-less, because she lets her moral disposition carry her through her actions, while showing no real commitment to morality since she deems it a necessary evil and acts morally halfheartedly. I will describe her "motive" as "going through the motions," for short. The motive skeptic, then, believes that it is rationally permissible merely to go through the motions in acting morally, and denies that rationality requires that an agent act from an ideal moral motive. "Going through the motions" is not a moral motive because the object of the agent's actions is not truly a moral one, though she acts morally. Kant's distinction between moral rightness and moral goodness is helpful on this point: the agent does what is morally right, but she and her acts lack moral goodness or worth because she lacks the appropriate motives. She falls short of the truly moral agent, but because of her disposition she acts morally in every possible situation in which acting morally could be required.

Now philosophers might be reluctant to broaden the skeptical project to defeating motive skepticism. After all, it is difficult enough to defeat action skepticism, particularly if we broaden the action skeptic's position to be grounded in privilege more generally rather than self-interest more narrowly. But there might be good reason to extend the project of defeating skepticism to include a rational requirement about the motives that agents must acquire and from which they must act. For one thing, motives have bearing on achieving the practical goal of people's acting morally. If we can show that merely going through the motions in acting morally is irrational, and that having and acting from the motive that a theory deems ideal is rationally required, those persons who follow reason and acquire the relevant ideal motive are more likely to act morally than otherwise. Further, if we can demonstrate that merely going through the motions in acting morally is irrational, then we will have defeated the motive skeptic who believes that this is rationally permissible. We want to show for a complete defeat of skepticism that rationality requires that a person *be moral*, that is, be a moral person who both acts morally and who acts from a certain motive. One of the main insights from care ethicists is that morality demands that people act in ways that are richer or fuller in ways related to motivation than merely overcoming self-interest or respecting rights, which is what rule-oriented theories require. Motives are not captured by rules, and if we require agents to act from the motive of care in particular, they will have richer moral lives when they do, and our moral theories will be richer. Having the right motive, whatever it is, and being a moral person in the full sense, might even be intrinsically desirable, as Kant believes.

The arguments of this chapter do not show *which* motive it is rational to acquire and act from, but only that motives are appropriate targets for skepticism, and that merely "going through the motions" would leave a person who has this "motive" in a position of irrationality. There are two main arguments. The first aims to refute a major objection to the view that motives are appropriate targets for skepticism, namely, that we cannot rationally require a person to adopt and act from certain motives if she cannot do so. I conclude from this that we need to defeat motive skepticism, and so we should broaden the skeptical project accordingly. The second aims to show that if we defeat action skepticism, but not motive skepticism, we will sometimes have to hold agents to be obliged to perform rational actions from irrational motives. I conclude from this that motive skepticism is an untenable position, and this serves as a way to defeat the motive skeptic.

As a point of clarification, one might think that my claim that endorsing motive skepticism would leave the agent in a position of irrationality because her reasons and motives would not be in harmony, commits me to endorsing Kantian internalism, the view that the reason to act morally must itself motivate the agent to act. But the motive skeptic holds the view that one has a reason to act morally, yet lacks the right motive, *whether or not the motive comes from the reason to act morally.* The motive that a given moral theory deems to be ideal might come from the reason to act, as in the Kantian motive of acting for the sake of duty, or it might be prior to the reason to act morally, as in the Humean motive of care that is necessary for prompting acting in a caring way, or it might be entirely independent of the reason to act morally, as in Mill's utilitarian motive that is generated from moral education. Because we believe that fully moral persons should have moral motives whatever these may be, and because we believe that reasons should motivate (rational) agents though they need not nor do not always do so, as I have already argued, we should believe that a disharmony between reasons and motives is schizophrenic, as Stocker claims, and so irrational. In short, it does not matter, for describing and for defeating the motive skeptic, how agents acquire moral motives or whether motives are logically related to the reason for acting morally; what matters is that when agents who act on moral reasons lack moral motives, they are irrational because of the disharmony between their reasons and their motives. The problem arises not just for the theories I have discussed, but for any moral theory.

2 REASONS TO DEFEAT THE MOTIVE SKEPTIC

An important objection to the idea that motives are an appropriate target for skepticism is most often leveled against the motive of caring about others. The objection is that it is not within the power of a person to come to adopt certain—or for that matter, any—motives. Given the dictum "'Ought' implies 'can,'" it follows that we cannot rationally require a person to come to adopt the moral motives at issue. The objection usually comes up in the context of the motive of caring because it is thought that we cannot make a person such as the one who merely goes through the motions in acting morally come to care about others. Some people just lack this motive, so we cannot rationally require that they acquire it. Indeed, one of Kant's objections to Hume is that it is false that everyone has benevolence or sympathy, and since morality must be teachable, it must not be based on this or any other feeling but on reason.[13]

But the objection could, of course, be raised also against the Kantian motive of acting for the sake of duty. Again, acting for the sake of duty amounts to recognizing what your duty is, and then being prompted to act by the fact that something is your duty. The prompting requires no prior motive such as caring about doing your duty. Yet it seems to be as out of place as in the case of caring about others to say that the person who is indifferent to morality ought rationally to acquire the Kantian motive. Perhaps Mill is right to think that we must bring up people in a utilitarian environment in order for them to come to acquire utilitarian consciences and motives—short of this, they cannot become so motivated. The objection, then, is that since we cannot rationally require that a person acquire moral motives, we cannot judge a person who merely goes through the motions to be irrational. Motives are beyond the scope of rationality.

Whether the objection that it is difficult, if not psychologically impossible, for a person to acquire motives she lacks, is true, turns, I believe, on the motive, the object of the motive, and the person herself. For instance, a person who was never interested in football might come to desire watching it after the home team wins a crucial and exciting playoff game. A person might be able to motivate herself to lose weight after moving to a city in which many people are physically fit, or by listening to a physician's advice. A person who strongly dislikes the town he has to live in because of his job might come to like it and to be motivated to stay when he compares it to the alternatives. Some people who harbor racist or sexist beliefs are able to shake them and change their behavior and motives after they reflect seriously on arguments against prejudice. Still, it might be difficult for a person to like what is evil, or to motivate herself to do things that require a huge time commitment or a great deal of energy. And it is difficult to imagine Hitler's being motivated to care about the Jews, or being motivated not to commit the heinous crimes he did, since his character seems to stand in the way. Hitler might have been, as Gilbert Harman says, beyond the pale, lacking even the *capacity* to be motivated to act morally.[14] But this kind of extreme case is rare; commonplace immoralists might be more susceptible to acquiring moral motives.

The acquisition of these motives can come about by argument and other ways. A hunter might come to care for animals after reading Peter Singer's exposition about the unethical treatment of animals in experimentation, or after working in an animal shelter, or even after acquiring a pet. A racist might come to care about blacks after reading about the treatment of slaves in the southern states, or after working side by side with blacks. Some cases will be more challenging than others, partly because some people are set in their ways, and partly because the kind of motive involved may be difficult to acquire for a variety of reasons. For instance, a person might find it difficult to acquire a desire for Chilean sea bass if she realizes that this fish is on the endangered species list. A person might find it hard to want to shop at a discount store when she learns that it exploits its workers. Or a person might resist the object of the motive because of short-term self-interest, such as when a junk food junkie cannot see past the pleasure she gets from eating junk food and fails to be motivated to eat food that is better for her health. Unless we identify something peculiar to moral motives such that persons cannot come to acquire them in the ways that they acquire the nonmoral motives in the cases just described, then they, too, are candidates for acquisition. It is legitimate, then, to require that we demonstrate that we are rationally required to acquire them. Despite the difficulty with acquiring the moral motives of care, of respect for morality, and for promoting the general welfare, unless the person is a Hitler-type—and perhaps even then—it is at least possible.

All of this aside, and more to the point, the worry we have about motives—whether we can rationally require people to acquire them—is a worry we should have also about actions. Yet many moral philosophers seem to have no hesitation in saying that in order to defeat action skepticism we must show that every morally required act is a rationally required one; that is, we rationally require people to act morally even if they believe they cannot. We certainly assume this in attempting to defeat action skepticism, so this assumption is not unique to motive skepticism.

Regarding action skepticism, one ought, rationally speaking, to do the morally required act. Since "ought" implies "can," we must believe that acting morally is something we can do, that is, are capable of doing. And we do not readily excuse anybody from its dictates: from the ordinary person who on occasion acts immorally, down to Hitler-types who commit heinous acts, many moral theorists, including Kant, Mill, and Bentham, intend to show that every person has reason to act morally. Whether the person is a Hitler-type who might be incapable of acting morally to the same extent that he is incapable of acquiring moral motives is irrelevant, according to such theorists, to whether acting morally is rationally required.

Of course, neo-Humean internalists would disagree, not because they think people should be off the hook because they cannot act morally, but because of the logical link between reasons and previously held motives. I said that for some neo-Humean internalists, the project of defeating action skepticism extends only to those with the relevant motives. Recall Brink's objection that agent internalism forces us to revise our beliefs about reasons and obligations; it leaves off the hook, or frees from duty or reason, persons who lack the relevant motive, or, in Harman's case, persons who lack the capacity to be motivated. Harman believes that unless one has at least the capacity to be motivated to act morally, then if one does not already have the motive, one does not have a reason or an obligation to act morally. Perhaps what leads Harman to say this is his belief in the dictum "'Ought' implies 'can.'" He holds a two-step internalism, according to which having an obligation to act implies having a reason to act, and this implies having a motive, or at least the capacity to be motivated, to act: "If someone S says that A (morally) ought to do D, S implies that A has reasons to do D and S endorses those reasons . . . such reasons would have to have their source in goals, desires, or intentions that S takes A to have and that S approves of A's having because S shares those goals, desires, or interests."[15]

There are two ways to read Harman's internalism, each of which is problematic for defeating skepticism. On one version, the person must actually possess the relevant motive to act in order to have a reason to act. This is the stronger reading of Harman's internalism. But then Brink's point stands: for anyone who lacks the relevant motive on any occasion, she lacks a reason to act morally as well. Although many of us are unlike Hitler in that we do have moral desires, on those occasions when we lack such desires, we lack a reason to act morally. This leaves a lot of instances of a person's acting morally not backed by reason, and thus compromises a defeat of action skepticism.

Interestingly, and significant for defeating skepticism fully, neo-Humean internalists have a good reason to defeat skepticism about motives.[16] The neo-Humean internalist who believes that having a reason to act morally is dependent on having a prior motive should want to show that rationality requires having that motive. For the neo-Humean internalist in particular, demonstrating the rationality of moral motives might lead to establishing the rationality of acting morally because it will mean that if one has a motive to act morally, then one has a reason to do so. Of course, it would be a further step to show that this reason overrides competing reasons to act otherwise, or, that rationality *requires* acting morally.

A second version of Harman's internalism, which is a weaker version of internalism that I did not discuss in the last chapter, is the view that one has a reason to act morally only if one has the *capacity* to be motivated to act morally—one need not actually have the motive.[17] The problem with this version of internalism is that everyone seems to have at least the capacity to be so motivated. We would think otherwise if we believed, implausibly, that people are so hardwired that they cannot in any way adjust their psychologies. In some sense, even Hitler has the capacity to change: if he were raised differently, if he had undergone cognitive psychotherapy, or if he converted to Judaism, he may not have been motivated to do the things he did. So even Hitler can have a reason to act morally in virtue of having the capacity to be motivated to act morally. But if this is right, it leaves the Humean-type internalism that Harman may be advocating in the position of externalism, according to which everyone has a reason to act morally, no matter what his or her actual motivations are. In addition, it is difficult to see what function the capacity to be motivated has in determining whether one has a reason to act. For what is it about Hitler's having merely the capacity to be motivated to act morally that gives him a reason to act morally? It seems that Harman's versions of internalism either exclude too many people from the bounds of morality—those who are not motivated to act morally on any given occasion—or include too many people within the bounds of morality: those who have only the capacity to be motivated to act morally but who are not actually so motivated.

These internalists aside, other internalists as well as externalists about reasons and motives believe that all persons are rationally required to act morally no matter whether they are motivated so to act. They, of course, believe in the dictum "'Ought' implies 'can,'" in that they probably would not judge a person to be irrational if she failed to act morally because she was held under force or was physically incapacitated. So why the discrepancy? Why do they believe that a person does not have a reason to act morally if she is under force or is physically incapacitated, but that she does have a reason even if, in the case of externalists, she lacks the relevant motive, or in the case of Kantian internalists, she lacks a prior motive to act morally? One reason might be that they believe that everyone, or at least anyone who is rational, is capable of being motivated to act morally, and that lacking moral motives, prior or otherwise, will not get them off the moral hook: they still have reason to be moral. But more to the point, both Kantian internalists and externalists believe that the rationality of acting morally is decided *independently* of motives. For externalists, reason is one thing, motivation another; reasons and motivation are not logically related. One ought, rationally speaking, to act morally whether or not one is motivated to act this way. Kantian internalists also believe that one is rationally required to act morally, no matter whether one is motivated with a prior motivation. They believe that if one is rational, one will be motivated, but by the reason itself. Recall Korsgaard's view that skepticism about practical reason does not threaten the view that one has a reason to act morally since the latter is decided independently of one's motivation.

It is interesting to note a parallel between acts and motives for both neo-Humean internalists and for Kantian internalists and externalists. About acts, neo-Humean internalists say that if you lack either moral motives or the capacity to be motivated, you are off the hook: you are not rationally required to act morally. If neo-Humean internalists believe this at least partly because they believe that we cannot rationally require people to act in ways that they are not motivated to act, then it would be incoherent for neo-Humean internalists not to let a person off the hook also in the case of motives. If a person like Hitler is off the hook about acting morally because he lacks moral motives, he will be off the hook about acquiring moral motives if it is too difficult for him to do so.

Kantian internalists and externalists want to extend the project of defeating action skepticism to everyone who is rational, independent of their motives (or previously held motives, in the case of Kantian internalists). One response they might give to the neo-Humean internalist who believes that it does not make sense to say that a person has a reason to act morally if she cannot acquire the motive to do so is that anyone can acquire this motive. Kantian internalists believe that the reason for acting morally will itself necessarily motivate a rational person; weak externalists believe that this reason can, but need not, motivate a person; strong externalists believe that reasons and motives are separate, and that if we ascribe reasons even to those who lack motives, then we should be able to require rationally that those who lack motives acquire them. The point is that whatever any of these positions say in relation to people's capacities about acts as targets for skepticism, each will say the same thing about motives as targets for skepticism.

I have objected to neo-Humean internalism in the previous chapter, and to Harman's version of it in this section. In addition, I have said that neo-Humean internalists have reason to defeat motive skepticism, that it might lead to defeating action skepticism. Since both Kantian internalists and externalists believe that acts are appropriate targets for skepticism, they should think that motives are as well. Thus, at least not for neo-Humean internalist reasons, we will need to show that for a complete defeat of skepticism, rationality requires in addition to acting morally that an agent acquire and act from certain motives, and not merely go through the motions.

3 DEFEATING THE MOTIVE SKEPTIC

There is another argument that cuts across the internalism/externalism debate, that might be offered in response to the objection that it does not matter what a person's motives are so long as she acts morally. If the objection is right, then there is no reason to think it necessary to defeat the motive skeptic. The argument tries to show that it does not matter what a person's motives are. More important for our purposes, we can develop the central point of the argument to show that it serves as a defeat of the motive skeptic by showing that his position is untenable. The argument can be generated from Stocker's view. Fleshing out his view a bit further, Stocker argues that modern moral theories are guilty of "moral schizophrenia" because they ignore motives and focus instead on reason, justification, duty, and the like. Moral schizophrenia is a split between one's motives and one's reasons: either one is not moved by what one values or has reason to do or one does not value what one's motives seek.[18] Stocker does not characterize the issue as the internalism/externalism debate all over again, but believes instead that schizophrenia between motives and reasons is bad because it would lead to a life that is not in harmony, but is essentially fragmented and incoherent.[19] Stocker believes that one motive in particular, namely, care for one's family and friends, has been largely ignored by modern moral theories, including egoism, utilitarianism, and Kantianism, but is essential for fellow feeling and community.[20] Either these theories do not value the beloved for the beloved's sake, but only insofar as doing so promotes one's own welfare or is a general source of pleasure, or they altogether leave out motives such as love, or care, more generally. None of these theories properly values the beloved; rather, they treat people as replaceable.[21]

The motive of care underlies moral schizophrenia. For suppose that a person is rational and adopts the motive of care. She will lead a schizophrenic life if she tries both to act on this motive and to follow any modern moral theory. Stocker's view is a strong one: he believes that modern moral theories *cannot* incorporate the motive of care in the right way. Since schizophrenia is necessarily a problem for such theories— assuming as Stocker does that we have and act from the motive of care—the person must give up either her motive or the theory in order to have a life in which her reasons and motives are in harmony.[22] I believe that Stocker would jettison modern moral theories in favor of a theory such as the ethic of care, since on this theory, one's motives and reasons are in harmony: one has reason to act in a caring way and from the motive of care.

Our concern is whether we can defeat the motive skeptic by showing that acting on moral reasons and not from a moral motive but merely going through the motions is schizophrenic in ways I will describe, and thus irrational. So I will leave aside the details of Stocker's argument, but rely on his notion of moral schizophrenia as a way of showing that the motive skeptic's position is untenable. I will understand Stocker's notion of schizophrenia more generally to be a disharmony between the reasons a person has for acting morally and her motives for acting this way, and not just a disharmony between the motive of care and reasons to act according to the dictates of modern moral theories. This disharmony is one that any theory faces, and it is not peculiar to any version of internalism or externalism. The issue is not whether a person must be motivated by her reasons, but that her reasons and motives prompting moral action do not go hand in hand. I will go in to explain in the rest of this section that when a person's reasons and motives fail to go hand in hand, the person is irrational in an important way.

Suppose we defeat action skepticism for either modern moral theory or the ethic of care. Suppose that a person then acts morally but merely goes through the motions, without either respecting morality or caring about others or wanting the general welfare. The claim is that her reasons and her motives are not in harmony and so she exhibits schizophrenia, which is a kind of irrationality. There seem to be two ways an agent can exhibit schizophrenia, neither of which Stocker elaborates on. One occurs when the agent does not value what his motives seek, such as when a mother loves her son but acts only for self-interested reasons. A second way the agent exhibits schizophrenia is when he is not moved by what he values or has reason to do, as when the agent believes he has reason to act in his own self-interest, knows that doing x is in his self-interest, and does x, but is moved not by concerns of self-interest but by a concern to appear prudent. I am concerned only with the second kind of case, since we are assuming that we have defeated action skepticism and want to know whether rationality requires having and acting from the relevant motive. The task before us is to show why the person whose motives and reasons are in disharmony is indeed irrational. Since the arguments I will present show that the disharmonious person is irrational in different ways, and since I am not defending a full-fledged theory of rationality that is needed for a complete defeat of skepticism, I will rely on an intuitive notion of rationality.

I will examine several explanations for why a person whose motives and reasons are not in harmony does not acquire moral motives so as to achieve this harmony. I will try to show that in each explanation, either this is not what is going on with the person or the person is irrational. I conclude that going through the motions is irrational when one both believes that acting in morally required ways is rationally required and one acts morally. If I am right that this is irrational, then demonstrating the irrationality of being at once a nonaction skeptic and a motive skeptic serves as a way to defeat motive skepticism.

So first, perhaps acquiring moral motives does not occur to the person suffering disharmony. But then she displays irrationality because she does not consider all the options that would allow her to achieve her goal, particularly ones that would provide obvious and excellent ways to

generate moral action, such as acquiring moral motives. Further, it is necessarily false that the idea of acquiring moral motives would not occur to her,
for if she wants merely to be *seen* as a morally good person, she must be
aware of the alternative of actually being a person with moral motives, since
it is this alternative that she rejects. So this is not what goes on in her case.

So perhaps she is just lazy. She might believe that having and acting
from moral motives takes too much energy—for instance, it is too hard to
care about others in the way that Stocker suggests, seeing them as irre-
placeable. But then it is likely that she expends more energy trying to fight
off acquiring moral motives than acquiring them and acting from them.
And this is irrational, too. But would the disharmonious person have to
fight off moral motives? It seems that she would, since it seems that our
actions shape our dispositions, which in turn influence our reasoning, our
motives, and subsequent actions. In the case of the agent at issue, the
person's acting morally influences her motives, causing her to acquire
moral motives. Thus she must fend off moral motives throughout her
lifetime as she continues to act morally. This is a third possibility of what
goes on in her case. I will say more in chapter 8 about the influence of
moral actions on one's dispositions, but we can now consider some cases
removed from morality in which actions influence motives. Consider a
person who is not interested in sports who works with people who talk
about sports all day long and take her to sporting events, and then acquires
a desire to go to these events and to talk about sports. Or consider a
person who lacks a desire for material goods, but gets a job that pays well,
finding herself surrounded by good quality, high-priced items, and being
treated by her clients and colleagues to expensive nights on the town and
fancy lunches. She comes to desire these things and activities because she
is surrounded by them or engages in them frequently. In such cases, prima
facie it is rational for the person to acquire these motives because her
actions bring them about. Unless she has some reason for not acquiring
these motives, such as that they are deformed by an unjust system and the
result of adaptation to her circumstances, she is rational to acquire them
because they cohere with her actions. Presumably the same kind of thing
happens in moral cases—acting morally influences the motives a person
acquires. Suppose a person would rather not exercise patience with
slower people. She recognizes this about herself, and decides not to
move to the front of the line to get on the bus, but waits for the elderly
and parents with young children to board. She waits in traffic, too, and
takes her place in line in stores instead of cutting to the front. Her actions
can make her want to be patient because she comes to appreciate why it
takes certain people longer to do these things. Since we are assuming that
the disharmonious person acts morally, she must fend off moral motives
that her actions tend to make her acquire. One way she could do this is
to bind herself not to acquire moral motives in the same way that an
indulgent person who wants to stop overeating binds himself to modify
his behavior in the future.

Jon Elster sets out a number of conditions that must be met in order for a behavior to be an instance of binding oneself.[23] One is that the person must "carry out a decision at time t1 in order to increase the probability that [the person] will carry out another decision at time t2."[24] And "the effect of carrying out the decision at t1 must be to set up some causal process in the external world."[25] For example, the indulgent professor who wants to lose weight decides to work at his campus office rather than at home so as to make food less available. The case of the disharmonious person is slightly different from the indulgent professor's case. If she is to bind herself, she would need to set up a causal process to modify her desires, or more accurately in this case, to prevent a modification in her desires, but not to modify her behavior. After all, she still wants to act morally to achieve the goals stated. So she needs to set up some causal process in order to prevent herself from acquiring moral motives.

Binding oneself can be rational or irrational. The indulgent professor's binding himself by working at his campus office and avoiding the cafeteria and places with vending machines is rational, but becomes irrational if he must stay in his campus office all his waking hours. Elster's view about the rationality of binding oneself is that "the resistance against carrying out the decision at t1 must be smaller than the resistance that would have opposed the carrying out of the decision at t2 had the decision at t1 not intervened."[26] Applying this to the case of the indulgent professor, the resistance against deciding to work at his campus office must be smaller than the resistance against not overindulging. Staying at his campus office all his waking hours would provide greater resistance than the resistance against not overindulging, and so would be irrational. The disharmonious person's case is again slightly different from the case of the indulgent professor who has to fight off a preestablished inclination to overeat. Unlike the indulgent professor, the disharmonious person does not have moral motives. Rather, she has a desire to have others believe that she is a moral person, which is a desire whose satisfaction she can achieve only by acting morally. But since acting morally is likely to issue in moral motives, she ends up in a position similar to that of the indulgent professor in that she has an inclination she has to fend off, though the inclination has not already been formed as it has for the indulgent professor. In the disharmonious person's case, since she acts morally most of the time, the influence of her actions on her desires is likely to be strong. She would have to set up some external causal process such that every time, or almost every time, she acts morally, it prevents her from acquiring moral motives. There is an oddness, though, in saying that she comes to be inclined to do x by doing x, rather than doing x because she is inclined to do x. So I will reformulate what she must do in the following way: the disharmonious person must be able to get herself voluntarily to act morally (when there is no penalty for not acting morally, but only for not being inclined to do so) without getting herself to prefer to act morally.[27]

On the face of it, it seems to make sense to say that one can voluntarily do things one does not prefer to do, such as going to a friend's funeral or waking up early in the morning. This is because acting voluntarily does not mean that one wants to do what one does; rather, it means merely that one acts willingly. The real problem—the one that arises for the disharmonious person—is whether one can get oneself voluntarily to do x, *without preferring* to do x. Can the disharmonious person get herself to act morally without preferring to act morally? Notice this inconsistency: doing x voluntarily suggests that one is willing to do x; getting oneself to do x suggests that one is not willing to do x. This tension suggests that getting oneself to do x voluntarily, without preferring to do x, is implausible.

But this may be too quick. Consider this example: suppose one realizes that one prefers having the best job, and that the only way to get the best job is to live in an undesirable place. It seems as if one *can* get oneself voluntarily to do x, without coming to prefer doing x. What one prefers is y, and one realizes that doing x is necessary for having y. In the case of the disharmonious person, she prefers having people believe she is a moral person (y), so she gets herself voluntarily to act morally (do x), without preferring to act morally. So it seems that a person's binding herself to acquire moral motives is not irrational.

But on closer inspection, I think it is misleading to say that the disharmonious person really does get herself voluntarily to act morally. Put aside whether she prefers to act morally, that is, whether she has moral motives. There is something else amiss in this case: the voluntariness of her action. I think that what really happens is that she voluntarily gets herself in the state of having y (having others believe she is a moral person). After all, were she not able to convince people that she is a moral person by acting morally, as I have described her, she would not act morally. We cannot read off from her behavior that she is acting morally voluntarily, willingly. That would be like reading off of women's behavior when they act in sexist ways that they voluntarily did so, ignoring the role of deformed desires in their actions. I do not think it makes sense in the case of the disharmonious person that she gets herself voluntarily to act morally. In general, it is implausible for a person voluntarily to get himself to do x, without preferring to do x. So this is not what is going on in the disharmonious person's case after all.

A fourth explanation for what is going on in with the disharmonious person is that she simply cannot acquire moral desires, so in order to act morally, she just makes herself believe that she is a morally good person in the full sense. In fact, Elster describes going through the motions as acting as if you believe in order to generate the real thing.[28] "The real thing" means two different things, each of which is problematic. On the one hand, if "the real thing" amounts merely to acting morally, the disharmonious person does not need to make herself believe that she has moral desires in order to generate "the real thing" because her desires to benefit the world and herself are sufficient for her adopting a moral disposition that prompts moral action.

Yet "the real thing" might mean being a moral person with moral motives. Here, though it might be true that the disharmonious person cannot come to develop moral motives, it is not true that she makes herself believe that she is a moral person in order to generate "the real thing." As I have described her, she does not want to acquire moral motives, but prefers to dupe others. She does not want to acquire moral motives because she fears that if it turned out that she could no longer expect benefits from the world where most people followed morality, and she were disposed to acting morally from moral motives, she would not be able to change. She would act morally even in this case, and thus would lose out as others could take advantage of her. She is the opposite of Gauthier's "trustworthy person," or, truly moral person, who disposes herself to act morally and does so even when it turns out that the system no longer provides her an expectation of benefit.[29] Of course, on the face of it, this makes it seem as if it can be rational to want to be disposed to go through the motions, but not to be moral in the full sense. If so, motive skepticism would be a rational position. But it is false, because the disharmonious person's fear of being taken advantage of in a moral world is unwarranted: she *would* benefit. And, if the whole system of morality collapsed, and she could no longer expect to benefit, then she could change her motives. So going through the motions by making oneself believe that one is a moral person in the full sense is not rational because it is based on a false fear. So the disharmonious person is not making herself believe that she is a moral person in order to generate "the real thing."

A fifth possibility is that the disharmonious person acts from a desire to benefit the world and herself, but *believes* she is a morally good person with the best of motives. But if this is what is going on in her case, then either she is simply refusing to face the facts, which is irrational, or she is involved in some kind of self-deception. She is involved in self-deception if she manages to believe and not to believe the same ideas.[30] Self-deception, according to Elster, is an intentional project to deceive oneself; it is a paradox.[31] The agent entertains incompatible beliefs simultaneously by overlooking the stronger reasons for one of the beliefs.[32] Consider the woman who is raised in a patriarchal society to believe that all men will be her protectors, and later in life is physically abused by her male partner. She comes to believe that men are not her protectors: she intentionally decides this, but decides also to forget it when it is too difficult for her to admit to herself that the man she is with is not a good person. When she cannot face the fact about his being an abuser, such as when she believes that she will be lonely and penniless without him, she forgets her belief that he is an abuser. When she does this, and thinks of the abuser as a good person, she must be hiding from herself the fact that she does not believe that men are not her protectors.

A similar thing might go on with the disharmonious person, but it begins as a disparity in a preference and a belief rather than a conflict in beliefs. That is, since the disharmonious person does not want to develop moral motives—she prefers not-x—she sets out to deceive herself that she already has moral motives—she believes x. Whenever she is reminded, either by others or by herself, of her falling short of the ideal moral person, she forgets the fact that she lacks moral motives and believes she has them. Her preference for not-x generates a belief in x. But since x is not true of her, and she knows this, she believes not-x too. She believes that she is the best kind of moral agent, yet she also believes that she falls short because she lacks moral motives. This defense mechanism helps her avoid adopting moral motives that she does not want.

But Elster rightly finds self-deception to be problematic: it involves a lack of continuity in the self, and a lack of integrity.[33] The objection is that a person who has at once incompatible beliefs cannot be a "whole" person. The objection must be that when it comes to beliefs about matters as serious as whether one is a moral person in the full sense, a person who is self-deceived in the way described lacks integrity. Sometimes deceiving oneself, and having incompatible beliefs, is not irrational, such as when an enslaved person convinces himself for reasons of survival that he will someday be free if he does exactly what his master wants, despite his belief that his fate is sealed. But the disharmonious person is not like this: she deceives herself about the kind of person she is because she does not want to acquire moral motives, preferring merely to go through the motions and reaping the benefits of morality without being a truly moral person. Certainly this kind of person seems immoral because she "skimps" on morality in an important way. But she is also irrational, because she deliberately causes herself to have incompatible beliefs in order to keep her reasons for acting morally and motives disharmonious, not having the right attitude toward morality, and not in the presence of an overriding reason for something as significant as survival.

Unless there is some better explanation of what goes on in the disharmonious person, we can conclude that she is irrational. Not having reasons and motives that are in harmony is irrational, and thus merely going through the motions, while believing that acting in morally required ways is rationally required, is irrational. Thus, the motive skeptic's position is untenable, since he believes that acting in morally required ways is rationally required, yet believes that it is rationally permissible merely to go through the motions in so acting. So, having and acting from the motives deemed ideal by the moral theory at issue is rationally required, since only these reasons and motives are in harmony. Technically, I have not shown directly that reasons and motives must be in harmony, but only that when they are not, the agent exhibits irrationality.

4 CONCLUSION

I have argued that we need to defeat motive skepticism for a full defeat of skepticism, and have offered an attempt to defeat the motive skeptic by showing that his position that going through the motions when acting in morally required ways is untenable.

Extending the skeptical project in this way, though it makes defeating skepticism a more onerous task, is important, since not doing so would mean that it is possible for a person who acts in morally required ways to be rational even when she does her duty halfheartedly. But our moral theories demand more than our merely acting in morally required ways, since they describe the ideal or full moral agent as one who also exhibits moral motives. In addition, defeating motive skepticism provides the ethic of care a strategy that allows it rationally to require the motive of care while freeing it from the problems arising from its endorsing the version of internalism it does. And for this and other theories, if we defeat skepticism fully, we will have shown that rationality requires being a moral person in a fuller and richer sense than we will have shown with only a defeat of action skepticism.

8

The Interdependency Thesis

This chapter defends an alternative theory for assessing the rationality of both dispositions and actions, which I call the Interdependency Thesis, according to which we assess the rationality of an agent's actions not independently of the agent who performs them, but as actions performed by a certain kind of agent. It defends a tight connection between dispositions and actions such that it makes sense, in assessing the rationality of one, that we at the same time assess the rationality of the other. It defends a model of rationality that relies on various levels of consistency, primarily in the sense of coherence existing between an agent's reasons for adopting a moral disposition; the argument for the moral theory or set of principles that the agent adopts, which relies on the Kantian notion of the intrinsic worth of persons; the agent's reasons for acting; and the agent's desire to be a moral person as reflected in the maxim the agent adopts. If we establish the Interdependency Thesis, and show either the rationality of being morally disposed or of acting morally, we will have defeated both disposition and action skepticism at once. There is reason to construe the skeptic as accepting reasons of consistency and not being wedded to EU.

1 INTRODUCTION

In this chapter, I want to make good on some promissory notes I have earlier alluded to. First, I defend the Interdependency Thesis, according to which the rationality of actions and dispositions is determined interdependently. Second, I defend a view of moral integrity that reflects a tight connection between an agent's moral disposition and the acts expressing it. This view, I argue, provides a richer picture of moral agency and moral action than SIB contractarianism allows. Third, I offer a consistency model of rationality as one that together with the Interdependency Thesis provides more promise of defeating action skepticism, as well as a more plausible view of ideal rational agency than that offered by the traditional view of the skeptic. This model builds on the requirement for consistency in respecting one's own humanity and that of others that I detailed in chapter 5, but it understands consistency mainly in the sense of coherence between an agent's reasoning about the justification of the moral theory or principles she adopts and her disposition, actions, and desires—what I have called "practical consistency" to distinguish it from logical consistency.

I acknowledge up front the Interdependency Thesis's apparent disadvantages, namely, that it does not give us as straightforward an answer as EU as to when an agent and her actions are rational, and that it makes rationality a matter of degree. But these are outweighed, I believe, by the Interdependency Thesis's advantages, including that it avoids problems about the connection between agents and their acts that the other accounts face, it is consistent with a more plausible view of moral agency, and it shows, significantly, that if the rationality of acting morally and of being morally disposed are interdependent matters, then to defeat action skepticism would be to defeat disposition skepticism, and vice versa; neither could be defeated without defeating the other.

2 FURTHER PROBLEMS WITH THE INDEPENDENCY THESIS AND THE DEPENDENCY THESIS

Recall Parfit's Independency Thesis, which he defends partly with the case of Kate, whose strongest desire is to make her books as good as possible, which will make her life go as well as possible. The Self-Interest Theory of rationality, S, gives to each of us the aim that our lives go, for each of us, as well as possible. Although it is rational for Kate, given her desires, to dispose herself to work very hard, when she works to exhaustion and depression, Parfit judges Kate, or, more accurately, Kate's disposition, to be rational, but her act to be irrational. Parfit makes independent assessments of dispositions and acts, and he endorses what Darwall calls an end or value-based theory of rationality.[1] Darwall defines a value-based theory of rational conduct or person as any theory that takes rationality "to derive from an independent view about what rational conduct or being a rational person should bring about or accomplish."[2] Value-based theories contrast with both ones that begin with an ideal of the rational (or moral) agent and define rational (or right) action in terms of it and ones in which the rationality (or goodness) of a disposition derives from that of the conduct manifesting it.[3] A comparison with value-based consequentialist theories of morality is helpful: these theories "begin with an independent conception of the good," or "a substantive aim" to which they answer, "which is then taken to provide a fundamental justification for any moral theory, whether of the right or of moral character."[4] On consequentialism, for example, the independent standard of good conduct is producing the best overall consequences. Thus value-based theories of rationality (or morality) allow us to assess dispositions and acts according to whether they meet an independent conception of rationality (or of the good). According to Parfit's theory, S, the independent standard of rational conduct is the promotion of one's self-interest, or, what makes a person's life go best.

In chapter 2, I raised problems with the Independency Thesis. One notable problem is that so long as Kate-type cases where having a disposition, but not every instance of acting on it, is rationally required are logically possible, this thesis in conjunction with S (or EU) will not defeat action skepticism. Here I want to raise an additional problem that concerns the connection between a disposition and the acts expressing it. This problem inspires my defense of the Interdependency Thesis.

There are two readings of the Independency Thesis; the weak reading assesses acts as "actions as performed"; the strong reading assesses acts as "bare acts." Assessing acts in the weak way does not separate the act from the agent; rather, the judgment refers to the agent performing the action. Assessing acts in the strong way judges only "the product," as it were, of what the agent does, that is, the bare act in itself, and thus separates the agent from the act.[5] Value-based theories may conflate these readings. On the strong reading, the assessments that the Independency Thesis yields do not adequately reflect *any* connection between dispositions and actions, not even a causal relation that Parfit might endorse, as I showed in the case of Kate, whose disposition causes her to work hard on days when it is better for her to take a break; nor does the Independency Thesis reflect the connection between dispositions and actions that we believe should exist in the rationally or morally ideal person. Specifically, value-based theories of rationality do not connect rationality with the agent's *reasons for acting*, whether justificatory or explanatory or both. Assessing Kate's actions independently of her disposition fails to capture the diversity of explanations for why Kate does or does not act on her disposition, including caring about making her life go well, luck, causation, being threatened, suffering from weakness of will, having a desire to dupe others, or even merely going through the motions. Indeed, since the strong interpretation ignores the agent's reasons for acting, on it Parfit is committed to the view that Kate's irrational act of working to exhaustion is just as irrational as the same act performed by the person who is disposed always to act in ways that make her life go worse. Further, the weak reading of the Independency Thesis is equally problematic, since it still judges the action according to a standard or value independent of the agent. Although the Independency Thesis sensibly takes actions to be performed by agents instead of considering them as mere events in the universe as on the strong reading, what matters is still only whether the act achieves the independent value. To press the point, consider that this value need not even be held by the agent. Kate might not have the aim that her life go as well as possible, but the weak reading assesses the rationality of her actions, as actions performed by Kate, strictly according to whether they promote this aim.

Independent judgments of acts and dispositions supported by value-based theories are thus decidedly empty ones: they tell us merely whether an agent or act meets a certain standard, and may at best offer agents a general guide to follow, namely, to aim to meet the standard. But they fail to reflect any deep facts about agency. What makes us interesting moral and rational agents and reveals our commitment to morality are features about ourselves such as, in addition to our reasons for acting, whether our reasons are linked to moral principles and can be described in maxims that guide our lives, whether these reasons relate to how we want to live our lives, our deliberations about our dispositions, whether acting a certain way will change our disposition or make us firm up our resolve, and whether we are open to revision about our dispositions. A plausible theory of moral and of rational action should reflect these complexities. I will elaborate on these points in connection to rationality throughout this chapter. *Agency-related judgments* reflect these deep facts about ourselves. Unlike judgments generated by value-based theories, agency-related moral and rational evaluations judge acts strictly *as they are performed by* a certain kind of agent who is committed to morality; and they do not conflate these with judgments of "bare acts." Further, they judge dispositions *in light of* the kinds of acts the agent performs and by whether the acts shape her disposition. Agency-related judgments would thus yield different moral (and rational) assessments of the following agents: a person who harms another so that even more people are spared harm, a person who harms another when he does not realize he is harming them, and a person who has it as her maxim to harm others for its own sake and refuses to change when others bring this to her attention. If we are going to defeat skepticism successfully, we want our rational judgments to reflect something about *agents*, more precisely, about things that matter for *moral agency*, not just whether their acts meet a certain standard, as value-based theories propose. We want rich, not empty, judgments, because if we defeat action skepticism, we will have shown something more significant than we would with a value-based judgment. In addition, we need a theory of rationality that supports rich judgments. The fact that EU is consistent with psychopathic reasons makes us suspicious that the value-based judgments it yields will not cut it.

I want to motivate the discussion of the nature of a moral disposition with Ann Davis's account of what it means to say that a person acts *as* a utilitarian.[6] Davis uses utilitarianism as an example, but her point is the general one that "living a life in accord with a moral theory is not simply living a life that is valuable in the theory's terms."[7] Davis asks us to suppose that Kant led a life that maximized utility, even though his motives, aims, beliefs, and philosophical works were decidedly nonutilitarian. Kant would have failed to act *as* a utilitarian, since acting in utilitarian ways is necessary, but not sufficient, for being a utilitarian. To be a utilitarian, one needs to be directed at or concerned in the right way with the realization of utility. One's choices must stem from, or be an expression of, a commitment to utilitarianism. One must deliberate as a utilitarian, which, in Davis's words, is to make utilitarianism "practically central." Although Davis is concerned particularly with the psychology of a utilitarian agent, and I am not, we can infer from her remarks about practical centrality a more general point about assessments of dispositions and actions, which is that even value-based theories of morality—and, we might expect, value-based theories of rationality—call out for richer assessments of dispositions and acts than those the Independency Thesis or its moral counterpart provides. In the example of utilitarianism, whether a person is a utilitarian or whether his act is utilitarian will be more than, or even other than, a matter of whether his disposition or act merely conforms to the principle of utility.

We would expect non-value-based theories to be able to accommodate richer assessments even more readily than value-based theories such as utilitarianism. Gauthier's Dependency Thesis, a purported non-value-based theory of rational action, is a promising candidate because on it the rationality of acts comes from the rationality of the dispositions they express rather than from an independent conception of what rational agency or conduct should achieve. But the Dependency Thesis is not straightforwardly a non-value-based theory of rationality because on it, the rationality of dispositions is determined by whether they meet an independent standard of utility-maximization. It is just that for Gauthier, only the rationality of actions is determined by the rationality of the disposition they express rather than by a further independent standard. Still, because of the dependency of the rationality of acts on the rationality of dispositions, dispositions and acts must be related.[8] The question is whether they are related in a way that captures Davis's insights about a theory's being practically central. As I have shown, Gauthier argues that it is rational, because in one's self-interest, to adopt the disposition of constrained maximization, as long as enough others in the population are similarly disposed. Constrained maximizers, who cooperate when doing so provides a greater expected utility than universal noncooperation, can expect to reap the benefits of morality unavailable to straightforward maximizers, who always act in ways they expect to bring them the greatest utility.[9] But in order to defeat skepticism fully, Gauthier needs to defeat action skepticism in addition to disposition skepticism. Recall that the Dependency Thesis is designed to show that acts expressing constrained maximization are rationally required, though not in a self-interested sense, since Gauthier rejects grounding the rationality of actions in self-interest. To show how the rationality of dispositions carries over to acts, we need to see how Gauthier construes the moral disposition of constrained maximization; and we need to assess whether it will allow us to make the richer assessments we want.

The mechanism interpretation of constrained maximization takes it to be a hardwired psychological trait or strong habit that forces or causes an agent to act according to it, independent of what her preferences might be at the time.[10] Along these lines, Gauthier remarks: "a [constrained maximizer] is not able, given her disposition, to take advantage of the 'exceptions'";[11] "and the entire point of disposing oneself to constraint is to adhere to it in the face of one's knowledge that one is not choosing the maximizing action."[12] A constrained maximizer is disposed to comply even when compliance "results in a real disadvantage to herself," because a disposition to comply affords her greater expected utility than being noncompliant on the occasion.[13] These passages suggest that something must "take hold of" the self-interested agent and make her comply. But if constrained maximization is psychological compulsion, it falls way short of what we think a genuine moral disposition ought to be. A genuine moral disposition requires commitment to a moral theory, deliberation about one's dispositions and actions, and performing routine checks on one's disposition to see whether one measures up to the kind of person one has chosen to be. A morally disposed person can suffer from occasional weakness of will, which a purely causal account of the relation between dispositions and actions rules out. Thus the mechanism interpretation makes dispositions and actions *too* related. So even if the Dependency Thesis linked the mechanism interpretation of constrained maximization with actions, if it were to demonstrate the rationality of acting morally, it would do so by invoking a moral disposition that is problematic.

Gauthier might hold a weaker view than the mechanism interpretation that would support the Dependency Thesis, namely, the view that actions are not caused by, but are mere expressions of, dispositions. But this must mean that the agent has a strong tendency to act, because Gauthier is defending a view of a moral disposition that would make a person act morally in response to Hobbes's Foole, who lacks such a disposition and so cannot legitimately be received into society. Gauthier argues that we need an internal moral constraint that ensures compliance in the presence of external, political constraints that fail, and that makes the solution moral, not merely political.[14] What this amounts to is unclear. On the one hand, Gauthier suggests, though ambiguously, that the moral person does not even reason about acting morally: "[the moral person] makes a choice about how to make further choices; he chooses, on utility-maximizing grounds, not to make further choices on those grounds."[15] And: "a constrained maximizer has a conditional disposition to base her actions on a joint strategy, *without considering* whether some individual strategy would yield her greater expected utility."[16] On one reading, these passages suggest that the morally disposed agent lets her disposition "lead" her to act, without considering the options. But since on this view the agent lacks reasoning when it comes to particular moral actions, this view is consistent with the agent's not having a commitment to act in the relevant way, but acting accidentally or indifferently, much like Kant's sympathetic man who helps others in need from an immediate inclination that he has fortuitously while being indifferent to morality because he is not concerned with whether his action is correct or required.[17]

On the other hand, Gauthier suggests that the moral agent does, indeed, reason about particular actions instead of letting his disposition control him: the constrained maximizer is not a straightforward maximizer in disguise, but reasons differently.[18] The problem, though, is that he reasons on grounds of self-interest, although, of course, not in terms of expected benefit from the particular action—he is disposed to comply with morality when he expects to benefit from the practice of compliance even if by chance he does not benefit on this occasion.[19] But self-interest is an inappropriate object of a moral disposition or action. Barbara Herman explains that what makes the moral motive special for Kant is that "it must provide the agent with an interest in the moral rightness of his actions."[20] Borrowing this idea, I propose that in order for a disposition and action to be moral, they must reflect a *commitment* to morality, which must entail knowing and not being indifferent about what morality demands, and having an interest in morality expressed in one's reasons for being morally disposed and acting accordingly. Further, these actions must reflect a choice, not a habit or learned response. If the Dependency Thesis supports either the causal or the weaker interpretation of the connection between dispositions and actions, it fails to make the assessments we want and fares no better on this score than the Independency Thesis.

I am not sure what a more plausible version of the Dependency Thesis that would capture the notion of dependency would look like. The Dependency Thesis is used to show how the rationality of a disposition carries over to the actions expressing it. Thus, Dependency theorists need a strong connection between a person's having a disposition and acting on it. For it not to be an Independency Thesis, or a value-based theory, the work must be done by the connection itself between the disposition and the actions expressing it, and not by the independent value, like self-interest, that weakly "links" the disposition and action. Indeed, the *strength* of the disposition and its effect on the actions seems to do the work. But strength, as Herman argues in the context of the Kantian moral motive, has nothing to do with the moral worth of an action, which is decided just by the fact that it takes duty as its object, or, that the agent has an interest in the moral rightness of his actions.[21] In other words, actions that get their rationality merely from the strength of the disposition they express lack the appropriate commitment to morality. But notice that value-based theories cannot invoke the agent's interest in the moral rightness of his actions instead of strength, since on such theories the object of the agent's action is the goal to be attained, such as self-interest, even if, as in Gauthier's case, the agent aims at the goal not in the individual action but in the practice in general. And this fact alone means that value-based theories give an account of dispositions and actions and their connection that does not square with what many of us think a moral disposition should be.

In addition, I have shown that neither the Independency Thesis nor the Dependency Thesis will defeat action skepticism. Again, the Independency Thesis fails because if it showed that all morally required acts were rationally required, it would make moral reasons otiose, and because it cannot show this after all due to the many cases of conflict. I suspect that other value-based theories of rationality would fail for similar reasons, since by definition they contrapose another value with morality. And the Dependency Thesis fails because of cases like the toxin case, which morality is more similar to than the smart pill case, leaving it open to the possibility that no morally required acts are rationally required. Indeed, we should not want either to succeed, since neither links dispositions and actions in the right way.

Yet to defeat skepticism fully, we need to defeat both disposition and action skepticism. So we need a better way of making rational assessments that reflects a plausible view of moral dispositions and the deep facts about agency. The view I defend in this chapter makes rationality and integrity a matter of consistency in the sense of coherence in an agent's desires, dispositions, and actions. Along the way, I reconstrue the requirements of morality that the skeptic takes as his target, from the mere morally required act to the complex connection between dispositions and actions expressed in a commitment to morality. My view reflects the notion that moral goodness comes in degrees, and that our rational assessments should reflect this. But first I need to say more about moral dispositions, since my view about dispositions undergirds the Interdependency Thesis.

3 MORAL DISPOSITIONS

Examining in more detail what it is to have a disposition will help us to see what is missing in assessments generated from the Dependency and Independency Theses. Generally speaking, to have a disposition is to have a commitment, which involves having "an integrated long-term loyalty to projects, persons, and/or values."[22] Some of the specific features of a disposition are the following. Dispositions are deep-seated, and cannot, psychologically speaking, be changed at will or in a short time because they are ways of life, distinguishing them from intentions like the intention to drink a toxin that will make you sick for a day but will bring you $1 million. Dispositions reflect a complex set of beliefs, attitudes, and rules or guidelines for behavior that generally do not provide situation-specific answers to how an agent should act. Dispositions necessarily involve acting in the relevant ways—for instance, one is not a Catholic if one never acts in ways dictated by Catholicism, just as one is not a fan of a sports team if one never watches or listens to the games. This is at least partly because, as I will argue, actions shape dispositions by influencing an agent's reasoning and motives. Dispositions reveal significant facts about the kind of person one is and, typically, wants to be. For instance, dispositions distinguish an athlete who intends to win this one game or to have the winningest record of the season from an athlete who is a winner. And dispositions might also entail having certain motives, such as when a feminist cares deeply about equality for women, in contrast to a person who merely intends to act in a feminist way.[23]

Next we need to examine in more detail the nature of a *moral* disposition. Davis's account of practical centrality is again instructive. For Davis, practical centrality means two things about a moral theory or set of principles: (1) its decisiveness, and (2) its motive force. Consider decisiveness first. Davis remarks that a utilitarian, for example, takes utilitarianism to be "the final and decisive test of the value and deontic status of a proposed course of action," that is, he regards it as the final word in determining what he ought to do.[24]

This view, I believe, is consistent with Herman's view of the Kantian moral motive, which gives the agent an interest in the moral rightness of his actions. Essentially this means that the moral motive requires having a maxim. As Herman says, "it is only when an agent has a maxim that we can talk about his motive."[25] This is the case with the sympathetic man who responds to suffering *and* takes this response to give him a reason to help: he finds the act to be the right thing to do, and its rightness is his reason for acting. He acts from the motive of duty, with a maxim that has moral content. The maxim, that is, is the decisive test of what he ought to do.

Two points in Herman's analysis are important for our purposes: the moral motive reflects reasons for action, and the reasons are expressed in a maxim. I believe that Herman's analysis of the moral motive can be applied equally to moral dispositions, so that a moral disposition also reflects reasons for action. This view is captured by yet another account of the Kantian moral motive, one held by Marcia Baron. Baron's insight is that the moral motive is not held "before the agent's mind" just prior to acting, but is a *commitment* to doing what is right that is captured in the agent's general character rather than his single actions.[26] I take this general character or disposition to reflect the agent's reasons for action, as expressed in a general maxim that she would use to describe her commitment. For instance, a person who is disposed not to harm animals might have the maxim "Do not cause needless pain or suffering to any sentient being." The moral motive, for Baron, is a long-term, wide-ranging commitment to morality: duty attaches to how a person lives, and only derivatively to individual actions.[27] It requires not always thinking about what is right before each action, but periodic reflection on one's character, and openness to change whenever one judges it to be necessary to shore up one's character. It guides and regulates one's conduct.[28] Compare it to the motive of the money manager who quarterly assesses his investments and makes changes when overall dips require it versus one who checks his stocks daily and makes decisions on this basis. This is not to say that the moral motive never functions as a primary motive that supplies the agent with the motivation to do the act in question;[29] it does, notes Baron, when it prompts the agent to refrain from doing something that she recognizes to be wrong but is tempted to do, or in the context of a character check, when she wants to make sure she is not slipping from morality or from the kind of person she wants to be. But since it is a long-term, wide-ranging commitment that governs all of one's actions, it usually functions as a secondary motive, one that provides limiting conditions on what may be done from other motives,[30] telling the agent that she may or may not do as she wishes.[31]

Consolidating these views of the moral motive, I propose that to have a moral *disposition* is (at least) to have a commitment to act according to a moral theory or set of principles, which is to endorse reasons to act in these ways, and to use these reasons in deliberation about acting morally. The reasons can be expressed in a maxim that guides the agent's actions and reveals the kind of person the agent wants to be. To *act* morally, then, is for one's actions to reflect the same commitment, or, to express one's moral disposition, but neither mechanistically nor causally. Good maxims order the lives of moral persons, but immoral maxims order the lives of racists ("Blacks are to be despised or hurt"), egoists ("No one's interests but my own are to count"), and the like. Even seemingly good maxims, though, must be scrutinized: recall that the kind of maxim held by a conscientiously wicked person might appear good but can take an immoral form. For example, the maxim "Everyone should be treated equally" might mean that an employer does not support maternity leave for women. The maxim specifies a kind of action or attitudinal response in accordance with what the person takes as a rule of life, which, for a moral person, is a moral theory or set of principles. Specifically, and in line with the Kantian view of the moral motive, the maxim should in some way refer to reasons for, or a defense of, the theory or principles. For example, a feminist's maxim might be "Respect women." This maxim, although it seems to oversimplify the complexities of feminism, is actually basic to all feminist thought: it is generated by and reflects a fundamental tenet of feminism that men and women are equal in humanity. To be a feminist is to adopt and follow such a maxim because you endorse reasons that justify the basic principles of feminism. These are theory-related reasons rather than merely inclination. In general, one who is morally disposed displays a penchant for morality: he understands morality and has an interest in following it for the right reasons. Morality guides his will, and he takes the theory or principles to be decisive in determining his actions.

My account of a moral disposition may seem overly intellectual.[32] Admittedly, many people neither engage in this kind of reasoning nor summarize their reasons for action in terms of a maxim. Some people might, for example, act simply out of concern for women rather than from a justified maxim requiring respect. I take my account merely to be explicating the philosophical underpinnings that a layperson *could* offer, even if not in terms of sophisticated arguments, were she to reflect on the way she wants to, and does, live her life. I am not suggesting that we hold laypersons to the same standards of justification that we hold philosophers. Rather, first, I share Kant's worry that a moral person still needs reasoning to guide him and to support his inclinations, even if he has good motives, for if he merely had, say, a concern for women, and acted from this motive, we could not expect that he would always act in ways exhibiting respect for women. And second, a person has to have and be at least somewhat cognizant of his reasons for acting just to be able to change, to firm up his resolve, to catch himself at mistakes, and so on. To be moral in the sense required for defeating skepticism about moral *reasons*, a person must to some extent be reflective, and not act simply on inclination.

My view of a moral disposition as a general commitment to morality excludes being *obsessed* with morality: the moral person is neither "hobbled" by her moral theory, trying to follow it more frequently and deliberately than others would,[33] nor is she preoccupied with duty, reflecting on it each and every time she acts,[34] nor does she engage in rule fetishism, memorizing and making habitual moral rules.[35] Rather, her maxim merely generally guides her life, but it need not tell her what to do in each situation. John McDowell's account is useful—it explains that a virtuous person knows what to do even in complex new circumstances in which the rules do not apply, because she has a certain perception of a situation that she gets by exercising sensitivity.[36] Her perception allows her to see certain aspects of a situation as generating a reason for acting in some way, which is apprehended not as outweighing other reasons for acting but as silencing them.[37] For instance, a feminist sees that denying women access to abortion is a violation of autonomy and a way of failing to respect women. Her perception silences concerns about fetal survival at all costs, and allows her to see reasons for action in other complex situations, such as whether women should fight in combat given the probability of rape by the enemy, or whether it is permissible from a feminist point of view for women to be pornography stars.

I have explained the decisiveness of a moral disposition. Next I need to explain the second feature of Davis's notion of practical centrality, that the moral theory or set of principles has motive force for the morally disposed agent, meaning that the agent *wants* it to determine how she acts, and it often does. Although Davis does not say, this must mean that the agent *reflects* on whether she should become disposed in the relevant way, and *chooses* to be a certain kind of person, such as a utilitarian or a feminist. Reflective deliberation is central to having a moral disposition and to agency in general.[38] It involves self-perception,[39] and takes place at a metalevel independent of one's moral beliefs. Were a person never to deliberate reflectively on her life, but instead simply move through life guided by her desires, we would doubt that she had the right reasons for acting, or even that she had a self-identity. Her character would be even more empty than that of the person who goes through the motions but at least has reasons for being morally disposed. Only agents who reflectively deliberate at some level can have a self-conception.[40] Reflection comes in degrees, sometimes being jarred by a bluntly critical comment from a friend, other times being the result of soul searching. The reflective person tries to change her behavior when it does not match the kind of person she wants to be. Being reflective entails knowing that one is not the kind of person who does certain things, but this need not require being philosophical in the strict sense about one's theory. Being reflective allows one sometimes to be inconsistent, to have principles that sometimes conflict or that are otherwise problematic. My point is that reflection is an essential feature of dispositions that are constitutive of moral agency, and it is these that are at stake in defeating skepticism.

My account of reflective deliberation bears similarity to Frankfurt's account of second-order desires or volitions, which is to want one of one's first-order desires to be one's will and to be effective, or, to motivate action.[41] My view of a moral disposition requires engaging in at least some level of reflective deliberation: one must have a second-order volition to be a certain kind of person, and must square this with one's first-order desires, interests, and beliefs. One must have a sense of oneself, morally speaking. In Frankfurt's words, one must identify oneself, through the formation of a second-order volition, with one rather than another desire. The maxim one adopts reflects one's second-order volition. Thus, if a feminist adopts the maxim "Respect women," yet has a first-order desire to be slavish to men, she must try to rid herself of the first-order desire since it conflicts with her second-order volition, revealed in her maxim, to be a feminist. Some people fail at or are incapable of reflective deliberation, and so lack moral dispositions and agency in the full sense. These include the psychopath who lacks the concept of moral wrongness and an understanding of the complexities of morality because he lacks certain values and emotions, the person who follows morality habitually, the person who is indifferent to evaluating her life, and young children.

Reflective deliberation involves reflecting not just on the maxim one adopts, but on the reasoning, or more specifically, the justification for the moral theory or set of principles that yields the maxim. In Frankfurt's terminology—and here I am expanding on his view—one must reflective-ly deliberate on what determines one's own will that allows one to identify more with one desire rather than another. Recall that without this further condition, a woman who is a person in Frankfurt's sense can want to make her deformed desires more truly her own than her other desires, and so identify herself with them. To avoid this result, one must consider the reasons that generate the maxim in the first place, since to do otherwise is not really to reflect on the kind of life one wants to lead but to adopt and follow a rule aimlessly or for the wrong reasons. That is, one must engage in at least a minimal level of reflection on what one takes to be a general guide to one's actions or commitment captured in one's character. Indeed, this is just what it means to have a maxim, since a maxim is a product of deliberation about the justification for the theory, principles, or general guide one follows, and it captures the reasons one has for acting and for being such a person. For instance, the maxim "Respect women" reflects the fact that the agent thought about what it means to respect women and why this way of treating women is how she wants to act. Reflective deliberation is an exercise in rationality; it can make one realize that the reasoning that yields a maxim is erroneous, as is the case with the racist who derives his maxim about how black persons are to be treated from false descriptive claims about their intelligence.[42] If there is no good justification for the theory or principles one believes, one should change one's maxim and disposition accordingly.

My account yields several further features of a moral disposition. The first has to do with how we acquire a moral disposition and the facility with which we can do so and make changes to it. Moral dispositions obviously are not instilled at birth, but since they necessarily involve reflection, they, like actions, are largely a matter of choice even though they are influenced by one's upbringing, experiences, and culture. These factors, together with the fact that a person sees reasons from the perspective she has adopted, the extent to which she reflects, and the fact that reflection requires that she extrapolate from her actions and examine the reasoning behind the disposition that shapes these actions, all contribute to the difficulty in acquiring and maintaining a moral disposition. The inconsistencies and shortcomings that reflection inevitably reveals can make it difficult for a person to face her disposition and adjust it accordingly. For instance, a person who is raised by abusive parents will find it hard to be self-respecting, a misogynist will find it hard to abandon his hatred for women in favor of feelings of equality, and a hunter who is steeped in self-vindication will find it difficult to see that he is the kind of person who gets pleasure out of stalking and killing animals for sport. Reflection is key to having a disposition and revising it rather than being resistant to change. A person's moral disposition is in constant formation due in part to character checks and subsequent changes and reaffirmations.

Since maxims are mere guides to action, and since agents are not hobbled by their moral theory or principles, a moral disposition allows for backsliding. Backsliding occurs when a person does not completely understand the complexities of morality that he should, does not focus on what is morally required, or succumbs to emotion, such as when he suffers from weakness of will or even jealousy. These are some of the kinds of immorality discussed in chapter 5. Backsliding is an inevitable feature of our humanity, for none of us is perfect. Yet backsliding must be met with a reasoned response in the person who reflectively deliberates and exhibits full agency. A person who is truly morally disposed will fess up to herself and firm up her resolve if she wants to continue endorsing her maxim. If she backslides too often, we have reason to suspect that she is not morally disposed, in which case she no longer endorses and guides her life according to a moral maxim. It is difficult and not necessary to say how much backsliding a person must do for it to be the case that she is not morally disposed, much like deciding how often a person who purportedly has a penchant for being in good health can indulge in too much food or inactivity or lose too much sleep before we question her resolve. In either case, the person's having the disposition depends on her reasoning, and how serious is the offense and its effect on the person's character or health.

A third feature is that moral dispositions are reflected over time in a pattern of actions. This view accommodates occasional backsliding and acting "out of character," and is consistent both with Baron's view of the moral motive as mainly a secondary motive or general commitment, and with dispositions being "works in progress." Patterns of behavior tell a much more accurate story about a person's disposition than do individual acts that might otherwise be explained away, since they best reveal the agent's reasoning. This is not to say that a person's disposition cannot be revealed in particular actions—sometimes new situations tell us who we really are, as in the case of the person who accidentally dents a parked car and takes off, or the person who misses the merits of his coworker's work and denies he did by conjuring up falsehoods. Grievous acts, too, are typically indicative of a person's true character, despite the kind of life he has led until then, as in the case of a professor who teaches feminism but sexually harasses a student. But it would be a mistake to focus solely on the most sensational acts, since run-of-the-mill acts, especially when viewed as part of a pattern of behavior, typically display the same reasoning that is revealed in a pattern that often is predictive of bigger things to come. Sensational acts of violence against women display the same hostility as everyday threats, rapes, and abuse, especially when these are part of a pattern.[43]

The account of a moral disposition that I have defended in this section is much richer than that offered by value-based theories, and the causal and weaker interpretations of the connection between dispositions and actions supported by the Dependency Thesis. This account provides the right connection between dispositions and actions, and ultimately should yield a nonempty defeat of skepticism. I now turn to this issue, which I have left hanging since chapter 2.

4 THE INTERDEPENDENCY THESIS

In this section, I propose an alternative theory for assessing the rationality of dispositions and actions as a way of defeating action and disposition skepticism. First I aim to establish that *joint* rational assessments of dispositions and actions best reflect my account of a moral disposition. Then

I defend in some detail what it would take to defeat the fuller sense of skepticism on my account.

4.1 Interdependent Moral Judgments

One reason to assess the rationality of dispositions and actions interdependently is that this kind of judgment parallels interdependent *moral* judgments that we often make. Here I am appealing to an intuitive sense of moral judgments that I will in the next section analogize to rational judgments. We often excuse, praise, or blame *agents* for their acts on the basis of their commitment to morality: the typically honest elderly woman who walks out of a thrift store wearing an inexpensive sweater she did not pay for is off the moral hook. We acknowledge that reflective deliberation comes in degrees by being lenient with those who are in the process of developing their moral dispositions, which are complex: thus the teenager who breaks a date with a less attractive fellow in order to date a more attractive one is cut more slack than a middle-aged person who does the same. We judge more favorably the person who is willing to face the fact that he uses others for money and tries to change this trait than one who digs himself more deeply into self-deception about his character by conjuring up stories about others' ability to be duped. Grievous acts, though, seem to be an exception: the first-time rapist or sexual predator is judged the same as a repeat offender. Here we question, rather than affirm, the person's commitment to morality.

We also often judge *acts* in light of the agent's disposition. We judge the promise-breaker's broken promise as more evidence of her character, but tend to write off some promises that are not kept by those who are generally promise-keepers, searching for reasons they may have broken their promise. We judge as antifeminist the legislators' adding gender to the list of biases in order to make a bill outlawing discrimination fail, despite the act's apparent fairness.[44] But again, the grievous nature of some acts seems to be independent of the agent's disposition or at least reveals the agent's lack of commitment to morality: an act of murder or assault is no less than that when performed by a first-time offender. Unlike independent judgments generated by value-based theories, interdependent judgments of agents and at least nongrievous acts are grounded in the agent's reasoning, her commitment, her choice to be a certain kind of person, including her willingness to recognize her mistakes and make the necessary adjustments, and her resolve. These factors go hand in hand with a richer view of morality than, for instance, SIB contractarianism.

There are good reasons that we *should* make interdependent judgments in morality. For one thing, dispositions and actions inform each other. Philosophers typically take for granted that dispositions influence actions. I argued in chapter 7 that actions influence motives. I believe that actions also shape our dispositions, by shaping our motives and, more significantly, our reasoning. Acting in morally good ways can help to make a person morally disposed. Prisoners who are forced to apologize to their victims might change their ways because they come to recognize the equal humanity of their victims; children who are made to share toys or care for younger siblings might come to be benevolent; a person who harbors racist stereotypes but who avoids racist literature and talk shows and interacts more frequently with minorities might learn to abandon his racism; and an environmentally conscious person who does not use pesticides and recycles his newspapers performs acts that may influence his reasoning and motives to drive a fuel-efficient car. Unfortunately, acting in morally bad ways can also inform one's reasoning and motivations, and consequently one's dispositions. Young men who mimic aggressive dating behavior they see in movies, and who, in the company of their male friends, mutter obscenities on the streets or cheer rape scenes in movies "may be testing the waters, and getting the message that it's clear sailing ahead"[45] to become sexists who act in more grievous ways. In general, dispositions and actions mutually affect each other; our actions help to form our dispositions, which in turn influence our reasoning, motives, and actions following from them. We most often choose from our dispositions to act in ways that reflect, support, and strengthen our dispositions. Since dispositions and actions are intimately connected through the agent's reasoning, and not merely by causal relations as the mechanism interpretations of Gauthier and Parfit suggest, it makes sense to assess them interdependently. We want our moral assessments of agents to reflect the whole package, since moral agency is about both being disposed a certain way and acting in certain ways, and the reasoning underlying both.

Second, and more important, the ideal moral person, in addition to having certain motives, is marked by both having the right disposition and performing the right actions; neither is independently sufficient, and they must be related in a certain way. Only interdependent judgments give us sufficient information about a person and her actions, so only these judgments appropriately capture the ideal. Consider the alternatives. Character-based theories make central the notion of a moral person; good acts are derivative from this. Value-based theories make central the defining characteristics of a right or good act; the ideal moral person is defined as one who performs right or good acts. The judgments that either theory invokes are like two sides of a moral coin,[46] but I believe that they are not related in the way needed for capturing the ideal moral person. My account makes neither acts nor agents prior to the other but judges them interdependently; so we need a basis for judging persons and their actions and explaining their interconnection.

I propose that integrity fuses together in the right way the two sides of the moral coin. Both moral and personal integrity factor in. One mark of integrity is consistency in a person's desires, dispositions, and actions. To repeat, by "consistency" here I mean coherence between a person's desires, disposition, and actions. *Moral* integrity is marked by consistency between an agent's moral disposition and actions, that is, this kind of consistency is necessary for an agent's having moral integrity; a person's reasons for committing to a moral theory are reflected in a maxim governing her actions. If the person's moral disposition and actions as revealed in a pattern over time conflict, she lacks moral integrity since she shows a disparity in her reasoning, as in the case of a person who wants not to be a liar but often lies.[47] Those who display inconsistent dispositions and actions, including the unreflective, the persistently weak-willed, and the self-deceived, fail to exhibit moral integrity, which requires cultivating and revising one's disposition in light of reflective deliberation. Evil persons, too, lack moral integrity since they either do not acquire a commitment to morality as expressed in a maxim or do not live up to the maxim they claim to endorse.

Personal integrity requires that a person reflect on whether her desire set is consistent, and ensure that her disposition and actions are chosen in light of her desires. Where there is an inconsistency, she needs to assess and revise her disposition and/or desires and actions accordingly. So a woman with deformed desires who wants to be a feminist must rid herself of them because they aim to lower her value as a person, which is inconsistent with the feminist requirement that women be valued equally to men. Moral integrity, then, defined partly by consistency in one's moral disposition and actions, presupposes personal integrity, defined partly by consistency in one's desires to be a certain kind of person and the disposition one forms and acts from.[48] An immoral person, then, might have personal integrity because her desire to be immoral is consistent with her disposition and actions; but she lacks moral integrity because she either lacks or fails to act on a moral disposition. The ideal moral person, in contrast, must have both moral and personal integrity.

I am proposing that we make deeper moral judgments about dispositions and actions than those espoused by traditional moral theories, especially value-based ones, since the former will be tied to integrity by reflecting the rich view of a moral commitment or disposition that I presented in the last section. Consider our judgments about agents and their actions. A morally good *person* will be one who is guided by moral principles and who has integrity, which is measured by consistency in desires, disposition, and actions. Moral evaluations of a person will reflect her reasons for being disposed and for acting, which are captured in a maxim and make reference to the moral principles to which she subscribes. These evaluations are sympathetic to the fact that our dispositions are in constant formation and subject to revision, and that reflectiveness comes in degrees. They also allow for occasional mistakes, and respect our resolve. Goodness, then, will come in degrees, according to the agent's reasoning. A person who reasons correctly according to the moral maxim she adopts is morally better than one who does not; a person who does not always act morally but is willing to listen to reasons for acting differently and to revise her disposition accordingly is morally better than one who acts morally but merely goes through the motions; and so on. A morally good *act*, then, will be one that contributes to an agent's integrity along the same lines: that is, the act will contribute to her reasoning and consistency in her desires, disposition, and actions. Goodness of acts, too, will come in degrees. An act that contributes to an agent's integrity is better than the same act that has no effect on its agent; an act that is done for the right reasons and by a person with moral integrity is better than a similar one performed by an immoral person, contra Parfit; and so on. Grievous acts and persons who commit them, though, will never be good, since they are not guided by moral principles. My view avoids value-based measurements of the goodness of individual acts that are grounded in conformity to a given moral principle. It embraces the commitment view of the moral motive, since it assesses acts in light of this commitment and in light of the agent's integrity.

The skeptic wants it to be shown that every morally required act is rationally required. The view I have been putting forward defends a different notion of what is morally required from that invoked by value-based theories. What is required by morality is not simply that a person act a certain way, or have a certain disposition, but that a person have a commitment to morality, which involves deliberating about one's disposition, actions, and desires, performing routine character checks, firming up one's resolve, and making sure that one's reasoning about the character one wants to be is in line with one's reasoning about how to act. In short, what is *morally required* is that an agent have *integrity* in the sense I have described.

This account of what is morally required seems to weaken the demands of morality because it allows for occasional backsliding, is sensitive to the nuances of character formation, and in general is responsive to the inevitable moral failings of our humanity. It also excludes acts that are dictated by the moral theory at issue, yet are not performed for the right reason. Whereas on value-based theories, morally required acts are ones that are dictated by the moral theory at issue and meet an independent standard of the good, on my view morally required acts are ones that foster moral integrity in the way described. Thus when an agent, in acting, slips from her moral commitment, but reflects on this fact and firms up her resolve, she does what is morally required. This is determined not by the act itself, but by its connection with the other features of moral integrity. In this way, my view actually *strengthens* the demands of morality, since it includes as morally required not just that the agent act in certain ways, but that she act morally for the right reasons, and be reflective about her character and open to revision. What is morally required is determined by a more stringent criterion than on value-based accounts. At issue in defeating skepticism is that we demonstrate that it is rationally required to act in morally required ways, that is, in ways fostering integrity.

Our *rational* judgments should parallel our moral judgments: where we blame, excuse, and praise in morality, prima facie we should do likewise in rationality: richer moral judgments require richer rational judgments. So if we should morally assess dispositions and actions jointly, we should also make interdependent rational assessments. Since I have modified our view of what is morally required to be that one has integrity, what is rationally required needs to shift accordingly. The Dependency Thesis was introduced for the purpose of defeating action skepticism: if we could show that rationality requires adopting a moral disposition, and could establish the Dependency Thesis, it would follow that all morally required acts expressed by the moral disposition are rationally required. Now Dependency theorists might agree that we must make parallel moral and rational judgments. Recall that they would judge a straightforward maximizer's and a constrained maximizer's act of promise-keeping differently, rationally speaking, and probably also morally speaking. But the reason for making different rational judgments is whether the act stems from a disposition that is rational or not, a reason that I reject. Instead, I think that a better reason for making interdependent rational assessments is that moral dispositions and actions are tightly connected by the agent's *reasoning*: dispositions and actions shape each other *through* the agent's reasoning. This is the basis for the Interdependency Thesis that I aim to establish in the next section. This is not captured by either the Dependency Thesis or by the Independency Thesis; neither reflects the right commitment to morality that an ideally moral and rational person should have. I invoke the Interdependency Thesis in order to capture in a better way the connection between the rationality of a moral disposition and moral actions. The rationality of dispositions and of acts will be a measure of this reasoning, and will reflect the agent's commitment, but not mere conformity, to morality. An agent who engages in the right reasoning but fails to act on it, or vice versa, would be rationally disjointed in the same way he would be morally disjointed if his disposition and actions were generally inconsistent. Further, I want to propose that consistency rather than self-interest or some other end-based value be the standard of rationality we use to determine whether doing what is morally required is rationally required. Just as consistency is required for integrity, and integrity for moral agency, so consistency is required for *rational* agency. Our evaluations of dispositions and actions should reflect these deep facts I have mentioned about agency, about the kinds of moral—and rational—agents we want to be. More specifically, moral integrity captures the notion of practical consistency or coherence reflected in a person's commitment to morality, including her deliberations about her disposition, whether she firms up her resolve, and whether her reasons for acting are linked to moral principles or a theory described in a maxim by which she guides her life, and whether she wants to live a moral life and has reflected on this. To show that fostering integrity is *rationally* required, we can employ as the standard of rationality consistency as coherence in the agent's reasoning, as I will now explain.

4.2 Interdependent Rational Judgments

I have arrived at the point of addressing the disposition and action skeptic, and it bears repeating that I am not attempting actually to defeat the skeptic, but merely to lay out explicitly what any moral theorist must show for a successful defeat. The traditional view of the action skeptic who demands that we show that every morally required act is rationally required by focusing just on the act itself unfairly favors value-based theories of morality, since it takes morally required acts to be those that merely conform to a given theory, and ignores the complexities of acts discussed here. Assessing acts and dispositions merely on the grounds of whether they meet a certain goal such as maximizing self-interest does not give us the correct, morally significant information about an agent. Like moral assessments, rational assessments need to reflect the complex picture of what it means to have a moral disposition and to act from it, and the connection between a person's reasons for adopting a moral disposition, and for having and acting from it. Being a moral person and acting morally, I have argued, have to do with making a theory practically central, which includes the agent's reasoning about the kind of person she wants to be, whether she endorses some justifications for certain moral principles, her resolve, and her being open to revision.

The traditional skeptic endorses EU as the standard of rationality, which is Parfit's version of S, the Self-Interest Theory, according to which the rationality of an action is determined by whether it produces outcomes that would be best for the agent and that would make his life go for him as well as possible, described in terms of preferences. Parfit relies on S, in conjunction with the Independency Thesis, but at the expense of defeating skepticism fully, since he acknowledges cases of Rational Irrationality. Gauthier, too, invokes S, but only at the level of dispositions, in conjunction with the Dependency Thesis; and he also fails to defeat skepticism fully. We have seen additional problems with EU regarding deformed and psychopathic desires, minimalist morality, incomplete description of immorality, and failure at defeating action skepticism. Thus, we need a better model of rationality than self-interest, and a better thesis than either the Dependency or Independency Thesis, to explain the connection, if any, between the rationality of a moral disposition and actions. The arguments in this chapter suggest that we need a standard better than whatever it is that Gauthier employs for actions. The standard I endorse as one that holds promise for defeating action skepticism is consistency, and it can be used in conjunction with the Interdependency Thesis, according to which the rationality of dispositions and actions is assessed interdependently. Here I want to add to the model of consistency as a lack of contradiction that I defended in chapter 5, and employ an additional sense of consistency as coherence.

Consistency is what Elster calls a thin theory of rationality, the conditions of which I believe we must satisfy at the bare minimum in order to defeat disposition and action skepticism. According to Elster, a thin theory of rationality

> leaves unexamined the beliefs and desires that form the reasons for action whose rationality we are assessing, with the exception that they are stipulated not to be logically inconsistent. Consistency, in fact, is what rationality in the thin sense is all about: consistency within the belief system; consistency within the system of desires; and consistency between beliefs and desires on the one hand and the action for which they are reasons on the other hand.[49]

Of course, I deny the first sentence in this passage, in favor of scrutinizing desires for their being consistent with a person's worth, as I have argued in chapter 4. The sense in which my model of rationality is thin is that it relies just on practical consistency. But since consistency comes in at different levels, the model is, after all, a fairly thick one. So, first, a rational requirement for being a person with integrity is that a person display consistency or coherence between her reasons for being morally disposed and the justification for the moral theory or principles she endorses. Indeed, the reasons for adopting a moral disposition must come directly from the agent's rational acceptance of the argument(s) for the theory. To be more concrete, the reasons for being disposed to feminism, for instance, might stem from an argument about women's and men's equality. Again, the agent need not construct the argument to herself, and it need not be very sophisticated when she does—in the feminism example, it could be as simple as recognizing a disparity in the treatment of women and men. A successful defeat of skepticism will appeal to the justification for the moral theory or set of principles, since this in part makes adopting a moral disposition (and acting from it) rationally required. In accepting the theory or set of principles, the agent makes it "theoretically central"; that is, she makes it part of her belief system. But morality requires that she make it practically central. She can do this partly by becoming morally disposed. If the reasons for adopting a disposition are grounded in self-interest or anything other than the justification for the set of principles or main tenets of the theory, then the agent does not make the theory practically central, at least not in the correct sense; she adopts it for non-theory-related, external reasons, and these guide her actions. In Davis's words, her choices would not stem from, or be an expression of, a commitment to morality. This method of coming to make a theory practically central is bound to run into problems such as those Hobbes and ultimately Gauthier and any value-based theorist face in attempting to defeat action skepticism.

The first kind of consistency is explained by the fact that a person's *reason* for disposing herself in the relevant way and acting accordingly is not separate or different from the justification of the moral theory she adopts. The agent who accepts such reasons and disposes herself accordingly exhibits a mark of rationality, since she exhibits consistency in her beliefs, her dispositions, and likely her actions. Contrast this with the alternative view, according to which one's reasons for being disposed and acting can be different from the justification for the theory. Such is the case with the person who believes in divine command theory, according to which what makes right acts right is the fact that God commands them, but whose reason for doing the right thing or being motivated correctly is to get to heaven or avoid going to hell. Here the reason for acting according to divine command theory parts company from the reason an act or disposition is the right one. On my view, if you have a reason to endorse a justification for a moral theory, then you necessarily have a reason to be disposed and to act accordingly. Note that my view is *not* that if a person accepts the justification for the moral principles at issue, she necessarily disposes herself accordingly, since, again, I endorse weak externalism, according to which a person may not be moved to act or to be disposed by a justification for the principles despite her having a reason to do so. My claim is merely that she necessarily *has a reason* to be disposed in the relevant way, if she endorses the justification.

A second level at which consistency comes in is in the argument for the principles or main tenets of the moral theory to which the agent sub-scribes. This kind of consistency contributes to the theory's being good and rational to endorse. The idea is one familiar from chapter 5: morality must be impartial in the sense that it acknowledges that persons are equal in being rational, autonomous beings possessing dignity and deserving of respect. The moral principles or theory must be rooted in the kind of consistency that involves seeing others as equal in the basic facts about humanity—they cannot, on grounds of the principle of consistency that requires that there be no contradiction, involve privileging in the sense of advantaging oneself, including doing so in a way that disrespects others' humanity. Our friend who adopts the maxim "Respect women" acknowl-edges the basic facts about humanity in men and women alike, which is reflected in the justification for feminism. The justification is consonant with the reasons for adopting and acting from the maxim. Thus grievous acts of a sexist nature are not likely to escape on my model as being even rationally permissible, since they violate this level of consistency by privileging men and discounting, ignoring, or not focusing on women's humanity, or even by benefiting from institutional sexism. The moral, and hence rational, status of less grievous acts will have to be decided on a case-by-case basis.

The first two ways consistency factors in speak to the skeptic's demand that we demonstrate the rationality of *adopting* a moral disposition. The third way consistency factors in is that it is a rational requirement that a person's desires cohere with her choice to be a certain kind of person as reflected in the maxim she adopts. This speaks to the skeptic's require-ment that we demonstrate the rationality of *having* a moral disposition. On my view, this requires that the disposition be consistent with the agent's desires: a rational agent chooses to be a certain kind of person,

consistent with her desires. She reflectively deliberates in the way I described in the previous section about the kind of life she wants to lead, and
disposes herself to follow a maxim or guideline that fits into a coherent
life plan. Her choice to become morally disposed stems from a second-
order desire or volition to be a moral person, to live a life guided by moral
concerns. Having a moral disposition is rationally required, then, when
adopting it is rationally required and having and acting from it is consistent with one's desire set. If a person who wants to be morally disposed
has desires that are inconsistent with this higher order volition, she must
try to rid herself of them. For example, if she wants to please only herself,
this is inconsistent with her higher order volition to be a moral person
who is appropriately self-sacrificing; if she has deformed desires, this is
inconsistent with her wanting to be a self-respecting person, which morality calls for. If such desires continue to resurface, this could indicate
that she does not sincerely have the second-order volition. Performing
occasional character checks tells an agent if her desires and reasoning in an
action or series of actions is consistent with her choice to be a moral
person, and as such, is a condition of rationality. Both the psychopath,
who cannot make the choice because he does not properly understand his
options, and the unreflective person, who does not attend to his options
but instead is merely what he was raised to be, fail to exhibit moral agency
and integrity, and are not rational in the sense required for moral beings.
My model of rationality as consistency meets Duff's charge against EU,
that it counts as rational psychopathic interest-satisfying actions. A person
who engages in the complex reasoning required for ensuring consistency
in her dispositions, maxims, moral theory, and so on must have interests
and values in the full sense.

Fourth and finally, a rational requirement for *acting* morally is that the
agent's actions are consistent or cohere with her disposition and her
desires. Our judgments of acts should be agent-dependent: morally required acts are rationally required when they contribute to an agent's
leading a life guided by morality, and being consistent in her desires,
disposition, and actions. That is, morally required acts are those that
contribute to an agent's integrity, and so by my definition of integrity
they are ones that reflect coherence with the agent's disposition and
desires in the way I have described. Whether a morally required act is
rationally required turns out on my view to be a measure of consistency,
rather than self-interest or some other value-based standard of rationality. Consistency is necessary for integrity, and it is the standard of rationality. Using consistency as the standard for rationality when it comes to
acts plays out as follows. The agent's reasons for choosing to be a moral
person who lives her life guided by a moral maxim should be the same
reasons for acting from her disposition. It is her *reasoning* that must be
consistent across her disposition, actions, desires, and maxim. The agent
need not hold the reasons before her mind each time she acts, but she
must be able to show that her act expresses her deliberations about the

kind of person she wants to be and the maxim she endorses. For example, a male professor's coming to the aid of his female colleague when she is treated rudely by their chairperson is rationally required when he wants to be nonsexist and guides his life by a maxim endorsing respect for all. Acts that foster integrity by contributing to the agent's leading a life consistent in her desires and disposition and the reasoning underlying these are ones we must demonstrate to be rationally required as measured by the consistency displayed in the reasoning. A person whose reasons for making a moral theory practically central do not carry over to her actions is rationally disjointed in the same way she is morally disjointed. Note that my view is not that an agent acts morally *in order to be consistent*, so that the reasons for becoming morally disposed and so acting line up. This agent has the wrong aim. Rather, the agent should act from the moral theory or set of principles she endorses that are reflected in her disposition and because she wants to be a moral person. Her aim is to be a moral person who guides her life by the moral maxim her theory or principles generates. Consistency as a standard of rationality of the agent's act should reflect whether she acts *from* the theory or set of principles, rather than merely in accord with it. Moreover, the requirement that one's desires, disposition, and actions be consistent precludes the possibility that one merely go through the motions in acting morally. This level of consistency, when met, would defeat motive skepticism.

I have argued that what is morally required is that an agent have integrity. I have argued further that acts come in degrees of goodness as measured by their contribution to an agent's integrity. What is rationally required is that an agent be consistent in her desires, disposition, and actions, that is, in her reason for choosing to be a moral person expressed in a maxim guiding her life that itself displays consistency about persons' worth. Acts may also come in degrees of rationality, depending on their contribution to an agent's consistent life plan. A morally good agent who acts out of character performs an act that exhibits some degree of goodness and rationality if it affects the agent's reasoning in such a way as to contribute to her leading a consistent life, and does not violate other forms of consistency that I have discussed. This may happen when, for instance, the agent performs a character check, sees that her act is out of line with the person she wants to be, and makes the relevant adjustments. But we would not judge as rational the same act performed by the same agent if it had *no* effect on her deliberations, because it does not contribute to her having a life consistent in the relevant respects. The person who cuts off another driver in traffic, realizes that his behavior was bad, shores up his resolve not to have road rage, and apologizes to the other at the next traffic light performs an act that is better morally and rationally than the same act performed by a person who never checks his aggression. Similarly, the agent who is not morally disposed, but who in one of his actions reasons in a way that would support a moral maxim, performs an act that has some degree of rationality if his reasoning goes some way toward shaping his deliberations about being a person who guides his life by a moral maxim. Such is the case with the self-absorbed person who offers his seat on the train to someone burdened with heavy packages, and uses his reasoning in this case as a springboard to be more other-concerned. And, in the ideal case, acts performed by a morally good agent whose reasoning about the kind of person he wants to be is consistent with his reasons for acting are rational. Here the agent reflects on his act, and realizes that it conforms to and supports the maxim he endorses and his second-order volitions about his life; his act reinforces his disposition and thus contributes to his leading a consistent life. Grievous acts are just going to fail because they are not supported by a moral theory requiring equal respect for persons based on their worth. But in more ambiguous cases where it is difficult to say exactly how an act might disrespect someone's value—for example, prohibiting abortion—we have to tell a longer story, and assess the act in the complex way I am suggesting. In general, we should assess actions for rationality in light of the agent's reasoning, the nature of the act, how the agent responds to the reasoning she endorses in the act, and so on. The degree of rationality an act has depends on its contribution to the agent's leading a life consistent in the ways suggested, rather than whether they promote some aim, as in value-based theories. Note, finally, that a defeat of skepticism on this account of rationality, unlike a defeat of skepticism on EU, potentially would not lead to an individualistic or atomistic view of persons who seek to maximize the satisfaction of their own interests. Instead, it presents a rational person as one with a coherent life plan.

Let me clarify the view I am putting forward in light of defeating action skepticism. According to the Independency Thesis, the rationality of an act can be assessed *independently* of the rationality of the disposition it expresses. I attributed this thesis to Parfit, who defends it partly with the case of Kate. Parfit uses S as the standard of rationality of an act and of a disposition, and the rationality of an act is decided independent of that of a disposition. To defeat action skepticism on this view, we need to show that every morally required act is rationally required because it meets the standard set by S that performing it makes one's life go as well as possible. This will be determined independently of the rationality of the disposition expressing the acts. Gauthier rejects both the Independency Thesis and S as a standard of rationality for morally required actions. He defends the Dependency Thesis, according to which the rationality of an act *depends on* the rationality of the disposition expressing it. To defeat action skepticism on this view, we need both to establish the Dependency Thesis, and to show that a morally required disposition is rationally required in some sense other than S, or self-interest. But we saw that the arguments for the Dependency Thesis fail, and that morality is threatened by the case of Kate and similar cases where having a rational disposition and an irrational act is a real possibility. I proposed the Interdependency Thesis, according to which the rationality of acts and dispositions are assessed *interdependently*, in light of each other. Making interdependent judgments in morality reflects a significant fact about us as moral agents, whether we have integrity, not just whether we act or are disposed a certain way. Making interdependent judgments in rationality reflects a crucial fact about our rational agency, whether we have the right reasoning. The Independency Thesis does not capture this feature of rational agency, and the Dependency Thesis, as proposed by Gauthier, does not have the right take on it. The Interdependency Thesis captures what I think Gauthier wanted to show but could not because he accepts S at the level of dispositions. He claims that one's reason for adopting constrained maximization *includes* the fact that one must act on it, and so the rationality of one's disposition carries over to the acts expressing it.[50] This might suggest that what carries over from the rationality of the disposition to the act is the agent's reasoning. But Gauthier never explains this, and the reason for adopting the disposition is self-interest, which, as he rightly points out, cannot be the reason for acting morally if we want to defeat action skepticism. On the Interdependency Thesis, the rationality of the disposition carries over to the acts, or better, is assessed jointly with the rationality of acts, because of the agent's reasoning, and is grounded in consistency rather than self-interest.

In addition, I have argued that we use consistency or coherence in the agent's reasoning as the standard of rationality. On the model I am proposing, to defeat action skepticism, we need to establish the Interdependency Thesis, and demonstrate that acting morally is rationally required in the sense of consistency in the agent's reasoning. It turns out that if we defeat disposition skepticism, we will at once defeat action skepticism, and vice versa. This is because whether an act or a disposition is rationally required is a matter of whether it forms part of a coherent package reflecting the agent's integrity. In defeating skepticism, we are concerned to show that for morally required acts, they are rationally required. What makes an act morally required is that it fosters integrity. What makes an act rationally required is that the reasoning for acting is consistent, forming part of a coherent package. My view is that this very reasoning, if it is present in the disposition of an agent who has integrity, must be present in the action. The reasoning is an affirmation of the maxim the agent endorses and wants to follow in guiding her life. To determine whether the agent's reasoning in her disposition and actions is consistent, we need to assess the rationality of each jointly, and whether it does turn out to be consistent is a matter of both reflecting the same affirmation. What it is actually to have consistent reasoning just is that the reasoning in each forms part of a coherent package: it is the whole thing going together. Consistency is a relational concept. Since on the Interdependency Thesis if we defeat either disposition skepticism or action skepticism, we defeat both, this thesis is a major move forward in fully defeating skepticism.

Another advantage of the Interdependency Thesis is that it gets rid of cases like Kate's, of Rational Irrationality. Kate's choices stem from a commitment to S, even when she acts in non-self-interested ways, such as when she works to exhaustion. The Independency Thesis forces separate judgments of dispositions and acts. Since the Interdependency Thesis assesses dispositions and actions in light of each other, and makes the same judgments of them, we do not end up with cases in which a person's disposition is rational, but her acts irrational. My argument has been in terms of a *moral* disposition, so this is one factor that makes it difficult to apply my view to the case of Kate. Another factor is that I have said that Kate does not have too many options from which to choose—any weaker disposition will not cause her to work as hard as she needs to for a good life, and any stronger one will make her work too hard all the time. Presumably, the moral case will be different—there are different ways of being committed to morality, and I have allowed room for backsliding and still being a morally good and rational person. These points aside, on the Interdependency Thesis, we do not judge as irrational Kate's working to exhaustion and depression on Friday on the grounds that her act fails to meet a certain standard. Rather, we judge whether Kate takes things a step further and shores up her disposition, revises it, or whatever. Kate will realize that, in assessing her disposition, it may give her a tendency to act in ways that on the Independency Thesis would be irrational because the acts do not meet a certain standard. But her act is rational on the Interdependency Thesis when it makes her consistent between her disposition, actions, desires, and maxim by which she guides her life. Kate's acts do not get their rationality because they meet a certain standard. Nor do they get their rationality from the disposition they express. Her disposition does not get its rationality from the acts expressing it, either. Her acts and her disposition are rational because they are consistent with each other, in light of her desires and maxim. To think otherwise is to be wedded to the value-based standard of rationality that I have rejected.

5 CONCLUSION

I have come a long way in tightening the skeptic's position. I have argued that we need to broaden the skeptic's position by addressing both the amoralist and the motive skeptic, in addition to the action skeptic. But we should have a broader model than self-interest, that it is rationally required to act in a way that privileges oneself. Finally, we should endorse the Interdependency Thesis and the consistency model of rationality, and assume that the skeptic accepts reasons of consistency, since doing so promises that if we defeat either disposition or action skepticism, we will at once defeat the other.

I have endorsed the consistency model of rationality over EU in the hope that it will provide a successful defeat of skepticism that favors a richer account of morality, and according to which, if we defeat skepticism, we defeat it for all immoral acts, leaving no further legitimate skeptical challenge remaining. We still have some way to go: a successful defeat of any skeptic about moral action, including this revised skeptic, can only be carried out in the context of a full-blown moral theory. Defending such a theory and defeating the skeptic are projects philosophers I hope will undertake in light of each other, since this approach promises the best chance of success.

Notes

Chapter 1

1. According to Russ Shafer-Landau, this kind of skeptic is either a nihilist, one who denies that there are any moral truths, or a moral subjectivist, one who allows for moral truth but believes that each person determines it, or a moral relativist, who also allows for moral truth but believes that each culture determines it. See Shafer-Landau, *Whatever Happened to Good and Evil?* (New York: Oxford University Press, 2004), 8.

2. David Gauthier, *Morals by Agreement* (New York: Oxford University Press, 1986), 158.

3. Gauthier, *Morals by Agreement*, 2.

4. Michael Smith, *The Moral Problem* (Oxford, Blackwell, 1994), 68–71.

5. Christine M. Korsgaard, *The Sources of Normativity* (New York: Cambridge University Press, 1997), 142–44 and the surrounding discussion.

6. Stephen Darwall, *The Second-person Standpoint: Morality, Respect, and Accountability* (Cambridge, Mass.: Harvard University Press, 2006), 5.

7. Darwall, *The Second-person Standpoint*, 3.

8. Darwall, *The Second-person Standpoint*, 10.

9. Darwall has more to say by way of response to the skeptic in chapter 11 of *The Second-person Standpoint*.

10. Compare David Copp's argument about skepticism about the existence of moral requirements, in *Morality, Normativity, and Society* (New York: Oxford University Press, 1995), 48–49.

11. David Copp, "The Ring of Gyges: Overridingness and the Unity of Reason," in *Self-Interest*, ed. Ellen Frankel Paul, Fred D. Miller, Jr., and Jeffrey Paul (New York: Cambridge University Press, 1997), 86–106, esp. 86–87.

12. David O. Brink, "Rational Egoism, Self, and Others," in *Identity, Character, and Morality: Essays in Moral Psychology*, ed. Owen Flanagan and Amelie Oksenberg Rorty (Cambridge, Mass.: MIT Press, 1990), 339–78, esp. 339 and 370–71.

Chapter 2

1. Of course, SIB contractarians need not believe that people are, in fact, mutually disinterested, but as I will say later, they assume this for the sake of argument for purposes of taking what they consider to be the worst-case scenario against morality.

2. Thomas Hobbes, *Leviathan* (1651), ed. Michael Oakeshott (New York: Collier Books, 1962). Kurt Baier, *The Moral Point of View* (New York: Random

House, 1965). Geoffrey Grice, *The Grounds of Moral Judgement* (New York: Cambridge University Press, 1967). David Gauthier, *Morals by Agreement* (New York: Oxford University Press, 1986).

3. Hobbes, *Leviathan*, 101, 103.

4. Hobbes, *Leviathan*, 48.

5. Gauthier, *Morals by Agreement*, 100. See also 83, 103.

6. Hobbes, *Leviathan*, chap. 14, 103.

7. Gauthier, *Morals by Agreement*, 8.

8. Gauthier, *Morals by Agreement*, 102–3.

9. Gauthier, *Morals by Agreement*, 87, 100–104. The assumption of nontuism is broader than it need be for SIB contractarians, since it means that a person is not intrinsically concerned with another's good or bad. SIB contractarians could restrict this assumption to not taking an intrinsic interest only in another's good, since they intend for it to exclude any moral interests, as Gauthier's discussion in *Morals by Agreement*, chap. 10, sec. 2.5, suggests.

10. Gauthier uses the term "expresses." See, for example, *Morals by Agreement*, 183.

11. Henry Sidgwick, *The Methods of Ethics* (1884), 7th ed. (Indianapolis: Hackett,), bk. 2, chap. 5, 175.

12. Gauthier, *Morals by Agreement*, 1.

13. Gauthier, *Morals by Agreement*, 1.

14. Gauthier, *Morals by Agreement*, 167.

15. For some criticisms, see Holly Smith, "Deriving Morality from Rationality," in *Contractarianism and Rational Choice: Essays on David Gauthier's Morals by Agreement*, ed. Peter Vallentyne (New York: Cambridge University Press, 1991), 229–53; Geoffrey Sayre-McCord, "Deception and Reasons to Be Moral," 182–95, in the same volume, reprinted from *American Philosophical Quarterly* 26 (1989): 113–22; and my dissertation, "The Self-Interest Based Contractarian Response to the Why-Be-Moral Skeptic" (University of Illinois at Chicago, 1990), especially chap. 3.

16. Gauthier, *Morals by Agreement*, 184–87.

17. Gauthier, *Morals by Agreement*, 186.

18. David Gauthier, "Afterthoughts" (part of the series "Responses to the Paradox of Deterrence"), in *The Security Gamble: Deterrence Dilemmas in the Nuclear Age*, ed. Douglas MacLean (Totowa, N.J.: Rowman and Allanheld, 1984), 159–61, at 159. Note that Gauthier does not say "rationally required" because in this context he is talking about the rationality of *any* disposition carrying over to the acts expressing it. When it comes to a moral disposition, though, he believes that it and the acts expressing it are rationally required.

19. I understand Gauthier's view to be that we can dispose ourselves to being moral by an act of will. The view of a disposition that I defend in chapter 8 takes a disposition to be much more complex than an intention, which can be a one-shot deal to perform the action at hand and need not be acted on in order for it to be rational. I leave aside these points for the present discussion.

20. Derek Parfit, *Reasons and Persons* (New York: Oxford University Press, 1984). Parfit is not in his discussion responding to skepticism. Rather, he is trying to show that the Self-Interest Theory of rationality should not be rejected for the reason that it is indirectly self-defeating. It is indirectly self-defeating because, in spite of its telling us to have a certain set of motives and thus a certain disposition, our having the disposition might cause us on occasion to act in ways that the

theory itself holds to be irrational. Parfit's view is that *the theory* does not tell us to act irrationally, but it is "a separate fact about reality" that we will act irrationally, given our disposition. So we should not reject the theory on these grounds. I am using his discussion to motivate the alternative view to Gauthier's.

21. Parfit, *Reasons and Persons*, 3.

22. It should be noted that it is not entirely clear that the Kate case really is a counterexample to Gauthier's view. Gauthier's claim is that if it is rational to dispose oneself to do x in c, then it is rational for one to do x in c. Consider the devil case again: being disposed to take a pill to dispel the devil might cause one to kill others in order to get the pill. Surely Gauthier would not claim that killing others to get the pill was rational because it is an act caused by a disposition it is rational to have. Only acts of doing x in c count. Thus, a relevant counterexample to Gauthier's view would have to be an instance of doing x in c, an expression of the disposition it is rational to adopt.

23. This phrase is coined by Richmond Campbell, "Moral Justification and Freedom," *Journal of Philosophy* 85 (4) (1988): 192–213, at 199.

24. Again, Parfit does not directly discuss this, but I believe it is his view.

25. This argument appears in the context of nuclear deterrence, in David Gauthier, "Deterrence, Maximization, and Rationality," *Ethics* 94 (3) (April 1984): 474–95, at 487.

26. David Lewis, "Devil's Bargains and the Real World," in MacLean, *The Security Gamble*, 141–54. Lewis casts his argument in terms of morality, but I will put it in terms of rationality.

27. Lewis, "Devil's Bargains," 143.

28. Regarding the intention to retaliate, Lewis believes that the commander-in-chief and people in the armed forces are right to form the intention to retaliate, but having this intention makes them ready to commit massacres. They are vengeful, but true patriots. Lewis remarks, "It seems artificial to try to take the package apart, despise part of it, and treasure the rest. And it seems repellent to desire the whole package." ("Devil's Bargains," 144.) In the end, he does not want to make any moral judgment of the person *as a whole*.

29. In the next few paragraphs I will deal with judgments made of a person, though my main concern is with *actions*. This temporary switch in emphasis is not critical: a rational action is backed by reasons; a rational person is one who acts in ways backed by reasons.

30. See Duncan MacIntosh, "Two Gauthiers?" *Dialogue: Canadian Philosophical Review* 28 (1) (1989), 43–61, esp. 45.

31. Gregory Kavka, "The Toxin Puzzle," *Analysis* 197 (January 1983): 33–36.

32. This point was motivated by discussion with David Copp.

33. Gauthier has what many regard as a "thin" moral theory: the moral code it dictates has to meet only two requirements, namely, impartiality and rationality. He might say that the contractors would not find agreeable significant sacrifices to their well-being. But it would be unlikely for the bargainers to fine-tune the rules on which they agree to exclude such cases—for instance, there will be a time when keeping a promise demands significant sacrifices, even life itself, no matter how thin a moral theory or code we agree to follow.

34. This argument appears in Gauthier, "Afterthoughts," 160. It is posed as an objection to Lewis, and is given in the context of nuclear deterrence, though I think that the same argument can apply to the case of morality. Kavka makes the same point in "The Toxin Puzzle," 33–36.

35. Kavka offers the view in "Some Paradoxes of Deterrence," *Journal of Philosophy* 75 (6) (June 1978): 285–302, at 293. But Kavka offers a contradictory view in his paper "Responses to the Paradox of Deterrence," in Maclean, *The Security Gamble*, 155–159, at 156, where he says that he rejects the view that an intention is irrational because the action it causes is irrational. Finally, Kavka offers a rather odd view that the intention is both rational and irrational. It is rational in that adopting it is rational, and irrational in that it sometimes causes one to act in irrational ways.

36. That is, there is reason for doubting the rationality of both forming and having the disposition. Kavka suggests both in "Some Paradoxes of Deterrence," 293.

37. Gauthier offers two more, but less central, arguments for the Dependency Thesis. Against his opponent who insists that it is rational to adopt a disposition if and only if one maximizes one's expected utility both in adopting it and in acting on it, and that the rationality of acting on the disposition must take precedence over adopting it, Gauthier insists that the fully rational actor "is not the one who assesses her actions from now but, rather, the one who subjects the largest, rather than the smallest, segments of her activity to primary rational scrutiny, proceeding from policies to performances, letting assessment of the latter be ruled by assessment of the former." ("Deterrence, Maximization, and Rationality," 488.) Gauthier's point is that constrained maximization is the rational choice over straightforward maximization. This might be correct, but it does not establish that the actions a constrained maximizer performs are rational because of their dependency on the disposition. Gauthier must be assuming the truth of the principle: "Whenever you act from a disposition it is rational for you to have, you act rationally." But the truth is just what is up for dispute, as the Kate case shows.

In a second argument, Gauthier claims that performance-maximization, by which an individual assesses each action, but not the disposition, on the basis of its utility maximization, "fails to take individuals seriously by dividing their unified concerns into disparate parts" (Gauthier, "Afterthoughts," 161). The idea is that performance-maximization "divides up" the goal of utility maximization that characterizes an individual as a unified whole, not a mere aggregation. But this metaphorical argument fails, too. A straightforward maximizer is a "unified whole" in having a policy that governs all of his actions: "Maximize expected utility in every action." And the argument does not establish the Dependency Thesis, even if it supports the rationality of adopting constrained maximization rather than straightforward maximization. This view does not follow *logically* from the view that if a disposition is rational to adopt, all the actions expressing it are rational, as well. But it is implicit in Gauthier's view, mentioned in the passage cited earlier, that the fully rational actor, in deciding the rationality of particular actions, proceeds from policies to performances, letting assessment of the latter be ruled by assessment of the former ("Deterrence, Maximization, and Rationality," 488).

Chapter 3

1. See a brief discussion of these points in Rosemarie Tong, *Feminine and Feminist Ethics* (Belmont, Calif.: Wadsworth, 1993), 63–79.

2. John Rawls, *A Theory of Justice* (Cambridge, Mass.: Harvard University Press, 1971), 137.

3. See, for instance, Alison Jaggar, "Feminist Ethics: Some Issues for the Nineties," *Journal of Social Philosophy* 20 (1–2) (Spring–Fall 1989): 91–107, at 104.

4. Virginia Held, "Feminist Transformations of Moral Theory," *Philosophy and Phenomenological Research* 1, supp. (Fall 1990): 321–44, at 325.

5. Jean Hampton responds to this feminist complaint with a feminist construal of contractarianism, one tempered with the Kantian assumption that everyone is equal in worth. The actions agreed on in the contract are ones that should not violate anyone's worth. Hampton intends for the contract to govern private as well as public relations, and indeed, the contract provides a good way to eradicate exploitation that exists in private relations. See her "Feminist Contractarianism," in *A Mind of One's Own: Feminist Essays on Reason and Objectivity*, 2nd ed., ed. Louise M. Antony and Charlotte E. Witt (Boulder, Colo.: Westview Press, 2002), 337–68. Marilyn Friedman agrees that contractarianism ought to cover personal relationships. See Friedman, "Beyond Caring: The De-moralization of Gender," *Canadian Journal of Philosophy* 13, supp. vol., *Science, Morality and Feminist Theory*, ed. Marsha Hanen and Kai Nielsen (Calgary, Alberta: University of Calgary Press, 1987): 87–110, at 99.

6. For this distinction, see Tong, *Feminine and Feminist Ethics*, esp. 4.

7. Carol Gilligan, *In a Different Voice: Psychological Theory and Women's Development* (Cambridge, Mass.: Harvard University Press, 1982); Carol Gilligan, "Moral Orientation and Moral Development," in *Women and Moral Theory*, ed. Eva Feder Kittay and Diana T. Meyers (New York: Rowman and Littlefield, 1987), 19–33.

8. Gilligan, "Moral Orientation," 25–26.

9. Gilligan, "Moral Orientation," 22 and 30.

10. Held, "Feminist Transformations."

11. Gilligan, "Moral Orientation," 17. Gilligan says that women define themselves in terms of their ability to care—as nurturers, caretakers, and helpmates. These are the roles they play in men's lifecycles, but men, in turn, in their theories devalue this care.

12. Gilligan's endorsement of the duck/rabbit view of perspectives means that this cannot be her own view.

13. Held, "Feminist Transformations," 332; see also 349–50 and 331.

14. Seyla Benhabib, "The Generalized and the Concrete Other: The Kohlberg-Gilligan Controversy and Moral Theory," in Kittay and Meyers, *Women and Moral Theory*, 154–77, at 160.

15. Cheshire Calhoun, "Justice, Care, and Gender Bias," *Journal of Philosophy* 85 (9) (September 1988): 451–63, at 458–59.

16. Gilligan, *In a Different Voice* and "Moral Orientation"; Nel Noddings, *Caring: A Feminine Approach to Ethics and Moral Education* (Berkeley: University of California Press, 1984); Sara Ruddick, "Maternal Thinking," in *Women and Values: Readings in Recent Feminist Philosophy*, ed. Marilyn Pearsall (Belmont, Calif.: Wadsworth, 1986), 340–51; Annette Baier, "What Do Women Want in a Moral Theory?" in *An Ethic of Care: Feminist and Interdisciplinary Perspectives*, ed. Mary Jeanne Larrabee (New York: Routledge, 1993), 19–32; Marilyn Friedman, "Beyond Caring"; Joan Tronto, "Beyond Gender Difference to a Theory of Care," in Larrabee, *An Ethic of Care*, 240–57, at 249; Owen Flanagan and Kathryn Jackson, "Justice, Care, and Gender: The Kohlberg-Gilligan Debate Revisited," *Ethics* 97(3) (April 1987): 622–37; and Lawrence Blum, "Gilligan and Kohlberg: Implications for Moral Theory," *Ethics* 98 (3) (April 1988): 472–91.

17. See Annette Baier, "The Need for More Than Justice," in *Canadian Journal of Philosophy* 13, 14–56, especially 47. See also Friedman, "Beyond Caring," 99.

18. Jeffrey Blustein offers a number of interpretations in his recent book *Care and Commitment: Taking the Personal Point of View* (New York: Oxford University Press, 1991).

19. Rita Manning suggests that caring for does not require any particular emotion toward the one cared for. See her *Speaking from the Heart: A Feminist Perspective on Ethics* (Lanham, Md.: Rowman and Littlefield, 1992), 64.

20. According to Blum, "Gilligan and Kohlberg," 476.

21. Blum, "Gilligan and Kohlberg," 491.

22. Annette Baier, "Hume, the Women's Moral Theorist," in Kittay and Meyers, *Women and Moral Theory*, 37–55, at 41.

23. Calhoun, "Justice, Care, and Gender Bias," 460.

24. Noddings, *Caring*, 86.

25. Flanagan and Jackson, "Justice, Care, and Gender," 623.

26. Benhabib, "The Generalized and the Concrete Other," 155.

27. Blum, "Gilligan and Kohlberg," 475.

28. Blum, "Gilligan and Kohlberg," 486.

29. The feminists cited in this section may no longer hold the views I discuss, as there has been considerable debate since these early views were put forward, particularly about the distinction between a feminist and a feminine theory.

30. Held, "Feminist Transformations," 322.

31. Genevieve Lloyd, *The Man of Reason: "Male" and "Female" in Western Philosophy* (Minneapolis: University of Minnesota Press, 1984). See especially ix and x.

32. Tong, *Feminine and Feminist Ethics*; Held, "Feminist Transformations;" and Nancy Tuana, *Women and the History of Philosophy* (New York: Paragon House, 1992).

33. But I am less certain than Lloyd that the philosophers she discusses really do strictly dichotomize reason and emotions. For instance, Marcia Homiak argues that Aristotle advocates a life in which reason and emotion are compatible and interactive. For Aristotle, "being caring and compassionate must be expressed within a life lived according to the rational ideal, or else these traits become destructive and unhealthy." See Marcia L. Homiak, "Feminism and Aristotle's Rational Ideal," in *A Mind of One's Own: Feminist Essays on Reason and Objectivity*, ed. Louise M. Antony and Charlotte E. Witt (Boulder, Colo.: Westview Press, 1993), 1–17, at 3. Barbara Herman argues that for Kant, reasons and motives can be complementary. According to Herman, Kantian motives reflect an agent's reasons for acting. Desires are merely incentives. The motive of duty, which is a reason, sets limits on whether and how other motives may be acted on. It is a limiting condition rather than an opposing tug. See Barbara Herman, "On the Value of Acting from the Motive of Duty," in *The Practice of Moral Judgment*, ed. Barbara Herman (Cambridge, Mass.: Harvard University Press, 1993), 1–22, at 14.

34. Lloyd, *The Man of Reason*; Held, "Feminist Transformations," 323.

35. Held, "Feminist Transformations," 323.

36. See Debra DeBruin, "Identifying Sexual Harassment: The Reasonable Woman Standard," in *Violence against Women: Philosophical Perspectives*, ed. Stanley G. French, Wanda Teays, and Laura M. Purdy (Ithaca, N.Y.: Cornell University Press, 1998), 107–22.

37. See, for instance, Marcia Baron, "Killing in the Heat of Passion," in *Setting the Moral Compass: Essays by Women Philosophers*, ed. Cheshire Calhoun (New York: Oxford University Press, 2004), 353–78. Baron takes up the topic of whether killing in the heat of passion should be a legal defense, and argues against feminists who favor rejecting it. Baron believes that we should instead narrow it since there are cases in which it is a good defense, as when a wife shoots her husband who rapes their baby daughter (362).

38. Nancy Tuana, "The Maleness of Reason," chap. 3 in *Women and the History of Philosophy*, 34–55, at 40.

39. Tuana, "The Maleness of Reason," 41.

40. Approximately 37 percent of PhDs in philosophy were awarded to women in 1997. For further statistics, see my "Welcome to the Boys' Club: Male Socialization and the Backlash against Feminism in Tenure Decisions," in *Theorizing Backlash: Philosophical Reflections on the Resistance to Feminism*, ed. Anita M. Superson and Ann E. Cudd (Lanham, Md.: Rowman and Littlefield, 2002), 89–117, at 90.

41. Patricia Hill Collins notes that black women have worked first as slaves, then as low-wage earners. See *Black Feminist Thought: Knowledge, Consciousness, and the Politics of Empowerment* (New York: Routledge, 1990), at 43–66.

42. See Kristin Luker, *Abortion and the Politics of Motherhood* (Berkeley: University of California Press, 1984), who gives evidence that stay-at-home (Christian) mothers are the loudest activists for the antiabortion cause. Their small but strong network was responsible for launching the "prolife" movement several decades ago that is alive and well today.

43. Held, "Feminist Transformations," 326.

44. Homiak, "Feminism and Aristotle's Rational Ideal," 2.

45. Tuana, "The Maleness of Reason," 41. I doubt that Tuana still holds this view.

46. See also Joan Tronto, who contrasts traditional moral theories that "rely on rational tests to check self-interested inclinations … [in which] the rational and the moral become identified" with contextual moral theories that "stress moral sensitivity and moral imagination as keys to understanding mature moral life." Tronto, "Beyond Gender Difference to a Theory of Care," 249. Tronto's view on justification is not clear in this essay.

47. Noddings, *Caring*, 50.

48. Noddings, *Caring*, 95.

49. Noddings, *Caring*, 95.

50. Noddings, *Caring*, 5.

51. Noddings, *Caring*, 104.

52. Noddings, *Caring*, 18.

53. Noddings, *Caring*, 99.

54. Noddings, *Caring*, 104.

55. Noddings, *Caring*, 83.

56. Noddings, *Caring*, 50.

57. Noddings, *Caring*, 81.

58. Noddings, *Caring*, 46.

59. Noddings, *Caring*, 83.

60. Noddings, *Caring*, 50. I state the question vaguely, instead of the more precise question "Why should I act morally on this occasion?" Defeating the action skeptic requires answering the more precise question. Noddings would have to

show, in order to defeat the action skeptic, that acting morally on every occasion contributes to being a moral person.

Note also that Noddings admits that the moral imperative is categorical only in relations (I assume) with intimates. If there is no relation, or when a relation may be "properly refused" (e.g., when it is abusive), the imperative is hypothetical: "I must if I wish to (or am able to) move into relation" (86).

61. David Hume, *An Enquiry Concerning the Principles of Morals* (1777), ed. J. B. Schneewind (Indianapolis: Hackett, 1983), 81–82.

62. Noddings, *Caring*, 2.

63. Noddings, *Caring*, 95.

64. Noddings, *Caring*, 98.

65. Noddings, *Caring*, 104.

66. Friedman says that this is how justice arises out of relations ("Beyond Caring," 104).

67. Tronto, "Beyond Gender Difference to a Theory of Care," 250, 251.

68. Noddings, *Caring*, 23, my emphasis.

69. Calhoun, "Justice, Care, and Gender Bias," 459.

70. Jean Hampton, "Rethinking Reason," *American Philosophical Quarterly* 29 (3) (July 1992): 219–36, at 222–24.

71. Ruddick, "Maternal Thinking," 341.

72. Hampton, "Rethinking Reason," 222–23.

73. Hampton, "Rethinking Reason," 222.

74. See Duncan MacIntosh, "Categorically Rational Preferences and the Structure of Morality" in *Modeling Rationality, Morality and Evolution*, ed. Peter Danielson Vancouver Studies in Cognitive Science 7 (New York: Oxford University Press, 1995), 282–301. MacIntosh's main objective is not to make EU consistent with feminist aims, but this view falls out of his argument.

75. Bernard Williams, "Internal and External Reasons," in *Moral Luck*, ed. Bernard Williams (New York: Cambridge University Press, 1981), 101–13, at 101.

76. He dubs the general thesis "sub-Humean internalism" because Hume's views, he believes, are more sophisticated than this. Williams's own view, then, is a modified sub-Humean internalism.

77. Bernard Williams, "Internal Reasons and the Obscurity of Blame," in *Making Sense of Humanity and Other Philosophical Papers 1982–1993*, ed. Bernard Williams (New York: Cambridge University Press, 1995), 35–45, at 35.

78. As I will discuss in chapter 6, other internalists believe that if one lacks the relevant motive, one must be irrational, yet one still has the reason to act morally.

79. Bernard Williams, "Internal and External Reasons."

80. Gilbert Harman, "Moral Relativism Defended," *Philosophical Review* 84 (1) (January 1975): 3–22, at 8. Harman says: "Inner judgments have two important characteristics. First, they imply that the agent has reasons to do something. Second, the speaker in some sense endorses these reasons and supposes that the audience also endorses them."

81. Assuming it is justified to act in the relevant way, of course. The capacity to be motivated by itself will not give a reason to act.

I believe that Hume shares this view, given his emphasis on the "seeds and first principles" that motivate us to act even if we do not have full-blown sympathy or benevolence. See Hume, *Enquiry*, 15, 45, 74, and 75.

82. David Hume, *A Treatise of Human Nature* (1888), 2nd ed., ed. L.A. Selby-Bigge (New York: Oxford University Press, 1992), 457–58 and 462–65; and *Enquiry*, especially app. 1 and sec. 1.

83. For a thorough discussion of this point, see Charlotte Brown, "Is Hume An Internalist?" *Journal of the History of Philosophy* 26 (1) (January 1988): 69–87, at 79.

84. Hume, *Enquiry*, 74, 45.

85. Hume, *Enquiry*, 80.

86. Hume, *Enquiry*, 80.

87. Hume, *Enquiry*, 54, 68.

88. Hume, *Treatise*, sec. 9, pt, 2, 81.

89. Jaggar, "Feminist Ethics: Some Issues for the Nineties," 91–107, at 102, referring to Gilligan and Noddings.

90. Ruddick, "Maternal Thinking," 348.

91. Benhabib, "The Generalized and the Concrete Other," 164.

92. Larry Blum, Marcia Homiak, Judy Housman, and Naomi Scheman, "Altruism and Women's Oppression," in Special Issue on Women and Philosophy, *Philosophical Forum* v (1–2) (Fall–Winter 1973–74): 222–57, at 222.

93. Marilyn Friedman, "Liberating Care," in *What Are Friends For?* ed. Marilyn Friedman (Ithaca, N.Y.: Cornell University Press, 1993), 142–83, at 174.

94. Michael Stocker, "The Schizophrenia of Modern Moral Theories," *Journal of Philosophy* 73 (14) (August 1976): 453–66, at 456–57.

95. Manning, *Speaking from the Heart*,158.

96. Noddings, *Caring*, 50.

97. Noddings, *Caring*, 5, 98.

98. Noddings, *Caring*, 104, 79.

99. Noddings, *Caring*, 104.

100. Noddings, *Caring*, 81.

101. Noddings, *Caring*, 17.

102. Noddings, *Caring*, 52.

103. Noddings, *Caring*, 95.

104. Noddings's view is confusing on this point. She says that the imperative in relation is categorical (*Caring*, 86), but she endorses partialism. Again, she believes that Americans do not have obligations to care for starving children in Africa "because there is no way of caring [for them] to be completed in the other unless [one] abandon[s] the caring to which [one is] obligated" (86).

105. Noddings, *Caring*, 96.

106. Noddings, *Caring*, 24.

107. Noddings, *Caring*, 81.

108. Friedman, "Liberating Care," 175.

109. Friedman, "Liberating Care," 177.

110. Sandra Bartky, "Feeding Egos and Tending Wounds: Deference and Disaffection in Women's Emotional Labor," in *Femininity and Domination*, ed. Sandra Bartky (New York: Routledge, 1990), 99–119. See especially her discussion of female flight attendants (104–5).

111. Blum et al., "Altruism and Women's Oppression," 231–32, 235, and 236.

112. Blum et al., "Altruism and Women's Oppression," 235.

113. Blum et al., "Altruism and Women's Oppression," 239.

114. Friedman, "Liberating Care," 152, and Susan Sherwin, "Ethics, 'Feminine' Ethics, and Feminist Ethics," chap. 2 in *No Longer Patient: Feminist Ethics*

and Health Care, ed. Susan Sherwin (Philadelphia: Temple University Press, 1992), 35–57, at 50.

115. Sarah Lucia Hoagland, "Some Thoughts about 'Caring,'" in *Feminist Ethics*, ed. Claudia Card (Lawrence: University Press of Kansas, 1991), 246–63, at 252–54. See also Ruddick, "Maternal Thinking," 348.

116. Friedman, "Liberating Care,"147, 182.

117. See Blum et al., "Altruism and Women's Oppression," through 237, for a detailed and very plausible account of these features of patriarchy.

118. Bartky, "Feeding Egos and Tending Wounds," 109–10.

119. I describe this phenomenon in "Right-Wing Women: Causes, Choices, and Blaming the Victim," *Journal of Social Philosophy* 24 (3) (Winter 1993): 40–61, at 49.

Chapter 4

1. Elizabeth Anderson describes the formal version of EU as one in which people tend to maximize their utility; it disregards the contents of the preferences and reasons for having them. See Anderson, "Should Feminists Reject Rational Choice Theory?" in *A Mind of One's Own: Feminist Essays on Reason and Objectivity*, ed. Louise M. Antony and Charlotte E. Witt, 2nd ed. (Boulder, Colo.: Westview Press, 2002), 369–97, at 373–74. Gauthier and Rawls take EU to require only that desires be consistent and properly ordered. See David Gauthier, *Morals by Agreement* (New York: Oxford University Press, 1986); John Rawls, *A Theory of Justice* (Cambridge, Mass.: Harvard University Press, 1971). Debra Satz and John Ferejohn say that on EU's formal version, the agent's reasons for having her preferences are irrelevant because the theory does not judge the rationality of the agent's preferences but only the relations among them, specifically, whether they are consistent with each other, which turns out on some accounts to be a requirement of transitivity. See Satz and Ferejohn, "Rational Choice and Social Theory," *Journal of Philosophy* 91 (2) (February 1994): 71–87, at 73.

2. Feminists and race theorists make a similar point about the alleged neutrality of the dominant ideology taken to be the norm by social institutions—on closer inspection, it is not neutral, and its alleged neutrality makes it seem as if, for example, affirmative action policies favor minorities rather than give them a fair starting point.

3. See Thomas E. Hill, Jr., "Servility and Self-Respect," in *Dignity, Character, and Self-Respect*, ed. Robin S. Dillon (New York: Routledge, 1995), 76–92, at 78; reprinted from Monist 57 (1973), 87–104. I will discuss this case in more detail in chapter 6.

4. See Evelyn P. Stevens, "*Marianismo*: The Other Face of *Machismo* in Latin America," in *Gender Basics: Feminist Perspectives on Women and Men*, ed. Anne Minas (Belmont, Calif.: Wadsworth, 1993), 484–90.

5. See my "Right-Wing Women: Causes, Choices, and Blaming the Victim," *Journal of Social Philosophy* 24 (3) (Winter 1993): 40–61. The conclusions I draw about the role of religion, particularly Christianity, on women's being right-wing, are based on evidence presented by Kristin Luker in *Abortion and the Politics of Motherhood* (Berkeley: University of California Press, 1984).

6. Uma Narayan, "Minds of Their Own: Choices, Autonomy, Cultural Practices, and Other Women," in Antony and Witt, *A Mind of One's Own*,

418–432. The dupes of patriarchy completely subscribe to the patriarchal norms and practices of their culture because of internal coercion of their deformed desires; the prisoners of patriarchy have these norms imposed on them by external forces against their will and consent.

7. Elizabeth Anderson, "Is Women's Labor a Commodity?" chap. 8 in Anderson, *Value in Ethics and Economics* (Cambridge, Mass.: Harvard University Press, 1995), 168–89, at 180–81, rev. version; originally published *Philosophy and Public Affairs* 19 (1990): 71–92.

8. Narayan, "Minds of Their Own," 420.

9. Christina Hoff Sommers, *Who Stole Feminism? How Women Have Betrayed Women* (New York: Simon and Schuster, 1994). For a discussion (and rejection) of Sommers's view, see Martha Nussbaum, "American Women," in *Sex and Social Justice*, ed. Martha C. Nussbaum (New York: Oxford University Press, 1990), 130–53, at 149.

10. Marilyn Friedman, "Autonomy and Social Relationships: Rethinking the Feminist Critique," in *Feminists Rethink the Self*, ed. Diana Tietjens Meyers (Boulder, Colo.: Westview Press, 1997), 40–61.

11. Narayan, "Minds of Their Own," 425.

12. Ann E. Cudd, *Analyzing Oppression* (New York: Oxford University Press, 2006). "Opportunity inequality" refers to women's being seen as inferior to men and so less worthy of investment in health and education. "Oppression by choice" refers to the way women willingly contribute to their own oppression, as when they sacrifice a career for family for expected higher male wages, perpetuating the stereotype that women are unreliable wage workers.

13. Sandra Bartky, "Narcissism, Femininity, and Alienation," in *Femininity and Domination: Studies in the Phenomenology of Oppression*, ed. Sandra Lee Bartky (New York: Routledge, 1990), 33–44, at 42.

14. Martha Nussbaum, "American Women." Nussbaum is referring to John Stuart Mill's view, which she discusses at 149.

15. Jon Elster, "Sour Grapes," in *Sour Grapes: Studies in the Subversion of Rationality*, ed. Jon Elster (New York: Cambridge University Press, 1987), 109–40, esp. 109. Nussbaum endorses this view of adaptation.

16. Nussbaum, "American Women," 149.

17. Bartky, "Narcissism, Femininity, and Alienation."

18. I mentioned this description by Duncan MacIntosh in chapter 3. See MacIntosh, "Categorically Rational Preferences and the Structure of Morality," in *Modeling Rationality, Morality and Evolution*, ed. Peter Danielson, Vancouver Studies in Cognitive Science 7 (New York: Oxford University Press, 1995), 282–301.

19. See Bartky, "Narcissism, Femininity, and Alienation," and Naomi Wolf, *The Beauty Myth: How Images of Beauty Are Used against Women* (New York: Anchor Books, 1992).

20. Elster, "Sour Grapes," 116.

21. Lois Pineau, "Date Rape: A Feminist Analysis," *Law and Philosophy* 8 (1989): 217–43, at 239.

22. See Catharine MacKinnon, "Desire and Power," in *Feminism Unmodified: Discourses on Life and Law*, ed. Catharine MacKinnon (Cambridge, Mass.: Harvard University Press, 1987), 46–69, at 54; "Sexual Harassment: Its First Decade in Court," in *Feminism Unmodified*, 103–16, at 114; "Francis Biddle's Sister: Pornography, Civil Rights, and Speech," in *Feminism Unmodified*, 163–97, at 180 and 194.

23. Ann Cudd, "The Paradox of Liberal Feminism: Choice, Rationality, and Oppression," in *Varieties of Feminist Liberalism*, ed. Amy Baehr (Lanham, Md.: Rowman and Littlefield, 2004), 37–61, at 47–48.

24. Kant endorses (at least) two levels of self-respect: (1) respect for yourself as a person, in virtue of your capacity for rationality, and (2) respect for yourself according to how you measure up morally (i.e., using your freedom in the right way, not succumbing to inclination). I am concerned with the first. See Immanuel Kant, "Dignity and Self-Respect," in *Lectures on Ethics*, trans. Louis Enfield (New York: Harper and Row, 1963 and 1830), 526–35, at 533–34; from the edition of P. Menzer (Berlin, 1924).

25. Bernard Williams, "Internal and External Reasons," in *Moral Luck*, ed. Bernard Williams (New York: Cambridge University Press, 1983), 101–13.

26. Michael Smith, *The Moral Problem* (Malden, Mass.: Blackwell, 1998), 154–55. According to *The American Heritage Dictionary of the English Language* (Boston: Houghton Mifflin, 1980), "accidie" is "spiritual torpor" or "ennui."

27. Richard B. Brandt, *A Theory of the Good and the Right* (Amherst, N.Y.: Prometheus Books, 1998), 111–12.

28. R. B. Brandt, "Rational Desires," *Proceedings and Addresses of the American Philosophical Association* 43 (September 1970): 43–64, at 46, emphasis in original.

29. Brandt, "Rational Desires," 46, 63; *A Theory of the Good and the Right*, 112.

30. Peter Railton, "Moral Realism," *Philosophical Review* 95 (2) (April 1986): 163–207, quotation at 173–74, first italics mine.

31. James Griffin, *Well-Being: Its Meaning, Measurement and Moral Importance* (New York: Oxford University Press, 1990). Elizabeth Anderson, *Value in Ethics and Economics* (Cambridge, Mass.: Harvard University Press, 1995).

32. Railton also discusses Beth, the successful and happy accountant who wants to quit and devote herself to full-time writing. See Peter Railton, "Facts and Values," *Philosophical Topics* 14 (2) (Fall 1986): 5–31, at 12. Railton also gives the example of Lonnie, the traveler in a foreign country who wants to overcome his ill feelings by drinking the milk that would make him more dehydrated. See Railton, "Moral Realism," 174–75. Brandt's examples are of a student who seeks an academic profession because he thinks his professor parents would be disappointed if he did not, and a professor raised in the depression who is not wealthy but spendthrifty. See Brandt, *A Theory of the Good and the Right*, 115, 123.

33. A number of passages are relevant. First is Kant's statement that every rational being exists as an end it itself, not merely as a means to be used by another's will at its discretion. See Immanuel Kant, *Groundwork for the Metaphysics of Morals* (1785), in *Practical Philosophy: The Cambridge Edition of the Works of Immanuel Kant*, trans. and ed. Mary J. Gregor, (New York: Cambridge University Press, 1996), 43–108, at 79, AKA 4:428. Kant says further that "the lawgiving itself, which determines all worth, must for that very reason have a dignity, that is, an unconditional, incomparable worth; and the word *respect* alone provides a becoming expression for the estimate of it that a rational being must give. *Autonomy* is therefore the ground of the dignity of human nature and of every rational nature." (*Groundwork*, 85, AKA 4:436.) He claims that rational nature is distinguished from the rest of nature by this, that it sets itself an end (the matter of every good will). (*Groundwork*, 86, AKA 4:437.) In *The Metaphysics of Morals*, he says:

"Hence there is also bound up with the end of humanity in our own person the rational will, and so the duty, to make ourselves worthy of humanity by culture in general, by procuring or promoting the *capacity* to realize all sorts of possible ends, so far as this is found to be in the human being himself." (*The Metaphysics of Morals*, in *Practical Philosophy*, trans. Gregor, 522, AKA 6:392.) Regarding servility, he says that a human being can set himself ends. As an end in itself, he possesses dignity, an absolute inner worth by which he exacts respect for himself from all other rational beings in the world. (*The Metaphysics of Morals* 557, AKA 6:435.)

34. This characterization of Kant's view mitigates the following concerns raised by some feminists: (1) that a person is an exceedingly thin being wholly consisting of the capacity for rationally autonomous moral agency; (2) that the morally significant feature of persons is something abstract and generic and distinguishes us from each other; and (3) that the abstract view of a person does not take seriously the person as an individual because it does not pay attention to the particular circumstances of a person's life, particularly the subordinating circumstances of women's lives. For a discussion of these objections, see Robin Dillon, "Toward a Feminist Conception of Self-Respect," in *Dignity, Character, and Self-Respect*, ed. Robin S. Dillon (New York: Routledge, 1995), 290–310, at 295. Reprinted from *Hypatia* 7 (1992), 52–69.

35. Judith Jarvis Thomson, "Trespass and First Property," in *The Realm of Rights* (Cambridge, Mass.: Harvard University Press, 1990), 205–26.

36. Thomson, "Trespass and First Property," 215.

37. Harry G. Frankfurt, "Freedom of the Will and the Concept of a Person," *Journal of Philosophy* 68 (1) (1971): 5–20. The relevant discussion can be found at 10–14.

38. She likely has sex with clients to preserve her life, to avoid bodily harm, or to achieve a higher standard of living, and without any interest or desire for connection to her clients, without any response to her own sexual needs, and so on, and detaching herself from the bodily event. See Clelia Smyth Anderson and Yolanda Estes, "The Myth of the Happy Hooker: Kantian Moral Reflections on a Phenomenology of Prostitution," in *Violence against Women: Philosophical Perspectives*, ed. Stanley G. French, Wanda Teays, and Laura M. Purdy (Ithaca, N.Y.: Cornell University Press, 1998), 152–58.

39. Narayan, "Minds of Their Own," 422.

40. Narayan, "Minds of Their Own," 422.

41. I argue for this in "The Deferential Wife Revisited: Agency and Responsibility," unpublished manuscript. I return to the Deferential Wife in chapter 6.

42. Narayan, "Minds of Their Own," 420. "Veiling" includes wearing a burqua.

43. Narayan, "Minds of Their Own," 422–23.

44. Dillon, "Toward a Feminist Conception of Self-Respect," 302.

45. Dillon, following Stephen Darwall but expanding on his account, defines "recognition self-respect," the respect that all persons are owed simply in virtue of being persons, as involving "(1) recognizing that something is a person, (2) appreciating that persons as such have intrinsic moral worth and status, (3) understanding that the fact that something is a person constrains us morally to act only in certain ways in connection with him or her, and (4) acting and being disposed to act in those ways out of that recognition, appreciation, and understanding." (See "Toward a Feminist Conception of Self-Respect," 293.)

46. I think my account avoids the problem of circularity raised by Richmond Campbell in conversation. Campbell says: Suppose that a person respects herself and takes herself to have intrinsic worth. She would believe that some of her desires, namely, those in her real self-interest, are worthy of satisfaction. But which desires are these? They must be those that are not deformed. But how do we decide this? Presumably they are the desires that are consistent with regarding oneself as having intrinsic worth. The problem is that we have defined intrinsic worth and nondeformed desires in terms of each other, in a way that illuminates neither the nature of deformed desires nor that of treating oneself as having intrinsic worth.

My response to this circularity is that in order for a desire to be deformed, it must satisfy other conditions aside from being associated with lack of intrinsic worth, and that having intrinsic worth is a more complicated matter than not having deformed desires, as I have just explained in the text.

47. Frankfurt, "Freedom of the Will," 445.

48. Narayan might be arguing that the desire to veil is not a deformed desire after all, in virtue of its being a desire that one has even after "bargaining" with patriarchy. But I think this is wrong because it satisfies the five conditions outlined in the previous section.

49. Compare her to a person who wants to save the lives of others at the cost of his own by giving them his seat in the lifeboat. While he does not benefit from satisfying this desire since he no longer exists, he benefits the ones rescued, and not the established order of domination, if his desire is not caused by unjust social conditions.

50. Brandt, *A Theory of the Good and the Right*, 113.

51. Immanuel Kant, *Grounding for the Metaphysics of Morals* (1785), trans. James W. Ellington (Indianapolis: Hackett, 1981), AKA 429, at 36. Kant does not actually say what the conditions are for "full rationality."

52. Sandra Bartky discusses conflicting messages in "Toward a Phenomenology of Feminist Consciousness," in *Femininity and Domination*, 11–21. See also Susan J. Brison, who says that messages of inferiority such as those given in rape can undo an entire lifetime of self-esteem. See Brison, *Aftermath: Violence and the Remaking of a Self* (Princeton, N.J.: Princeton University Press, 2002), 63.

53. Williams, "Internal and External Reasons," 104–5.

54. Railton, "Moral Realism," 174.

55. Railton, "Moral Realism," 177.

56. Williams, "Internal and External Reasons," 101–13; Williams, "Internal Reasons and the Obscurity of Blame," 35.

57. Williams, "Internal and External Reasons," 105.

58. Williams, "Internal and External Reasons," 105.

59. Railton, "Moral Realism," 177.

60. Brandt, "Rational Desires," 46.

61. Williams, "Internal and External Reasons," 103.

62. Griffin, *Well-Being*. Anderson, *Value in Ethics and Economics*.

63. Sommers, *Who Stole Feminism*, 260. See also Nussbaum's critique of Sommers's argument, in "American Women," 146–53.

64. Susan Estrich, "Rape," in *Feminist Jurisprudence*, ed. Patricia Smith (New York: Oxford University Press, 1993), 158–87.

65. Mary Gibson, "Rationality," *Philosophy and Public Affairs* 6 (3) (Spring 1977): 193–225, quotation at 209. Jean E. Hampton, *The Authority of Reason*,

ed. Richard Healey (New York: Cambridge University Press, 1998), 205. See also her "Feminist Contractarianism," in Antony and Witt, *A Mind of One's Own*, 236. Susan Moller Okin, *Is Multiculturalism Bad for Women?* (Princeton, N.J.: Princeton University Press, 1999). Martha C. Nussbaum, *Women and Human Development: The Capabilities Approach* (New York: Cambridge University Press, 2000), chapter 1.

66. Philosophers have gone in both directions, for feminist or other reasons. MacIntosh, whose view inspired the informed desire test I offer here, favors keeping it. ("Categorically Rational Preferences and the Structure of Morality.") Hampton favors keeping the theory for the feminist reason that it protects women from surrendering their self-interest to the requirements of a morality that makes them the prey of others. ("Feminist Contractarianism," 245.) Anderson favors abandoning it for a number of reasons in favor of her expressivist theory. (*Values in Ethics and Economics*.) Thomas Hill offers some competing theories of rational action, including a consequentialist model, a Kantian model, and a common sense model. See Thomas E. Hill, Jr., "Reasonable Self-Interest," in *Self-Interest*, ed. Ellen Frankel Paul, Fred D. Miller, Jr., and Jeffrey Paul (New York: Cambridge University Press, 1997), 52–85.

Chapter 5

1. David Copp, "The Ring of Gyges: Overridingness and the Unity of Reasons," in *Self-Interest*, ed. Ellen Frankel Paul, Fred D. Miller, Jr., and Jeffrey Paul (New York: Cambridge University Press, 1997), 86–106, at 90–91.

2. David Gauthier, *Morals by Agreement* (New York: Oxford University Press, 1986), 17.

3. Plato, Republic, in *The Collected Dialogues of Plato*, ed. Edith Hamilton and Huntington Cairns, trans. Paul Shorey (Princeton, N.J.: Princeton University Press, 1980), bk. 2, 360c, 575–844, at 608.

4. David Hume, *An Enquiry Concerning the Principles of Morals* (1877), ed. J. B. Schneewind (Indianapolis: Hackett, 1983), 81–84, at 81 and 82. As Gerald Postema puts it, "Hume's knave, like Hobbes's 'Foole,' is often thought to pose a fundamental challenge to the rationality of morality (or, more precisely, a challenge to the rationality of internalizing the principles, attitudes, and perspective proper to morality)." See Postema, "Hume's Reply to the Sensible Knave," *History of Philosophy Quarterly* 5 (1) (January 1988): 23–40, at 23. For a similar theme, see David Gauthier, "Three against Justice: The Foole, the Sensible Knave, and the Lydian Shepard," in *Moral Dealing: Contract, Ethics, and Reason*, ed. David Gauthier (Ithaca, N.Y.: Cornell University Press, 1990), 129–49; reprinted from *Midwest Studies in Philosophy* 7, ed. P. A. French, T. E. Uehling, Jr., and H. N. Wettstein (Minneapolis: University of Minnesota Press, 1982), 11–29.

5. Gauthier, *Morals by Agreement*, 311.

6. Gauthier, *Morals by Agreement*, 7.

7. Gauthier, *Morals by Agreement*, 22.

8. Gauthier, *Morals by Agreement*, 36.

9. Jean Hampton, for one, disagrees. According to Hampton, preferences are not merely behavioristically related through determinate choices but also something "in the head" that is in some way causally responsible for the choices we make. See Jean E. Hampton, *The Authority of Reason* (New York: Cambridge University Press, 1998), 171.

10. Gauthier, *Morals by Agreement*, 4, 6, and 17.

11. Gauthier, *Morals by Agreement*, 8.

12. David Gauthier, "Morality, Rational Choice, and Semantic Representation: A Reply to My Critics," *Social Philosophy and Policy* 5 (2) (Spring 1988): 173–221, at 213.

13. When self-interest and morality do not conflict, the moralist can still grant that acting self-interestedly is rational.

14. Elizabeth Anderson, "Should Feminists Reject Rational Choice Theory?" in *A Mind of One's Own: Feminist Essays on Reason and Objectivity*, 2nd ed., ed. Louise M. Antony and Charlotte E. Witt (Boulder, Colo.: Westview Press, 2002), 369–97, at 370.

15. Recall from chapter 3 that women's caring too much is the proper counterpart to acting morally. This might become a way that a person does not count her own interests and reasons as much as others'—she privileges others and their interests and reasons, and does not take her own worth to give her a reason not to let others take a position of privilege against her. But since I do not endorse the ethic of care, which would best defeat this way of acting, I will leave this out. My proposal does not wed us to the ethic of care, but keeps open the moral theory we adopt.

16. One is self-interested when one acts in ways that promote one's interests, where these interests may, when satisfied, promote the ends of others, or even are self-destructive. Self-interest is a matter of pursuing the satisfaction of one's desires, whatever they may be.

17. But even Hobbes, who endorses a subjectivist and relativist notion of the good, believes that acting on certain desires is against one's interest on the grounds that satisfying them jeopardizes one's self-preservation.

18. Plato, *Republic*, bk. 2, 359c, Shorey trans., 608; emphasis mine. The case initially dichotomizes moral and self-interested *actions*, but later dichotomizes being a moral or just *person* and being an unjust *person*.

19. Thomas Hobbes, *Leviathan* (1651), ed. Michael Oakeshott (New York; Collier Books, 1962), chaps, 13 and 14.

20. Hobbes, *Leviathan*, 101.

21. Hume, *Enquiry*, 81.

22. Even genetically "determined" traits, such as diabetes, can be altered, and not expressed in a persons' phenotype, due to diet, exercise, and so on.

23. Ronald D. Milo, *Immorality* (Princeton, N.J.: Princeton University Press, 1984), 185; Stanley I. Benn, "Wickedness," *Ethics* 95 (1985): 795–810, at 797–98.

24. Plato, *Republic*, bk. 2, 360a–c.

25. Gauthier describes in terms of a Prisoner's Dilemma Hobbes's view about whether it is rational in a self-interested sense to act morally. David Gauthier, "Morality and Advantage," *Philosophical Review* 76 (1967): 460–75.

26. Peter Vallentyne, "Contractarianism and the Assumption of Mutual Unconcern," in *Contractarianism and Rational Choice: Essays on David Gauthier's Morals by Agreement*, ed. Peter Vallentyne (New York: Cambridge University Press, 1991), 71–75, at 75. Reprinted with minor modifications from *Philosophical Studies* 56 (1989): 187–92.

27. Benn, "Wickedness," 805–10. Milo categorizes malignity as a form of moral indifference (*Immorality*, 185).

28. Christopher Morris, "The Relation between Self-Interest and Justice in Contractarian Ethics," *Social Philosophy and Policy* 5 (2) (Spring 1988): 119–53, at

135. L. Wayne Sumner agrees: "The worst case for morality is not the agent who is purely self-regarding but the agent whose other-regarding concerns take the form of envy, spite, misanthropy, racial hatred, and the like." See Sumner, "Justice Contracted," *Dialogue: Canadian Philosophical Review* 26 (3) (1987): 523–48, at 533.

29. Gauthier, "Morality, Rational Choice," 213.

30. Gauthier, "Morality, Rational Choice," 213.

31. Gauthier, *Morals by Agreement*, 317, 327.

32. For one such statement of this view, see Mark Timmons, *Moral Theory: An Introduction* (Lanham, Md.: Rowman and Littlefield, 2002), 104–5.

33. John Cottingham, "Ethics and Impartiality," *Philosophical Studies* 43 (1983): 83–99, at 83.

34. John Rawls, *A Theory of Justice* (Cambridge, Mass.: Harvard University Press, 1971), 141.

35. Rawls, *A Theory of Justice*, 19.

36. I have more to say in "Moral Luck and Partialist Theories," *Journal of Value Inquiry* 30 (1–2) (June 1996): 213–27.

37. Perhaps care ethicists believe that the property of being in a relation is the significant feature determining duties, and that since everyone is in some kind of relation, each is owed certain treatment. That is, the theory is impartialist after all.

38. See my "Privilege, Immorality, and Responsibility for Attending to the 'Facts about Humanity,'" *Journal of Social Philosophy* 35 (1) (Spring 2004): 34–55. I will borrow some of my discussion about the various immoralities from this essay.

39. Jean Hampton, "Feminist Contractarianism," in Antony and Witt, *A Mind of One's Own: Feminist Essays on Reason and Objectivity*, 337–68.

40. Darwall develops this notion in "Moral Obligation and Accountability," in *The Second-person Standpoint: Morality, Respect, and Accountability* (Cambridge, Mass.: Harvard University Press, 2006). Also, see his response to my "Privilege, Immorality, and Responsibility for Attending to the 'Facts about Humanity,'" *Symposia on Gender, Race, and Philosophy* 2 (1) (January 2006):1–5; http://web.mit.edu/sgrp.

41. Darwall, *The Second-person Standpoint*, 120.

42. Thomas E. Hill, Jr., "Must Respect Be Earned?" in *Respect, Pluralism, and Justice: Kantian Perspectives*, ed. Thomas E. Hill, Jr. (New York: Oxford University Press, 2000), 87–118.

43. Christine M. Korsgaard, "Kant's Formula of Humanity," in *Creating the Kingdom of Ends* (New York: Cambridge University Press, 1996), 106–32.

44. Korsgaard, "Kant's Formula of Humanity," 114, 117, 119.

45. Korsgaard, "Kant's Formula of Humanity," 123.

46. Korsgaard, "Kant's Formula of Humanity," 128.

47. Korsgaard, "Kant's Formula of Humanity," 124.

48. Robin Dillon, "Kant on Arrogance and Self-Respect," in *Setting the Moral Compass: Essays by Women Philosophers*, ed. Cheshire Calhoun (New York: Oxford University Press, 2004), 191–216, at 193.

49. Jean Hampton, "Defining Wrong and Defining Rape," in *A Most Detestable Crime*, ed. Keith Burgess-Jackson (New York: Oxford University Press, 1999), 118–56, at 135.

50. Dillon, "Kant on Arrogance," 198.

51. Dillon, "Kant on Arrogance," 208 and 209.

52. See Christine M. Korsgaard, "The Right to Lie: Kant on Dealing with Evil," in *Creating the Kingdom of Ends* (New York: Cambridge University Press, 1996), 133–58.

53. For an excellent discussion of these views, see Susan Estrich, "Rape," in *Feminist Jurisprudence*, ed. Patricia Smith (New York: Oxford University Press, 1993), 158–87.

54. Milo, *Immorality*; Benn, "Wickedness." I discuss some of these examples in "Privilege, Immorality, and Responsibility."

55. Milo, *Immorality*, 185; Benn, "Wickedness," 797–98.

56. Milo categorizes malignant wickedness not as immorality stemming from bad preferences or values, but as a kind of moral indifference because the malignantly wicked person fails to have a "con-attitude," or negative attitude, toward what he believes to be wrong. See *Immorality*, 185.

57. Benn, "Wickedness," 805–10.

58. Milo, *Immorality*, chap. 2. Milo discusses both cognitivist and noncognitivist versions of perverse wickedness. On the cognitivist version, we can have moral knowledge; moral judgments can be true or false. Here the perversely wicked person does the wrong thing because he is ignorant that it is wrong: he is ignorant of moral knowledge. His ignorance can occur at two levels: that of basic moral principles and that of derivative moral principles. Milo believes that if the agent knows what moral wrongness is, then he cannot be ignorant of basic moral principles—knowing what is morally required entails knowing what moral wrongness is. A person who claims to be ignorant of basic moral principles must really be disinterested or self-interested. The agent can be confused only about derivative moral principles. On the noncognitivist version, according to which there is no moral knowledge, and moral principles therefore are not capable of being true or false, there is nothing to be ignorant about, which excludes the possibility of perverse wickedness.

59. Milo, *Immorality*, chap. 3.

60. Antony Duff, "Psychopathy and Moral Understanding," *American Philosophical Quarterly* 14 (3) (1977): 189–200.

61. Hervey Cleckley, *The Mask of Sanity: An Attempt to Clarify Some Issues about the So-called Psychopathic Personality*, 5th ed. (St. Louis: Mosby, 1976), esp. 337–64.

62. Shaun Nichols, "How Psychopaths Threaten Moral Rationalism," *Monist* 85 (2) (2002): 285–303, at 299–301.

63. Nichols, "Psychopaths," 288, 295.

64. Duff, "Psychopathy," 197. See also Hervey Cleckley, "A Clinical Profile," in Cleckley, *The Mask of Sanity*, 353–380.

65. Cleckley says that the psychopath throws away excellent opportunities to make money or gain any other end that he at other times spent a lot of time trying to achieve (*The Mask of Sanity*, 343).

66. Cleckley, *The Mask of Sanity*, 340–41.

67. Benn, "Wickedness," 799.

68. Benn, "Wickedness," 799; Cleckley, *The Mask of Sanity*, 343. Nichols rejects this explanation because he thinks that the psychopath's taking another's perspective is part of what makes him so successful at manipulating others. ("Psychopaths," 297.)

69. Duff, "Psychopathy," 195, 196, 197.

70. Duff, "Psychopathy," 197.

71. Milo rejects this account by Duff. Milo believes that the psychopath is simply *indifferent* to the rightness or wrongness of his acts, but that he can understand what it is to have a reason to avoid an act. He believes that the psychopath can understand that others are affected by their own pain caused by a pin prick, and that this gives *them* a reason to avoid such acts. But I think Milo gets this wrong. As Duff says, the psychopath can understand simple moral facts such as its being wrong to cause pain from a pin prick, but fails to understand complex moral facts. Further, perhaps the psychopath can see that pain yields a *prudential* reason, but he does not see that it yields a *moral* reason for action. Most significantly, the psychopath can see that others link up moral reasons and avoiding pain, but he does not understand what they mean when they use the language of reasons since this entails having the deep interests and values that put one in the moral game.

72. Milo, *Immorality*, chap. 6. According to Milo, internalists deny the possibility of moral indifference since they believe that if an agent believes that an act is wrong, he must have a negative attitude toward it (142). Milo believes that moral indifference is possible, so he denies internalism.

73. Milo, *Immorality*, 183.

74. Benn, "Wickedness," 801. Alternatively, conscientious wickedness can occur when the agent's end itself is very bad. Benn's example is Hitler, whose end of killing people was bad because it did not cohere with his other beliefs—he did not apply them to Aryans or to himself. The conscientiously wicked person does things that, for instance, cause others' death in a matter-of-fact way, and he is not pained by them.

75. Benn, "Wickedness," 800.

76. Benn, "Wickedness," 801.

77. Benn, "Wickedness," 801.

78. Donald Davidson, "How Is Weakness of the Will Possible?" in *Essays on Actions and Events*, ed. Donald Davidson (New York: Oxford University Press, 1980), 21–42.

79. Milo, *Immorality*, chap. 4.

80. This example comes from Larry May, "Shared Responsibility and Racist Attitudes," in *Sharing Responsibility*, ed. Larry May (Chicago: University of Chicago Press, 1992), 36–54.

81. This example comes from Marcia Baron, "What Is Wrong with Self-Deception?" in *Perspectives on Self-Deception*, ed. Brian McLaughlin and Amelie Rorty (Berkeley: University of California Press, 1988), 431–49.

82. Neither Benn nor Milo categorizes this kind of immorality.

83. I owe the phrase "individual malfeasance" to Louise Antony. See See "Commentary on Anita Superson's "Privilege, Immorality, and Responsibility for Attending to the 'Facts about Humanity',"" *Symposia on Gender, Race, and Philosophy* 2 (1) (January 2006): 1–5; http://web.mit.edu/sgrp.

84. For an interesting discussion of stereotypes of black women and men and sex, see Adele Logan Alexander, "'She's No Lady, She's a Nigger': Abuses, Stereotypes, and Realities from the Middle Passage to Capitol Hill," in *Race, Gender, and Power in America*, ed. Anita Faye Hill (New York: Oxford University Press, 1995), 3–25.

85. Peggy McIntosh, "White Privilege and Male Privilege," in *Gender Basics: Feminist Perspectives on Women and Men*, ed. Anne Minas (Belmont, Calif.: Wadsworth, 1993), 30–38. See pp. 32–34 for the list. The language of "wild

card" comes from Alison Bailey, "Privilege: Expanding on Marilyn Frye's 'Oppression'," *Journal of Social Philosophy* 29 (3) (1998): 104–19.

86. See Ann Cudd, *Analyzing Oppression* (New York: Oxford University Press, 2006), 25, for an excellent analysis of oppression.

87. Charles R. Lawrence III, "If He Hollers Let Him Go: Regulating Racist Speech on Campus," in *Words That Wound: Critical Race Theory, Assaultive Speech, and the First Amendment*, ed. Mari J. Matsuda et al. (Boulder, Colo.: Westview Press, 1993), 53–88, at 61.

88. See my "Privilege, Immorality, and Responsibility for Attending to the 'Facts about Humanity'," *Journal of Social Philosophy* 35 (1) (Spring 2004): 34–55, as well as my "Response to Four Commentaries: (Antony, Darwall, Thomas, Uleman) on "Privilege, Immorality, and Responsibility for Attending to the 'Facts about Humanity',"" *Symposia on Gender, Race and Philosophy* 2 (1) (January 2006): 1–12; http://web.mit.edu/sgrp.

89. Hobbes, *Leviathan*, 108.

90. Hobbes, *Leviathan*, 115.

91. Hume, *Enquiry*, 81–82.

92. See Henry Sidgwick, *The Methods of Ethics*, bk. 1, chap. 9, sec. 3, reprinted in Kelly Rogers, ed., *Self-Interest: An Anthology of Philosophical Perspectives* (New York: Routledge, 1997), 199.

93. Gauthier, *Morals by Agreement*, 23, 37.

94. Gauthier, *Morals by Agreement*, 8.

95. Hampton, *The Authority of Reason*, 234.

96. Elizabeth Anderson, *Value in Ethics and Economics* (Cambridge, Mass.: Harvard University Press, 1993), 1.

97. Kelly Rogers, ed., *Self-Interest: An Anthology of Philosophical Papers*, (N.Y.: Routledge, 1997), 169, quoting Bentham, "A Table of the Springs of Action," in *The Works of Jeremy Bentham*, ed. John Bowring, vol. 1 (New York: Russell and Russell, 1962), sec. 1(f).

98. Rogers, *Self-Interest*, 169–170.

99. Hampton, *The Authority of Reason*, 238.

100. Hampton, *The Authority of Reason*, 234–41. Hampton aims to show in her book that EU really is normative, and that this puts it into the "less scientific" sphere of moral reasons.

101. Anderson, *Value in Ethics and Economics*, chap. 6.

102. Hampton, "Feminist Contractarianism," 234.

103. Thomas Nagel, *The Possibility of Altruism* (Princeton, N.J.: Princeton University Press, 1970), 87.

104. James P. Sterba, *Three Challenges to Ethics: Environmentalism, Feminism, and Multiculturalism* (New York: Oxford University Press, 2001), 6.

105. See Sterba, *Three Challenges to Ethics*, 9; and Jesse Kalin, "In Defense of Egoism," in *Morality and Rational Self-Interest*, ed. David Gauthier (Englewood Cliffs, N.J.: Prentice-Hall, 1970), 64–87.

106. One might think I have collapsed these two views because I have said that the privileged person privileges his *reasons*. But this is not so. The account I favor, that the privileged person takes himself to have more worth than others, is about reason-giving. The objector's view is about reasons per se, that the privileged person favors his reasons over the reasons others give him.

107. Jim Sterba believes that the universal egoist can escape the inconsistency charge, but that he still acts contrary to reason in rejecting morality. But Sterba

starts by granting the prima facie relevance of both self-interested and moral reasons so as not to beg the question against either morality or egoism (self-interest). This approach is not open to me since I am following the tradition that takes the skeptic to endorse reasons far removed from moral ones. See Sterba, *Three Challenges to Ethics*, 10–19.

Chapter 6

1. See, for instance, David Brink, "Externalist Moral Realism," *Southern Journal of Philosophy* 24, supp. (1986): 23–41, at 30.

2. Note that the amoralist need not be an immoralist: the amoralist simply denies that moral reasons motivate him, but he might nonetheless act morally for nonmoral reasons, such as when self-interested reasons also justify moral action. Some immoralists who act contrary to the dictates of morality might not be amoralists—e.g., the weak-willed person might see that she has reason to act morally, and be moved to act morally, but have a stronger motivation to act otherwise. But there is an overlap: an amoralist could be an immoralist because he is moved to act immorally by nonmoral considerations, but is not moved by moral reasons.

3. Miles F. Burnyeat, "Aristotle on Learning to Be Good," in *Essays on Aristotle's Ethics*, ed. Amelie Oksenberg Rorty (Berkeley: University of California Press, 1980), 69–92, at 81.

4. Aristotle, *Nicomachean Ethics*, in *The Basic Works of Aristotle*, ed. Richard McKeon, trans. W. D. Ross (New York: Random House, 1941), 928–1112; bk. 1.4, at 1095b.

5. I am relying on Richard Kraut's interpretation of this passage. He takes this passage to yield the strongest of three interpretations of Aristotle's position about the composition of his target audience. (From my notes to Richard Kraut's lecture at the University of Illinois at Chicago, February 27, 1986.)

6. Aristotle, *Nicomachean Ethics*, bk. 10.9, at 1179b.

7. Gregory S. Kavka, "The Reconciliation Project," in *Morality, Reason and Truth: New Essays on the Foundations of Ethics*, ed. David Copp and David Zimmerman (Totowa, N.J.: Rowman and Allanheld, 1985), 297–319, at 306–7. Debra A. DeBruin concurs with Kavka that rationalists, who aim to justify morality in a way that demonstrates that each of us in virtue of our rationality has reason to act morally, cannot convince amoralists to be moral, since amoralists are not open to conversion. See DeBruin, "Can One Justify Morality to Fooles?" *Canadian Journal of Philosophy* 25 (1) (March 1995): 1–31, at 16–18.

8. Aristotle, *Nicomachean Ethics*, bk. 1.7, at 1098b.

9. I owe the reference for this passage and interpretation of it to Richard Kraut. He takes this to offer an intermediate interpretation about to whom the argument should be addressed.

10. Charlotte Brown, "Is Hume an Internalist?" *Journal of the History of Philosophy* 26 (1) (January 1988): 69–87, at 74, 75.

11. Christine M. Korsgaard, "Skepticism about Practical Reason," *Journal of Philosophy* 83 (1) (January 1986): 5–25, at 8.

12. Stephen L. Darwall, *Impartial Reason* (Ithaca, N.Y.: Cornell University Press, 1983), 54–55.

13. David Hume, *A Treatise of Human Nature*, 2nd ed., ed. L. A. Selby-Bigge (Oxford: Oxford University Press at Clarendon, 1992), 415.

14. See Brown, "Is Hume an Internalist?" 76.

15. Brown, "Is Hume an Internalist?" 76.

16. I construe Kantian internalism to be a kind of rationalist internalism. Christine Korsgaard might disagree, since on her view Kantian internalism requires that the agent be motivated by the reason to act itself, and not some further thought about the rightness of the act. She offers the definition of Kantian internalism in "Skepticism," 9–10. Moreover, Kant's own view is unclear. Korsgaard says in this essay that Kant may be either an externalist or an internalist, though she thinks that he is an internalist because in the third section of the *Groundwork* he tries to show that we have an autonomous will that can be motivated by reason (the Categorical Imperative) itself. Brown does not comment on whether Kant is a rationalist internalist. I will use Korsgaard's label of Kantian internalism. I construe Kantian internalism to be a kind of rationalist internalism in order to separate it from Humean internalism.

17. Different versions of internalism define the connection between reasons and motivations in one of these ways, as I will explain shortly.

18. Korsgaard, "Skepticism," 25.

19. William Frankena, "Obligation and Motivation in Recent Moral Philosophy," in *Perspectives on Morality: Essays by W. K. Frankena*, ed. Kenneth E. Goodpaster (South Bend, Ind.: Notre Dame University Press, 1976), 49–73, at 51 and 49; reprinted from *Essays in Moral Philosophy*, ed. A. I. Melden (Seattle: University of Washington Press, 1958), 40–81.

20. Frankena, "Obligation and Motivation," 50.

21. Brown, "Is Hume an Internalist?" 74; Frankena cites C. L. Stevenson, who says that ethical terms "must have, so to speak, a magnetism," and that any analysis of them must provide for this. See "Obligation and Motivation," 57.

22. As William Frankena puts it, "the statement, 'I have an obligation to do B,' means or logically entails the statement, 'I have, actually or potentially, some motivation for doing B.'" ("Obligation and Motivation," 60.) Michael Smith says that on internalism, believing that I should do x seems to bring with it my being motivated to do x. See Smith, *The Moral Problem* (Oxford: Blackwell, 1994), 60.

23. Korsgaard, "Skepticism," 10.

24. Brink, "Externalist Moral Realism," 27.

25. Brink, "Externalist Moral Realism," 28.

26. See Korsgaard, "Skepticism," 9; Brown, "Is Hume an Internalist?" 74.

27. Rachel Cohon, "Internalism about Reasons for Action," *Pacific Philosophical Quarterly* 74 (1993): 265–88, at 268.

28. Jean Hampton calls this *straightforward motivational internalism*. See *The Authority of Reason* (New York: Cambridge University Press, 1998), 65ff.

29. Brink, "Externalist Moral Realism," 27. Appraiser internalism might also be what Darwall calls *judgment internalism*, according to which it is a "necessary condition of a genuine instance of a certain sort of *judgment* that the person making the judgment be disposed to act in a way appropriate to it." See Darwall, *Impartial Reason*, 54.

30. Korsgaard suggests exactly this way of thinking: "The Kantian must go further, and disagree with Hume on both counts, since the Kantian supposes that there are operations of practical reason which yield conclusions about actions and which do not involve discerning relations between passions (or any pre-existing sources of motivation) and those actions." Korsgaard, "Skepticism," 8.

31. Cohon, "Internalism," 269, my emphasis.

32. Korsgaard, "Skepticism," 11 and 12. Peppered throughout the essay are more instances of this kind of talk.

33. Korsgaard also mentions this view: "Modern intuitionists, such as W. D. Ross and H. A. Prichard, seem also to have been externalists, but of a rather minimal kind. They believed that there was a distinctively moral motive, a sense of right or desire to do one's duty. This motive is *triggered by* the news that something is your duty, and only by that news, but it is still separate from the rational intuition that constitutes the understanding of your duty. It would be possible to have that intuition and not be motivated by it. The reason why the act is right and the motive you have for doing it are separate items, although it is nevertheless the case that the motive for doing it is 'because it is right.' This falls just short of the internalist position, which is that the reason why the act is right is the reason, and the motive, for doing it: it is a practical reason." ("Skepticism," 9, my emphasis.)

34. Brown, "Is Hume an Internalist?" 73, 75. Brown argues that in order for his argument that morality is grounded in sentiment rather than reason to be successful, Hume needs to be an internalist, as he is largely regarded as being. But she argues that he is really a trigger theorist. Were he an internalist, he would construe the moral feelings of approval and disapproval as themselves possessing motivational influence, such that when the agent approves of some action, this entails having some desire to act in the ways approved. She argues further that Hume does not show this, and that his view is not internalist because at best the feelings of approval and disapproval trigger the desire to be happy and the feeling of pride, which together with the moral sense, prompt the agent to act morally. This happens in two cases: (1) the case of the unsound person who lacks the natural common feeling of sympathy—a moral motive comes to the rescue to prompt action, and (2) the case of artificial duties such as justice, when a single instance of justice is not in a person's self-interest—the person is motivated by the sense of duty, but only because it triggers pride and the desire to be happy, which themselves motivate. See also 76, 82–83.

35. Hume, *Treatise*, 416; *Enquiry*, 84.

36. Hume, *Treatise*, 457.

37. Brown rightly argues that the epistemological conclusion does not follow from Hume's premises about reason not being the basis of morality. See "Is Hume an Internalist?" 71–78.

38. Hume, *Enquiry*, 74, 45.

39. Hume, *Enquiry*, 80.

40. At least not in the normal case. Recall the cases when a person lacks the appropriate natural, nonmoral motive, and then the sense of duty, which is independent of motives, kicks in. See Brown, "Is Hume an Internalist?" 81–82.

41. Hume, *Enquiry*, 47.

42. Brown, "Is Hume an Internalist?" 82–83. The phrase "naturally morally sound person" is Brown's. Brown argues that Hume's view is really that the sense of duty is created by the moral sense, together with pride about being virtuous and the desire for the happiness that is promoted by being virtuous. The motive for acting morally, then, is a desire to be proud of one's character, since this contributes to a person's happiness. Thus a person's regard for the moral worth of an action motivates in the end not by itself, but by triggering pride and the desire for happiness.

43. Hume, *Enquiry*, 81.

44. Hume, *Enquiry*, 82.

45. Hume, *Enquiry*, 81. I am suggesting that Hume portrays the sensible knave not merely as an action skeptic, but as an amoralist who is not moved by reasons for acting morally once they are shown to him.

46. Brink, "Externalist Moral Realism," 29. Frankena makes the same point: "Externalism, [the externalist] will say, in seeking to keep the obligation to act in certain ways independent of the vagaries of individual motivation, runs the risk that motivation may not always be present, let alone adequate, but internalism, in insisting on building in motivation, runs the corresponding risk of having to trim obligation to the size of individual motives." See "Obligation and Motivation," 73.

47. Smith, *The Moral Problem*, 68–71, quotation at 68.

48. Smith, *The Moral Problem*, 62.

49. Smith, *The Moral Problem*, 61.

50. Smith agrees with Korsgaard, as I will show, about "the practicality requirement," but Korsgaard thinks the amoralist goes wrong in being irrational. An alternative reading of Smith's view from the one I present in the text is that the amoralist is irrational because he does not understand moral judgments, or that his not understanding moral judgments is what explains or underlies the manifestation of the irrationality he suffers. Since Smith does not talk this way about the amoralist in the section of his book in which he explicitly addresses the amoralist, I favor the former interpretation of his view.

51. Brink, "Externalist Moral Realism," 30, citing Richard M. Hare, *The Language of Morals*, 124–26, 163.

52. Smith, *The Moral Problem*, 68–71.

53. Smith, *The Moral Problem*, 71–76.

54. Michael Smith, "The Humean Theory of Motivation," *Mind* 96 (381) (January 1987): 36–61, at 36.

55. Smith, "The Humean Theory," 39. In separating motivating and normative reasons, Smith's view is different from Bernard Williams's view. As I have shown, Williams endorses a kind of Humean internalism, but he believes that there is no such thing as an external reason. All (practical) reasons are internal because they are motivating. An agent who is not motivated can deliberate from his motivational set and bring about motivation. See Williams's "Internal and External Reasons," which I discuss more fully in chapter 4.

56. Smith, "The Humean Theory," 39.

57. Brown, "Is Hume an Internalist?" 70, 81. Brown points out that for Hume, a sound person acts from the motives of approval or disapproval, but an unsound person acts from the motives of pride and a desire to be happy, which are generated by the moral sense that all persons have. Neither acts from a sense of duty, which would involve reason itself motivating, which Hume disallows.

58. I say "rational amoralist" because as I said at the start of this subsection, Smith's argument against the amoralist must be addressing an amoralist who does not suffer from some irrationality, since otherwise he would reject the amoralist as irrational because the amoralist violates "the practicality requirement" that an agent has reason to act in a certain way just in case she would be motivated to act in that way if she were rational. Since Smith does not reject the amoralist as irrational, and since he goes on to give the arguments against the amoralist that I have addressed in this subsection, I can only assume that he takes the amoralist not to suffer any kind of irrationality.

59. Korsgaard, "Skepticism," 11, my emphasis.

60. Korsgaard, "Skepticism," 11. Jean Hampton calls this a "reason-making" condition. See Hampton, *The Authority of Reason*, chap. 2.

61. Again, I think Smith agrees with the irrationality claim, but since he gives other arguments against the amoralist, he must be taking up an amoralist who is not irrational.

62. Korsgaard, "Skepticism," 21. She thinks that Williams begs the question against Kantian internalism by assuming that everything in a person's motivational set must be an end or a desire since this closes off the possibility that reason itself can motivate.

63. Korsgaard, "Skepticism," 25.

64. Korsgaard, "Skepticism," 14.

65. True irrationality is "a failure to respond appropriately to an available reason." Also, she says that factors such as rage, passion, depression, and so on could cause us to act irrationally, that is, "to fail to be motivationally responsive to the rational considerations available to us." See Korsgaard, "Skepticism," 12 and 13.

66. Korsgaard, "Skepticism," 12.

67. Korsgaard, "Skepticism," 14–15, including n. 10.

68. Korsgaard, "Skepticism," 13–14, n. 9.

69. Hampton, *The Authority of Reason*, 71.

70. Thomas E. Hill, Jr., "Servility and Self-Respect," in *Dignity, Character, and Self-Respect*, ed. Robin S. Dillon (New York: Routledge, 1995), at 78; reprinted from *Monist* 57 (1973): 87–104. I discuss whether the Deferential Wife is responsible for being servile, and rely on that discussion here, in "The Deferential Wife Revisited: Agency and Moral Responsibility," unpublished.

71. Immanuel Kant, *Grounding for the Metaphysics of Morals*, trans. James W. Ellington (Indianapolis: Hackett, 1981), 36, AKA 429.

72. Susan J. Brison, *Aftermath: Violence and the Remaking of a Self* (Princeton, N.J.: Princeton University Press, 2002), 63. The probability of being a victim is based on the following kinds of statistics. Every six minutes in the United States, a woman is raped (ABC Nightly News, March 5, 2004; Amnesty International). Eighty-eight percent of women have experienced some form of sexual harassment. See Rosemarie Tong, *Women, Sex, and the Law* (Savage, Md.: Rowman and Littlefield, 1984), 66. Seventy-six percent of girls in grades 3–11 said they have been the target of sexual comments, jokes, or gestures or looks from teachers and other students, and 65 percent said they were touched, fondled, or pinched in a sexual manner (*Chicago Tribune*, January 2, 1994, sec. 6, 11; American Association of University Women [AAUW]). Every 15 seconds an American woman is battered (*Chicago Tribune*, November 6, 1994, sec. 6, 8). An AAUW study reports that elementary and middle school boys call out answers eight times more often than girls, and teachers allow them to continue, while girls who call out answers are rebuffed and told to raise their hands. See "How Schools Shortchange Girls," *Better Homes and Gardens* 71 (4) (April 1993): 40–41.

73. Ann E. Cudd argues this position in "Oppression by Choice," *Journal of Social Philosophy* 25 (1988): 22–44.

74. Jean Hampton exempts only Kantianism from the list of moral theories that require altruism to the point of disrespect for one's self. See Hampton, "Selflessness and the Loss of Self," *Social Philosophy and Policy* 10 (1) (1993): 135–65, at 151. Susan Wolf criticizes all moral theories, but particularly utilitarianism and Kantianism, on this score, in "Moral Saints," *Journal of Philosophy*

79 (8) (August 1982): 419–31. Interestingly, Kant himself displays confusion about women's worth: his moral theory dictates that we ought to treat any rational being as an end in itself, yet he believes that women's education should be directed to their "appropriate" roles of wives and mothers rather than to their rational development, thereby treating them as mere means to men's rational capacities, which ought to be fully developed. It is no surprise that the Deferential Wife is confused. See Nancy Tuana's interesting discussion of Kant's point in her *Women and the History of Philosophy* (New York: Paragon House, 1992).

75. Uma Narayan, "Minds of Their Own: Choices, Autonomy, Cultural Practices, and Other Women," in *A Mind of One's Own: Feminist Essays on Reason and Objectivity*, ed. Louise M. Antony and Charlotte E. Witt (Cambridge, Mass.: Westview Press, 2002), 418–32, at 420.

76. Cynthia Stark, "The Rationality of Valuing Oneself: A Critique of Kant on Self-Respect," *Journal of the History of Philosophy* 34 (1) (January 1997): 65–82, at 74, quotation on 77.

77. Susan Wolf, "Asymmetrical Freedom," in *Moral Responsibility*, ed. John Martin Fischer (Ithaca, N.Y.: Cornell University Press, 1986), 225–40, at 233–34; reprinted from *Journal of Philosophy* 77 (March 1980): 151–66.

78. Wolf defends a much more deterministic view than I do about the Deferential Wife.

79. It might be that in cases like the belief in God, we can construct two or more arguments that draw competing conclusions, and so Korsgaard's view of rationality stands. But I do not think she would endorse this view, since there should be one argument or set of reasons that overrides the other(s) and determines rationality.

80. Wanda Teays argues for rejecting a plea of self-defense when it is construed as an excuse rather than a justification, because the excuse defense denies the status of moral agency to the woman by perceiving her to be a potentially dangerous, not reasonable person. See Wanda Teays, "Standards of Perfection and Battered Women's Self-Defense," in *Violence against Women: Philosophical Perspectives*, ed. Stanley G. French, Wanda Teays, and Laura M. Purdy (Ithaca, N.Y.: Cornell University Press, 1998), 57–76.

81. In the first section of her essay, Korsgaard talks in general of the motivational force of reason, but in the second section, she borrows from Frankena, Falk, and Nagel in defining internalism as the view that there is a necessary connection between a *moral* judgment and the existence of a motive.

82. Korsgaard, "Skepticism," 10.

83. Korsgaard, "Skepticism," 10.

84. Jean Hampton argues for this view. For Hampton, the agent is motivated in virtue of the authority of the reason she has. For instance, a person will go to the doctor if she wants to be well, even though she hates to go, because she has a reason to go. See *The Authority of Reason*.

85. The notion of "world-traveling" comes from Maria C. Lugones, "Playfulness, 'World' Traveling, and Loving Perception," in *Free Spirits: Feminist Philosophers on Culture*, ed. Kate Mehuron and Gary Percesepe (Englewood Cliffs, N.J.: Prentice-Hall, 1995), 121–28; reprinted from *Making Face, Making Soul—Hacienda Caras: Creative and Critical Perspectives by Feminists of Color*, ed. Gloria Anzaldua (San Francisco: Aunt Lute, 1990), 390–402.

86. See my web response (posted 2/21/06) to Sue Campbell's response to the web-based symposium commentaries on Superson, "Privilege, Immorality, and

Responsibility for Attending to the 'Facts about Humanity,'" *Journal of Social Philosophy* 35 (1): 34–55, *Symposia on Gender, Race, and Philosophy* 2 (1) (January 2006): 1–12; http://web.mit.edu/sgrp.

Chapter 7

1. Barbara Herman, "Rules, Motives, and Helping Actions," *Philosophical Studies* 45 (3) (May 1984): 369–77, at 371.

2. Immanuel Kant, *Grounding for the Metaphysics of Morals* (1785), trans. James W. Ellington (Indianapolis: Hackett, 1981), at 3 (AKA 390) and 2 (AKA 411).

3. Marcia Baron, "On De-Kantianizing the Perfectly Moral Person," *Journal of Value Inquiry* 17 (1983): 281–93, at 285 and 288.

4. Michael Stocker, "The Schizophrenia of Modern Moral Theories," *Journal of Philosophy* 73 (14) (August 1976): 453–66, at 456–57. We can find similar claims about act utilitarianism in Bernard Williams, "A Critique of Utilitarianism," in *Utilitarianism: For and Against*, ed. J. J. C. Smart and Bernard Williams (New York: Cambridge University Press, 1973), 77–150, and in Peter Railton, "Alienation, Consequentialism, and Morality," *Philosophy and Public Affairs* 13 (2) (1984): 134–71.

5. See Annette Baier, "What Do Women Want in a Moral Theory?" *Nous* 19 (1) (March 1985): 53–63, at 57.

6. Nel Noddings, *Caring: A Feminine Approach to Ethics and Moral Education* (Berkeley: University of California Press, 1984).

7. Noddings, *Caring*, 86.

8. Noddings, *Caring*, 81.

9. Noddings, *Caring*, 81.

10. John Stuart Mill, *Utilitarianism* (1861), ed. George Sher (Indianapolis: Hackett, 1979), at 30–33.

11. Christine M. Korsgaard, "Skepticism about Moral Motives," *Journal of Philosophy* 83 (1) (January 1986): 5–25, at 9.

12. David Gauthier, *Morals by Agreement* (New York: Oxford University Press, 1986), 184, 186, 336, 337, and 355. Because Gauthier describes the liberal individual, we might think he believes that we need to defeat motive skepticism in order to defeat skepticism fully. But his view seems to be that defeating action skepticism is sufficient for defeating skepticism fully.

13. Kant, *Grounding for the Metaphysics of Morals*. Kant says that indirection cannot be commanded, but morality can (12, AKA 399), and that knowledge of duty must be available to every man, even the most ordinary (16, AKA 404).

14. Gilbert Harman, "Moral Relativism Defended," *Philosophical Review* 84 (1) (January 1975): 3–22.

15. Harman, "Moral Relativism Defended," 8–9.

16. I owe this point to Ann Cudd.

17. Perhaps this is what Hume wanted to say, since he believes that we all have at least the first seeds of the universal sentiment of benevolence. Harman acknowledges that he is following Hume, not Kant, in his view about reasons and motives.

18. Stocker, "Schizophrenia," 453–54.

19. Stocker, "Schizophrenia," 455.

20. Stocker wrote his article when the ethic of care was in its rudimentary stages, so his objection is not directed to it.

21. Stocker, "Schizophrenia," 459. This seems to be Peter Railton's complaint about act utilitarianism and traditional moral theories. See Railton, "Alienation, Consequentialism, and the Demands of Morality," 134–71.

22. Stocker, "Schizophrenia," 453.

23. Jon Elster, *Ulysses and the Sirens* (New York: Cambridge University Press, 1984), 36–47.

24. Elster, *Ulysses*, 39.

25. Elster, *Ulysses*, 42.

26. Elster, *Ulysses*, 44.

27. I thank Duncan MacIntosh for this formulation.

28. Elster, *Ulysses*, 48.

29. David Gauthier, "Morality and Advantage," *Philosophical Review* 76 (1967): 460–75.

30. Elster, *Ulysses*, 157. According to Amelie Rorty, x is self-deceived if x believes p and not-p, or denies that he believes p. See Amelie Rorty, "Self-Deception, Akrasia and Irrationality," in *The Multiple Self: Studies in Rationality and Social Change*, ed. Jon Elster (New York: Cambridge University Press, 1986), 115–31, at 125.

31. Elster, *Ulysses*, 174.

32. Elster, *Ulysses*, 174.

33. Elster, *Ulysses*, 176.

Chapter 8

1. Stephen Darwall, "Rational Agent, Rational Act," *Philosophical Topics* 14 (2) (Fall 1986): 33–57, at 55 n. 24.

2. Darwall, "Rational Agent," 34.

3. Darwall, "Rational Agent," 34, 39.

4. Darwall, "Rational Agent," 41.

5. I thank David Copp for prompting this distinction.

6. Nancy (Ann) Davis, "Acting Utilitarians," *Pacific Philosophical Quarterly* 66 (1985): 125–40. The ensuing discussion comes from 126–28. Davis is suggesting that the judgments rendered by value-based theories need to be richer than they usually are.

7. Davis, "Acting Utilitarians," 125.

8. This in fact may be one reason Gauthier offers his thesis, but clearly his main motive is to provide a theory that is grounded in self-interest so as to address the skeptic who accepts only self-interested reasons for action.

9. Gauthier, *Morals by Agreement*, 167.

10. Duncan MacIntosh, "Two Gauthiers?" *Dialogue: Canadian Philosophical Review* 28 (1) (1989): 43–61, at 45.

11. Gauthier, *Morals by Agreement*, 182. See MacIntosh, "Two Gauthiers?" for a good list of other relevant passages, at 46.

12. Gauthier, *Morals by Agreement*, 186.

13. Gauthier, *Morals by Agreement*, 169.

14. Gauthier, *Morals by Agreement*, 164, 165.

15. Gauthier, *Morals by Agreement*, 158.

16. Gauthier, *Morals by Agreement*, 167, my emphasis.

17. Barbara Herman, "On the Value of Acting from the Motive of Duty," *Philosophical Review* 90 (3) (July 1981): 359–82. The relevant discussion can be found on 363–66.

18. Gauthier, *Morals by Agreement*, 169.

19. Gauthier, *Morals by Agreement*, 169.

20. Gauthier, *Morals by Agreement*, 366.

21. Herman, "On the Value of Acting from the Motive of Duty," 368–69.

22. Joel Kupperman, "Character and Ethical Theory," in *Midwest Studies in Philosophy*, vol. 12, *Ethical Theory: Character and Virtue* (Notre Dame, Ind.: University of Notre Dame Press, 1988), 115–25, quotation on 120.

23. The distinction between dispositions and intentions offered here does not affect my arguments against the Dependency Thesis in chapter 2.

24. Davis, "Acting Utilitarians," 128.

25. Barbara Herman, "On the Value of Acting from the Motive of Duty," rev. version in *The Practice of Moral Judgment*, ed. Barbara Herman (Cambridge, Mass.: Harvard University Press, 1993), 1–22, quotation on 11–12.

26. Marcia Baron, "The Alleged Moral Repugnance of Acting from Duty," *Journal of Philosophy* 81 (4) (1984): 197–220. See especially 198n. 2, and the discussion on 208–9.

27. Baron, "The Alleged Moral Repugnance," 209.

28. Marcia Baron, "Is Acting from Duty Morally Repugnant?" rev. version of the original essay, chap. 4 of Baron, *Kantian Ethics Almost without Apology* (Ithaca, N.Y.: Cornell University Press, 1995), 117–45, esp. 129.

29. Baron, "The Alleged Moral Repugnance," 207.

30. See Herman, "On the Value of Acting from the Motive of Duty" (1981), 359–82.

31. Herman agrees. Her account of the moral motive allows for the presence of nonmoral interests. In these "overdetermined" actions, the agent must be moved by the moral motive in order for her action to have moral worth. In the case of morally permissible actions, the moral motive functions as a limiting condition by limiting the ways in which nonmoral motives may be acted on. That is, the moral motive gives the agent a commitment to act on nonmoral motives only if she judges that her action complies with the Categorical Imperative. (See part 4 of the original version of "On the Value of Acting from the Motive of Duty.") One main difference between Herman's and Baron's views is that while Herman believes that a morally good person *can* have nonmoral motives present when she acts in morally good ways, Baron believes that in order to be a perfectly moral person, one *must* have nonmoral motives along with the moral motive, since the latter is a way of life.

32. David Copp and Ann Cudd proposed this objection.

33. Davis, "Acting Utilitarians," 127–28. A similar view is expressed by Robert Louden, who objects to Susan Wolf's characterization of a moral saint as one who spends as much time as possible producing as much moral good as possible. In opposition to this view, Louden characterizes the moral person as "one who is disposed to live according to principles she reflectively accepts. The more strongly one is disposed to stand fast by one's reflectively chosen principles when tempted by considerations that are morally irrelevant, the more one conforms to the ideal of the moral person." See Louden, "Can We Be Too Moral?" *Ethics* 98 (2) (January 1988): 361–78, at 371–72.

34. Baron, "The Alleged Moral Repugnance," 205, 208.

35. Barbara Herman, "Integrity and Impartiality," in Herman, *The Practice of Moral Judgment*, 23–44, esp. 26.

36. John McDowell, "Are Moral Requirements Hypothetical Imperatives?" *Proceedings of the Aristotelian Society*, supp. vol. 52 (1978): 13–29, esp. 21.

37. John McDowell, "Virtue and Reason," *Monist* 62 (3) (July 1979): 331–50, esp. 334–35.

38. See Louden, "Can We Be Too Moral?" 373.

39. Davis, "Acting Utilitarians," 128. See also George Sher, "Ethics, Character, and Action," *Social Philosophy and Policy* 15 (1) (Winter 1998): 125–40, at 14.

40. Elizabeth Spelman argues that the self and self-conception are central to treating a person as a person. See Spelman, "On Treating Persons as Persons," *Ethics* 88 (1978): 150–61.

41. Harry G. Frankfurt, "Freedom of the Will and the Concept of a Person," in *Moral Responsibility*, ed. John Martin Fischer (Ithaca, N.Y.: Cornell University Press, 1986), 65–80, esp. 70–73.

42. See Charles Johnson and Patricia Smith, *Africans in America: America's Journey through Slavery* (New York: Harcourt Brace, 1998), 301. According to Julien Joseph Virey's theory, blacks were ugly and savage, and their heads were shaped more for eating and not for thinking. Charles White believed that blacks were closer to apes. Such racists were able to spread propaganda and breed hatred for blacks, and distance them from Caucasians in order to facilitate ill treatment of them.

43. Katha Pollitt, "Violence in a Man's World," in *Reasonable Creatures: Essays on Women and Feminism*, ed. Katha Pollitt (New York: Vintage Books, 1995), 26–30.

44. Apparently this happened with Title VII of the Civil Rights Act of 1964, which outlaws discrimination on grounds of race, color, religion, sex, or national origin. Sex discrimination was a late amendment to the bill, proposed by Southern congresspersons who attempted to defeat the entire bill, a plan that backfired. See Joel T. Anderson, "Employment Discrimination—The Expansion of Scope of Title VII to Include Sexual Harassment as a Form of Sex Discrimination: *Meritor Savings Bank, FSB v. Vinson*," *Journal of Corporation Law* 12 (3) (Spring 1987): 619–38, esp. 620–21.

45. Pollitt, "Violence," 30.

46. The phrase comes from Gregory Kavka, "Some Paradoxes of Deterrence," *Journal of Philosophy* 75 (6) (June 1978): 285–302.

47. See Lynne McFall, "Integrity," in *Ethics and Personality: Essays in Moral Psychology*, ed. John Deigh (Chicago: University of Chicago Press, 1992), 79–94, at 81; originally published in *Ethics* 98 (1) (October 1987): 5–20.

48. My point is a modified version of McFall's, "Integrity," 90. See also Nancy Schauber, "Integrity, Commitment and the Concept of a Person," *American Philosophical Quarterly* 33 (1) (January 1996): 119–29. Schauber mentions what she calls the self-unification view of integrity that includes both moral and nonmoral commitments. An agent remains true to herself by keeping both kinds of commitments.

49. Jon Elster, *Sour Grapes: Studies in the Subversion of Rationality* (New York: Cambridge University Press, 1983), 1.

50. Gauthier, "Deterrence, Maximization, and Rationality," *Ethics* 94 (3) (April 1984): 474–95, at 436. For a similar view, see Gauthier, "Rethinking the Toxin Puzzle," in *Rational Commitment and Social Justice: Essays for Gregory Kavka*, ed. Jules L. Coleman and Christopher W. Morris (New York: Cambridge University Press, 1988), 47–58.

References

Alexander, Adele Logan. 1995. "'She's No Lady, She's a Nigger': Abuses, Stereotypes, and Realities from the Middle Passage to Capitol Hill." *In Race, Gender, and Power in America*, ed. Anita Faye Hill, pp. 3–25. New York: Oxford University Press.

Anderson, Elizabeth. 1995. "Is Women's Labor a Commodity?" In Anderson, *Value in Ethics and Economics*, pp. 168–89. Cambridge, Mass.: Harvard University Press. Rev. version; originally published in *Philosophy and Public Affairs* 19 (1990): 71–92.

———. 1995. *Value in Ethics and Economics*. Cambridge, Mass.: Harvard University Press.

———. 2002. "Should Feminists Reject Rational Choice Theory?" In *A Mind of One's Own: Feminist Essays on Reason and Objectivity*, 2nd ed., ed. Louise M. Antony and Charlotte E. Witt, pp. 369–97. Boulder, Colo.: Westview Press.

Anderson, Joel T. 1987. "Employment Discrimination—The Expansion of Scope of Title VII to Include Sexual Harassment as a Form of Sex Discrimination: Meritor Savings Bank, FSB v. Vinson." *Journal of Corporation Law* 12 (3): 619–38.

Antony, Louise. 2006. "Comments on Superson: Commentary on Anita Superson's "Privilege, Immorality, and Responsibility for Attending to the 'Facts about Humanity'."" *Symposia on Gender, Race, and Philosophy* 2 (1) (January 2006): 1–5. http://web.mit.edu/sgrp.

Aristotle. 1941. Nicomachean Ethics. In *The Basic Works of Aristotle*. Ed. Richard McKeon. Trans. W. D. Ross, pp. 928–1112. New York: Random House.

Baier, Annette. 1987. "Hume, the Women's Moral Theorist." In *Women and Moral Theory*, ed. Eva Feder Kittay and Diana T. Meyers, pp. 37–55. New York: Rowman and Littlefield.

———. 1987. "The Need for More Than Justice." *Canadian Journal of Philosophy* 13: 14–56.

———. 1993. "What Do Women Want in a Moral Theory?" In *An Ethic of Care: Feminist and Interdisciplinary Perspectives*, ed. Mary Jeanne Larrabee, pp. 19–32. New York: Routledge.

Baier, Kurt. 1965. *The Moral Point of View*. New York: Random House.

Bailey, Alison. 1998. "Privilege: Expanding on Marilyn Frye's 'Oppression'." *Journal of Social Philosophy* 29 (3): 104–19.

Baron, Marcia. 1983. "On De-Kantianizing the Perfectly Moral Person." *Journal of Value Inquiry* 17: 281–93.

———. 1984. "The Alleged Moral Repugnance of Acting from Duty." *Journal of Philosophy* 81 (4): 192–220.

Baron, Marcia. 1988. "What Is Wrong With Self-Deception?" In *Perspectives on Self-Deception*, ed. Brian McLaughlin and Amelie Rorty, pp. 431–49. Berkeley, Calif.: University of California Press.

———. 1995. "Is Acting from Duty Morally Repugnant?" Rev. version in Baron, *Kantian Ethics Almost without Apology*, pp. 117–45. Ithaca, N.Y.: Cornell University Press.

———. 2004. "Killing in the Heat of Passion." In *Setting the Moral Compass: Essays by Women Philosophers*, ed. Cheshire Calhoun, pp. 353–78. New York: Oxford University Press.

Bartky, Sandra. 1990. "Feeding Egos and Tending Wounds: Deference and Disaffection in Women's Emotional Labor." In *Femininity and Domination*, ed. Sandra Lee Bartky, pp. 99–119. New York: Routledge.

———. 1990. "Narcissism, Femininity, and Alienation." In *Femininity and Domination: Studies in the Phenomenology of Oppression*, ed. Sandra Lee Bartky, pp. 33–44. New York: Routledge.

———. 1990. "Toward a Phenomenology of Feminist Consciousness." In *Femininity and Domination: Studies in the Phenomenology of Oppression*, ed. Sandra Lee Bartky, pp. 11–21. New York: Routledge.

Benhabib, Seyla. 1987. "The Generalized and the Concrete Other: The Kohlberg-Gilligan Controversy and Moral Theory." In *Women and Moral Theory*, ed. Eva Feder Kittay and Diana T. Meyers, pp. 154–77. New York: Rowman and Littlefield.

Benn, Stanley I. 1985. "Wickedness." *Ethics* 95: 785–810.

Blum, Larry, Marcia Homiak, Judy Housman, and Naomi Scheman. 1973–74. "Altruism and Women's Oppression." In "Special Issue on Women and Philosophy," *Philosophical Forum* 5 (1–2) (Fall–Winter 1973–74): 222–57.

Blum, Lawrence. 1988. "Gilligan and Kohlberg: Implications for Moral Theory." *Ethics* 98 (3): 472–91.

Blustein, Jeffrey. 1991. *Care and Commitment: Taking the Personal Point of View*. New York: Oxford University Press.

Brandt, Richard B. 1970. "Rational Desires." In *Proceedings and Addresses of the American Philosophical Association* 43 (September 1970): 43–64.

———. 1998. *A Theory of the Good and the Right*. Amherst, N.Y.: Prometheus Books.

Brink, David. 1986. "Externalist Moral Realism." *Southern Journal of Philosophy* 24 supp.: 23–41.

———. 1990. "Rational Egoism, Self, and Others." In *Identity, Character, and Morality: Essays in Moral Psychology*, ed. Owen Flanagan and Amelie Oksenberg Rorty, pp. 399–78. Cambridge, Mass.: MIT Press.

Brison, Susan J. 2002. *Aftermath: Violence and the Remaking of a Self*. Princeton, N.J.: Princeton University Press.

Brown, Charlotte. 1988. "Is Hume an Internalist?" *Journal of the History of Philosophy* 26 (1): 69–87.

Burnyeat, Miles F. 1980. "Aristotle on Learning to Be Good." In *Essays on Aristotle's Ethics*, ed. Amelie Oksenberg Rorty, pp. 69–92. Berkeley: University of California Press.

Calhoun, Cheshire. 1988. "Justice, Care, and Gender Bias." *Journal of Philosophy* 85 (9): 451–63.

Campbell, Richmond. 1988. "Moral Justification and Freedom." *Journal of Philosophy* 85 (4): 192–213.

Cleckley, Hervey. 1976. *The Mask of Sanity: An Attempt to Clarify Some Issues about the So-called Psychopathic Personality.* 5th ed. St. Louis: Mosby.

Cohon, Rachel. 1993. "Internalism about Reasons for Action." *Pacific Philosophical Quarterly* 74: 265–88.

Copp, David. 1995. *Morality, Normativity, and Society.* New York: Oxford University Press.

———. 1997. "The Ring of Gyges: Overridingness and the Unity of Reason." In *Self-Interest,* ed. Ellen Frankel Paul, Fred D. Miller, Jr., and Jeffrey Paul, pp. 86–106. New York: Cambridge University Press.

Cottingham, John. 1983. "Ethics and Impartiality." *Philosophical Studies* 43: 83–99.

Cudd, Ann E. 1988. "Oppression by Choice." *Journal of Social Philosophy* 25: 22–44.

———. 2004. "The Paradox of Liberal Feminism: Choice, Rationality, and Oppression." In *Varieties of Feminist Liberalism,* ed. Amy Baehr, pp. 37–61. Lanham, Md.: Rowman and Littlefield.

———. 2006. *Analyzing Oppression.* New York: Oxford University Press.

Darwall, Stephen. 1983. *Impartial Reason.* Ithaca, N.Y.: Cornell University Press.

———. 1986. "Rational Agent, Rational Act." *Philosophical Topics* 14 (2): 33–57.

———. 2005. "Moral Obligation and Accountability." Paper presented at the Metaethics Workshop, Madison, Wisconsin.

———. 2006. "Comments on Superson: Commentary on Anita Superson's "Privilege, Immorality, and Responsibility for Attending to the 'Facts about Humanity'."" *Symposia on Gender, Race, and Philosophy* 2 (1) (January 2006): 1–3. http://web.mit.edu/sgrp.

———. 2006. *The Second-person Standpoint: Morality, Respect, and Accountability.* Cambridge, Mass.: Harvard University Press.

Davidson, Donald. 1980. "How Is Weakness of Will Possible?" In *Essays on Actions and Events,* ed. Donald Davidson, pp. 21–42. New York: Oxford University Press.

Davis, Nancy (Ann). 1985. "Acting Utilitarians." *Pacific Philosophical Quarterly* 66: 125–40.

DeBruin, Debra A. 1995. "Can One Justify Morality to Fooles?" *Canadian Journal of Philosophy* 25 (1): 1–31.

———. 1998. "Identifying Sexual Harassment: The Reasonable Woman Standard." In *Violence against Women: Philosophical Perspectives,* ed. Stanley G. French, Wanda Teays, and Laura M. Purdy, pp. 107–22. Ithaca, N.Y.: Cornell University Press.

Dillon, Robin. 1995. "Toward a Feminist Conception of Self-Respect." In *Dignity, Character, and Self-Respect,* ed. Robin S. Dillon, pp. 290–310. New York: Routledge. Reprinted from *Hypatia* 7 (4) (Fall 1992): 52–69.

———. 2004. "Kant on Arrogance and Self-Respect." In *Setting the Moral Compass: Essays by Women Philosophers,* ed. Cheshire Calhoun, pp. 191–216. New York: Oxford University Press.

Duff, Antony. 1977. "Psychopathy and Moral Understanding." *American Philosophical Quarterly* 14 (3): 189–200.

Elster, Jon. 1983. *Sour Grapes: Studies in the Subversion of Rationality.* New York: Cambridge University Press.

———. 1984. *Ulysses and the Sirens.* New York: Cambridge University Press.

———. 1987. "Sour Grapes." In *Sour Grapes: Studies in the Subversion of Rationality,* ed. Jon Elster, pp. 109–40. New York: Cambridge University Press.

Estrich, Susan. 1993. "Rape." In *Feminist Jurisprudence*, ed. Patricia Smith, pp. 158–87. New York: Oxford University Press.

Flanagan, Owen, and Kathryn Jackson. 1987. "Justice, Care, and Gender: The Kohlberg-Gilligan Debate Revisited." *Ethics* 97 (3): 622–37.

Frankena, William. 1958. "Obligation and Motivation in Recent Moral Philosophy. In *Perspectives on Morality: Essays by W. K. Frankena*, ed. Kenneth E. Goodpaster, pp. 49–73. South Bend, Ind.: Notre Dame University Press. Reprinted from *Essays in Moral Philosophy*, ed. A. I. Melden, pp. 40–81. Seattle: University of Washington Press, 1976.

Frankfurt, Harry G. 1971. "Freedom of the Will and the Concept of a Person." *Journal of Philosophy* 68 (1): 5–20.

Friedman, Marilyn. 1987. "Beyond Caring: The De-moralization of Gender." *Canadian Journal of Philosophy* 13: 87–110.

———. 1993. "Liberating Care." In *What Are Friends For?* ed. Marilyn Friedman, pp. 142–83. Ithaca, N.Y: Cornell University Press.

———. 1997. "Autonomy and Social Relationships: Rethinking the Feminist Critique." In *Feminists Rethink the Self*, ed. Diana Tietjens Meyers, pp. 40–61. Boulder, Colo.: Westview Press.

Gauthier, David. 1967. "Morality and Advantage." *Philosophical Review* 76: 460–75.

———. 1984. "Afterthoughts." In *The Security Gamble: Deterrence Dilemmas in the Nuclear Age*, ed. Douglas MacLean, pp. 159–61. Totowa, N.J.: Rowman and Allanheld.

———. 1984. "Deterrence, Maximization, and Rationality." *Ethics* 94 (3): 474–95.

———. 1986. *Morals by Agreement*. New York: Oxford University Press.

———. 1988. "Morality, Rational Choice, and Semantic Representation: A Reply to My Critics." *Social Philosophy and Policy* 5 (2): 173–221.

———. 1990. "Three against Justice: The Foole, the Sensible Knave, and the Lydian Shepard." In *Moral Dealing: Contract, Ethics, and Reason*, ed. David Gauthier, pp. 129–49. Ithaca, N.Y.: Cornell University Press. Reprinted from *Midwest Studies in Philosophy* 7, ed. P. A. French, T. E. Uehling, Jr., and H. N. Wettstein, pp. 11–29. Minneapolis: 1982, University of Minnesota Press, 1982.

———. 1998. "Rethinking the Toxin Puzzle." In *Rational Commitment and Social Justice: Essays for Gregory Kavka*, ed. Jules L. Coleman and Christopher W. Morris, pp. 47–58. New York: Cambridge University Press.

Gibson, Mary. 1977. "Rationality." *Philosophy and Public Affairs* 6 (3): 193–225.

Gilligan, Carol. 1982. *In a Different Voice: Psychological Theory and Women's Development*. Cambridge, Mass.: Harvard University Press.

———. 1987. "Moral Orientation and Moral Development." In *Women and Moral Theory*, ed. Eva Feder Kittay and Diana T. Meyers, pp. 19–33. New York: Rowman and Littlefield.

Grice, Geoffrey. 1986. *The Grounds of Moral Judgement*. New York: Cambridge University Press.

Griffin, James. 1990. *Well-Being: Its Meaning, Measurement and Moral Importance*. New York: Oxford University Press.

Hampton, Jean. 1992. "Rethinking Reason." *American Philosophical Quarterly* 29 (3): 219–36.

———. 1993. "Selflessness and the Loss of Self." *Social Philosophy and Policy* 10 (1): 135–65.

————. 1996. "On Instrumental Rationality." In *Reason, Ethics, and Society: Themes from Kurt Baier, with His Responses*, ed. J. B. Schneewind, pp. 84–116. Chicago: Open Court.

————. 1998. *The Authority of Reason*. New York: Cambridge University Press.

————. 1999. "Defining Wrong and Defining Rape." In *A Most Detestable Crime*, ed. Keith Burgess-Jackson, pp. 118–56. New York: Oxford University Press.

————. 2002. "Feminist Contractarianism." In *A Mind of One's Own: Feminist Essays on Reason and Objectivity*, 2nd ed., ed. Louise M. Antony and Charlotte E. Witt, pp. 337–68. Boulder, Colo.: Westview Press.

Harman, Gilbert. 1975. "Moral Relativism Defended." *Philosophical Review* 84 (1): 3–22.

Held, Virginia. 1990. "Feminist Transformations of Moral Theory." *Philosophy and Phenomenological Research* 1: 321–44.

Herman, Barbara. 1981. "On the Value of Acting from the Motive of Duty." *Philosophical Review* 90 (3): 359–82.

————. 1984. "Rules, Motives, and Helping Actions." *Philosophical Studies* 45 (3): 369–77.

————. 1993. "Integrity and Impartiality." In *The Practice of Moral Judgment*, ed. Barbara Herman, pp. 23–44. Cambridge, Mass.: Harvard University Press.

————. 1993. "On the Value of Acting from the Motive of Duty." Rev. version in *The Practice of Moral Judgment*, ed. Barbara Herman, pp. 1–22. Cambridge, Mass.: Harvard University Press.

Hill, Thomas E., Jr. 1995. "Servility and Self-Respect." In *Dignity, Character, and Self-Respect*, ed. Robin S. Dillon, pp. 76–92. New York: Routledge. Reprinted from *Monist* 57 (1973): 87–104.

————. 1997. "Reasonable Self-Interest." In *Self-Interest*, ed. Ellen Frankel Paul, Fred D. Miller, Jr., and Jeffrey Paul, pp. 52–85. New York: Cambridge University Press.

————. 2000. "Must Respect Be Earned?" In *Respect, Pluralism, and Justice: Kantian Perspectives*, ed. Thomas E. Hill, Jr., pp. 87–118. New York: Oxford University Press.

Hill Collins, Patricia. 1990. *Black Feminist Thought: Knowledge, Consciousness, and the Politics of Empowerment*. New York: Routledge.

Hoagland, Sarah Lucia. 1991. "Some Thoughts about 'Caring.'" In *Feminist Ethics*, ed. Claudia Card, pp. 246–63. Lawrence: University Press of Kansas.

Hobbes, Thomas. 1962. *Leviathan*. Ed. Michael Oakeshott. New York: Collier Books. (Originally published 1651)

Homiak, Marcia L. 1993. "Feminism and Aristotle's Rational Ideal." In *A Mind of One's Own: Feminist Essays on Reason and Objectivity*, ed. Louise M. Antony and Charlotte E. Witt, pp. 1–17. Boulder, Colo.: Westview Press.

"How Schools Shortchange Girls." 1993. *Better Homes and Gardens* 71 (4): 40–41.

Hume, David. 1983. *An Enquiry Concerning the Principles of Morals*. Ed. J. B. Schneewind. Indianapolis: Hackett. (Originally published 1777)

————. 1992. *A Treatise of Human Nature*. 2nd ed. Ed. L. A. Selby-Bigge. New York: Oxford University Press. (Originally published 1888)

Jaggar, Alison. 1989. "Feminist Ethics: Some Issues for the Nineties." *Journal of Social Philosophy* 20 (1–2): 91–107.

Johnson, Charles, and Patricia Smith. 1998. *Africans in America: America's Journey through Slavery*. New York: Harcourt Brace.

Kalin, Jesse. 1970. "In Defense of Egoism." In *Morality and Rational Self-Interest*, ed. David Gauthier, pp. 64–87. Englewood Cliffs, N.J.: Prentice-Hall.

Kant, Immanuel. 1963. "Dignity and Self-Respect." In *Lectures on Ethics*, trans. Louis Enfield, pp. 526–35. New York: Harper and Row. From the edition of P. Menzer (Berlin, 1924). (Originally published 1830)

——. 1981. *Grounding for the Metaphysics of Morals.* Trans. James W. Ellington. Indianapolis: Hackett. (Originally published 1785)

——. 1996. *Groundwork for the Metaphysics of Morals.* In *Practical Philosophy: The Cambridge Edition of the Works of Immanuel Kant*, trans. and ed. Mary J. Gregor, pp. 43–108. New York: Cambridge University Press. (Originally published 1785)

——. 1996. *The Metaphysics of Morals.* In *Practical Philosophy: The Cambridge Edition of the Works of Immanuel Kant*, trans. and ed. Mary J. Gregor, pp. 370–540. New York: Cambridge University Press. (Originally published 1797)

Kavka, Gregory. 1978. "Some Paradoxes of Deterrence." *Journal of Philosophy* 75 (6): 285–302.

——. 1983. "The Toxin Puzzle." *Analysis* 197: 33–36.

——. 1984. "Responses to the Paradox of Deterrence." In *The Security Gamble: Deterrence Dilemmas in the Nuclear Age*, ed. Douglas MacLean, pp. 155–59. Totowa, N.J.: Rowman and Allanheld.

——. 1985. "The Reconciliation Project." In *Morality, Reason and Truth: New Essays on the Foundations of Ethics*, ed. David Copp and David Zimmerman, pp. 297–319. Totowa, N.J.: Rowman and Allanheld.

Korsgaard, Christine M. 1986. "Skepticism about Practical Reason." *Journal of Philosophy* 83 (1): 5–25.

——. 1996. "Kant's Formula of Humanity." In *Creating the Kingdom of Ends*, ed. Christine M. Korsgaard, pp. 106–32. New York: Cambridge University Press.

——. 1996. "The Right to Lie: Kant on Dealing with Evil." In *Creating the Kingdom of Ends*, pp. 133–58. New York: Cambridge University Press.

——. 1997. *The Sources of Normativity.* N.Y.: Cambridge University Press.

Kupperman, Joel. 1988. "Character and Ethical Theory." *Midwest Studies in Philosophy*, vol. 12, *Ethical Theory: Character and Virtue*, pp. 115–25. Notre Dame, Ind.: University of Notre Dame Press.

Lawrence, Charles R., III. 1993. "If He Hollers Let Him Go: Regulating Racist Speech on Campus." In *Words That Wound: Critical Race Theory, Assaultive Speech, and the First Amendment*, ed. Mari J. Matsuda et al., pp. 53–88. Boulder, Colo.: Westview Press.

Lewis, David. 1984. "Devil's Bargains and the Real World." In *The Security Gamble: Deterrence Dilemmas in the Nuclear Age*, ed. Douglas MacLean, pp. 141–54. Totowa, N.J.: Rowman and Allanheld.

Lloyd, Genevieve. 1984. *The Man of Reason: "Male" and "Female" in Western Philosophy.* Minneapolis: University of Minnesota Press.

Louden, Robert. 1988. "Can We Be Too Moral?" *Ethics* 98 (2): 361–78.

Lugones, Maria C. 1995. "Playfulness, 'World' Traveling, and Loving Perception." In *Free Spirits: Feminist Philosophers on Culture*, ed. Kate Mehuron and Gary Percesepe, pp. 121–28. Englewood Cliffs, N.J.: Prentice-Hall. Reprinted from *Making Soul—Hacienda Caras: Creative and Critical Perspectives by Feminists of Color*, ed. Gloria Anzaldua, pp. 290–402. San Francisco: Aunt Lute.

Luker, Kristin. 1984. *Abortion and the Politics of Motherhood*. Berkeley: University of California Press.

MacIntosh, Duncan. 1989. "Two Gauthiers?" *Dialogue: Canadian Philosophical Review* 28 (1): 43–61.

———. 1995. "Categorically Rational Preferences and the Structure of Morality." In *Modeling Rationality, Morality and Evolution*, ed. Peter Danielson, pp. 282–301. Vancouver Studies in Cognitive Science 7. New York: Oxford University Press.

MacKinnon, Catharine. 1987. "Desire and Power." In *Feminism Unmodified: Discourses on Life and Law*, ed. Catharine MacKinnon, pp. 46–69. Cambridge, Mass.: Harvard University Press.

———. 1987. "Francis Biddle's Sister: Pornography, Civil Rights, and Speech." In *Feminism Unmodified: Discourses on Life and Law*, ed. Catharine MacKinnon, pp. 163–97. Cambridge, Mass.: Harvard University Press.

———. 1987. "Sexual Harassment: Its First Decade in Court." In *Feminism Unmodified: Discourses on Life and Law*, ed. Catharine MacKinnon, pp. 103–16. Cambridge, Mass.: Harvard University Press.

Manning, Rita. 1992. *Speaking from the Heart: A Feminist Perspective on Ethics*. Lanham, Md.: Rowman and Littlefield.

May, Larry. 1992. "Shared Responsibility and Racist Attitudes." In *Sharing Responsibility*, ed. Larry May, pp. 36–54. Chicago: University of Chicago Press.

McDowell, John. 1978. "Are Moral Requirements Hypothetical Imperatives?" *Proceedings of the Aristotelian Society*, supp. vol. 52: 13–29.

———. 1979. "Virtue and Reason." *Monist* 62 (3): 331–50.

McFall, Lynne. 1992. "Integrity." In *Ethics and Personality: Essays in Moral Psychology*, ed. John Deigh, pp. 79–94. Chicago: University of Chicago Press. Originally published in *Ethics* 98 (1) (1987): 5–20.

McIntosh, Peggy. 1993. "White Privilege and Male Privilege." In *Gender Basics: Feminist Perspectives on Women and Men*, ed. Anne Minas, pp. 30–38. Belmont, Calif.: Wadsworth.

McKeon, Richard. 1941. *The Basic Works of Aristotle*. New York: Random House.

Mill, John Stuart. 1979. *Utilitarianism*. Ed. George Sher. Indianapolis: Hackett. (Originally published 1861)

Milo, Ronald D. 1984. *Immorality*. Princeton, N.J.: Princeton University Press.

Morris, Christopher. 1988. "The Relation between Self-Interest and Justice in Contractarian Ethics." *Social Philosophy and Policy* 5 (2): 119–53.

Murphy, Jeffrie G. 1972. "Moral Death: A Kantian Essay on Psychopathy." *Ethics* 82: 284–98.

Nagel, Thomas. 1970. *The Possibility of Altruism*. Princeton, N.J.: Princeton University Press.

Narayan, Uma. 2002. "Minds of Their Own: Choices, Autonomy, Cultural Practices, and Other Women." In *A Mind of One's Own: Feminist Essays on Reason and Objectivity*, 2nd ed., ed. Louise M. Antony and Charlotte E. Witt, pp. 418–32. Boulder, Colo.: Westview Press.

Nichols, Shaun. 2002. "How Psychopaths Threaten Moral Rationalism." *Monist* 85 (2): 285–303.

Noddings, Nel. 1984. *Caring: A Feminine Approach to Ethics and Moral Education*. Berkeley: University of California Press.

Nussbaum, Martha. 1990. "American Women." In *Sex and Social Justice*, ed. Martha C. Nussbaum, pp. 130–53. New York: Oxford University Press.

———. 2000. *Women and Human Development: The Capabilities Approach*. New York: Cambridge University Press.

Okin, Susan Moller. 1999. *Is Multiculturalism Bad for Women?* Princeton, N.J.: Princeton University Press.

Parfit, Derek. 1984. *Reasons and Persons*. New York: Oxford University Press.

Pineau, Lois. 1989. "Date Rape: A Feminist Analysis." *Law and Philosophy* 8: 217–43.

Plato. 1980. Republic. In *The Collected Dialogues of Plato*, ed. Edith Hamilton and Huntington Cairns, pp. 575–844, trans. Paul Shorey. Princeton, N.J.: Princeton University Press.

Pollitt, Katha. 1995. "Violence in a Man's World." In *Reasonable Creatures: Essays on Women and Feminism*, ed. Katha Pollitt, pp. 26–30. New York: Vintage Books.

Postema, Gerald. 1988. "Hume's Reply to the Sensible Knave." *History of Philosophy Quarterly* 5 (1): 23–40.

Railton, Peter. 1984. "Alienation, Consequentialism, and Morality." *Philosophy and Public Affairs* 13 (2): 134–71.

———. 1986. "Facts and Values." *Philosophical Topics* 14 (2): 5–31.

———. 1986. "Moral Realism." *Philosophical Review* 95 (2): 163–207.

Rawls, John. 1971. *A Theory of Justice*. Cambridge, Mass.: Harvard University Press.

Rogers, Kelly, ed. 1997. *Self-Interest: An Anthology of Philosophical Perspectives*. New York: Routledge.

Rorty, Amelie. 1986. "Self-Deception, Akrasia and Irrationality." In *The Multiple Self: Studies in Rationality and Social Change*, ed. Jon Elster, pp. 115–31. New York: Cambridge University Press.

Ruddick, Sara. 1986. "Maternal Thinking." In *Women and Values: Readings in Recent Feminist Philosophy*, ed. Marilyn Pearsall, pp. 340–51. Belmont, Calif.: Wadsworth.

Satz, Debra, and John Ferejohn. 1994. "Rational Choice and Social Theory." *Journal of Philosophy* 91 (2): 71–87.

Sayre-McCord, Geoff. 1989. "Deception and Reasons to Be Moral." *American Philosophical Quarterly* 26: 113–22. Reprinted from *Contractarianism and Rational Choice: Essays on David Gauthier's Morals by Agreement*, ed. Peter Vallentyne, pp. 182–95. New York: Cambridge University Press, 1991.

Schauber, Nancy. 1996. "Integrity, Commitment and the Concept of a Person." *American Philosophical Quarterly* 33 (1): 119–29.

Shafer-Landau, Russ. 2004. *Whatever Happened to Good and Evil?* New York: Oxford University Press.

Sher, George. 1998. "Ethics, Character, and Action." *Social Philosophy and Policy* 15 (1): 125–40.

Sherwin, Susan, ed. 1992. *No Longer Patient: Feminist Ethics and Health Care*. Philadelphia: Temple University Press.

Sidgwick, Henry. 1981. *The Methods of Ethics*. 7th ed. Indianapolis: Hackett. (Originally published 1884)

———. 1997. "*The Methods of Ethics*." In *Self-Interest: An Anthology of Philosophical Perspectives*, ed. Kelly Rogers, pp. 197–204. New York: Routledge.

Smith, Holly. 1991. "Deriving Morality from Rationality." In *Contractarianism and Rational Choice: Essays on David Gauthier's Morals by Agreement*, ed. Peter Vallentyne, pp. 229–53. New York: Cambridge University Press.

Smith, Michael. 1987. "The Humean Theory of Motivation." *Mind* 96 (381): 36–61.

———. 1994. *The Moral Problem*. Malden, Mass.: Blackwell.

Smyth, Clelia Anderson, and Yolanda Estes. 1998. "The Myth of the Happy Hooker: Kantian Moral Reflections on a Phenomenology of Prostitution." In *Violence against Women: Philosophical Perspectives*, ed. Stanley G. French, Wanda Teays, and Laura M. Purdy, 152–58. Ithaca, N.Y.: Cornell University Press.

Sommers, Christina Hoff. 1994. *Who Stole Feminism? How Women Have Betrayed Women*. New York: Simon and Schuster.

Spelman, Elizabeth. 1978. "On Treating Persons as Persons." *Ethics* 88: 150–61.

Stark, Cynthia. 1997. "The Rationality of Valuing Oneself: A Critique of Kant on Self-Respect." *Journal of the History of Philosophy* 34 (1): 65–82.

Sterba, James P. 2001. *Three Challenges to Ethics: Environmentalism, Feminism, and Multiculturalism*. New York: Oxford University Press.

Stevens, Evelyn P. 1993. "*Marianismo*: The Other Face of *Machismo* in Latin America." In *Gender Basics: Feminist Perspectives on Women and Men*, ed. Anne Minas, pp. 484–90. Belmont, Calif.: Wadsworth.

Stocker, Michael. 1976. "The Schizophrenia of Modern Moral Theories." *Journal of Philosophy* 73 (14): 453–66.

Sumner, L. Wayne. 1987. "Justice Contracted." *Dialogue: Canadian Philosophical Review* 26 (3): 523–48.

Superson, Anita M. 1990. "The Self-Interest Based Contractarian Response to the Why-Be-Moral Skeptic." Ph.D. diss., University of Illinois at Chicago.

———. 1993. "Right-Wing Women: Causes, Choices, and Blaming the Victim." *Journal of Social Philosophy* 24 (3): 40–61.

———. 1996. "Moral Luck and Partialist Theories." *Journal of Value Inquiry* 30 (1–2) (June 1996): 213–27.

———. 1999. "Sexism in the Classroom: The Role of Gender Stereotypes in the Evaluation of Female Faculty." *American Philosophical Association Newsletter on Feminism and Philosophy* 99 (1): 46–51.

———. 2002. "Welcome to the Boys' Club: Male Socialization and the Backlash against Feminism in Tenure Decisions." In *Theorizing Backlash: Philosophical Reflections on the Resistance to Feminism*, ed. Anita M. Superson and Ann E. Cudd, pp. 89–117. Lanham, Md.: Rowman and Littlefield.

———. 2004. "Privilege, Immorality, and Responsibility for Attending to the 'Facts about Humanity'." *Journal of Social Philosophy* 35 (1): 34–55.

———. 2006. "Response to Four Commentaries: (Antony, Darwall, Thomas, Uleman) on "Privilege, Immorality, and Responsibility for Attending to the 'Facts about Humanity'."" *Symposia on Gender, Race and Philosophy* 2 (1) (January 2006): 1–12. http://web.mit.edu/sgrp.

———. 2008. "The Deferential Wife Revisited: Agency and Moral Responsibility." Unpublished manuscript.

Teays, Wanda. 1998. "Standards of Perfection and Battered Women's Self-Defense." In *Violence against Women: Philosophical Perspectives*, ed. Stanley G. French, Wanda Teays, and Laura M. Purdy, pp. 57–76. Ithaca, N.Y.: Cornell University Press.

Thomson, Judith Jarvis. 1990. "Trespass and First Property." In *The Realm of Rights*, pp. 205–26. Cambridge, Mass.: Harvard University Press.

Timmons, Mark. 2002. *Moral Theory: An Introduction*. Lanham, Md.: Rowman and Littlefield.

Tong, Rosemarie. 1984. *Women, Sex, and the Law*. Savage, Md.: Rowman and Littlefield.

———. 1993. *Feminine and Feminist Ethics*. Belmont, Calif.: Wadsworth.

Tronto, Joan. 1993. "Beyond Gender Difference to a Theory of Care." In *An Ethic of Care: Feminist and Interdisciplinary Perspectives*, ed. Mary Jeanne Larrabee, pp. 240–57. New York: Routledge.

Tuana, Nancy. 1992. *Woman and the History of Philosophy*. New York: Paragon House.

Vallentyne, Peter. 1991. "Contractarianism and the Assumption of Mutual Unconcern." In *Contractarianism and Rational Choice: Essays on David Gauthier's Morals by Agreement*, ed. Peter Vallentyne, pp. 71–75. New York: Cambridge University Press. Reprinted from *Philosophical Studies* 56 (1989): 187–92.

Williams, Bernard. 1973. "A Critique of Utilitarianism." In *Utilitarianism: For and Against*, ed. J. J. C. Smart and Bernard Williams, pp. 77–150. New York: Cambridge University Press.

———.1981. "Internal and External Reasons." In *Moral Luck*, ed. Bernard Williams, pp. 101–13. New York: Cambridge University Press.

———. 1995. "Internal Reasons and the Obscurity of Blame." In *Making Sense of Humanity and Other Philosophical Papers 1982–1993*, ed. Bernard Williams, pp. 35–45. New York: Cambridge University Press.

Wolf, Naomi. 1992. *The Beauty Myth: How Images of Beauty Are Used against Women*. New York: Anchor Books.

Wolf, Susan. 1982. "Moral Saints." *Journal of Philosophy* 79 (8): 419–31.

———. 1986. "Asymmetrical Freedom." In *Moral Responsibility*, ed. John Martin Fischer, pp. 225–40. Ithaca, N.Y.: Cornell University Press.

Index